The Australian Colonists

The Australian Colonists

An exploration of
social history 1788–1870

K. S. INGLIS

MELBOURNE UNIVERSITY PRESS 1974

First published 1974
Printed in Australia by
Wilke and Co. Ltd, Clayton, Victoria 3168 for
Melbourne University Press, Carlton, Victoria 3053
USA and Canada: ISBS Inc., Portland, Oregon 97208
Great Britain, Europe, Middle East, Africa and the Caribbean: International Book Distributors
Ltd, 66 Wood Lane End, Hemel Hempstead, Hertfordshire HP2 4RG, England

National Library of Australia
Cataloguing in Publication data

Inglis, Kenneth Stanley, 1929–
    The Australian colonists: an exploration
    of social history, 1788–1870/ [by] K. S.
    Inglis.—Carlton, Vic.: Melbourne
    University Press, 1974.
    Index.
    Bibliography.
    ISBN 0 522 84072 8.
    1. Australia—Social conditions—1788–1870.
    I. Title.
    309.194

To my mother and father,
grandchildren of Australian colonists

CONVERSION FACTORS
(to three decimal places)

1 acre	0.404	hectare
1 inch	2.54	centimetres
1 foot	0.304	metre
1 yard	0.914	metre
1 furlong	201.168	metres
1 mile	1.609	kilometres
1 pint	0.568	litre
1 gallon	4.546	litres
1 ounce	28.35	grams
1 pound	0.453	kilogram
1 hundredweight	50.802	kilograms
1 ton	1.016	tonnes

Fahrenheit to Celsius $°C = \frac{5}{9}(°F-32)$

ACKNOWLEDGMENTS

Most of this book was written while I was a Visiting Fellow at the Australian National University in 1971–2. I greatly appreciate the generosity of that institution, and of the University of Papua New Guinea for letting me take leave.

I am grateful to the following friends and colleagues who have helped me in various ways to write the book: D. W. A. Baker, G. N. Blainey, C. M. H. Clark, A. G. Daws, G. Fischer, T. M. Fitzgerald, W. L. Gammage, R. A. Gollan, J. T. Gunther, Sir Keith Hancock, Barbara Hau'ofa, J. A. La Nauze, Di Langmore, Judy McQueen, B. Nairn, H. N. Nelson, J. D. Pringle, P. A. Ryan, F. B. Smith, H. Stretton, Maya Tucker.

For typing the manuscript I thank Marie Gehde, Diane Goodwin, Jan Hicks, Sheila Kemish, Audrey Liebenow, Hane Pascoe, Pat Romans and June Watkins.

My wife, Amirah, has been exploring the subject with me ever since we first talked about it on Cup Day 1962.

Introduction

This book is conceived as the first in a series of volumes about Australia from the first days of British settlement to the present. Chronologically the study begins on 26 January 1788; but as a historical enquiry it starts from 25 April 1915. At dawn on that day, men from Australia landed on the Gallipoli peninsula, in Turkey, as part of a British and French force which was supposed to capture Constantinople. In the months of fighting that followed, the place where they came ashore was known by the invaders as Anzac Cove, after the initials of the Australian and New Zealand Army Corps. The campaign failed. The survivors of Anzac Cove were withdrawn before the year was out; but by that time Gallipoli was a household word in Australia and the name of Anzac was on its way to becoming sacred.

The first anniversary of the landing was called Anzac Day. In churches, halls and theatres, in parks and streets, in the columns of newspapers, and at Westminster Abbey, where Anzacs from Gallipoli sat in places of honour, men spoke of the soldiers' achievement in loftier language than had ever been used of any deeds in the history of Australia since that other landing of convicts and gaolers had begun it all at the place the white occupiers named Sydney Cove. The men and women and children of Australia were told that at Gallipoli their country had become a nation. Some said that it had undergone baptism, others that it had come of age. After the war 25 April became Australia's national day. In all the six states, which had been separate colonies until 1900, returned soldiers assembled on the day to meet each other, to receive tributes, and to mourn the men who had not returned.

To serve the ceremonies of Anzac Day and to express all the year round what the day stood for, monuments were raised throughout the country, from vast shrines in capital cities to modest columns, clock towers and statues in every suburb and country town, bearing the names of the men from the neighbourhood who had gone to the Great War, and marking for grief and honour the names of the men who had died for king and country. The statues were of a digger, as the soldier of the Australian Imperial Force had come to be called, sometimes in a belligerent posture but more often in repose, the mourner and the mourned. An English visitor, D. H. Lawrence, contemplated one in 1922 which had been lately dedicated by the people of a town south of Sydney 'a statue in pale, fawnish stone, of a Tommy standing at ease, with his gun down at his side, wearing his puttees and his turned-up felt hat. The statue itself was about life size, but standing just overhead on a tall pedestal it looked small and stiff and rather touching'. The digger was Australia's hero.

Children who grew up after 1916 learned from their teachers and their reading books that Anzac had been the making of the nation. Schools were shut on 25 April; but on the last day of school before each anniversary, pupils stood in their asphalt playgrounds to hear headmaster or mayor or representative of the Returned Sailors and Soldiers Imperial League of Australia tell them what the day meant, or should mean, to them all. The left lapel of the speaker's suit coat bore either the Returned from Active Service badge conferred by a grateful government, or the badge that showed him to be a financial member of the R.S.S.I.L.A., and he wore also the medals and ribbons of whatever awards he had won for gallantry or service. Every child whose father had been in the A.I.F. had his medals and ribbons pinned to coat or shirt for the day, and was envied by friends who had none.

The Anzac ceremonies at North Preston State School, No. 1494 of the Victorian Education Department, are among my most vivid memories of the years from 1935, when I was five, to 1939. Later the Anzac tradition began to attract me as a theme to write about, a base from which to explore areas of Australian history not yet well mapped. The more I learned of it and thought about it, the more its ceremonies, monuments and rhetoric seemed to me to constitute in some respects a civic religion. I was interested to notice that many Christian clergymen were uneasy about the solemnities of Anzac, and some were hostile to them, and that some custodians of the tradition, creating and executing homage to dead mates, regarded churches as at best unnecessary and at worse divisive. Yet in so far as the recent history of Christianity in Australia had attracted students, I did not find that the contest between the churches and the men of Anzac had interested them. Looking at the history of the labour movement, I noticed during and after the Great War conflicts and confusions of allegiance: did a man stand beside all other workers in a struggle between classes, or all other Australians (or Britons, or adherents of the right) in a struggle between nations (or empires, or right and wrong)? But historians of labour were apt to give this dilemma less weight than it occupied in the minds of the men they studied, and were reluctant, I thought, to recognize the popularity of the Anzac tradition among Australians whom they allocated to the working class.

When I gave a lecture on the Anzac tradition in Canberra in 1964 which happened to be reported in the newspapers, I found myself in touch with a variety of people who were surprised that an academic historian should be interested in the subject. The papers had given prominence to my remark that a history of Australia that did not explore the meaning of Anzac Day was too thin, and my opinion that the work of C. E. W. Bean, official historian of the A.I.F., had been paid too little attention by other writers of history. This lecture led me into correspondence and acquaintance with veterans of Gallipoli, relatives holding soldiers' diaries and letters, and admirers of Bean as writer and man. I was sure now that I wanted to write a book on the subject.

In 1965 I travelled as *Canberra Times* correspondent with about three hundred Australians and New Zealanders who had served in the Great War—or World War I, as it had become by now—on a pilgrimage to coincide with the fiftieth anniversary of the landing at Gallipoli. The journey lasted three weeks on a chartered Turkish ship. In that time I had the privilege of talking with many men about their experiences of war and peace, and at dawn on 25 April 1965, I stepped on to the sands of Anzac Cove in the company of men who had been there on 25 April 1915. They were welcomed by Turks, all bald or white-haired and some leaning on sticks, who also remembered the first landing. Back in Australia I went on learning from correspondence and conversation with the pilgrims. Their ranks are now thinning fast, and I am sorry that it is taking me so long to write about their experience as I promised them.

25 April 1915 was said to be a consummation. Of what? Trying to set out the themes of my book, I met questions that kept turning me back. The rhetoric of Anzac was both imperial and national. What had Australians thought about themselves before 1915 as Britons, colonists, and members of their own nation? At last, people said after Gallipoli, we have a national day. What other occasions had it been their custom to celebrate as holidays? If Australians wanted a national day, why had no other satisfied them? The Australian Imperial Force was said to have been an army of unusual qualities: egalitarian, informal, its ordinary soldiers self-directed to a degree not known in the British army. Was that true? In so far as the expeditionary force did have peculiarities, how had they got there? What had been the previous military and naval arrangements for the defence of Australia and for participation in imperial wars and skirmishes? How far, if at all, did the Anzac tradition have roots in Australian participation in the Boer War of 1899–1902, or for that matter in the momentary involvement of soldiers from New South Wales in the Sudan in 1885? How had people in Australia responded to earlier imperial wars, from the struggle against Napoleon to the campaign in the Crimea, and to the intermittent threats of war during the nineteenth century? And what was the Australian experience of domestic violence, in which armed force was used against a variety of objects, from aborigines to gold diggers? Did none of these interruptions to the peace of colonial life elicit a memorable valour? Were there, finally, activities other than war or internal conflict that produced candidates for the status of Australian hero before the digger was raised on his plinth?

These questions have sent me farther into early Australian history than I expected. 1788 to 1870 was the age of exploration in this continent, and I hope that the reader will accept this volume as an exploratory journey necessary to the purpose of my study. In Part I, landmarks already familiar to many readers are described in order to get bearings on territory less well charted. In the later parts, my questions have been made harder to answer by the historians' habit of writing what J. H. Hexter has described as tunnel history. 'They split the past into a series of tunnels', he writes, 'each continuous from the remote past to the present, but practically self-contained at every point and sealed off from contact with or contamination by anything that was going on in any of the other tunnels'. In the tunnel of labour history, readers can learn readily about men at work but not about men and women at leisure. The tunnel of political history contains much about the making of laws but little about the legal system and the police force by which the laws are administered and enforced; nor would one guess how much political energy and public money in Australia before 1914 went into preparations for defence. Along the tunnel of religious history one rarely finds an account of how people spent their Sundays, or how seriously every generation of Australians until 1914 took funerals. Not only the funerals but the ceremonies of all sorts, solemn or joyous, local or national, in which the people of colonial Australia expressed aspects of their identity, are too seldom to be glimpsed in the tunnels our historians have dug. That grand work the *Australian Dictionary of Biography* is helping to stop the tunnelling habit, by showing again and again how much richer were the lives of colonial worthies than most of us knew. (Try Barry, Sir Redmond; or Douglas, Henry Grattan; or Mitchell, Sir Thomas; or Wills, Horatio Spencer.) Historians will get further encouragement to stay out of their burrows when we have, for example, a proper dictionary of Australian English and a thorough study of place-names.

I hope to follow this volume with a second, which I think of as *The Little Boy From Manly*, carrying the themes of the work to 1900, and a third, *Australia Will Be There*, which ends on the first anniversary of the landing at Gallipoli. In a fourth volume, *Anzac Day*, I hope to write about the world I began to know at North Preston State School and thereabouts.

Contents

Illustrations

For help in finding illustrations I thank Suzanne Mourot, the Mitchell Librarian; Patricia Reynolds, the La Trobe Librarian; G. Fischer, Archivist of the University of Sydney; R. D. Marginson, Vice-Principal of the University of Melbourne.

Illustrations are reproduced with permission as follows:

National Library of Australia: pages 11, 26, 34, 35, 45, 70, 71, 78, 80, 81, 84, 91, 92, 95, 96, 98, 99, 100, 102, 106, 110, 114, 115, 121, 128, 134, 135, 140, 141, 147, 155, 156, 159, 162, 166, 172, 173, 174, 175, 193, 204, 208, 214, 223, 225, 229, 231, 242, 251, 268
National Library of Australia, Rex Nan Kivell collection: pages 6, 9, 24, 68, 79, 94, 180, 192, 196, 198, 216, 217, 222, 258
Mitchell Library: pages 76, 144, 183, 201, 244
Library of New South Wales: page 22
Art Gallery of New South Wales: page 32
University of Sydney: pages 247, 248
New South Wales Government Printer: pages 59, 243, 245
La Trobe Collection, State Library of Victoria: pages 83, 158, 186, 260
University of Melbourne: page 264

The People

The British occupation of Australia was proclaimed at Sydney Cove in 1788 by a naval captain in command of about a thousand convicts, soldiers and dependants. For the next half-century most new-comers to the great island and Tasmania were people sent out by British courts. What were a convict's rights in this country, once his sentence had expired? The first political controversy was over that question. What kind of society would be made out of such a population? When people in England noticed Australia, they spoke about its future with apprehension, and looked with some hope to the sons and daughters of the felons.

Convicts and their children regarded emigrants as interlopers; but after 1830 free men and women were to alter the character of the colonies. 'The rich stay in Europe,' wrote Crèvecoeur in his Letters from an American Farmer (1782), 'it is only the middling and the poor that emigrate.' It was just as true of nineteenth-century Australia. Helped by governments through the sale of land, and attracted after 1850 by the prospect of gold, hundreds of thousands of the middling and the poor left the United Kingdom for the Australian colonies. Some would return; most would settle and die here, either because they could not do otherwise or because they preferred the new life. Contented or not, they would go on calling the old country 'home'.

People born here, identifying themselves in relation to emigrants, liked to say that they were Australians. Their protagonist in the 1820s and 1830s was William Charles Wentworth, almost but not quite the son of a convict, who encouraged his fellow-Australians to think of their land not as a dump but as a new centre of British civilization. As free emigrants and native-born adults became more numerous, birthplace tended to become a less important fact about a man than it had once been. In politics, colonial-born and emigrants found themselves on both sides of debates about the disposal of public lands, the constitutional ties between mother country and colony, and the franchise. It was settled by 1850 that the colonies would be self-governing. The old legislative councils, with advice from newspapers and public meetings, proposed more or less democratic arrangements for the new parliaments; and by 1860 most colonies had ministries responsible to parliaments elected by manhood suffrage in secret ballot.

By 1870 Australia was the home of a flourishing colonial society. The population of the six colonies had passed one million by 1860 and would reach two millions before 1880. Colonists found much cause for pride in what they had made; but to one imperial visitor in about 1870, their democracy appeared less an achievement than an accident, and another, hearing colonists brag, thought that he detected in them a sense of inferiority to people at home.

The affairs of every colony were conducted largely by emigrants. Most of the queen's Australian subjects in 1870 were actually colonial-born, but it was the native youth who enabled emigrants to be outnumbered. The education of the young was a large preoccupation of the politicians, for colonists wanted their children to have a better schooling than themselves. By 1870 systems of state schools were being constructed; but there were large questions yet to be answered about what teachers should try to put into the heads and hearts of the rising generation, the young Australians who would inherit what the convicts, the emigrants and the colonial-born had made of the land since 1788.

1 Convicts

BOTANY BAY

This was the last of continents to be entered and labelled by European man. Terra Australis Incognita, the whole area had been named in early maps; then sometimes Terra Australis Nondum Cognita—not *yet* known—as Europeans moved out across the oceans. In 1606 Pedro Fernandez de Quiros offered the region to the Holy Spirit and (by a Spanish pun) to Philip III of Austria, as Austrialia del Espiritu Santo. Men of the Dutch East India Company from Java found stretches of coast which they named Compagnis Niew Nederland or Hollandia Nova. Far to the south, Abel Tasman named Anthonio van Diemensland in 1642 to honor the governor-general of the Dutch company. He also discovered the islands that the Dutch called Nieuw Zeeland. William Dampier, exploring southern waters in 1688, wrote of New Holland as part of Terra Australis Incognita. James Cook, sent to Tahiti to observe the transit of Venus across the sun in 1769, looked in vain for the continent supposed to be somewhere south of his track, then took the *Endeavour* west from New Zealand for the unknown east coast of New Holland. On 19 April 1770 his men saw land. They followed it north, and on 29 April sailed into a sheltered bay and went ashore. Cook noted 'fine meadow'. The men of science in his party, Joseph Banks and Daniel Solander, gathered so many plants that Cook called the place Botany Bay. Sailing north, Cook noticed but did not enter a bay which he named Port Jackson, after the judge-advocate of the fleet. On 22 August, before passing south of the land a Spaniard had named Nueva Guinea, Cook took possession for King George III of the coast he had been charting since April. During the voyage home, and without explaining why, he named it New South Wales. The official account of his voyage included a chart of 'the Sea Coast of New South Wales on the East Coast of New Holland.' What land and water lay between it and the west coast of New Holland, and between it and Van Diemen's Land, nobody knew.

New South Wales was the name of the penal colony Captain Arthur Phillip of the navy was sent to establish at Botany Bay in 1787. Its territory was greater than the area Cook had claimed, stretching from the northern tip of the coast down to the south of Van Diemen's Land and west to the 135th parallel of longitude, which ran midway between the coasts mapped by Cook and the Dutch. There were differences of opinion about where this most remote piece of empire actually was, one newspaper placing it on the *west* side of New Holland.

Phillip's fleet reached Botany Bay in January 1788, in the middle of the southern summer. Unable to see the fine meadow Cook had observed in a wet autumn, and judging the place generally unsuitable for settlement, Phillip searched for a better site and found it at Port Jackson, which seemed to him 'the finest harbour in the world'. He put his charges ashore on a part of the harbour which he named Sydney Cove, after the secretary of state for the colonies.

Before the convicts left England their intended home had been known informally as Botany Bay; and that name, neat and euphonious, was used in early accounts of the colony even though no settlement had been made at the place it marked. But publishers soon avoided it: 'the word "Botany Bay" ', David Collins explained in *An Account of the English Colony in New South Wales* (1798), 'became a term of reproach that was indiscriminately cast on every one who resided in New South Wales.' In conversation and ballad at home, Botany Bay meant convicts. The words 'New South Wales', however lacking in poetry or sense, seemed preferable to a name by which every free man connected with the colony felt himself polluted. Their kinsmen were slow to respond to this nicety of nomenclature: 'by the great body of the public,' a colonial author wrote of the 1790s, ' "New South Wales" was absolutely unknown, and "Botany Bay" was looked upon merely as the fit receptacle of national crime.'

Van Diemen's Land, which Matthew Flinders and George Bass proved in 1798 to be an island, became a penal dependency of New South Wales in 1803. Because the worst offenders were sent down there, and convicts were always a large proportion of the population, Van Diemen's Land became even more of a byword for criminality than Botany Bay. The name was kept when the colony was separated from New South Wales in 1825, but it was deeply disliked by inhabitants. In Dutch it sounded agreeable; to English ears it sang of an evil spirit lurking in the place. People in the colony and at home preferred Tasmania, which recognized the Dutch discovery and was not tarnished by later history. Books carried such titles as *Godwin's Emigrant's Guide to Van Diemen's Land, more properly called Tasmania* (1823). The imperial government allowed the popular name to be attached to a Church of England diocese formed in 1824 and a royal society in 1843. Men and women born in the colony were distinguished from the European-born by being called Tasmanians; Vandemonians meant not its children but its felons. When John West published his history of the island in 1852, he called it Tasmania in the title and explained why: Tasmania, he wrote, had a melodious and simple sound; Van Diemen's Land was harsh, complex, infernal, and associated among all nations with the idea of bondage and guilt. Official nomenclature surrendered to general usage in the act of 1854 which granted responsible government. Postage stamps costing sixpence and a shilling recorded the change in 1858; but as those of lower value did not follow at once, letters bearing a fourpenny and a sixpenny stamp took the dirty old name and the clean new one side by side to England until 1870. It was an appropriate message to carry: for long after the last convict reached the island, the stink of Van Diemen's Land hung in the crisp Tasmanian air.

Conjecture that the coasts discovered by the Dutch and Cook formed part of a single great island was proved true when Matthew Flinders sailed all the way round it in 1802–3. That discovery seemed to Flinders to invite a new name for the continent. 'New Holland', he wrote in 1804, 'is properly that portion of it from 135° of longitude westward; and eastward is New South Wales, according to the Governor's patent.' To call the whole by either name would be unjust, he believed, to the navigators of one or other country. Flinders began to write of the continent as Australia, a formation from Terra Australis which had been used occasionally, and with varying reference, during the eighteenth century. In his book about the voyage, Flinders was persuaded to use Terra Australis instead (for New Holland and New South Wales including Van Diemen's Land), on the ground that the name was familiar to the public. But he added in a footnote: 'Had I permitted myself any innovation upon the original term, it would have been to convert it into Australia; as being more agreeable to the ear, and an assimilation to the names of the other great portions of the earth.' *A Voyage to Terra Australis* was published on the day Flinders died, aged forty, in 1814. Many of its readers shared his preference for Australia. Colonel Lachlan Macquarie, governor of New South Wales, received a copy early in 1817 and wrote to the Colonial Office in December of 'the Continent of *Australia*, which I hope will be the Name given to this Country in future, instead of the very erroneous and misapplied name, hitherto given to it, of "New Holland", which properly speaking only applies to a part of this immense Continent.' When Macquarie was buried back in Scotland in 1824, 'Australia' was written on the tomb. New South Wales and New Holland remained the official terms; but Australia replaced them both in popular colonial usage after 1820 and had some formal use as a synonym for New Holland after 1830.

By that time the name New South Wales, like Botany Bay before it, was associated in English minds with convicts. Peter Cunningham, a surgeon on convict ships and a landowner in the colony, wrote in 1827 that if you were conversing amiably in an English stagecoach with someone who discovered that you had been to New South Wales, your companion would move away, and under pretence of fumbling for a penknife or a toothpick assure himself that all his pockets were safe.

The word 'Australia' went into the names of two new colonies outside New South Wales founded not for convicts but for free settlers. An act of 1829 establishing the Swan River colony spoke of 'His Majesty's settlements in Western Australia', and the names Swan River and Western Australia were used interchangeably for a long time. For the colony between New South Wales and Western Australia created by systematic colonizers in 1836, one patron, Jeremy Bentham, proposed the name Felicitania or Liberia; but sober settlers made it South Australia. The name was a little misleading, as the colony did not include the most southern part of the continent; and it became more so after 1863 when South Australia extended its border to the north coast. But it had a pleasing music to citizens of a colony which never received a convict, for nothing in the name hinted at any connexion with their tainted eastern neighbours.

The name Australia Felix was given by Major Thomas Mitchell, surveyor-general, to flowery plains and green hills which he crossed in the south of New South Wales in 1836. But the name Port Phillip had been applied already, in 1802, to a harbour on the south coast; and when men from Van Diemen's Land and the north converged to settle in the area discovered by Mitchell, it became part of the Port Phillip District of New South Wales. Several new names were canvassed as separation approached, among them Phillipsland; but the devisers of the new colony rejected any word that alluded to the penal past. From 1837, when Victoria came to the throne, makers of names for new parts of the British empire looked to the queen above all other sources of inspiration. As the first English colony had been named Virginia in honour of Queen Elizabeth, so this one became Victoria. In the north of New South Wales, Moreton Bay (named by Cook for the president of the Royal Society) was established as a penal settlement in 1824. The name soon reeked of the convict system, and when the Moreton Bay District was

HELL OR BOTANY BAY
An English view of New South Wales, 1829

separated from New South Wales in 1859 it became the colony of Queensland.

Yet Botany Bay would not die. Long after Australia had been covered with other names, many of them chosen deliberately to affirm that the land they defined was not contaminated ground, the old term and its associations lingered in the minds of people at home.

THE TRANSPORTED

Phillip set out across the world in May 1787 with 759 convicts—568 men and 191 women. His eleven ships sailed out to Tenerife, across the Atlantic to Rio de Janeiro, back to Cape Town, through the Indian Ocean to the bottom of Van Diemen's Land and up the coast to Botany Bay. The voyage took eight months, six of them at sea and two in ports for supplies and repairs. Twenty-three convicts died on the way.

On Saturday 26 January 1788 Phillip had a flagstaff erected at Sydney Cove. The Union Jack, bearing the cross of St George for England and St Andrew for Scotland, was hoisted to the top by a marine. Officers, marines and convicts assembled beneath the flag and toasts were drunk to King George III and to the success of the colony. Its establishment was proclaimed formally on Thursday 7 February at a ceremony which all the convicts attended, sitting on the ground surrounded by marines. All possible solemnity,

Phillip noted, was given to the occasion. The marines received him with flying colours and a drum-and-fife band. The judge-advocate, David Collins, unsealed and read out his commission as captain-general and governor-in-chief of New South Wales. The marines fired three volleys, and their band played 'God Save the King'. Then Phillip gave an address, most of which was directed at the convicts. If they behaved well and worked hard, he said, they might in time regain the advantages and estimation in society of which they had deprived themselves. If they did not work they would not eat; and if they stole any-thing, or if they presumed to offend against the peace and good order of the settlement, they would be punished without mercy. After the ceremony Phillip and his officers had what passed here for a feast: a plate of cold and maggoty mutton eaten in a tent. Some convicts who tried to arrange a feast of their own were caught and treated as the governor had warned. They were flogged, and one of them was put to grow hungry in the harbour on Rock Island, beginning a tradition which would gain it the name of Pinchgut.

The first published account of the journey out and the beginnings of settlement, *The Voyage of Governor Phillip to Botany Bay*, appeared in London in 1789. Its title-page bore an impression of a vignette which Josiah Wedgwood had made out of a piece of clay carried home from the new colony. It showed the female figure of Hope 'encouraging Art and Labour, under the influence of Peace, to pursue the employment necessary to give security and happiness to an infant settlement.' The philosophic poet Erasmus Darwin wrote lines inspired by the picture which appeared as a preface to the volume, entitled 'Visit of Hope to Sydney-Cove, Near Botany-Bay'. Hope, having calmed the water and stilled the winds, looks into the colony and sees broad streets, bright canals and solid roads, colossal bridges, villas, golden farms and blushing orchards.

> *There* shall tall spires, and dome-capt towers ascend,
> And piers and quays their massy structures blend;
> While with each breeze approaching vessels glide,
> And northern treasures dance on every tide!

In the colony as it actually was in 1789 and 1790, the hope of convicts and their keepers was directed towards the coming of a second fleet with food to keep them alive. On 3 June 1790 the *Lady Juliana*, eleven months out of Plymouth, arrived with a few provisions and 221 female convicts, and at the end of the month three ships brought more supplies and 683 male and 67 female convicts. Another 267 had died during the voyage.

More shiploads of convicts followed. When ill-health made Phillip retire at the end of 1792 he could report a secure population of three thousand at Sydney Cove, Parramatta and Toongabbee, and another thousand on Norfolk Island—one thousand miles north-east of Sydney, and found and named by Cook in 1774. He had persuaded the authorities at home to encourage free settlers; he had granted land for agriculture to officers and soldiers, and he had set convicts to work for them. He had freed more than fifty of the convicts and given them land. Only a poet could imagine the spires and towers and quays of Erasmus Darwin's vision; but the place was at least beginning to resemble the picture on its first official symbol, the silver seal for use on official documents which arrived in 1791. Oxen are ploughing. A town rises on a hill, protected by a fort and a church. The presiding spirit is not Hope but Industry, sitting on a bale of goods with a distaff, a beehive, a pickaxe and a spade. She is receiving convicts and releasing them from their fetters.

The number of convicts transported to Australia rose steadily from decade to decade. There were nearly 400 a year on average from 1793 to 1810 and more than 1000 a year by 1815. The flow increased greatly after the wars ended: some 2600 a year arrived from 1816 to 1825, and nearly 5000 a year from 1826 to 1835. From the mid-1830s the number declined, though there were still some 4000 a year from 1841 to 1845, most of whom went now to Van Diemen's Land. In all, more than 160 000 convicted men and women—about six men for every woman—were sent to the Australian colonies. More than half had been sentenced for seven years, about a quarter for life, and most of the rest for fourteen years. Among those who did not die as prisoners, many were released before their time expired. Few went home. The return of convicts who had served their sentences could not legally be prevented; but 'it should be distinctly understood', Phillip was told, 'that no steps are likely to be taken by Government for facilitating their return.'

Most convicts were transported for stealing. Among prisoners from England and Wales most were unmarried men in their twenties from London and the manufacturing cities of the midlands and north who had been found guilty of some sort of larceny and who had one or more previous convictions. Scotland did not contribute many convicts, the Scots being less prone to criminality than the English. Ireland provided about a quarter of the convict population directly—nearly 30 000 men and 9000 women—and another 6000 who were born in Ireland and arrested in England. The Irish were older than other convicts, included more married men and more women, had fewer prior convictions, and often received shorter sentences. They came more frequently from the country; and though most were thieves, a greater proportion than among convicts from elsewhere were rebels and agitators. Nearly a fifth of the Irish convicts were sent to Australia for crimes of protest against British domination and in particular against land laws. Their keepers had good reason to expect that they would be more troublesome than the rest.

A convict's fate in Australia depended on how docile he was and on many things over which he had no control, from the current state of penal theory in England to the temper of a public overseer or private employer. At first most male convicts were put to work on turning the new settlements from camps into towns, building houses, wharves, granaries, windmills and barracks, making carts and roads and bricks. As private farming spread, more and more convicts were assigned to work for respectable citizens. Many who worked for the government and many assigned servants gave such satisfaction that their names appeared in no judicial document other than the account of their trial at home. Many others were brought before magistrates and charged with drunkenness, disobedience, idleness, disorderly conduct or some other offence. The magistrate normally found them guilty and commonly ordered flogging as punishment. In New South Wales between 1833 and 1836 one male convict in every four was flogged each year, receiving an average of more than forty lashes. Governors as well as victims knew that the lash made men savage, but no other means of discipline was so cheap or so quick.

For more serious offences a convict in government or private service might be hanged after trial in the Supreme Court, or confined by order of two magistrates in a penal settlement, or—after 1826—put into a chain gang. Between 1826 and 1836 almost a quarter of all men transported to New South Wales spent some time undergoing one of these two punishments. The names of penal settlements became things of horror in colonial

CONVICTS AT WORK

and homeland folklore. The most famous of all was the settlement on Tasman's Peninsula, south of Hobart, to which Governor Arthur gave his name when he established it in 1830. Five years later more than a thousand men were incarcerated at Port Arthur. 'Constantly exhibited as a place of profound misery,' John West wrote in 1852, 'it carried the vengeance of the law to the utmost limits of human endurance.' The ambition of most convicts was to stay clear of penal settlements, avoid the lash, and sooner or later go free. The governor had power to make it sooner. From Phillip's time to Macquarie's the governor's instructions allowed him 'to remit, either absolutely or conditionally, whole or any part' of a prisoner's sentence. From 1823 the governor could not grant pardons, but could recommend them to London. Short of a pardon, the convict could look forward to a ticket-of-leave, a device introduced by Governor King, used widely by Macquarie, and regulated in 1823 so that a well-behaved prisoner might be allowed after four, six or eight years—according to the length of his sentence—to be released from compulsory labour and work for himself. Magistrates recommended, governors gave or withheld approval, and by 1837 a quarter of all convicts had these tickets. A holder could not have a convict assigned to work for him, he could not hold a publican's licence, and the ticket could be withdrawn if he misbehaved; but he was well on the way to freedom.

  The governor's powers to lighten the load of punishment were limited after Macquarie's time because he was judged to have used them too readily. There were allegations in the colony and in England that Macquarie was unduly lenient towards convicts, hostile towards free settlers, and extravagant. In 1819 John Thomas Bigge, formerly chief justice of Trinidad, was commissioned to advise how the punishment of convicts in New South Wales could be made more severe in order to deter crime at home, and how the cost of administering the colony could be reduced. He found Macquarie, as custodian of convicts, both too tender and capricious. He condemned the governor's public works for being inappropriately grand and for keeping in Sydney at the expense of the government many convicts who ought to be employed by settlers out in the country. Macquarie was on his way home after twelve years when the first of Bigge's reports was submitted to parliament in May 1822. The old governor believed himself maligned. Certainly Bigge's reports embodied a view of the colony profoundly antipathetic to his own. New South Wales was in Macquarie's eyes a place for the prisoners to inherit once they had undergone a time of humane punishment; to Bigge, as to the men at the Colonial Office who had sent him, the primary purpose of the punishment was to inspire terror among potential lawbreakers in the United Kingdom, and the colony was to belong not to the convicts but to free settlers. The next governor, Major-General Sir Thomas Brisbane, was instructed to act on Bigge's recommendations.

The dispatch of convicts to Sydney Cove was stopped in 1840. Under scrutiny at home the system of transportation appeared less and less defensible. Governors were supposed to reduce the number of convicts kept at public expense and assign as many as possible to free settlers. But once a convict was assigned, there was no way to make sure that he was treated with even-handed severity. 'A man is estimated by his capacity as a colonist,' observed an official in England, 'not by his crime as a felon.' Moreover, no matter how attentively convicts were punished, the system was not working unless it actually induced terror at home. Its purpose, as James Stephen of the Colonial Office mused in 1835, was to create misery on one side of the globe in order to prevent the perpetration of offences on the other. Short of interrogating poor but law-abiding men about why they had failed to become burglars, the debate about whether transportation deterred men from crime could not easily be resolved; but it seemed reasonable to suppose that fear of being sent to New South Wales was being undermined in the late 1830s by a policy which actually helped free men to emigrate there. Colonial opinion was divided on the system. Free labourers did not like the competition it provided, but their views had little force. Some employers did not want to be deprived of convict workers; others preferred free emigrants. A committee on transportation appointed by the House of Commons in 1837 judged it not wise 'to stigmatize emigration by associating it with the idea of degradation and punishment.' The system was an obstacle, moreover, to the self-government for which many colonists were now pressing. That aspect seemed of some weight to Lord John Russell, secretary of state in 1839. 'As I contemplate the introduction of free institutions into New South Wales,' he wrote, 'I am anxious to rid that colony of its penal character.' When he ordered the end of transportation to the colony in 1840 and of assignment in 1841 the decisions were well received in New South Wales.

Convicts were sent out to Van Diemen's Land until 1853, to Norfolk Island from 1844 to 1846, to Port Phillip from 1844 to 1849, and to Moreton Bay in 1849 and 1850. Van Diemen's Land was deluged with them: an average of more than four thousand a year was sent from 1841 to 1844, increasing the convict population by more than 40 per cent. Officials in the colony had to find work for the prisoners without offering them to employers as assigned servants, and at a time when the colonial economy was severely depressed. For two years the dispatch of male convicts was suspended, and when resumed it was under a plan by which convicted people were sent under the official designation of

THE PENAL SETTLEMENT AT PORT ARTHUR

exiles. The term was intended officially to convey that they were somewhere between convicts and emigrants, having spent time in reformatory prisons at home before matriculating to Australia.

Nearly two thousand of the exiles were sent to Port Phillip after confinement in the new prison of Pentonville. Not long after landing at Melbourne, Geelong and Portland, somebody gave them the name Pentonvillains. In 1849, when work was scarce in Port Phillip, there were protests against the unloading of exiles there. The convict ship *Hashemy* was sent on to Sydney in May without putting her passengers ashore, by officials who feared riots if they were landed at Melbourne. A shortage of labour in New South Wales had encouraged the secretary of state, Earl Grey, to think that exiles might be accepted at Sydney; but when the *Hashemy* entered Port Jackson with the first prisoners to arrive since 1840 she provoked vehement protests and petitions. The exiles when landed were removed prudently far from Sydney. No more convicts were sent to the mainland of eastern Australia. In New South Wales and Victoria as well as in Van Diemen's Land, free men agitated to have the traffic stopped altogether. They were supported at home by people who were convinced that it was more rational to punish offenders by putting them in new English prisons. Discoveries of gold in 1851 made it easy for the abolitionists to prevail. 'It would be a little too much even for Downing Street philosophy', remarked one of them, 'to transport a highwayman or a burglar to a gold mine!' The last load of convicts sailed for Van Diemen's Land on 27 November 1852. Only Western Australia, where rural employers were short of labourers, received convicts after 1853, some five hundred a year being sent until 1868.

In retrospect transportation was called convictism, an evil abstraction. 'No one who has not lived in Australia', English readers were told in 1864, 'can appreciate the profound hatred of convictism that obtains there.' Port Arthur became its zoo, where wild men were kept as grisly exhibits long after transportation had stopped. Anthony Trollope, collecting material in 1872 for a book on Australia and New Zealand, met some of the inmates, including an Irishman named Doherty who had been a convict since he was transported for mutiny in 1830. 'The record of his prison life was frightful', Trollope learned. 'He had been always escaping, always rebelling, always fighting against authority,—and always being flogged.' Mutiny, the visitor thought, was not an offence at which the mind revolted. 'I did feel for him, and when he spoke of himself as a caged bird, I should have liked to take him out into the world, and have given him a month of comfort. He would probably, however, have knocked my brains out on the first opportunity.' Trollope was told that within a few years Doherty and his fellows would probably be removed to a prison near Hobart. 'If this be done', he reflected, 'there can hardly, I think, be any other fate for the buildings than that they shall stand till they fall. They will fall into the dust, and men will make unfrequent excursions to visit the strange ruins.' In fact the buildings of Port Arthur would be restored one day and visited by tourists as a chamber of antiquarian horrors. Even by 1870 convictism was outside the personal experience of most people in every colony except Tasmania and Western Australia. In that year Marcus Clarke, a young gentleman who had reached Melbourne in 1863, began to reanimate its enormities in a novel. For readers who knew as little of the system as Clarke himself had known until he studied its documents in Victoria and visited its relics at Port Arthur, *His Natural Life* displayed the penal settlements of Australia's dark age as engines for breaking the spirit of man.

EMANCIPISTS

Phillip's instructions allowed him 'to emancipate and discharge from their servitude' convicts deserving of favour, and to make grants of farming land to 'convicts so emancipated': thirty acres for a man, another twenty if he had a wife, and ten for each child. The first man to be given such a grant was James Ruse, who had been a farmer at home before he was transported for burglary. Officials watched him keenly, hoping that here was the pioneer of a peasantry. Before long, Ruse had sold his land to pay for a passage home; but the money trickled away and he was given more land. After many ups and downs as a farmer, Ruse ended his life working for wages. It was a common progress. Of sixty freed convicts given land by Phillip, fewer than twenty were working it by 1798. Most of the 1284 convicts released by 1800 had been men of the towns at home, and most would be makers of towns out here.

Many of the emancipated were soon doing well for themselves. A surgeon noted in 1804 'good mechanics who had been convicts' now having plenty of work, and living with their families 'in great comfort and even luxury, comparatively speaking with the manner in which people of the same description live in England.' Skills precious out here could not be wasted merely because their possessors had broken the law. George

Howe, a printer transported for shoplifting, was put almost immediately in charge of the colony's only press and was commissioned by Governor King to begin the first newspaper, the *Sydney Gazette and New South Wales Advertiser* [*Sydney Gazette*], which began weekly publication on 5 March 1803. Some men flourished in private trade. Edward Wills, transported for highway robbery in 1799, was a rich merchant and ship-builder by the time he died in 1811. His widow then married George Howe. Daniel Cooper, sentenced for theft in 1815, pardoned by 1821, went into partnership with another freed convict, Solomon Levey, to make a fortune in commerce before he returned home in 1831. Cooper and Levey were famous for their rise from disgrace to prosperity. So was one female convict, Mary Haydock, transported in 1790 at the age of thirteen for stealing a horse and married in 1794 to Thomas Reibey, a free settler who became associated with the pardoned Edward Wills. Reibey died in 1811, the same year as Wills, leaving his widow with seven children. Mary Reibey managed and enlarged her husband's enterprises and became one of the richest people in New South Wales. Other emancipated convicts flourished modestly as tailors, harness-makers, tin-smiths and carpenters.

Respectable people worried about the future of a community composed so largely of men and women who belonged to it because they had been caught stealing. The convicts' morals, it was feared, accompanied them to freedom and comfort, and infected other members of the civil and military population. 'The circumstances under which the colony was settled, and the very purpose of the settlement,' wrote a visitor in 1805, 'has had a very visible effect upon the general manners, or what may be called the national character, of Botany Bay.'

The place of former convicts in New South Wales became a political issue under Governor Macquarie. This country, he declared in 1821, 'should be made the home AND A HAPPY HOME to every emancipated convict who DESERVES IT . . . My principle is, that when once a man is free, his former state should no longer be remembered, or allowed to act against him; let him then feel himself eligible for any situation which he has, by a long term of upright conduct, proved himself worthy of filling.' So Francis Greenway, architect, was eligible when pardoned to be treated as if he had never been transported for forgery; Simeon Lord and Andrew Thompson, convicted at home for stealing cloth, were appointed as magistrates and invited to dine at Government House; former convicts were admitted to practise as attorneys in the new Supreme Court. It was a policy necessary to induce reform, Macquarie thought; but it was a source of outrage to some free men, including the principal chaplain, Samuel Marsden, and the judge, Jeffery Hart Bent. Marsden refused to sit with emancipated magistrates as trustees of a new road; Bent would not let emancipated attorneys appear before him, and was dismissed. Chaplain and judge were among those whose complaints led to Bigge's mission of inquiry, and it became a widely received opinion in New South Wales that Bigge's report was a contrivance to keep the emancipists in a state of vassalage. Macquarie was remembered as their patron. In the words of Joseph Harpur, son of an emancipated highway robber:

> The exiled wanderer in a foreign land
> With tears confessed Macquarie's saving hand.

How a man happened to have come to New South Wales was the most delicate of topics in colonial conversation. The word 'convict' came to be forbidden from general discourse. Peter Cunningham observed in 1827 that the term was 'erased by a sort of general tacit compact from our Botany dictionary, as a word too ticklish to be pronounced in these sensitive latitudes.' He recalled a case in which a man who had been pardoned for meritorious conduct in Van Diemen's Land won fifty pounds in court from someone who called him 'd——d convict!' In a later case 'Irish convict' was thought to be especially offensive. There were various euphemisms, funny and serious. Convicts wearing a yellow outfit provided for newcomers were 'canaries'. 'Prisoners' was deemed a little less disagreeable than 'convicts'; but the alternative with the widest currency was, as Cunningham put it, 'the loyal designation of *government-men*'. The word presumably originated with convicts themselves, as did 'legitimates', with its sardonic implication that they were the only people with a proper reason for being here. In similar mood somebody thought of the remark, to be repeated for generations, that the first settlers of Australia were chosen by the best judges in England.

The freed convict was called an expiree, but he much preferred to be known as an emancipist. That word could describe a person pardoned short of his term as well as one who had served it out, and it spoke of his new liberty rather than his old servitude. It acquired, moreover, a political usage well beyond its original legal context, suggesting not just that a man had been made free but that he strove for the freedom of others. In the ears of an unspotted free man hostile to the pretensions of expirees, it could sound a violation of language to call them emancipists. James Mudie, a respectable landowner from Scotland, objected to it in 1837. 'Mr. Wilberforce may be honoured with the title of emancipist,' he wrote; 'but it is as absurd to give the same appellation to the emancipated felons of New South Wales as it would be to bestow it upon the emancipated negroes of the West Indies.' What affronted Mudie and others was the insinuation that these people had somehow freed themselves, and were resolved on freeing others and ultimately on delivering the colony into their own dirty hands. A new name for them was needed. 'The author has ventured to coin the word *felonry*', Mudie wrote, 'as the appellative of an *order* or class of persons in New South Wales,—an order which happily exists in no other country in the world.' It was, he suggested, a 'legitimate member of the tribe of appellatives . . . as *peasantry, tenantry, yeomanry, gentry*.'

'Felonry' was a word that appealed to the faction known in Botany English from 1825 as 'exclusionist' and later 'exclusive'—so named, Cunningham wrote, 'from their strict exclusion of the emancipists from their society'. The terms were associated above all with the family of John Macarthur, who had arrived as an army officer in 1790, became a landowner and trader, and flourished as a pastoral magnate after persuading the authorities at home in 1804 to give him five thousand acres on which to experiment with the growing of wool from Spanish merino sheep. The exclusionist was also called a 'pure merino'. Roger Therry, who came out from Ireland as a legal official in 1829, explained that this was 'a designation given to sheep where there is no cross-blood in the flocks', and was applied to 'a class who were not only free and unconvicted, but who could boast of having no collateral relationship or distant affinity with those in whose escutcheon there was a blot. These *pure merinos* formed the topmost round in the social ladder.' The have-nots in this unsettled society were proving clever at defining both themselves and the haves: for 'emancipist' gave dignity and 'exclusionist' sounded mean; 'pure merino', connecting the supposed aristocrats with their animals, must have been hard to say without a sneer. Some people with thoroughly blotted escutcheons liked to call themselves cross-breds.

However named, they were numerous enough by the 1820s to feel that they had a large stake in the colony. A census taken in 1828 showed that about half the people in New South Wales were convicts, and that former convicts made up nearly half of the free population. Between 1828 and 1841 the proportion of convicts declined sharply and the proportion of former convicts slightly. Most people in New South Wales now were free emigrants or had been born in the colony. In 1851 there were about eighty thousand convicts and former convicts still alive and living in Australia, or about one in five of the white population. Nearly half of them were in Van Diemen's Land. In New South Wales they became a small minority, convicts making up 1.5 per cent of the population and former convicts another 14 per cent.

The citizens of Victoria had little enough convictism in their past to speak with malice, if they wished, about the lineage of their northern neighbours. 'Of course, there are frightfully rich people there', a European visitor heard people in Melbourne say of Sydney in 1863, '—but mostly descended from convicts—and as for their behaviour!' Such talk might be only intercolonial banter; but it was apt to sound funnier in Victoria or South Australia than in New South Wales, where in 1870 one's parentage was a matter to be avoided in polite society just as the circumstances of one's arrival had been a perilous subject a generation earlier.

2 Emigrants

NEW CHUMS

Many emancipists regarded free emigrants as intruders, and told them so. Alexander Harris, an emigrant of 1825, heard himself called, soon after landing in New South Wales, 'one of the free objects—bad luck to 'em! What business have they here in the prisoners' country?' When a shipload of artisans from Scotland reached Sydney in 1831, it was said that they 'could not pass along the streets ... without hearing such observations as the following from almost every cottage they passed: "There are these bloody emigrants come to take the country from us".'

Emigrants were so far a small minority. At the census of 1828, New South Wales had fewer than 5000 people who had come out voluntarily, in a population of 36 598. Thousands more bought and read such books as William Charles Wentworth's *A Statistical, Historical and Political Description of the Colony of New South Wales, and its Dependent Settlements in Van Diemen's Land: with a Particular Enumeration of the Advantages which these Colonies Offer for Emigration and their Superiority in Many Respects over those Possessed by the United States of America* (London 1819). But for most prospective emigrants Australia had no advantage to outweigh the hard facts that it was thousands of miles farther away than North America and cost three or four times as much to reach. Only to men with some capital did New South Wales and Van Diemen's Land hold out attractions not available in the United States: free land and convict labourers. Settlers, as they were called, were given land for agriculture and pasture. In early colonial usage the word meant a freeholder, and it applied to men who had emigrated as private citizens, to military or civil officers who had decided to stay, and to pardoned convicts who had been granted land.

The imperial government decided in 1831 to stop giving land away to settlers, to sell it at not less than five shillings an acre, and to use money from land sales for the fares of emigrants. It suited authorities worried about the dangers of redundant population to have a means of inducing some poor families to leave the kingdom; and in New South Wales, as the secretary of state put it in 1838, the change of policy was intended 'to remedy the great want of labour, which was at that time complained of in the Colony, by providing the pecuniary means of assisting emigration, and at the same time preventing the undue dispersion of the Emigrants.' Australia now became the emigrants' country as well as the prisoners'. From 1831 to 1840 about 50 000 offenders were transported and about 65 000 free men and women chose to emigrate.

The minimum price of land in New South Wales was raised to twelve shillings an acre in 1838, providing more money for emigration and making sure that men would have to work longer for wages in regions already settled before they could hope to buy land farther out. In South Australia land was sold at one pound an acre, and in 1842 that price was made the minimum throughout the Australian colonies under an imperial act which reserved half the proceeds for carrying out emigrants who could not otherwise afford to go. The Australian colonies admitted more than 170 000 emigrants from the United Kingdom between 1831 and 1850, of whom about two-thirds were assisted out of land funds. The proportion of government-assisted emigrants varied from colony to colony, amounting to about three-quarters of people reaching New South Wales including Port Phillip, half those going to South Australia, and fewer to Van Diemen's Land and Western Australia. It varied also from year to year according to how much land was sold and to the demand for labour. New South Wales and South Australia stopped assisted emigration in 1841 during a severe depression, and the total number of emigrants reaching Australia from 1842 to 1846 was only half as many as had arrived during 1841. By 1847 the flow was increasing again.

The balance of sexes was more nearly equal among emigrants than among convicts; but even South Australia, which was wholly an emigrants' country, had only eight females to every ten males by 1850, and in Australia as a whole there were fewer than seven to every ten. The shortage of women had been a matter of official concern ever since 1787, when Phillip's instructions encouraged him to pick some up from Pacific Islands for his convicts. It appalled Caroline Chisholm, wife of an officer in the service of the East India Company, who reached Sydney in 1838. She met every shipload of emigrants, putting much energy into protecting single girls against the consequences of being in short supply. In England from 1846, she persuaded the Colonial Office to give free passages to wives and children of convicts emancipated in New South Wales, and she promoted plans for moving out poor people in family parties. But she was opposed by rural employers in the colony, who rightly judged that she was proposing to form a self-sufficient peasantry rather than to supply them with wage-labourers; and she was suspected of plotting to continue what seemed to many people another imbalance: an excess of Catholics, who made up more than twice as large a proportion of the Australian as of the English population. Her husband was a Scottish Catholic and she an English convert. When she visited Rome, Pope Pius IX received and praised her. In Sydney a Scottish Presbyterian minister called her 'an artful female Jesuit, the able but concealed agent of the Romish priesthood in Australia.' She was in truth respectful of other varieties of Christianity, having vowed to God that she would 'know neither country nor creed', and had chaplains for all the faiths represented among the families who sailed on ships she chartered. But that was no comfort to Protestants who saw so many Catholics of Irish origin arriving every year as reinforcements to the army of their fellow-countrymen and fellow-papists who had come out as convicts.

In convicts' rhyming cant the emigrant was a Jemmy Grant. As perceived by aggressive users of the word, he not only competed for work with the emancipist but was a lesser man, having taken a free passage out because he was helpless at home. 'I never wanted to leave England', an old Vandemonian was heard to boast. 'I wasn't like one of these "Jemmy Grants"; I could always earn a good living; it was the Government as took and sent me out.' Jemmy Grant became Jemmy, then Jimmy, as the newcomer was thought of not as a man leaving England but as a man coming here, not emigrant but immigrant (that word having been coined in the United States). He was also a new chum, a term in derogatory use by 1840 for the recently arrived free man, ignorant and incompetent alongside the old hand. 'What a queer lot most of these emigrants are', said a character in Alexander Harris's novel *The Emigrant Family* (1849). 'They seem like a set of children. They have no notion how to help themselves till they've been here half the length of a man's life.' That was a judgement more indulgent than Harris himself had suffered in 1825. The speaker was perceiving the emigrant as merely lacking skill, and colonial experience might put that right. In the observation of one traveller in 1847, the emancipists' feeling 'that the colony was theirs by right, and that the free emigrants were interlopers upon their soil . . . has now passed away.' New issues had arisen by that time, over which many emancipists and emigrants found themselves on the same side.

AN EXCELLENT SYSTEM FOR POOR GENTLEMEN

One in every three emigrants to Australia between 1831 and 1850 paid his own fare. Sometimes accident decided whether a person came out assisted or unassisted, as it did for William Deakin in 1849. Deakin, who worked for a grocer in Oxford, sought a free passage for himself and his wife; but because the New South Wales emigration fund happened to be low when they applied, the Deakins paid their own fares and chose to get off the ship at Adelaide. Other unassisted emigrants were people of greater wealth, booking cabins for the voyage out, dining with the captain, and hoping that they would prosper by having the poorer emigrants, jammed in below, work for them when they all reached Australia.

Among the cabin passengers were members of over-populated areas in the professions of law and medicine, army officers retired on half-pay, and people from families of precarious gentility struggling to keep up accustomed ways of life as income from farming declined. In 1828 James Henty, son of a Sussex farmer, himself manager of a family bank, wrote to his younger brother William who was studying law. 'After mature deliberation', he began, 'I have almost come to the conclusion that New South Wales will do more for our family than England ever will'. In England the Hentys would have to 'descend many steps in the scale of Society . . . which our feelings could ill stand, having at the same time an opportunity of doing as well and perhaps considerably better in New South Wales, under British Dominion and a fine climate.' Moreover, 'immediately we get there we shall be placed in the first Rank in Society, a circumstance which must not be overlooked as it will tend most materially to our comfort and future advantage.' James and William, five other brothers, a sister and their parents all sailed out in chartered ships to settle in Western Australia, Van Diemen's Land and Australia Felix. Thomas Mitchell was startled to find Hentys and their animals established at Portland Bay in 1836, most of them well on the way to flourishing exactly as James had hoped. An admiring neighbour wrote of them later as 'those representative Englishmen and distinguished colonists, the Hentys,' who 'commenced the Anglo-Saxon conquest of Australia Felix.' Scotland gave Australia Felix many pioneer graziers whose history, hopes and colonial fortunes were similar to those of the Hentys. Some two-thirds of the men who settled in the district were farmers from the lowlands. Ireland sent out plenty of lawyers such as Redmond Barry, who had been earning so little at the crowded Bar of Dublin that the prospect of practice in Sydney or Melbourne was attractive. Barry, son of a general, sailed out in

1839 at the age of twenty-six and became the second judge of the Supreme Court of Victoria in 1852.

While some gentlemen emigrated to make money, others went to restore their health. John Reid, a Scottish clergyman, sailed for Melbourne with his family in 1852 on medical advice that Australia would cure his bronchitis. It did; and his sons and daughters were grateful to the physician on other grounds. One son became managing director of a shipping company. Another, George, rose higher and higher in colonial politics. 'I think it was well for us all', George Reid wrote, 'that our chances in life were thus transferred to a new land containing so many resources, and offering so many advantages to those who could only inherit a good name.' It was on the advice of doctors that Robert Lowe, a young barrister in London, set off for Sydney in 1842, though for him Australia was supposed to provide an alternative career rather than a cure. He would be blind in seven years, they told him, and ought to take up outdoor work in a colony. The patient resolved to make a fortune in those years and come home secure. Out in Sydney, Lowe found himself involved like many other professional men in colonial politics. Among his allies was the Reverend Dr John Dunmore Lang who had left the Church of Scotland in 1822 because he disapproved of a system that put the choice of ministers in the hands of laymen, and who had chosen New South Wales because a younger brother wrote from Sydney to say that the colony had Scottish settlers and no Presbyterian clergy.

The passengers rarely included people who had been close to the top of society at home; for like all countries formed by the great migration from nineteenth-century Europe, Australia did not recruit those who had no need to better themselves. Many gentlemen could have said what an emigrant of the 1850s, Robert O'Hara Burke, was reported to have replied to a dancing partner who observed disparagingly that others in the company had come to Victoria to seek their fortunes: 'Why, my dear Mrs. G——, did not you and I come out here because we could not get so good a living at home?'

There were gentlemen who had left home in disgrace. Adam Lindsay Gordon, son of a retired cavalry officer, was a wild lad of nineteen when he sailed for Australia in 1853 in circumstances which he set down in verse:

> Across the trackless seas I go,
>   No matter when or where,
> And few my future lot will know,
>   And fewer still will care.
>
> My parents bid me cross the flood,
>   My kindred frowned at me;
> They say I have belied my blood,
>   And stained my pedigree.

There were some younger sons of aristocrats, not all of them black sheep. There were perhaps, but nobody could be sure, a few royal bastards endowed with common names and sent to the farthest part of the empire with or without parental patronage. Was William Augustus Miles, superintendent of police in Sydney, a son of King William IV? Was the merchant Prosper de Mestre a half-brother of Queen Victoria? Was Colonel Gibbes, collector of customs and father-in-law of Terence Murray of Yarralumla, a son of Mrs Fitzherbert and King George IV? These were questions to be cherished in the gossip of so plebeian a society.

When substantial free emigration was under way and the end of convict transportation in sight, any middle-class Englishman who happened to visit Australia was likely to wonder how it would serve as a home for people like himself. On 12 January 1836 H.M.S. *Beagle*, four years out from England on a surveying voyage around the world, brought Charles Darwin to Sydney. He was twenty-six, and had joined the *Beagle* as a naturalist after graduating from Cambridge. He was grandson both of Erasmus Darwin who had composed in 1789 the 'Visit of Hope to Sydney-Cove' and of Josiah Wedgwood whose vignette made of clay from the colony had inspired those lines. 'Before we came to the Colony,' he wrote in his diary, 'the things about which I felt most interest were, the state of Society amongst the higher & Convict classes, & the degree of attraction to emigrate.' A month in New South Wales and Van Diemen's Land made him proud of his nationality. 'It is necessary to leave England,' he wrote, '& see distant Colonies of various nations, to know what wonderful people the English are.' Sydney he found a good town, comparable to the suburbs of London or Birmingham but growing more quickly. Out at Parramatta he visited the house of Hannibal Macarthur, nephew of John, and judged that it 'would be considered a very superior one even in England.' After riding over the mountains to Bathurst and back he pronounced New South Wales 'a wonderful Colony; ancient Rome, in her Imperial grandeur, would not have been ashamed of such an offspring.' His grandfather's verse had 'prophecyed most truly.'

Charles Darwin felt, however, no degree of attraction to emigrate to New South Wales. The landscape bored him. The system of transportation, he allowed, was a success, 'converting vagabonds, most useless in one hemisphere, into active citizens of another, and thus giving birth to a new and splendid country—a grand centre of civilization'. But he disliked the rancorous divisions within colonial society which were a legacy of its penal origins. 'There is much jealousy between the children of the rich emancipist & the free settlers; the former being pleased to consider honest men as interlopers.' Above all he was revolted by the intimate association between free citizens and convicts, the confusion of relationships which made a gentleman both master and gaoler. 'How disgusting', Darwin wrote, 'to be waited on by a man, who the day before, was by your representation flogged for some trifling misdemeanour!' Van Diemen's Land pleased him and his companions more. The wetter climate made gardens and fields more like those of England. In Hobart Town the emancipists were less ostentatious and the servants, though convicts, more respectable. Several of the *Beagle*'s officers thought seriously of returning to this colony to raise sheep. Emigration, he reflected in Hobart Town, was an excellent system for poor gentlemen. If ever he had to undertake it himself, he would come to Van Diemen's Land. 'To a person not particularly attached to any particular kind, (such as literary, scientific &c) of society, & bringing out his family, it is a most admirable place of emigration.' But Charles Darwin would get from his family enough money to pursue as a gentlemanly scholar the puzzles about life that absorbed him; and he needed the company of the Geological Society, and correspondence with fellows only a few days away by post, to help him solve them. After eight dull days at King George Sound in Western Australia, England beckoned impatiently. 'Farewell, Australia!' he wrote on 14 March 1836; 'you are a rising child, and doubtless some day will reign a great princess in the South; but you are too great and ambitious for affection, yet not great enough for respect. I leave your shores without sorrow or regret.' Home he went to the country he loved, married his cousin Emma Wedgwood, and never left England again, even for a day. Thomas Mitchell named a mountain south of the Murray River after Darwin in 1836. The geologist Charles Gould honoured him alongside other Englishmen of science on a mountain in the west of Tasmania in 1862. On a later voyage of the *Beagle*, in 1839, his name was left on a harbour in the dry, hot, deserted north where Charles Darwin would have found it disagreeable to spend five minutes. Sometimes, though, he daydreamed of Van Diemen's Land. 'I am always building veritable castles in the air about emigrating', he wrote to a friend in 1854, five years before publishing *The Origin of Species*, 'and Tasmania has been my headquarters of late'.

Some eminent people considered going to an Australian colony as a last resort or even a way of punishing England. Charles Dickens, gloomy that such humbugs as Disraeli were in charge at Westminster, thought of 'flying to Australia and taking to the Bush.' Thomas Carlyle thought at least momentarily that the sovereign and the court and all the machinery of government should go to Australia 'where the field for national life was so wide, attractive and unencumbered, and so leave the contracted spaces and the murky atmosphere of England behind them.' The queen herself threatened to take her children and emigrate to Australia in 1870 if newspapers did not stop making rude remarks about her. Dickens did not think long or seriously of it, though he dispatched the Micawber family in 1849 and two of his own sons emigrated later, one to Victoria in 1865 and the other to New South Wales in 1869. The only acknowledged members of the queen's family who sailed to Australia in her lifetime came as visitors.

HENRY AND CLARINDA PARKES

Like masses of his compatriots Henry Parkes was born in the country and grew up in an industrial city. His father, a tenant farmer cultivating land which had been in the family for generations, was forced off it after 1815—the year in which the wars ended and Henry was born—and drifted into Birmingham, where his children tried to acquire skills that might fit them to climb a little way up the pyramid of society. From the sermons of the Nonconformist chapel, the lessons of the Mechanics' Institute, and the example of his respectable superiors, young Henry Parkes learned the gospel of self-improvement; and political radicals taught him that the obstacles in the path of such people as himself could be removed if—in Thomas Attwood's image—the masters and the workmen went hand-in-hand to the gates of government and demanded the redress of their common grievances. He served an apprenticeship to a turner of bone and ivory and looked about first in Birmingham and then in London, for a chance to set himself up in business. But he failed, and fell into debt; and his mind turned from improvement at home to emigration abroad, at a time when the governments of Australian colonies were seeking to populate them with sturdy free men. 'I am one of the many', he wrote to the *London Charter*, 'who cannot now obtain the means of living in their native country. In a fortnight's time I shall be gone to seek a better home in the wilderness of Australia.' On 26 March 1839, aged nearly twenty-four, Henry Parkes and his wife Clarinda boarded the *Strathfieldsaye*, of 476 tons, at Gravesend and began their long journey.

In Birmingham Parkes had discovered a taste for writing, both in prose and in verse, though lack of proper schooling had left his spelling and grammar shaky. To the

EMIGRANTS EMBARKING AT LIVERPOOL

London Charter he sent 'A poet's farewell', and among the books he bought for the journey
was a cheap edition of the poems of Thomas Campbell. There he found 'Lines on the
Departure of Emigrants for New South Wales' which became his favourite poetry:

> On England's shore I saw a pensive band,
> With sails unfurl'd for earth's remotest strand,
> Like children parting from a mother, shed
> Tears for the home that could not yield them bread . . .

In Parkes's case it was butter and jam rather than bread that England could not yield
him, but he preferred to speak now and later as if hunger rather than ambition had driven
him to New South Wales.

> Delightful land, in wildness ev'n benign,
> The glorious past is ours, the future thine!
> As in a cradled Hercules, we trace
> The lines of empire on thine infant face.

The pious young man could readily say 'Amen' to that.

Henry and Clarinda Parkes could have applied to go out as government emigrants.
They went instead as bounty emigrants, under a scheme introduced in 1835. Employers
in the colony had complained that too many of the people who had been paid to come out

since 1831 were useless as workers. Under the bounty system, an employer was paid by the colonial government if he brought out emigrants who were judged to be suitable when they landed. In practice by 1839 it was usually agents in London who did the choosing, and the ship's captain who collected the bounty in Sydney. John Marshall, the agent who selected Parkes and his wife, had two testimonials from Birmingham about their character and could see that they were healthy and decent. They were among forty thousand assisted emigrants who sailed for New South Wales between 1838 and 1841.

Some of the 205 emigrants on the *Strathfieldsaye* were gentlefolk paying their own passage. Live birds and animals, Parkes noticed, were taken on board for them; but down below it was beef and soup and biscuits in quarters designed for the poor and therefore, as Parkes wrote, most miserably uncomfortable to him. He and his pregnant wife had to live there for four months. In the view of John Dunmore Lang the long voyage out sometimes did irreparable damage to an emigrant's character, inducing habits of indolence and intemperance which were never shaken off ashore. The cause of morality in New South Wales would be served, Lang thought, if doctors could drug emigrants on embarkation and have them wake up in Port Jackson. Idleness and drink were not temptations to the aspiring young man from Birmingham, but an opiate would have spared him the horror of spending so long so close to his fellow-emigrants. 'I am more solitary and companionless than I ever was in all my life in this stagnant crowd of human beings', he wrote in a letter home. 'Some of them are of the most indecent and brutish description.'

The *Strathfieldsaye* entered Port Jackson late in July. Clarinda's child, a girl, was born two days before they landed. As they sailed into Sydney Cove the young poet was moved to pity and horror by his first sight of the convicts whom men such as himself were to replace in this society:

> A score of men, in coarse habiliments,
> Hewing the rock away. You may remember,
> Among the many evil-traced events
> Of a town life, some robbery, when December
> Brought on the long, dark nights—a neighbour's boy
> Tried for't, and banished. He, perchance, is one
> Who yonder lift the pickaxe in the sun
> To level Pinchgut Island! If e'er joy
> Gladden'd your heart on England's shore, oh! never
> Forget that Englishmen are banished here for ever.

An assisted emigrant who had lived through the years since Waterloo could easily imagine himself, or at least his neighbour, coming here as prisoner rather than emigrant.

If Henry and Clarinda Parkes had been government emigrants they and their baby could have lodged for up to two weeks in the Immigration Barracks while employers looked them over. As bounty emigrants, once inspected and deemed suitable additions to the population, they were on their own. Parkes hoped to find work in Sydney rather than the wilderness, but after two weeks he had sold his few possessions for expensive food and shelter and still had no job. About forty miles out of Sydney he was engaged as a labourer—a common labourer, he said in a letter home—at Regentville, the property of Sir John Jamison, who had named it for George IV. The raw and penniless newcomer happened to be working for one of the greatest landowners of the colony, its earliest

NEW CHUMS AT THE DIGGINGS

*'Many getting either disgusted with the difficulties of travelling or becoming heart
sick returned dispirited to Melbourne perfectly satisfied with their knowledge of gold
mining, resolving at the same time not to abandon the pen for the spade or as a young
Gentleman remarks in a Colonial song:*

I've got to work with all my might,	*If my mother could but see me now,*
And throw up nasty clay.	*Whatever would she say.'*

knight, and the leader of the first generation of free emigrant settlers. Six months of rural
life and convict's work was more than enough: at the first chance Parkes moved in to
Sydney. It was a common choice. Like convicts before them, assisted emigrants preferred
the town to the bush. Within two years Parkes had a set of turner's tools worth a hundred
pounds and was ready to go into business. In letters to Birmingham he was sometimes a
homesick exile, sometimes a buoyant colonist. Early in 1843 he vowed that while he lived
he would 'cling to the hope of returning to dear England.' A change of mood, and perhaps
a rise in income, and he could identify himself with the new land. 'Yes! henceforth the
country of my children shall be mine. Australia has afforded me a better home than my
motherland, and I will love her with a patriot's love.' He plunged into her politics,
agitating with Robert Lowe against the revival of transportation and in favour of a
popularly elected parliament. Lowe went home in 1850, his eyesight intact, to become
chancellor of the exchequer and Lord Sherbrooke. Parkes committed himself to a
colonial destiny.

GOLD SEEKERS

Gold doubled the population of Australia in less than ten years. Half a million people sailed out from the United Kingdom between 1852 and 1861—more in some years than went to the United States, for at last Victoria and New South Wales really did have an advantage as places of emigration. More than half—a higher proportion than ever before— were people paying their own fares. In the golden colony of Victoria, to which most of the newcomers rushed, seven in every ten were unassisted. Gold drew a higher proportion of men with education, professional experience and good connexions. Francis Augustus Hare, son of a captain in the Dragoons, cousin of the governor of Singapore, reached Melbourne from the Cape of Good Hope in April 1852. Thomas Woolner, sculptor, was seen off for the goldfields on 24 July 1852 by his pre-Raphaelite brethren, one of whom, Ford Madox Brown, was inspired by the scene at the dockside to paint his picture *The Last of England*. Charles Summers was another sculptor who went out in search of gold. So did Richard Horne, famous for a season as the author of the epic poem *Orion*. After reading that a man in Australia might take a bag from his pocket 'containing two pounds of gold he procured before dinner', Horne sailed out in his fiftieth year with a mountainous cargo of mining equipment and a letter of introduction from Charles Dickens to the husband of Caroline Chisholm. Henry Kingsley, younger brother of the fashionable clergyman, moralist and historian Charles, went to New South Wales after gold in 1853. Peter Lalor, a civil engineer, left Ireland for Melbourne in 1852. Joseph Reed, a Cornish architect, gave up practising in England to look for gold in Victoria. Thousands of men crossed the Pacific from California, many of whom had gone from Australia to look for gold there. Some came from continental Europe. Raffaello Carboni, a colonel under Garibaldi and since 1849 an exile from Rome, was attracted to Melbourne in 1852 by articles on gold in the *Illustrated London News*. Louis Monasch, aged twenty-five, son of a Hebrew publisher in Russian Poland, set off for Victorian gold in 1853. But most emigration to the goldfields, as to the colonies until 1850, was of people from Britain. Among them were many who left one Australian colony for another, as William Deakin moved from Adelaide to the Victorian goldfields in 1851.

The goldfields were the diggings, and the man after gold was a digger. 'Diggerdom', William Howitt wrote of Victoria after arriving in 1852, 'is gloriously in the ascendant here.' Governors, preachers and other moralists feared that the diggers would make poor citizens, as if there was something singularly wicked about a man who made his fortune in a moment without raising a sweat. That was, indeed, the digger's dream. As on goldfields elsewhere in the world, one place here, at Ballarat in Victoria, was named hopefully Eureka—'I have found it'. Thousands did find it. A golden boulder known as Kerr's hundredweight, dug up north of Bathurst in July 1851, earned its owner more than four thousand pounds. It was larger than any mass of gold found in California, but even greater nuggets were soon unearthed in Victoria. Not far from Eureka four men— four working men, as the governor told the secretary of state—struck early in 1853 a mass of gold which weighed more than two thousand ounces and was worth more than two thousand pounds to each man. Nugget after nugget on the Victorian fields became briefly the largest in the world. Gold worth three million pounds was found in New South Wales, and more than nine million pounds in Victoria, by the end of 1852, most of it before the emigrant ships began to disembark gold seekers from England.

By that time many men who had rushed for gold were turning already to other occupations. 'Carters, carpenters, storemen, wheelwrights, butchers, shoe-makers, &c.,'

THE LAST OF ENGLAND

wrote a visitor to the Victorian diggings in 1853, 'usually in the long run make a fortune quicker than the diggers themselves, and certainly with less hard work or risk of life.' Francis Augustus Hare and Richard Horne found that there was steadier money to be made by guarding the gold as it travelled to Melbourne than by digging for it. Louis Monasch opened a store (and became Monash, a British subject, in 1856). William Deakin went in for coaching. Joseph Reed began to design the grand civic buildings that gold made possible for Melbourne. But there were huge rushes to new Victorian goldfields in the later 1850s. The colony's digger population was probably at its peak—of about

140 000—in 1858. In that year a group of Cornish emigrants at Ballarat found the
Welcome Nugget, of 2217 ounces. After 1860 the amount of gold found in Victoria
declined gradually and the number of individual diggers declined fast. New South Wales
was the colony for rushes in the 1860s; but it was in Victoria that the most gigantic nugget
of all, the Welcome Stranger, was found in 1869. It weighed 2284 ounces and fetched a
Cornish emigrant and his mates £9436. Several of her majesty's ships visiting Port Phillip
that year provided illegal emigrants from their crews. 'Australia, and markedly Melbourne,
seemed such a joyous free-handed land', Midshipman William Creswell wrote indulgently.
'The diggings—Ballarat, Bendigo and others—were in full swing. One heard on all sides
of rich finds and ounces to the ton and great nuggets.' It was remarkable, he thought,
that the deserters were not far more numerous. Gold had given Victoria a greater power
than any other part of the British empire to attract emigrants.

SOJOURNERS AND STAYERS

'Emigrants may be divided into two classes,' wrote a traveller in the years just before gold,
'namely, those who intend to settle permanently in their adopted country, and those
who intend to return after having amassed a competency.' As Henry Parkes knew, both
intentions could jostle in the heart of an emigrant. Sir Charles Hotham, presiding as
governor of Victoria over the rush of newcomers, could see in them only the wish to
return. They were "essentially migratory,' he told the Colonial Office in 1855; 'the man of
commerce strives to accumulate wealth, the capitalist invests his money in land, the
miner works for gold, but none of these persons contemplate making this land their homes
or endeavour to do more than amass sufficient money to enable them to return to
England'. Government House, itself a sojourner's residence, was not the best place from
which to discover the thoughts and feelings of several hundred thousand men and
women about where to spend the rest of their lives, and Hotham knew less than most
governors of what his people thought and felt about anything. Redmond Barry, a judge
of the Supreme Court in Hotham's time, had settled happily the day he reached Melbourne
in 1839, and never thought of returning to the old world except as a visitor. It may
nevertheless have been true that most emigrants of the 1850s, like Henry Parkes earlier,
sailed for Australia hoping to get rich and go home. Henry Kingsley returned in 1858
after five years. The dedicatory passage to his parents in a novel about Australia, *The
Recollections of Geoffry Hamlyn* (1859), called the book the fruit of many weary years of
separation. 'It seems like a waste of existence', says one character, 'for a man to stay here
tending sheep, when his birthright is that of an Englishman: the right to move among
his peers, and find his fit place in the greatest empire in the world.' Thomas Woolner the
sculptor had by no means seen the last of England in 1852, for he was back in 1854. Like
other returned adventurers he was interrogated by prospective emigrants. When the
radical Irish member of the House of Commons, Charles Gavan Duffy, was thinking of
going out in 1855 he met Woolner at the Carlyles' house in Chelsea and asked him about
the flies, the climate and the company. 'The flies', Duffy was told, 'count for nothing; the
air is exhilarating; he was always in high spirits and ready for work. There were some
men of brains and culture in Melbourne, and he enjoyed life thoroughly. I laughed and
inquired, "Why did you quit this terrestrial Paradise?" "Well," he rejoined, "I am an
artist, and art won't be born there for a generation or two, and meantime I must live, if
possible." ' Charles Joseph La Trobe, who had preceded Sir Charles Hotham as

governor of Victoria, confirmed all the favourable things Duffy heard from Woolner and others. Duffy liked the sound of this society enriched by gold and on the edge of self-government. 'You would lead the colony', a friend had urged him, '—you would create a better Ireland there—you would become rich.' He sailed on one of the new American-built clippers, sailing ships which had begun to cut weeks from the journey, and got to Melbourne in just under eighty days. He went a long way towards fulfilling the friend's prophecies; but eventually he too returned.

By 1870 a number of emigrants who had become men of mark in the Australian colonies were back home living in affluent and even ostentatious retirement. Edward Wilson, an emigrant to Port Phillip in 1841, proprietor of the Melbourne *Argus* since 1850, settled in Kent in 1864 to live as a country gentleman in a small palace with its own zoo which kangaroos and emus shared with animals from other parts of the empire. In London Edward Wilson often met Sir Charles Nicholson, who had gone to Sydney as a young doctor in 1834 and returned in 1862 to live as nearly as possible like a lord. 'Residence in England', Nicholson wrote from Sydney in 1852, 'could afford me a thousand sources of enjoyment, not one of which is to be found here.' But residence in England would have been unlikely to make him, as residence in New South Wales did, a rich landowner and investor, speaker of a legislature, chancellor of a university, and a baronet. One thing making colonial life tolerable, as he remarked in a letter, was the opportunity it gave every individual of quality to affect the course of history. Having affected the course of history in New South Wales, Nicholson took home his accumulated wealth and prestige, hired Scottish forests to hunt deer, and gave advice to the Colonial Office on how to manage the empire. Absentee colonists, the Irish immigrant, George Higinbotham, called Nicholson and his friends and spoke of them in 1869 as men who had 'deserted the sphere of their natural duties'. Other emigrants returned in their prime to crown colonial careers by achieving eminence at home. Two of them, Robert Lowe and Hugh Childers, were in Gladstone's ministry of 1868. Old colleagues back in the colonies were not always sure whether to be proud or amused at such triumphs. Archibald Michie, an emigrant lawyer who stayed, smiled to think of Childers commanding the channel fleet, but went on: 'In sober earnest, let us express our gratification that England has apparently found a very efficient First Lord of the Admiralty in one who received his political and administrative education in this our own Colony of Victoria.'

Returned emigrants pressed Australian political interests in London. They joined a General Association for the Australian Colonies to support bills for new constitutions, to request better mail services and naval defence, and to oppose the dispatch of convicts to Western Australia. Wilson, Nicholson and Childers were among more than two hundred members of the association, which lasted from 1855 to 1862. When Canadian delegates came to London in 1867 to work out the terms of their confederation, Nicholson and others talked with them about forming a body that would enable men from self-governing colonies to meet each other in London for fellowship and discussion, to represent colonial interests, and to resist a tendency in governing circles to hold imperial possessions in low regard. The inaugural dinner of the Colonial Society was attended by about two hundred gentlemen on 10 March 1869. Two thirds of the company had some connexion with the Australian colonies, among them Wilson, Nicholson, Charles Sturt and William Henty (who had been colonial secretary of Tasmania and became, in 1862, the only member of his family to return home). They heard the prime minister, Gladstone, speak fruitily about handing down from generation to generation the unity of the British race. The Colonial Society became the Royal Colonial Institute in 1870. Peers agreed to preside over it; Edward Wilson was its first financial member, and men from Australia were prominent in its armchairs and at meetings that discussed how best to preserve the association between mother country and colonies.

Among the great majority of emigrants who stayed to be buried in Australia, many must have ended there only because they could not face the ocean again or lacked the fare home or did not want to admit that they had failed to make good; but many others had settled happily in the new environment, believing that their children had more chance there of growing up healthy, literate and comfortable. 'Oh, what a difference there is between this country and home for poor folks', a girl from London told Caroline Chisholm in 1846. 'I know I would not go back again,—I know what England is. Old England is a fine place for the rich, but the Lord help the poor.' This country was not only for the poor, but for anybody who felt himself a gainer from its greater freedom of social movement. 'The tendency of colonial life is to annul the prejudices of European society,' wrote John West in 1852, 'and to yield to every man the position which may be due to his talents or virtues.' Had West himself not emigrated, he might have spent his life in honourable obscurity as a Congregational minister in the south of England. Out here he discovered talents for politics, literature and journalism. Having led the campaign to stop convicts coming to Van Diemen's Land, he wrote a formidable history of the colony and left it in 1854, on the invitation of John Fairfax, to make the *Sydney Morning Herald* a powerful agent of education and opinion in New South Wales. He was still editing the paper when he died in 1873. 'Whilst the desire of returning lasts,' Archibald Michie observed in 1844, 'it is seldom that immigrants here have the ability to gratify it; and by the time the ability is acquired, the desire is lost.' He was then a young barrister in Sydney, five years out from London, and still had some desire of returning. He tried copper mining in South Australia, had desire and ability enough to go back to England in 1848, but sailed out again in 1852 and settled finally in Melbourne, where he edited the *Herald*, made up to eight thousand pounds a year at the Bar, and performed in parliament with a skill that moved Duffy to compare him with Disraeli. He became Sir Archibald in 1878 and died in his adopted country at the age of eighty-six, in 1899. Henry Kendall, born in New South Wales of emigrant parents in 1839, imagined in one of his earliest published poems the outlook of emigrants on their old and new homes:

> 'Tis true that emotions of temper'd regret,
> Still live for the country we'll never forget;
> But yet we are happy,—since learning to love
> The scenes that surround us—the skies are above,
> We find ourselves bound,—as it were by a spell,—
> In the clime we've adopted contented to dwell.

Those lines could almost have been written by Henry Parkes. He became a colonial patriot, a Briton thoroughly settled in New South Wales, deeply attached to the old country—though capable of rebellious rhetoric about its politicians—and ambitious for the new. He founded a daily newspaper, the *Empire*, and entered parliament. When he returned home in 1861 after more than twenty years away, it was only for fourteen months, to lecture in the cause of emigration. He grew a beard to keep out the cold of English winter. Henry Parkes, commissioner of emigration and member of the Legislative Assembly of New South Wales, had access to heights of society beyond the reach of any mere artisan from Birmingham. Nobles chaired his meetings. Carlyle invited him for oatmeal cakes and tea. Richard Cobden had him to stay and talk free trade. He formed 'quite a loving friendship' with the Christian socialist Thomas Hughes, who had written *Tom Brown's Schooldays* and whom he found the 'manliest of men'. In conversation he was both proud and deferential, representing in his person a great part of the empire but feeling civilized by the privilege of standing so close to its summit.

Parkes had been offered the assignment by members of a ministry who were happy to have him away from parliament for a while, and he had accepted it all the more eagerly because in 1858, with a wife and five children to support, his enterprise of publishing the *Empire* had failed and he had gone bankrupt. (The paper resumed under new ownership in 1859.) As a member of parliament he received no salary; as commissioner of emigration he was paid a thousand pounds a year and allowances. His eloquence made New South Wales an attractive place for working people; but prospective emigrants had to be told that the government of the colony would give money for their passages only if friends or relatives already out there would first nominate them and put up a deposit. Colonial politicians worried now about the widsom of paying for emigrants. Working men's hostility to emigrants as rivals for jobs became more potent as the franchise was widened; and shortly before Parkes embarked for England, artisans and labourers had been petitioning the government to suspend assisted emigration altogether. 'If I could have given free passages,' Parkes wrote, 'I might have sent out to the colony 10 000 emigrants.' Many of the applicants, he recalled, 'did not appear to care where they went if they could leave England without cost to themselves.' The fact that he and Clarinda had been given free passages was omitted from his autobiography.

The government of New South Wales increased assistance to emigrants in 1862, then reduced it drastically for a decade after 1865. In Victoria, radical friends of the workers argued in parliament that self-respecting colonies should not help England get rid of her unwanted population. The critics prevailed in Victoria when the vote for immigration was stopped in 1873. For the Australian colonies as a whole, the proportion of emigrants assisted by governments declined after 1870. Assisted and unassisted, emigrants would henceforth be a decreasing proportion of the colonial population. But the habit of referring to a country twelve thousand miles away as 'home' would be slower to diminish.

HOME

Australia was as far from the imperial homeland as a place on earth could be, and nature had made it stranger to European eyes than any part of the northern hemisphere. The seasons were upside-down, the animals were weird, and there were at first none of the oaks, elms, birches, beeches, poplars or willows which colonists had found in North America. Beyond the settled districts lay the bush, which had to be explained to people at home. '"The Bush",' an interpreter wrote in 1855, 'when the word is used in the towns, means all the uninclosed and uncultivated country . . . when in the country, "the Bush" means more especially the forest.' Bush vegetation unknown in England had to be identified. The various species of eucalyptus were called gum trees because of their sap, and acacias were known as wattles because their boughs and shoots were used for making walls by the method known at home as wattle-and-daub. For creatures of the bush the newcomers used some aboriginal words such as kangaroo, wallaby and dingo. Names drawn from other parts of the world were applied to animals or birds apparently related to species found elsewhere, such as the opossum (North America), the bandicoot (India) and the emu (South America). One animal was so singular that some naturalists at home suspected it to be a hoax, and men in the colonies were undecided whether to call it an ornithorhynchus or a duck-bill or a water-mole. They settled for platypus. There was only one Australian creature more fabulous, which aborigines knew as the bunyip. The *bête noire* of the Australian bush, a writer called it in 1865. It was half horse and half alligator, and lived in the swamps and lagoons of the interior; or it was like a bullock, and had tusks like a walrus; or it had countless eyes and ears, sharp claws, lurked in lakes and ran people down on land. The bunyip was one of the few elements in the aboriginal universe to enter the white men's imagination. Bushmen as well as blackfellows swore that they had seen it. Sceptical town dwellers made it by 1850 a synonym for impostor, pretender or humbug.

Nature was alien; but the social and political environment that newcomers found in this country was more familiar than the one that greeted most participants in the exodus from Europe. People who went to the United States and South America became at first aliens, and many of them had to learn a new language if they wanted to take on a new nationality. But people who sailed from the United Kingdom to colonies in Australia, Canada, southern Africa or New Zealand remained at the end of the journey subjects of the same monarch as at home and settled among people who spoke the same language. The longest journeys took emigrants to the least unfamiliar of new Britains. Unlike the colonists of Canada or southern Africa, those of Australia and New Zealand did not have to share the land with a people from another part of Europe; and white men met less resistance in Australia than in New Zealand from inhabitants of another race. After those long weeks at sea, emigrants to Australia stepped ashore in places they could recognize at once as provinces of Britannia, John Bull and Queen Victoria.

Britons annexed the new land by planting in it old names, chosen either because they saw resemblances or because they hoped that naming a place would domesticate it. A Scottish governor, Macquarie, named a river the Clyde; a Scottish surveyor, Mitchell, named a mountain range the Grampians. Victoria gained a Belfast, New South Wales a Swansea, and three colonies a Killarney. The principal cities all proclaimed their imperial character. Sydney and Hobart Town honoured two secretaries of state for the colonies, and Perth was named after the birthplace in Scotland of a third, Sir George Murray. Adelaide would have been Wellington had King William IV not preferred his queen's name to the duke's for the capital of South Australia. At Port Phillip, where one settlement appeared on the bank of a river and another on the bay, the former was called Melbourne after the prime minister and the latter Williamstown after the king. Brisbane, on Moreton Bay, commemorated the governor who put the penal settlement there. As these capital cities sprouted suburbs, names from home were attached to many of them. There were two Camberwells and three Cheltenhams, and every colony but Western Australia had a Brighton by the sea. Duffy thought it remarkable how far the makers of this society had gone in imitation of English conventions, the politicians of Melbourne having their words recorded in a Victorian Hansard, the laywers putting up their plates in Chancery Lane, and the citizens driving for recreation to Kew or Windsor. Visitors were amused to find children out here raised on English poetry which connected frost with January and hot weather with July; but according to one piece of emigrant folklore the colonial seasons actually followed those of England, a severe winter or a wet summer at home being followed by a similar season in Australia, as if the climate, like the people, had travelled

across the world from home. If so it warmed up on the way out, for Australian sunshine was no imitation of England's. Emigrants hated it or learned to love it, according to which part of the continent they inhabited and how happily in other ways they were settling into the place.

Cheerful or miserable, the emigrant could hunger intensely for news from home. The exiles of Phillip's day craved it as they waited month after month, all through 1788 and 1789 and into 1790, for a second fleet to bring supplies. When a sail was seen on 3 June 1790 an officer cried, 'Pull away, my lads! she is from Old England! a few strokes more and we shall be aboard! hurrah for a belly-full, and news from our friends!' They begged news from the men on the *Lady Juliana*. They shouted for letters and trembled as they tore them open. 'News', wrote Watkin Tench, 'burst upon us like meridian splendor on a blind man. We were overwhelmed with it'. Once newspapers were established, every ship that arrived at a colonial port from any other country was welcomed by men of the press hoping that it carried European or American papers whose reports they could disseminate. Newspapers in country towns copied their overseas intelligence from papers such as the *Sydney Morning Herald* or the Melbourne *Argus* or the *South Australian Register*. People who could afford it had their own subscriptions to English newspapers and periodicals. The most cultivated of them kept up with English literature and journalism as closely as the mail permitted, one emigrant perceiving as early as 1863 that *Punch* was falling off.

Private mail from home was even more precious than public news. An early settler of Swan River declared that 'no one but those so far from home, who have lived so long with, and loved so truly, so many of his own kin can fully appreciate a letter from one of the beloved.' Letters between motherland and colonies were 'the cherished link', an early emigrant to Melbourne wrote, 'that solaced the absent hearts yearning for intelligence at both extremes of the earth'. James Smith, looking back from the 1880s on the Melbourne of the gold rushes, recalled the pole on Flagstaff Hill standing ready to announce that a ship was in sight. 'We had been transplanted, but had not yet taken deep root in the country', he reflected. 'The ties formed in early life were still numerous and powerful. Men and women could not lightly forget the place of their birth'. So they watched eagerly for the mail from England. Each month the returning ships carried their replies. On average every person in Australia—man, woman and child, immigrant and colonial-born—posted one letter abroad in 1870. Anthony Trollope, who was postal official and inventor of the pillar box as well as novelist, perceived that the importance of mail for the people of these colonies was expressed in their splendid post offices.

News from home in the first issue of the *Sydney Gazette*, of 5 March 1803, had left England in May 1802. By 1850 mail was usually four months old when it arrived. When an exchange of letters took the best part of a year it could become hard to believe that one's correspondent was living in the same world. 'It is a sort of presumption to expect that one's thoughts should live so far', wrote Charles Lamb to his friend Barron Field, judge of the Supreme Court in Sydney from 1817 to 1824. 'It is like writing for posterity . . . news from me must become history to you.' The emigrants, one who came in 1841 recalled, 'were accounted by those who remained behind as undergoing a sort of premature interment. The immigrants after their arrival viewed the matter in much the same light'. The very

NEWS FROM HOME
Gold diggers reading a letter

POST OFFICE, BOURKE STREET, MELBOURNE
*'C.O.' on the flag gives news, received by telegraph, that a mail steamer has been
sighted off Cape Otway.*

time taken to communicate with the old world disposed people to feel themselves makers
of a new one.

Messages passed a little more quickly between the two worlds after 1850. The
Peninsular and Oriental Steam Navigation Company extended its mail service to Australia
in 1852, bringing articles which had travelled from Southampton to Alexandria by
steamship, overland to the Red Sea, and by steamship to Ceylon and Australia. 'The
immediate effect', the *Sydney Morning Herald* declared on 3 August 1852, 'will be to reduce

the distance between us and old England by at least one half.' The arrival of the mail
steamer from Ceylon was itself a piece of news. 'The gallant Chusan came into port last
night a little before eleven o'clock, the *Sydney Morning Herald* reported on 17 March 1854,
'bringing the English mails of the 10th of January, thus putting us in possession of
intelligence only 65 days old.' That was twenty days less than the fastest sailing ships, the
clippers, were advertised to take from England. Winds and mechanical breakdowns made
the service unreliable, and in 1854 it stopped altogether when the British government
turned the steamers into troopships for the Crimea; but by 1858 a monthly P. & O. mail
steamer was providing the quickest regular means for correspondence and newspapers to
move between England and Australia. After the Suez Canal was opened in 1869, mails
could be carried from London to Melbourne in forty-four days. People could travel with
the mails, but only if they were rich. Most passengers to and from Australia were carried
not on mail steamers but on ships under sail or steam around Africa or America, which
might take three months for the journey.

By 1870 some news was being sent part of the way by electricity. Wires along the
route from Europe to India by way of Suez carried messages which ships on the way to
Australia might pick up. Once a permanent cable connexion across the Atlantic was

THE STEAMSHIP *GREAT BRITAIN*
*She is being welcomed in Port Jackson after her first run to Australia in 1852 after
taking just over eighty days from Liverpool to Melbourne.*

achieved by 1865, a piece of European news might travel more quickly from London to New York and thence by telegraph to San Francisco and ship across the Pacific than a piece of news coming eastwards from London. When telegraph lines were put between Adelaide, Melbourne and Sydney in 1858, newspaper proprietors in the eastern cities made elaborate arrangements for information from England to go by wire for its last few hundred miles. At King George Sound in Western Australia, the steamer transferred mail for Adelaide into a branch boat. While the *Bombay* or one of her sisters steamed for Melbourne, the branch steamer *Balclutha* would make for Adelaide, carrying reporters whose job it was to open the packets addressed to their newspapers and have ten thousand words of news ready for transmission to Melbourne and Sydney when the boat reached Adelaide. At Port Adelaide they would hand their dispatches to couriers on horseback who raced for the telegraph office. At first, when only one message could be sent along the wire at a time, the man who got in first would try to book the line after he had finished his own message and pay for chapters of the Bible to be sent by intercolonial telegraph while the next man waited. Editors thought it worth paying to have God's words put into Morse code in order to be first on the streets of Melbourne or Sydney with news two months old from England.

The daily newspapers of the capital cities had colonial-born as well as emigrant readers. They printed news not only from the United Kingdom but from America and Europe, and they reported local affairs. People read them also for the advertisements which brought in a large part of their revenue and for the opinions on colonial issues in editorials, contributed articles and letters. But the press of London, and especially *The Times*, was the model for them all. English papers were the richest source of their news from abroad, providing, whenever a ship arrived, column after column of matter about English politics, commerce, religion, literature and recreation. Nearly all of them were owned and edited by men from England and Scotland. If an editorial in the *Sydney Morning Herald*, the *Empire*, the *Argus*, the *Age*, the *South Australian Register*, the *South Australian Advertiser* or the *Hobart Town Courier* referred to 'our country', only the context would show whether the writer meant the colony or England. The papers helped to preserve in emigrants and to communicate among their colonial-born children the sentiment that the old country was home.

3 Colonists

CURRENCY LADS

White people born in New South Wales were known by the 1820s as currency lads and currency lasses. Lads and lasses they still were; the very oldest, born to women of the first fleet, did not turn forty until 1828. 'Currency' began as a jest. Paper money issued in Sydney by private traders to eke out the supply of sterling coinage was described as currency. As these notes were judged to be worth less than their face value, somebody in Macquarie's time thought of applying the term 'currency' to the colonial-born, so branding them inferior to sterling people. The objects of the word embraced it happily. Peter Cunningham found the name 'a sufficient passport to esteem with all the well-informed and right-feeling portion of our population; but it is most laughable to see the capers some of our drunken old Sterling madonnas will occasionally cut over their Currency adversaries in a quarrel. It is then, "You saucy baggage, how dare you set up your *Currency* crest at me? I am *Sterling*, and that I'll let you know!"' The colonial-born were also called cornstalks, after the corn or maize which grew quickly tall when planted in New South Wales. Bigge reported them physically distinguishable from people born at home: 'generally tall in person, and slender in their limbs, of fair complexion, and small features. They are capable of undergoing more fatigue, and are less exhausted by labour than native Europeans; they are active in their habits, but remarkably awkward in their movements.'

They were about a quarter of the population: 4000 out of 17 000 in 1817, 9000 out of 37 000 in 1828. At least eight out of ten were children of convicts. 'Is there much difference to see', Charles Lamb asked Barron Field, 'between the son of a thief, and the grandson? or where does the taint stop?' About grandsons, it was too early to say. The sons appeared to Bigge and others not only physically but morally superior to their parents. They were far less inclined than convicts or emancipists to commit crimes, and even a little less so than free emigrants. When Bigge sailed from Sydney to Hobart Town, the authorities made sure of a trustworthy crew by manning the ship entirely with native-born men.

They had their own manner of speaking. In the society from which their parents had come, internal migration was producing rapid changes in patterns of language, including amalgamation of accents and vocabularies. A convict born of Irish emigrants in Liverpool, for example, had grown up learning the English of Ireland and of Lancashire. In the colony he might marry a woman from another part of England, and he would live among people from various regions of the United Kingdom. His own children would be exposed to a very wide range of voices. The currency accent was a new mixture of old sounds, in which particular influences from London, Birmingham, Dublin and elsewhere could be detected by ears familiar with the originals. There were also currency idioms, deriving often from the streets and dens of the criminals' world at home, and passed on by convicts not only to their own children but to those of free settlers to whom they were assigned as servants. Among such usages was 'bloody', to signify disapproval or belligerence or merely to make a statement more emphatic. There was no mistaking the hostility of 'bloody emigrants' as applied by emancipists to the Scottish artisans in 1831, or of 'bloody judge', a phrase applied to the chief justice of New South Wales by a convict who had killed Robert Wardell in 1834. But in currency speech the word could have a far more casual application. Alexander Marjoribanks reported in 1847 that it was the favourite oath of New South Wales. One man would say that he married a bloody young wife, another a bloody old one. A bullock driver in Marjoribanks's hearing used the word twenty-five times in a quarter of an hour; at that rate, the disgusted listener estimated, he would have uttered it more than eighteen million times before he died. Frank Fowler wrote in 1859 that the Australian boy 'never speaks without apostrophising his "oath" and interlarding his diction with the crimsonest of adjectives.' Generation after generation, men born in this most peaceful of European lands sprinkled their speech with the blood they so rarely saw spilt in conflict. Even the aborigines, it was said, learned English oaths and curses. Very little of their own speech passed into currency language. The newcomers took over an aboriginal cry 'Coo-ee!', the first syllable slow, the second high-pitched and sharp. Like the older inhabitants of the continent, European travellers found it a useful sound to send whipping through the trees, especially when they were lost in the bush. 'Jirrand' was noted as the one aboriginal word in the slang of the 1820s. It meant 'afraid', and was presumably a term aborigines had occasion to use fairly often in the hearing of white men.

By 1840 it was the colonial-born whites who were known as natives, not the aborigines. For English readers it was necessary to explain the usage. The natives, Mrs Charles Meredith wrote in 1844, were 'not the aborigines, but the "currency" as they are termed'. But in the settled regions of the colonies the term could be used without confusion, for the aborigines—or as they were often called, blackfellows, or blacks—had been expelled from the places where most emigrants and white natives lived.

The native-born were sometimes called colonial, or colonials. When people from home used the adjective or the noun it was easy for them to sound patronizing. 'They were natives, and a little colonial, as might be expected', wrote Rachel Henning, a well-born emigrant, of two gawky girls travelling north through Queensland in 1863 with their father and twelve thousand sheep. 'They had just left school in Melbourne, they told me. I formed my opinion respecting the state of the fine arts in Melbourne ladies' schools from the specimens they exhibited'. If they suspected condescension, natives might respond with aggressive colonial patriotism. From the beginning, most currency lads thought of Australia as their home for life. Bigge, knowing other British colonies, was surprised to find that sentiment so widespread here. One of the earliest of colonial jokes made England a den of thieves, the place where all the convicts came from. Currency lads who visited England in the 1820s were not impressed by its weather, the milk and butter of its cows, or the speed and beauty of its horses. There was said to be one who told his hosts in London that a certain shop on Ludgate Hill was not as fine as Daniel Cooper's store in Sydney, and that not even Bond Street had anything to rival Mrs Rickards's Fashionable Repository.

Twenty years later, people in Sydney talked of a rich citizen, back after visiting London, who when asked if he had not admired its magnificent thoroughfares replied: 'Oh! very well; but nothing like George-street!' In a version heard by an emigrant of the 1850s, the man from Sydney puts up Dan Cooper's store for comparison with St Paul's Cathedral. Stories were told with relish in Australia of colonial visitors who astonished the natives of England with their rumbustious ways, such as shouting 'Coo-ee!' when bushed in London. According to colonial travellers' tales, ignorant people thought that all the inhabitants of Australia were aborigines. The touchy native could be irritated by the convention that made England home. When a solicitor employed it in a Sydney court in 1854, the police magistrate said: 'We Currency Lads call it *abroad* and this is our home.' The cultivated emigrant, treated as a helpless new chum, might well find the native insufferable. More than ten years after Henry Kingsley returned home, he wrote a fable in which a prince follows a boy named Gil round the world observing European colonization. They come to Australia. 'All the male adult colonists were down on the shore; and every man had brought his grandmother, and every man had brought an egg, and was showing his grandmother how to suck it. "Come here," they cried, as Gil and the Prince coasted along; "come here, you two, and learn to suck eggs . . . And we will teach you to suck eggs which we have never seen." '

Currency versus sterling was often a good-natured game. Indeed, the recreations of New South Wales in the 1820s and 1830s were in large part a series of sporting contests between representatives of the two groups. John Dunmore Lang complained in 1834 that the newspapers were 'stuffed, almost to nausea, with advertisements and accounts of races, cricket-matches, boxing-matches, and regattas; with challenges to fight, to run, or to row, addressed by one obscure candidate for notoriety to another; and with lengthy descriptions of contests, either by land or by water, between the colonial youth and natives of England, or, to use the phrase of the colony, between *currency and sterling*.' To a Scottish puritan it was all aimless and therefore wicked frivolity; but to the participants it was a matter of keen interest to discover how the natives compared with men born at home when their speed, strength and skill were put to a test.

As the first batch of natives aged, they were scrutinized with care by emigrants and visitors. An emigrant of the 1830s, the schoolmaster Thomas Braim, thought that by 1845 the semi-tropical climate was taking its toll. Rapid physical and intellectual growth was followed, he believed, by 'early and premature decay', especially among women. 'The girl of fifteen possessing all the charms, and many of the graces of womanhood, must, at the age of thirty, yield the palm to her, who realizing the triumphs of her sex at a later, preserves them to a more advanced, period of life. This appears to be a law belonging to all warm climates'. Only in New South Wales and Van Diemen's Land were natives of advanced years numerous by 1850. Elsewhere they were all children, except a few who had moved from an old colony to a new one. In New South Wales just before the crowd of gold-seekers began to come ashore, currency lads and lasses slightly outnumbered emigrants. In a population of 187 000, the native-born numbered 81 000 and free emigrants 77 000.

RISE, AUSTRALIA!

It was not with complimentary intent that E. S. Hall referred to people in the New South Wales of 1826 as Australians. Hall, an English settler of 1811 who had just established the *Monitor* to campaign for free institutions, used the term to describe people of British or colonial birth who would not stand up against Governor Darling for their rights. 'The people of New South Wales', declared the *Monitor*, 'are a poor grovelling race . . . their spirit is gone—the scourge and the fetters and the dungeon and the Australian inquisition have reduced them to a level with the negro—they are no longer *Britons*, but *Australians*!' Hall rubbed it in a week later. They had 'lost their English spirit', and had 'degenerated into *Australians*.' More commonly the word meant the colonial-born. 'Oh we are Australians & know nothing about England', the Macarthur girls told Charles Darwin in 1836. Such modesty, or archness, fell prettily from the lips of young ladies whom it would have been accurate but facetious to call currency lasses. Colonists of pure merino sires and dams were pure merino still, wherever they happened to be born. Among those natives who were not pure merino, the term Australian was used with more spirit as they assembled to affirm their common birth and sentiments. In the politics of the 1820s the men who called themselves Australians were those colonial-born who stood alongside the emancipists against the governor and the exclusives. Their champion was William Charles Wentworth.

Wentworth was one of the oldest natives, having been born in the colony in 1790. His Anglo-Irish father, Darcy Wentworth, sailed out as an assistant surgeon that year and became superintendent of the convict settlement at Norfolk Island. The son was sent to England for schooling in 1803, was met amiably by his father's kinsman and patron Lord Fitzwilliam, and returned to the colony in 1810 after trying in vain to get into the military academy at Woolwich and the East India Company. He was a large and powerful young man, active in his habits and awkward in his movements, restlessly ambitious for himself and uncertain how to make his mark. The colony's two frontiers, the mountains and the ocean, challenged him. In 1813 he found a way across the Blue Mountains with a settler, an army officer and four servants; the next year he sailed into the Pacific searching for sandalwood. He returned to England in 1816, his father hoping that he might make a career in the army; but the year after Waterloo was not a good time for that, and he decided instead to become a lawyer. His purpose, he said, was to acquaint himself 'with all the excellence of the British Constitution, and hope at some future period, to advocate successfully the right of my country to a participation in its advantages.' By 'my country' he meant New South Wales. He hoped to marry another native of that country, Elizabeth Macarthur, daughter of John. Darcy Wentworth was now principal surgeon, personal physician to Governor Macquarie, chief police magistrate, and holder of large land grants. His son was also a substantial landowner, Macquarie having granted him 1750 acres in 1811 and a further 1000 acres as a reward for crossing the mountains. The Macarthurs had more land, lucrative trading interests, and the stature of magnates. William Charles Wentworth hoped that the two families would make a grand connexion, but negotiations for the match were abandoned after he and John Macarthur junior quarrelled in 1818.

In that year Wentworth discovered that his father had very nearly been a convict. Four times in England young Darcy Wentworth was tried for highway robbery. Three times he was acquitted. When the prosecutor at the fourth trial told the court that the accused had taken a passage to Botany Bay, the judge discharged him. Among the female prisoners who travelled with him on the *Neptune* in 1790 was Catherine Crowley, transported for stealing clothes. Not long after the end of the journey she bore the child who grew up as William Charles Wentworth, and who was apparently ignorant of the circumstances in which both parents had come out. Whether or not he learned of his mother's history at the same time as his father's, Wentworth became protagonist of the convicts' children in 1819, when he published *A Statistical, Historical and Political Description of the Colony of New South Wales*. The book expressed eloquent admiration of Macquarie and hostility to 'a party in the colony . . . an aristocratic body, which would monopolise all situations of power, dignity and emolument, and put themselves in a posture to domineer alike over the governor and the people.' It was not a friendly characterization of the Macarthurs. The covert aim of these men, the author declared, was 'to convert the ignominy of the great body of the people into an hereditary deformity. They would hand it down from father to son, and raise an eternal barrier of separation between their offspring, and the offspring of the unfortunate convict.' He advocated for the colony a legislative assembly which would be elected on a broad franchise. The book found keen readers in the colony and at home, and went into three editions by the time Wentworth returned to Sydney in 1824. The title-page proclaimed that it was 'by William Charles Wentworth, Esq., a native of New South Wales.'

In the colony if not in England he gained by 1824 some reputation as a poet. At Cambridge University, where he was a member of a college, Peterhouse, but not enrolled for a degree, Wentworth entered in 1823 a competition for a poem on 'Australasia'. As a native, Wentworth declared in his verses, he felt obliged to compete for the chancellor's medal when his own country was the prescribed subject:

> And shall I now, by Cam's old classic stream,
> Forbear to sing, and thou propos'd the theme?
> Thy native bard, though on a foreign strand,
> Shall I be mute, and see a stranger's hand
> Attune the lyre, and prescient of thy fame
> Fortell the glories that shall grace thy name?

A stranger's hand wrote the winning poem, and Wentworth came second out of twenty-seven. The winner, William Macworth Praed, was an Englishman who had been winning prizes for poetry since he was a schoolboy at Eton, and who carried off the chancellor's prize again in 1824 when the subject set was 'Athens'. Wentworth did not quarrel with the judges' verdict; they were right, he conceded, 'not to inquire to whose lot a block of the richest marble has fallen, but to ascertain from whom the crude substance, without reference to its intrinsic qualities, has received the highest polish.' The winning poem offered a very remote view of the colonies. His own established in the first line that the author was born there and was homesick. He mixed colonial with classical imagery: Parramatta with Libya, kangaroo and emu with faun and dryad. He dwelt on the paradox that the bay named by Cook for its flora had become a byword for criminality, and he recalled that Rome rose high from seamy origins. He hoped that his compatriots would go on living in peace, neither invading nor being invaded; but he closed with the vision of another future than the pursuit of mere good living and wisdom. If Britannia should ever cease to rule the ocean, if the old lion should lose its might and be vanquished, then:

> May all thy glories in another sphere
> Relume, and shine more brightly still than here;
> May this, thy last-born infant,—then arise,
> To glad thy heart, and greet thy parent eyes;
> And Australasia float, with flag unfurl'd,
> A new Britannia in another world.

Britons before Wentworth had offered similar prophecy. 'Who knows', Joseph Banks had asked in 1797, 'but that England may revive in New South Wales when it has sunk in Europe.' An officer at Port Phillip in 1803 foresaw there 'a second Rome . . . giving laws to the world, and superlative in arms and in arts, looking down with proud superiority upon the barbarous nations of the Northern Hemisphere.' The novelty was the author: a currency lad, soon to return home after eight years in England to take up the cause of the emancipist and the colonial-born. Wentworth's Cambridge poem was to be quoted often in his native land, especially for the pithy patriotism, at once colonial and imperial, of the last couplet.

'Australasia' was the theme prescribed for the exercise, and when published the poem was 'by W. C. Wentworth, an *Australasian*'. The word 'Australasia' had been used in 1766 to mean that part of the supposed Terra Australis which lay in the Indian Ocean south of Asia. Of known lands it included New Holland, New Zealand and New Guinea. In an English work of 1794 it was used interchangeably with both New Holland and Australia as a name for the southern continent alone. Poets found that wings could be fitted to Australasia more easily than New South Wales or New Holland. Michael Massey Robinson, a convict engaged by Macquarie as laureate, used it in odes. The first scientific association in the continent, formed in 1821, was called the Philosophical Society of Australasia. The English winner of the Cambridge prize interpreted the name as including New Zealand. The competitor from New South Wales did not.

Wentworth had called the continent New Holland in the first edition of his book and referred in its title only to New South Wales and Van Diemen's Land. In the third edition, of 1824, he showed a preference for Australasia and Australia over New Holland, and the title became *A Statistical Account of the British Settlements in Australasia; including the colonies of New South Wales and Van Diemen's Land*. Like Macquarie, to whom the published version of his prize was dedicated, Wentworth thought Australia the best name. The ship which carried Wentworth back to his country in 1824 had among its cargo a printing press with which he and Robert Wardell planned to break the monopoly enjoyed for twenty years by the *Sydney Gazette*, published weekly under official auspices. Wentworth and Wardell named their paper the *Australian*. Its first issue appeared on 14 October 1824. The makers of the *Sydney Gazette*, seeing the competitor coming, registered their own colonial patriotism by beginning on 16 September 1824 to put the words 'Advance Australia' at the head of each issue. Before returning home Wentworth had called for an 'independent paper . . . which may serve to point out the rising interests of the colonists, and become the organ of their grievances and rights, their wishes and wants'. The *Australian* demanded from week to week that the king's colonial subjects be given more liberties than were allowed them under the act of 1823 which established a wholly nominated Legislative Council and the act of 1828 which enlarged the council but still composed it entirely of nominees. All Sydney knew Wentworth now: his massive form, his slouching walk, the cast in his eye, the raging at enemies of himself and the people, and the conviction that the principal obstacle to freedom was Governor Darling. The governor described Wentworth in dispatches as 'a vulgar, ill-bred fellow, utterly uncon-scious of the Common Civilities, due from one gentleman to another', 'a Demagogue', a man 'appearing desirous to lead the Public and degrade the Government on all occasions.' Wentworth flourished as tribune, barrister and pastoralist. He inherited his father's lands when Darcy Wentworth died in 1827. He bought in that year a harbour estate known as Vaucluse, and when Darling was recalled in 1831 the jubilant native was host there at a feast for four thousand celebrants. The *Australian* described and promoted rejoicings in town on the eve of Darling's departure: the fatted ox led in triumph through the streets; the bonfires blazing; the transparency glowing on the windows of the *Australian's* office and displaying the victory of the press over the tyrant, a printer's devil pulling him down by the coat tails, and a padlock dropping from the mouth of John Bull, who shouts 'Huzza—boys—Australia and Freedom for ever'. In his early forties, Wentworth was unchallenged leader of the Australians.

Friends and admirers liked that word. The *Currency Lad*, a literary journal founded in 1832, appeared as 'published by Horatio Wills, an Australian'. The publisher, born in 1811, was the posthumous son of Edward Wills, one of the convicts who had become rich in trade. His widowed mother named the baby after the hero of Trafalgar. When she married another emancipist, George Howe of the *Sydney Gazette*, the child became Horatio Spencer Howe Wills. He went to sea as a cabin boy, and was apprenticed to his step-brother, Robert Howe, from whose service he absconded three times. Later he named a son Thomas Wentworth Wills after Wentworth had defended him on a charge brought by Robert Howe. By 1832 Horatio Wills was himself a printer and publisher of the *Sydney Gazette*, and his own *Currency Lad* was printed on the *Sydney Gazette* press. He had chosen for its title, he explained, the term 'affixed as a mark of reproach—now become a boastful appendage', and observed that in this respect the *Currency Lad*'s history was like Yankee Doodle's. Each week the front page bore the last couplet of Wentworth's prize poem, amended a little, and two lines of Wills's own:

> See, AUSTRALASIA floats, with flag unfurl'd,
> A new BRITANNIA in another world!
> While every surge that doth her bosom lave
> Salutes her, 'Empress of the Southern wave!'

In the original poem the last two lines referred to a future time; Wills's version made the colonial nation a new Britannia already. Alongside the verse, above the title, he printed the invocation 'Rise Australia'.

Other natives followed Wills in aspiring to make a fresh civilization in this land to which their parents had come as prisoners. Among the writers whose work he published in the *Currency Lad* was Charles Harpur, born in 1813 to transported parents and summoned, he believed, to be the poet of his native country. In one of Harpur's poems a goddess with the word 'Australia' engraved on her helmet addresses an emigrant in words about the motherland and the colony which show her to be a true currency lass:

> 'O stranger!' she said, 'hast thou fled from the home
> Which thy forefathers bled for so vainly?
> Does shame for its past thus induce thee to roam,
> Or despair of its future constrain thee?
> In the far sunny South there's a refuge from wrong,
> 'Tis the Shiloh of freedom expected so long;
> Their genius and glory shall shout forth their song—
> 'Tis the evergreen land of Australia.'

Younger currency lads who believed that the arts could be cultivated in Australian ground looked to Harpur as model and guide. A contributor to the *Colonial Literary Journal*, a weekly magazine published in 1844–5, called him 'the guiding star of his countrymen in the glorious and soul-elevating paths of literature,—of a literature NATIONAL and Australian, for if it be worthy . . . the terms are synonymous!' The most learned of native-born literary men, Daniel Deniehy, born in 1828 to two Irish Catholic convicts, came to know Harpur and his work in the Sydney of the 1840s. When Deniehy gave public lectures after 1850, on literature, he encouraged colonial readers to appreciate not only the European masters but their own Harpur.

The native makers of a culture for Australia depended on help from well-read immigrants. Harpur's first volume of verse, *Thoughts, a Series of Sonnets*, was published by W. A. Duncan, a Scottish Catholic convert who had arrived in 1838 with experience of journalism and reforming politics and a rich knowledge of European languages and literatures. Harpur and Deniehy were both encouraged by N. D. Stenhouse, a friend of Thomas De Quincey, who had come out to practise as a solicitor in 1839 and befriended so many hopeful young writers that they thought of the Roman who had been patron to Horace and Virgil and called him the Maecenas of their literature. They borrowed from his library. Deniehy was articled to him. Among younger native writers Henry Kendall owed much to Stenhouse's encouragement and counsel. The older native could in turn lend a hand to under-educated immigrants with literary ambition. Henry Parkes, who had a book of poems, *Stolen Moments*, published in Sydney in 1842, spoke later of Harpur and Duncan as the 'chief advisers in matters of intellectual resource and enquiry' in his early colonial years. In a preface to these verses Parkes declared his wish to serve 'the cause of Australian literature'.

Harpur, Deniehy, Kendall, Duncan, Stenhouse and Parkes would all spend the rest of their lives in Australia. They laboured to make a literature that would express the common experience of native and settled immigrant, of all whose bodies would be buried here. The grave, symbol of kinship among men and women committed to the Australian earth, attracted colonial poets as a subject. Kendall wrote reverently about the very oldest grave in the white man's Australia, in which one of Cook's seamen, Forby Sutherland, was buried at Botany Bay:

> *There* tread gently—*gently* pilgrim; there with thoughtful eyes look round;
> Cross thy breast and bless the silence: lo, the place is holy ground!

When Harpur's muse commanded him to write, she spoke of Australia not as the place where the poet was born but the place where his emigrant father was buried:

> Be then the bard of thy country! O rather
> Should such be thy choice than a monarchy wide!
> Lo, 'tis the land of the grave of thy father!
> 'Tis the cradle of Liberty—Think and decide.

On that view of nationality the Australians were the people who chose to have their bones lie here.

Old lines of division in colonial society were fading by the year 1850. The word emancipist was rarely heard in Sydney, in opposition either to emigrant or exclusivist, for

THE UNKNOWN TONGUE.

OLD COLONIST : What's your weakness ? Nog, Knickerbocker, Sherry Cobbler,
Snowstorm, Nightingale, Claret Spider, Jenny Lind, Shandygaff, Brandy
Smash, or Sangaree ?
NEW CHUM is dumb-foundered, and looks round imploringly for an interpreter.

emancipists were not by then a group with specific interests, resentments and enemies.
Currency versus sterling was an archaic antithesis when the natives were no longer of
almost entirely convict parentage and most of the British-born were assisted emigrants.
It was common now for the settled residents of the country, whatever their birthplace and
whether or not they had once been prisoners, to be known as the colonists. The *Sydney
Gazette* had proposed that term for 'all the free inhabitants' as early as 1825, hoping that
to speak of all as colonists would diminish the antagonism of emancipists and emigrants.
John Dunmore Lang, an immigrant who wanted his fellows to develop a sense of patriotic
attachment to their adopted land, called the newspaper he founded in 1835 the *Colonist*.
It could be high praise of men to say that they 'had come to this country in the true spirit

of colonists'. The word could also carry memories of earlier imperial history, and be used to threaten politicians at home. 'The history of the American revolution', observed Archibald Michie, lecturing in 1859 on "Colonists: Socially, and in their relations with the mother country", 'shows us, that nothing offends colonists so much as contempt'. The colonist was a man of sturdy dignity, committed to a new life and determined that his rights be recognized.

DEMOCRACY

The imperial government did a service to Australian democracy when it put a consignment of convicts on the *Hashemy* in 1849. Since 1842 the Legislative Council of New South Wales had been partly nominated and partly elected by voters with property. Radicals, among them Robert Lowe and Henry Parkes, agitated for a wholly elected parliament. The day in 1848 when Lowe won a seat in the Legislative Council was hailed by Parkes as the birthday of Australian democracy. News that the *Hashemy* was on its way gave the democrats a grand issue, enabling them to declare that the imperial authorities' indifference to colonial opinion could be overcome only by vehement demonstration followed by political reform. For Parkes himself the episode was the beginning of a career in politics. 'The Great Protest Meeting', he wrote in the *People's Advocate and New South Wales Vindicator*, a weekly founded by reformers in December 1848, 'will, we are confident, be the most imposing meeting by far ever held in this part of the world . . . It will be an event that shall startle the Mother Country, and shall become a landmark in Australian history. It will be the first national movement in Australia.'

At the Circular Quay on Sydney Cove on Monday 11 June, in heavy winter rain, a protest was adopted by a crowd estimated by its enemies at seven hundred, by its organizers at five thousand, and by Parkes in his autobiography at between seven and eight thousand. The transportation of British criminals to the colony of New South Wales, the protesters resolved, was 'in violation of the will of the majority of the colonists'. The Great Protest Meeting, and other agitation that followed it until transportation was thoroughly abolished, represented an alliance of outraged emigrants and natives. Five emigrant ships lay near the *Hashemy* in Sydney's harbour. Ten years earlier Parkes himself, an emigrant about to come ashore, had been appalled at the sight of convicts breaking rock on Pinchgut. Now he invited the crowd at the quay to imagine what it was like for the people on the other five ships to see the polluted *Hashemy* alongside them. 'Let him ask that meeting did the fourteen hundred emigrants now afloat on the waters of Port Jackson suspect when they left Great Britain that they would find a convict ship in the midst of the vessels that brought them hither? Would they, had they dreamt of such a thing, have sacrificed all home ties and volunteered to degrade themselves?' Native-born orators at the quay, among them Robert Nichols and Robert Campbell, blended their oratory with that of Lowe, Parkes and other emigrants to denounce the restoration of a system which they hoped was dying with their fathers. Emigrant and native together expressed their anger so vividly that when it was reported by Governor FitzRoy, Earl Grey observed 'that even the worst of our convicts would find they had something to learn from the speakers at public meetings in despising truth and decency.'

The campaign became a national movement, as Parkes prophesied. The Australasian League for the Abolition of Transportation, formed to stop the dumping of convicts in Van Diemen's Land, adopted in 1851 its own flag bearing a Union Jack and the

stars of the southern cross. Charles Harpur wrote for the league an anthem which tran-
scended convictism and invited Australians to sing of loyalty

> To Man, to progress, and to all
>   The free things, nobly free,
> Of which their loved Australia shall
> The golden cradle be.

In verse and prose Harpur was now calling colonists to demand not merely the British
Constitution but republican democracy. To his son born in 1851, Harpur gave the name
Washington. There were moments when Parkes too, denouncing transportation, could
sound as if he had in mind to follow the American colonists of 1776.

Wentworth supported the resumption of transportation in 1849, and believed that
the crusaders against it were stirring dangerous passions. As he grew older and richer and
his country filled up with assisted immigrants, Wentworth came to think that legislators
should be chosen by voters with a higher property qualification than he had proposed in
1819. He made peace with the 'aristocratic body' which he had then denounced, and
appeared on the same platform as James Macarthur. The *Australian*, now in other hands,
said of its founder in 1842: 'His day is gone by . . . Certainly he first taught the natives
of this colony what liberty was, but he has betrayed them since and they have withdrawn
their confidence from him.' With the reformers around Robert Lowe he still shared some
ground: in the Legislative Council to which he was elected as a member for Sydney in
1843, Wentworth demand self-government for the colony. But self-government and
democracy were different notions. Parkes 'doubted whether the phrase so often idly used,
"The People", ever in his mind included the masses of his fellow-men . . . Constitutional
reform with him meant putting an end to government from Downing Street, and handing
over the affairs of the colony, including the public lands, to his own class.'

On the hustings in 1848, Wentworth and his supporters made much of their
Australian birth. He sneered at radical newcomers as 'migratory birds'. 'The old hands
and currency lads of the colony', he declared, 'can and will put in whom they please.'
But Robert Lowe's election suggested otherwise. 'Nativity is a mere accident', he had said.
Parkes used the word 'Australian' as a marker of sentiment rather than birthplace, saying
on one occasion that 'all present, little boy and white-headed old man, would from that
day forth be Australian in their feelings and aims.' In his paper the *Empire* Parkes abused
Wentworth for favouring transportation and called him 'a .taggering old traitor',
'renegade', and 'the turncoat of Sydney.' Harpur judged him still more severely, not as a
renegade but as one who had merely pretended to be a friend of liberty:

> In his well-masked displays of by-gone years,
> With democratic wrath he tore the ears
> Of Sydney's wealthy groundlings, being then
> Thwarted and snubbed by Darling's party-men!
> But now behold him in his native hue,
> The bullying, bellowing champion of the Few!
> A Patriot?—he who hath nor sense nor heed
> Of public ends beyond his *own* mere need!

Wentworth faced voters for the third and last time in 1851. The election was conducted under the Australian Colonies Government Act of 1850 which gave the younger colonies legislative councils one-third nominated and two-thirds elected, and enabled property qualifications for voters everywhere to be less exclusive than had applied in New South Wales at the elections of 1842 and 1848. The enlarged electorate was addressed by Wentworth in a tone 'so high and offensive,' FitzRoy told Grey, 'and so indiscriminate in his abuse of the lower class of voters, that many of them, who had hitherto supported him and were still inclined to do so, refused to vote at all or voted for other candidates.' He was nearly defeated, being returned last of the three members for Sydney. When the poll was declared he expressed regret that 'there was a spirit of democracy abroad, which was almost daily extending its limits; and which, he was afraid, would result in much mischief to the well-being and tranquility of the country.'

To his democratic opponents after 1851, Wentworth embodied the associated causes which they labelled nomineeism and squatterdom. Nomineeism was the principle that a certain element in colonial society should be granted political representation without having to face an electorate. Squatterdom was the element so represented. A squatter, Charles Darwin learned in January 1836, was a former convict, 'a freed or "ticket of leave" man, who builds a hut with bark in occupied ground, buys or steals a few animals, sells spirits without a license, receives stolen goods & so at last becomes rich & turns farmer: he is the horror of all his honest neighbours.' The word quickly changed meaning. By the early 1840s a squatter was not a disreputable emancipist but any man, whatever his character or origin, grazing animals beyond the nineteen counties which Governor Darling had proclaimed in 1829 as the limits within which settlers were permitted to select land. Respectable men as well as ruffians were driving sheep and cattle out to eat grass on land that nobody was allowed to buy. Governor Bourke saw that there was no stopping them. On his initiative, the Legislative Council introduced in 1836 a licence which for ten pounds a year authorized anybody not deemed undesirable to graze stock wherever he chose. 'The principal settlers are also the principal squatters,' wrote Judge Therry, 'settlers as to their own lands, squatters as to the Crown Lands they occupy.' In 1844 Governor Gipps wrote of 'the "Squatting Interest" as it is called'. The word 'squattocracy' was being used of the interest by 1846. Squatters were now seeking security of tenure without having to pay the one pound an acre which had been fixed as a minimum for the sale of land. Charles Harpur deplored their demands in a sonnet, 'On the Political and Moral Condition of Australia in 1845':

> Lo, in *what* hands seem now thy destinies!
>   Hands grasping all, through party means, to seize
> Some private benefit: and what should be
> Thy Freedom's dawn, but gives ascendancy
>   To lawless Squatters, and the Hacks of these!

A pastoral association formed to represent the squattocracy persuaded the imperial authorities to grant security in 1847 on terms which Gipps thought too lenient and Harpur and other radicals judged iniquitous. 'Be the capabilities of these lands what they may,' cried Robert Lowe, '*they are to be a sheepwalk for ever*!'

Wentworth hoped so, and believed it necessary to the health of New South Wales that the electoral act which conferred responsible government should entrench the pastoral interest. 'Being a squatter,' he said, 'the belief has grown among the deluded and ignorant mass that I cannot be a patriot,—that it was being a squatter which had caused the dereliction from what were termed the liberal and constitutional predilections of my former years, and which have made me a leading member in what it is popular to call the squattocratic oligarchy.' The old currency lad, now in his sixties, was presenting to the Legislative Council on 16 August 1853, on behalf of a select committee which he had dominated, a bill for 'a Constitution in perpetuity for the colony—not a constitution which could be set aside, altered and shattered to pieces by every blast of popular opinion.' It was not to be altered except by a two-thirds majority of its two houses. The electorates of the Legislative Assembly were to be so drawn as to represent 'not the mere population, but the great interests of the country'. The Legislative Council was to be fortified against popular opinion by having some of its members nominated by the governor and the rest chosen from among members of a hereditary colonial peerage composed of 'our Shepherd Kings'.

Wentworth's pastoral aristocracy was intended both to provide conservative wisdom for the legislature and to give to the best of colonists honours which would prevent them from leaving the country. What incentive, he asked, was there now for 'those who, having made their fortunes here, desire to see their sons occupied in higher pursuits than those of trade?' At present such people 'aspire to a speedy migration to other lands, seeing it is better for themselves and families to build up homes where the democratic and levelling principles so rapidly increasing here are scouted; and where there are high and honourable pursuits and distinctions to which the children of the prudent may aspire.' Make for the colony an institution like the House of Lords, Wentworth said, and the great gentlemen of the colony would remain to form an honourable, wealthy and educated aristocracy. Did his own parentage dispose Wentworth to devise this new peerage? When opponents threw his origins at him, he retorted that the paltry efforts of dirty revilers did not affect him. 'If it be true that there is any blot on my escutcheon (if I have one), which has not been of my handiwork, what blame on that account can attach to me?' He quoted Alexander Pope:

> Honour and shame from no condition rise,
> Act well your part; there all the honour lies.

He did, of course, see his own line as among the hereditary legislators. 'Whether I do or do not entertain that desire is a matter of very little moment; but admitting that I do, is it an improper object of ambition? Or am I to be denounced for cherishing the hope that some son of mine will succeed me in the councils of my country?'

If the house was against him, Wentworth declared, he would not persist with the hereditary peerage. 'Hear, hear', said some members. A petition against this and other aspects of his proposal was presented to the council from a public meeting held in the Victoria Theatre, Sydney, the day before he spoke. Parkes moved the resolution of protest. Daniel Deniehy, making his first political speech, subjected Wentworth's aristocracy to vivid ridicule. Botany Bay magnificos, he called the proposed peers of the colony; a new-fangled Brummagem aristocracy; Australian mandarins. He fancied James Macarthur as the Earl of Camden, a rum keg on his coat of arms. He was puzzled to know how to classify such creatures. 'But perhaps it was only a specimen of the remarkable contrariety that existed at the Antipodes. Here they all knew the common water mole was transformed into the duck-billed platypus, and in some distant emulation of this degeneration, he supposed that they were to be favoured with a bunyip aristocracy.' Deniehy's democratic audience was delighted by his associating Wentworth's idea of a nobility with the nasty animal of the bush which was the continent's one gift to faery mythology and a byword for humbug. The man whom his friend Charles Harpur called

> Little Dan Deniehy!
> Brilliant Dan Deniehy!

was well placed to appeal to both the currency lads and the newcomers who opposed an anti-democratic constitution, for he himself was both native and emigrant. His emancipated parents had taken him to England and Ireland and the family had returned as bounty emigrants in 1844, when Daniel was sixteen, father and son describing themselves as agricultural labourers and mother as a laundress. Deniehy, said his democratic friends, had killed Wentworth's peerage with scorn. 'The Bunyip *was*, and *is*, and is *to be*—nothing', Charles Harpur wrote. Radicals chuckled also over Harpur's parody of the young Wentworth's prize poem, which the author had quoted in the council as peroration to his speech on the constitution. Deniehy judged the poem 'as execrable a piece of trash as it has ever been my misfortune to read.' Harpur imagined Wentworth's nation taking over the job of ruling from a Britannia which had turned from empire to virtue:

> May this thy last born daughter then arise
> A barbarous Britain under other skies,
> And Australasia spread, with flag unfurled,
> All thy worst features through a wider world.

When the bunyip aristocracy entered legend, it was easy for democrats to exaggerate the difference between its creator and its clever critic. Deniehy shared Wentworth's conviction that this society needed to find some way of nurturing and recognizing distinction. Wentworth, to be sure, was looking in the wrong direction for nobility. His clique 'were not the representations of the spirit, the intelligence of the freemen of New South Wales.' But Deniehy believed in 'God's aristocracy', which appeared 'wherever man's skill is eminent, wherever glorious manhood asserts its elevation', and conferred 'honour upon the land that possesses it.' He regretted that Australia so far lacked such an aristocracy. Legend also forgot that although the bunyip aristocracy was aborted, it was not replaced by the elected Legislative Council whose democratic propensities Wentworth feared. The Constitution Bill passed by the council and approved in London contained, as Wentworth wished, the provision that it could not be changed except by two-thirds of the members of both houses. The franchise for the Legislative Assembly was well short of manhood suffrage, and its electorates were designed to protect rural interests; and despite popular protest the Legislative Council was to be composed of men nominated for life by the governor on the advice of the Executive Council.

Wentworth resigned his seat in the old Legislative Council and sailed for England to see the bill for the constitution through the imperial parliament. At the by-election for Sydney he was replaced by Henry Parkes, who would be one of the new men learning to work the new constitution. 'It has been alleged', Parkes said, 'that I am mainly supported in this election by the labouring and shop-keeping classes.' The latter Wentworth despised, the former he feared; and it was indeed on their votes that Parkes and his allies largely depended to gain a majority in the Legislative Assembly.

By 1860 the queen's representatives in New South Wales, Tasmania, South Australia, Victoria and Queensland governed on the advice of ministers who had a majority among elected representatives. The constitutions approved at Westminster varied a little from colony to colony. Guardians of property in Victoria devised not a nominated Legislative Council but one elected by about a tenth of the voters who chose the Assembly. Thanks to the demands of gold diggers the franchise for the Assembly in Victoria came closer than that of New South Wales to manhood suffrage. In Tasmania the right to vote for the elected Legislative Council was spread more widely than in Victoria, and the electorate for the House of Assembly was similar to that for the lower house in New South Wales. In South Australia thousands of men back from the Victorian diggings petitioned Westminster successfully for vote by ballot, an upper house with lower property qualifications than in other colonies, and a House of Assembly for which every man could vote. In a few years of responsible government, popular politicians in Sydney, Hobart, Melbourne and Brisbane also secured manhood suffrage and vote by ballot and gained more nearly equal electorates. The democrats in New South Wales removed the provision that any alteration of the constitution required a two-thirds majority of both houses. The mails carried news of these democratic innovations to Wentworth, living as an absentee colonist in England. But the colonial press brought also more pleasing news. The Legislative Councils nominated or elected by men of property were proving to be durable obstacles to change, and especially to efforts directed at unlocking the lands which had been made a sheepwalk. The new politicians were not finding it easy to make governments that were both democratic and stable: in the first five years, New South Wales had four general elections and seven ministries. Returning home briefly in 1861, Wentworth was gratified to be offered the presidency of the Legislative Council.

Stability in the new parliaments was rendered difficult both by the rule that a ministry fell once it lacked a majority in the Assembly and by the absence of any deep divisions of interest or principle in this society of emigrants and exiles and their children. 'All men—gentle or simple, educated or ignorant—came to work at something or other', Archibald Michie reflected in 1859. Trollope found in 1871–2 that the men near the top of the tree in Australia were 'they who came young from the old country, without much money, with great energy, and with a strong conviction that fortune was to be made by industry, sobriety, and patience.' Where all were in a sense workers, the conservative was not an inheritor of ancient privilege but simply the man who had got to the tree first, ascended most skilfully, and on the whole wished well to those below him. The Australian conservative, a Victorian colonist explained in London, was a man who had got four of the six points of the People's Charter and wanted to conserve them. The Australian radical was no expropriator of the rich: Henry Parkes and Charles Gavan Duffy and their friends were climbers, not fighters in a class struggle. When the queen opened the Order of St Michael and St George to colonists 'in consequence of the growth and advancement of Her Colonial Empire', neither Parkes nor Duffy would find it incompatible with a democratic outlook to become a Knight Commander.

Unstable ministries relieved a little the boredom and frustration of being a governor in this age of colonial democracy. Sir William Denison, who governed Van Diemen's Land from 1847 to 1854, the last years of autocracy, went to Sydney just in time to live with the new order. 'In these responsible governments', he confessed to his sister in 1860, 'one sees much going on which is most objectionable, yet one is powerless to do good or to prevent evil. One may make suggestions, but these, if adopted, which is by no means certain to be the case, are pretty sure to be marred in the working from the ignorance of the instruments, or from the inability of the Ministers to comprehend subjects upon which they have never thought'. He presided over a Philosophical Society, organized an Agricultural Society, and accepted readily the invitation to go as governor to Madras. 'I look forward with great pleasure', he wrote, 'to the idea of having something to do.'

The governor had to be careful not to *appear* to be usurping the responsibility of his callow ministers. Denison had his premier, Charles Cowper, threatening to resign in protest because the governor put the great seal of the colony on a document without consulting his Executive Council. The new men were bound to be touchy in the presence of imperial officials whom they knew to be privately judging them, however impeccable their formal relations. Newcomers and visitors inevitably measured them against politicians at home. Some were flattering. 'I passed from the House of Commons to the Commons of Victoria', wrote Duffy, 'and, deducting half-a-dozen exceptional statesmen, the latter, to my thinking, were as competent in debate and as well informed in the business it was their duty to know as the former'. Charles Dilke, a young English gentleman making an imperial tour of inspection in 1867, declared himself impressed with such men as Parkes. But these were published judgments. What might the inspector really think of politicians and other colonists?

Anthony Trollope, visiting in 1871–2 to see his emigrant son, a squatter in New South Wales, and to produce a book about Australia and New Zealand, wrote for publication: 'It was a very pleasant life that I led at these stations. I like tobacco and brandy and water, with an easy-chair out on a verandah, and my slippers at my feet. And I like men who are energetic and stand up for themselves and their own properties'. In a letter, to George Eliot and G. H. Lewes, he said: 'I am reduced to the vilest tobacco out of the vilest pipe, and drink the vilest brandy and water,—very often in very vile company.' He did commit to print one criticism which touched such tender nerves that it sprang to colonial minds whenever the novelist's name was mentioned. 'Colonists', he wrote, 'are usually fond of their adopted homes,—but are at the same time pervaded by a certain sense of inferiority which is for the most part very unnecessary . . . Men and women will apologize because they cannot do this or that as it is done in England. But this very feeling produces a reaction which shows itself in boasting of what they can do . . . You are told constantly that colonial meat and colonial wine, colonial fruit and colonial flour, colonial horses and colonial sport, are better than any meat, wine, fruit, flour, horses, or sport to be found elsewhere. And this habit spreads from things national to things personal; and men boast of their sheep, their cattle, and their stations;—of their riding, their driving, and their prowess . . . The colonists themselves have a term for it, and call it—"blowing."' Trollope set down his perception when writing about Queensland and returned to it when he got to Victoria. 'They blow a good deal in Queensland;—a good deal in South Australia. They blow even in poor Tasmania. They blow loudly in New South Wales, and very loudly in New Zealand. But the blast of the trumpet as heard in Victoria is louder than all the blasts, and the Melbourne blast beats all the other blowing of that proud colony. My first, my constant, my parting advice to my Australian cousin is contained in two words—"Don't blow."'

Why not? Whether called blowing or, as the Americans said, boosting, or under some other name, such blasting of trumpets was a traditional occupation among makers of new societies. 'Let them produce any colonie or commonwealth in the world,' said the magistrates of Massachusetts Bay in 1646, 'where more hath beene done in sixteen yeares.' It was surely commendable of the Victorians that they produced by 1870 the best statistics in the world, to enable the progress of their colony to be measured precisely. How else draw attention to colonial achievements than by blowing about them? The agents sent by Australian governments to London, becoming 'agents-general' from 1870, were paid to blow, so that suitable citizens of the homeland would want to emigrate and investors would have confidence in colonial railways. An informant wrote critically to Henry Parkes about his agent-general in 1878, saying that he 'blows but little about the colony and keeps himself too much in the background.' What caused Trollope's observation to be remembered with such bad temper in Australia was the suggestion that when colonists blew, they betrayed a fear that they were inferior to Englishmen.

SCHOOLING THE CHILDREN

Hope was invested in the first babies of New South Wales by the keepers of their parents. In 1794, when the oldest native white child was six, the chaplain to the colony judged that the only prospect of reformation lay in 'the rising generation'. The phrase went into official policy. When William Bligh was made governor in 1805, Lord Castlereagh advised him that in a settlement where the parents' habits were likely to leave children exposed to suffer from vices similar to their own, 'you will feel the peculiar necessity that the Government should interfere on behalf of the rising generation'. Two years later, Castlereagh allowed the governor to pay schoolmasters to teach in public schools. At home, public schools—Rugby, Harrow, Eton and others—were endowed institutions with clergymen as headmasters, run for boarding pupils whose wealthy parents paid fees. Here they were day schools for the poor, conducted by convicts or emancipists, maintained by the government and superintended by its Church of England chaplains. In the first generation of colonial-born children a larger proportion went to school than did so in many parts of England. Schoolmasters could well feel some pride when visitors praised the native youth for their bearing and character.

The reach of the public schools was limited both by the growth of the colony and by its social composition. The proportion of children in them dropped after 1800 as population increased and dispersed; and they were not attended by children whose parents could afford to buy a more respectable education. Some people sent sons and even daughters to England for schooling. It would be unjust to children, Elizabeth Macarthur wrote in 1795, 'to confine them to so narrow a society'. She reported that 'the little creatures all speak of going home to England with rapture. My dear Edward almost quitted me without a tear.' Darcy Wentworth sent his sons home to school, and so did some among the more affluent of emancipists. Isaac Nichols, transported in 1790 for stealing, became principal superintendent of convicts, then post master. His son Robert, born in 1809, went to school in England and stayed to qualify as a solicitor before returning to Sydney. Some families engaged private teachers. The Macarthurs had an aristocratic French emigré to teach their children before they could be taken to England, but most tutors and governesses had arrived as convicts. There were also, in Sydney and Parramatta after 1800, private academies which parents suspected were inferior to their English models.

The school was a revered institution in every land touched by the gospel of improvement, and colonists were more apt than most peoples to have embraced that gospel. The senior priest of the Catholic mission in Australia observed in the late 1830s: 'wherever I go, and I have largely traversed this country, I meet men of industrious domestic habits, solicitous to give their children an education superior to their own'. When John Martin, a steward of Castle Hyde, Fermoy, County Cork, was invited by Sir Thomas Brisbane to come out to New South Wales as his private trainer and groom, he accepted because he saw a better life in the colony for his children. The emancipist parents of Daniel Deniehy put him into an academy run by an able emigrant teacher, W. T. Cape; and when they took the boy to England in 1842 it was to seek for him a more advanced education than the colony could offer. For people raised poor and sent out in shame, the determination to give a child a good English education was perhaps like the urge which led Magwitch, the uncouth convict in Charles Dickens's *Great Expectations*, to make a gentleman of Pip.

The young gentlemen of Rugby in 1852 might have been surprised to know that they had among them the grandson of a Botany Bay convict. He was Thomas Wentworth Wills, whose father Horatio was as solicitous as any parent in the continent to give the boy an education superior to his own. Horatio Wills, rough and seamanlike in manner, had no formal education other than apprenticeship to a printer. As a young man he wrote bitterly in his magazine the *Currency Lad* about a so-called public library in Sydney to which poor mechanics were not admitted. 'Since the rich members of our state cannot afford to instruct the poor', he declared, 'let the latter do it themselves. For we beg to impress upon their minds, if they wish their children hereafter to move in society with respect, that nothing will conduce so much to this end as an education'. Before Thomas was born in 1837, Horatio left Sydney, took to squatting, and went overland to Port Phillip. In 1843, when Thomas was six, Horatio wrote in his diary: 'I never knew a father's care. My own youth faded out and I know nothing. But my son! May I be spared for him, that he may be useful to his country'. There was no school within reach of the Willses' property, Lexington. Father began to teach son reading, writing and arithmetic, and could soon report: 'Tom has advanced as far as six times one and is scribbling pot hooks and hangers'. When his station hands deserted to go to the diggings in 1852, Horatio Wills sold Lexington with its twenty-nine thousand sheep and three thousand cattle, and settled near Geelong. That year Thomas Wentworth Wills, grandson of the transported Edward, went to Rugby, and later to Cambridge.

Since 1830 parents, clergymen and schoolmasters, first in New South Wales and then elsewhere, had been trying to found schools which would make it unnecessary to send Australian boys to England for education. The Australian College, created by the Presbyterian minister John Dunmore Lang, was opened in Sydney in 1831. The King's School, a Church of England foundation at Parramatta, took pupils in 1832. The Sydney College was established in 1835 by a group of parents who agreed to subscribe fifty pounds each. James Martin, son of John the vice-regal groom, was enrolled there and heard the first headmaster, W. T. Cape, say in 1836 that from such boys as himself would be chosen 'the judges, the magistrates of the land, the clergymen, the lawyers, the legislators, the civil servants'. But these three schools had a struggle to stay open. They lacked the endowments that nourished schools for the sons of gentlemen in England; they were committed to costly buildings; the depression of the early 1840s prevented some parents from paying fees, and others preferred their sons to sail home. The Australian College closed in 1841, opened again in 1846, and lasted until 1854. When Thomas Braim, headmaster of Sydney College, published *A History of New South Wales* in 1846, the school was deep in debt and the historian devoted several pages to a prospectus for it, citing an examiners' report by two fellows of Cambridge as proof that it was now 'quite possible for youths to obtain a superior education without travelling beyond the limits of the colony'. He appealed to the sense of nationality among colonial-born parents. 'Australians! you profess attachment to the land of your birth, prove yourselves true patriots; rest not till education spread over the land'. But Sydney College had to close in 1848.

The King's School survived, to be joined between 1855 and 1870 by schools in all colonies influenced by Thomas Arnold's Rugby and staffed in due course by a new breed of muscular Christian emigrant schoolmasters. The government of Victoria granted forty thousand pounds to the main religious denominations between 1853 and 1856 to help them build secondary schools. The Anglican bishop of Melbourne, Charles Perry, laying the foundation stone of the Geelong Grammar School in 1857, said that he 'was glad to see a school established in this town, on the plan of their good old English public schools, and he hoped that this institution would bear such a character as that parents need no longer send their sons home to Harrow or Eton'. It and schools like it did bear such a character, and Australian parents, however rich and however devoted to the motherland, would rarely look beyond them. Taught by English, Scottish and Irish schoolmasters, in neo-Gothic or neo-classical buildings, from English books, Australian boys could learn well enough in their own colony how to grow into leaders of their fellows. Edmund Barton, son of an estate agent, born in Sydney in 1849, went to Sydney Grammar School in 1857. John Forrest, born in Western Australia in 1847, was sent by his father, a farmer with high hopes for his children, to board at Bishop Hale's School in Perth in 1860. William Deakin enrolled his son Alfred at the Melbourne Church of England Grammar School in 1864.

By 1870 the secondary schools were not providing many undergraduates for Australia's two universities. The first, in Sydney, owed its foundation to Wentworth, who proposed and chaired a select committee of the Legislative Council in 1849 to report upon the best means of instituting a university. One of its purposes, he believed, would be to help remove the stench of Botany Bay. 'In this colony of all others', he told the council, 'it was the paramount duty of the Government to provide for the instruction of the people, and to reclaim it from the moral taint attaching to it, by elevating and enlightening the minds of its inhabitants'. His committee reported with colonial patriotism and fatherly concern on the dispatch of young Australians over the sea for higher education, lamenting that 'for all beyond the mere rudiments of learning, we have still to send our sons to some British or Foreign University, at the distance of half the Globe from all parental or family control, and, as might be predicated, in most cases, with certain detriment to their morals; in few, with any compensating improvement to their minds'. Unfortunately Wentworth and his colleagues, among them Robert Lowe, Charles Nicholson and James Macarthur, gave no examples. They firmly recommended a university. Wentworth told the council that without it self-government would be useless, for until the native youth of the country could gain an education to fit them for high office in the state, the colony 'would be forced to employ people who came from abroad, and who could not feel the intense interest in the country which sons of the soil ought to feel.' Wentworth's bill for a university was defeated after he proposed that a former convict—Dr William Bland, transported for killing a man in a duel—should be a member of the senate, and that clergymen as a body should be ineligible for it. The composition of the senate was left open in a bill which the Legislative Council passed in 1850. William Woolls, a botanist who had taught at both The King's School and Sydney College, published a long poem expressing liberal delight at the prospect of this 'Alma Mater of the Southern Land':

> Rise, Rise! Australia, chase the mists away
> Which for too long have held the light of day . . .
> In that vast pile which near the Cove shall rise
> Pointing its Gothic turrets to the skies,
> The poet yet shall wear the laurel crown,
> And every Art some bright distinction own.

The University of Sydney opened in 1852, but the turrets rose faster than the enrolments. Henry Parkes was uncomfortable at the opening ceremony, which to his taste smacked of 'downright flunkeyism'. He found in Nicholson's speech as vice-provost a preference for 'antiquated absurdities', and he accused the enterprise of wearing 'an air of aristocratical predilection which with public money ought not to be indulged'. In 1870 the university had only forty-one students. 'They will seldom pursue learning for learning's sake', Thomas Braim wrote of Australian-born youths; 'they require an appeal to their interest, they need the recommendation of profit and advantage'. Undergraduates at Sydney were offered an arts degree with a heavy concentration of classics and mathematics; law began in 1859, but only for arts graduates and with no professional courses. A correspondent in the *Sydney Morning Herald* of 29 August 1870 was expressing a common view when he judged 'that, so far, the University has lamentably failed to realise the general benefits that were expected from it'. A kindly visitor could find little to praise but the architecture. Trollope pronounced the Great Hall, opened in 1859, to be 'the finest chamber in the colonies'.

The University of Melbourne, which admitted students in 1859, offered by 1870 professional degrees in medicine and law as well as an arts degree. Ninety-two students were attending lectures in 1869. It was serving the community a little more actively than its sister in Sydney and was esteemed a little more highly, but it was far from fulfilling the hopes of its founders. The University of Melbourne after 1870, and the University of Sydney after 1880, would grow in numbers and public regard as the secondary schools increased the flow of matriculants who saw profit and advantage in higher education, especially as training for a profession. Universities would open at Adelaide in 1875 and Hobart in 1893. The founding father and first chancellor at Melbourne, Redmond Barry, wanted professors to display 'such habits and manners as to stamp on their future pupils the character of loyal, well-bred English gentlemen'. Drawing most of their professors, ideas and customs from institutions at home, the colonial universities would become more formidable agents of imperial patriotism and British civilization as larger numbers of young men (and from the 1880s some young women) passed under their neo-Gothic arches.

What sort of education was to be given to the great majority of children who had no prospect of reaching the colonial versions of English public schools? The question occupied legislators more than any other matter except the disposal of public land. It was a divisive issue in every colony, touching as it did the great controversies of the age on science and religion and liberty and the state, and being argued out in a society where it came to seem almost self-evident that all children should have access to education when all men had the right to vote. In 1844 a select committee of the Legislative Council, whose chairman was Robert Lowe, reported that about half the children of New South Wales between the ages of four and fourteen were attending schools and half were not. Sir Richard Bourke, governor from 1831 to 1837, had hoped to raise the proportion by copying a system lately introduced in Ireland. Under the Irish National plan, the government gave aid and direction to schools in which children received a general elementary education, Christian but undenominational; clergy of different churches came in to impart religious instruction to children of their own persuasion. In New South Wales the public schools of early years had become parish schools of the Church of England. It was evident to Bourke—himself a liberal, Anglican Irishman—that a Church of England monopoly of public education was no longer appropriate for the free and denomi-nationally various society which this colony was becoming. But his recommendation of the Irish system outraged Protestant clergymen who were led, or misled, by the Church of England bishop, William Broughton, to believe that it made concessions to the Catholic minority which were intolerable in a British colony. Bourke abandoned the proposal.

Schools run by churches were given subsidies in Bourke's time and later. Lowe's select committee of 1844, which had been appointed 'to devise the means of placing the education of youth upon a basis suited to the wants and wishes of the community' recommended the Irish system as likelier to achieve that end than the current policy of giving public money to church schools wherever they happened to have been built. The Legislative Council adopted the committee's view by thirteen votes to twelve. It made sense to the governor, Sir George Gipps. 'The great dispersion of the population of New South Wales', he had said in 1839, 'renders perhaps more than in any country upon earth, a system of education necessary that shall be as comprehensive as possible'. Again clergymen objected, and again a governor let the scheme drop. Governor FitzRoy eventually introduced the Irish system in 1848 after satisfying himself that whatever clergymen said, most people in the colony now wanted it, and after assuring the churches that the new arrangement would complement, not replace, the making of grants to their schools.

For nearly twenty years public money was paid to a board of denominational commissioners which distributed it to church schools throughout New South Wales, and another board of national commissioners which encouraged communities to make schools of their own. Wherever people could promise to find one-third of the cost of putting up and fitting out a school, to superintend its building, to take a share in conducting it, and to deliver thirty children regularly into it for instruction, the commissioners would find two-thirds of the cost, appoint and pay a teacher, and provide such inspection as could be managed. But most of the teachers were incompetent, the schools squalid, and the work done in the name of the national commissioners was 'deplorable in the extreme'. That was the judgment in 1854 of three schoolmasters appointed to report on the school system of the colony for a select committee of the Legislative Council. They concluded that 'the Colony possesses no system of education at all, in the proper sense of the word. Primary education is divided into two great sections, repugnant, if not hostile, to each other in spirit, and independent of each other in every respect . . . There should be but one system, especially adapted to the wants of the country, and controlled and administered by one managing body'. The principal author of this indictment was William Wilkins, inspector and superintendent for the national commissioners. He had been trained at home in the Irish National system and came out in 1851 to be headmaster of the Model School in Fort Street, Sydney, from which the conductors of National Schools were supposed to learn how to run them. Wilkins became chief inspector for the national commissioners in 1860 and secretary in 1864. He did more than any other man, except one, to have the so-called dual system abolished.

The exception was Henry Parkes. By 1854 the middle-aged emigrant who had been offered no education by the government of his native land was declaring in his newspaper the *Empire* 'that . . . as education is necessary even to the physical and secular well-being of the State, it is as much within the province of the State to promote it as it is to provide police for our protection'. From 1854 until the *Empire* failed in 1858, Parkes used its columns to express the conviction he had come to share with Wilkins, that there had to be a unified system of state schools. After 1858 Parkes waited his chance in parliament to legislate for such a system. The chance came in 1866, when he and James Martin formed a ministry which lasted for three years.

The defects of the dual system inherited by Victoria and Queensland when they separated from New South Wales had led the parliament in Brisbane to pass a Primary Education Act in 1860, establishing a Board of General Education, and the parliament in Melbourne to pass a Common Schools Act in 1862. When Parkes was proposing change in New South Wales, he said of the Victorians: 'they found, as we have found, that the two systems together were at the same time expensive and ineffectual'. The speech in which Parkes moved the second reading of the Public Schools Bill in the Legislative Assembly on 12 September 1866 was the testament of a liberal democrat and a proud colonist, determined that the children of New South Wales should not be deprived of their right to the schooling which would make them free and responsible citizens, builders of a new nation. He spoke it, as always, in the manner of a self-educated man, anxious to pronounce every word correctly but often uncertain how to do it. He expressed in vividly local terms the liberal conviction that more education would mean less crime, inviting members to imagine 'children who, whilst ministers of religion are cavilling over a division of spoils are left destitute of all instruction, and often sink into the worst courses of evil as a consequence'. Of men hanged lately in Sydney he said: 'We know that some of those young natives, led step by step in crime till they forfeited their lives on the gallows, never had the slightest chance of instruction'. Did he mean that the denominational system was encouraging murder? It was the sort of rhetorical flourish which could goad Parkes's clerical opponents to fury; but the solid votes for this bill was to show that they now represented a minority. Against defenders of the dual system, Parkes wielded figures which showed, he declared, that nearly 100 000 of the colony's 150 000 children under fourteen were not in school. 'This cause cannot suffer from the feebleness of my appeal', he said after nearly three hours of powerful oratory; 'the voices of a hundred thousand children appeal to you'. Some of these hundred thousand voices could only gurgle and bellow, as they belonged to babies well below school age; but members could forgive hyperbole in so good a cause.

The act itself had much in it to conciliate church interests. A single Council of Education replaced the two boards. Denominational schools would still get public money, but on terms which proclaimed that the new public schools were the state's preferred agents of enlightenment. Parkes became the first president of the Council of Education,

PUBLIC SCHOOL, CASTLEREAGH STREET, SYDNEY

and Wilkins its permanent secretary. In two years the council established more than fifty new schools, among them the Castlereagh (later Cleveland) Street Public School, a massive baronial neo-Gothic structure which became a model for many others in the capital and in country towns. It might appear a grim and forbidding pile to later pupils and passers-by, who saw it as archaic and grimy and knew nothing of what it replaced— the 'wretched hovels' Wilkins had inspected in the old days. When schoolhouses 'resemble the miserable homes of the lower classes', Wilkins had written, 'it cannot be expected that the children will become more refined in their domestic arrangements when they grow up. The school is an evidence of what their superiors consider good enough for them'. A member of parliament remarked that some new schools in Sydney were like palaces. Parkes, who liked to lay their foundation stones and declare them open, could well have replied that there was no reason why a building designed to accommodate 750 children— the attendance at Castlereagh Street in 1868—should not look like a palace, unless it was thought wrong to encourage ambitious fancy in young colonial minds. The tower that rose over Cleveland Street was a monument to the faith of Henry Parkes and colonists like him that it was, as he said when opening another school in 1869, 'a great and holy work to educate this rising generation'.

The new schools, like the old, were vehicles of an emigrant culture. Unlike educators in the United States, the makers of public elementary schools in Australia did not see it as their job to propagate a sentiment of attachment to the land in which the children lived. Most teachers in 1870 were themselves emigrants. Their pupils read poetry written in an English landscape and in a hemisphere where June was summer and December winter. They could have been offered 'September in Australia', an experiment in national poetry which Henry Kendall undertook in 1867:

> Grey winter hath gone, like a wearisome guest,
>   And, behold, for repayment,
> September comes in with the wind of the West,
>   And the Spring in her raiment!

But it would be left to the syllabus-makers of later years to put those lines into school readers.

In 1870 all colonies except South Australia had denominational schools which received money from the state, and other schools, known variously as public, national or common, for which the government took a direct responsibility. The liberal Nonconformist politicians of South Australia had resolved against denominational instruction as early as 1851. The debate over whether governments should go on subsidizing church schools would arouse passion in the politics of other colonies for varying periods after 1870. It had also to be resolved whether the education offered in government schools should be compulsory, free and secular.

The education systems of 1870 were still reaching only about half the children of school age. In arguments about how to take in the other half, many people spoke as Parkes did of the association between ignorance and crime. Others were sceptical. 'Education gives people of no conscience more power to commit evil than before', said one critic of Parkes's argument (who nevertheless voted for his bill). Differing prophecies were made about the power of schooling to tame the gangs of larrikins who hung about the streets of Melbourne and Sydney by 1870. Students of the larrikin speculated about how his name originated, whether he was a high-spirited youth to be indulged or a criminal menace to be suppressed, and whether larrikinism—that word was current by 1870— would be dissolved by compulsory education. 'My inquiries into the origin and habits of that troublesome parasite the larrikin', wrote an inspector of schools in Melbourne in 1872, 'do not make me sanguine that compulsory, primary instruction can do much for him, unless indirectly'. According to the sceptic's view of education, it might only make them more potent. In Adelaide a year later, a member opposing a bill for compulsory education modelled on a Victorian measure of 1872 found 'a terrible warning in Victoria's compulsory schools; Melbourne's educated larrikins were organized with a secretary, who collected funds to pay their fees'.

Larrikins apart, defenders and opponents of the state schools would argue warmly after 1870 about the capacity of secular education to produce good citizens. The Catholic bishops of New South Wales would fling at Parkes in 1879 the accusation that his schools were 'seed-plots of future immorality, infidelity, and lawlessness, being calculated to debase the standard of human excellence, and to corrupt the political, social, and individual life of future citizens'. Parkes was sure that they were, on the contrary, makers of civic virtue. Scripture and military drill were both in the curriculum of his schools. Children had to be taught the ethics and traditions judged to be common to all varieties of Christianity, and they had to learn to march in step.

Holidays Old and New

'If the ballads of a people are the essence of its history', a patriot wrote in 1857, 'holidays are, on similar grounds, the free utterance of its character'. The author was an American, rightly fearful that the United States were about to disintegrate and scanning the calendar for festivals on which his countrymen could affirm their common sense of nationality. What did the days that Australian colonists set aside for ceremony, rhetoric and leisure express about their character as a people? Their celebration of the monarch's birthday, the most formal festival of the year in every colony, showed them to be children of empire. The colonists affirmed also that they were inheritors of Christian civilization. Here, as at home, the word 'holiday' might still be spelt 'holyday', and thus remind readers of its origin in the calendar of the ecclesiastical year. Days commemorating the birth, death and resurrection of Jesus were given both official and popular recognition. On Sundays nearly everybody stopped work and many attended worship. On 17 March the Irish part of the population displayed a powerful sentiment of attachment to their old homeland; for of all the saints' days, the one set aside for St Patrick was recognized most vigorously.

These were transported holidays, carried ashore by officers and convicts and emigrants and planted to grow in Australian soil. There were other holidays of local making, in which colonists revealed not what they had been but what they were becoming. One day in the year was set aside, first in Victoria and later elsewhere, to celebrate the achievement of artisans who had secured the right to work no more than eight hours a day. In Melbourne by 1870 there was a day on which men stayed away from work and attended to an increasingly popular form of play, the racing of horses. In New South Wales the anniversary of Arthur Phillip's landing was celebrated in oratory and festivity. It became a day for the native-born to talk and drink and play together; but they could not always agree about what it was appropriate to say. Nor could they expect people elsewhere in Australia to join them in commemorating the unloading of convicts at Sydney Cove. The citizens of other colonies preferred to celebrate their own later and cleaner beginnings.

Colonists expressed on their holidays a love of sunshine and seaside. The frequency of their respites from work, compared with those granted to most people at home before 1870, was remarked by visitors and newcomers. Christmas became not merely, as for most Englishmen, a single day off, but the occasion for a week or more of leisure. No other country had a festival quite like Eight Hours Day, when men took a day from work to celebrate a reduction in hours of work. Nor, as observers said with delight, amusement or disapproval, did any other people proclaim a public holiday for the running of a horse race.

4 The Monarch's Birthday

A FESTIVAL OF EMPIRE

One of the aboriginal inhabitants, watching and listening to the newcomers, thought that the name of the bemusing fluid they drank must be 'king', so often did they shout that word before draining their mugs. For King George III, New South Wales had been claimed by James Cook in 1770. In the king's name Arthur Phillip proclaimed the colony on 7 February 1788, and the first public holiday observed there was for his fiftieth birthday that year. The fourth of June, on English lips during his reign, meant the king's birthday; and it gave republican Americans after 1776 a special pleasure to refer to the anniversary of their declaring independence as the fourth of July. Each year in the Australian colonies, governors presided on the monarch's birthday over ceremonies affirming that they belonged to an empire on which (as a writer at home put it in 1829) the sun never set. The participants in 1788 were aware that they themselves represented an extension of the king's realm. 'Perhaps no birth-day was ever celebrated in more places,' one wrote, 'or more remote from each other, than that of his Majesty on this day.'

At home it was traditionally a day of good cheer; and Phillip had the fourth of June observed, as he wrote, 'with every demonstration of joy our situation permitted.' Union Jacks were displayed on ships and shore. Guns on H.M.S. *Sirius* and H.M.S. *Supply* fired royal salutes at sunrise, one o'clock and sunset. At noon the marines fired three volleys and the band played 'God Save the King'. The governor and his officers sat down to a dinner of mutton, pork, duck, fowl, fish and kangaroo—a richer feast than they had managed for the reading of Phillip's commission on 7 February—washed down with wines and porter. 'These went merrily round in bumpers', one officer wrote. There was merriment also for soldiers and sailors and even for convicts. Work was suspended for the day. At Phillip's expense every soldier had a pint of porter to drink the king's health; every seaman had an additional allowance of rum, and every convict was given a ration of it. For a few lucky convicts there was a larger gift, of freedom. It was a custom at home to exercise royal clemency towards prisoners on the monarch's birthday. Out here, Phillip saw, the gesture could assume a larger importance. At sunset the convicts assembled around bonfires, sang loyally of the king, and gave three cheers for the governor. Phillip was well pleased with his arrangements for celebrating the more benign aspects of the power which had sent the convicts and their custodians across the world. 'There was not', he wrote, 'one heavy heart in this part of His Majesty's dominions.' There was one split head, belonging to a man caught burgling an officer's tent during the evening.

The prince of Wales's birthday was recognized in August and the queen's in January. The royal feasts became lean during 1789 as supplies in the settlement ran down. It was on the day before the king's birthday in 1790 that the *Lady Juliana* brought some provisions and news of more, and news also that his majesty had recovered from an almost fatal illness. The anniversary was therefore even more than ordinarily a time to extend the royal clemency. Phillip pardoned all offenders who were under confinement or sentence of corporal punishment, and increased all rations for the day.

On the last king's birthday of Phillip's term, his liberality to convicts provoked antagonism from the rank and file of the New South Wales Corps, a regiment which had come out to replace the marines of the first fleet. When the governor ordered the same quantity of rum—half a pint—for each soldier and each convict on 4 June 1792, the soldiers felt slighted and at first refused their ration. They accepted it only when Major Francis Grose, their commander, asked them to take it. They were men who might well respond sensitively to such a gesture, for the line distinguishing them from convicts was none too wide. Acting as governor a year later, their commanding officer showed none of Phillip's concern to make the day a time of civic festivity. Grose arranged no dinner and no rum for the prisoners, and there were no bonfires. 'I believe never was such a King's birth day kept here as this one', Richard Atkins, a legal official, grumbled into his diary on 4 June 1793; '. . . that marked attention which G[overnor] P[hillip] shewed to every one whose rank entitled him to it, is totally laid aside, and a selfish partial principal [sic] substituted in the room of it. The Govr usually extended his mercy to such convicts as were in Irons, unless they were very hardened wretches indeed. No such thing at present.' It was an early sign that the officers of the New South Wales Corps had not much will to be public benefactors.

The traditions of festivity and clemency were resumed by Governor Hunter and carried on by Governor King, who made the monarch's birthday in 1801 the time to welcome the United Kingdom of Great Britain and Ireland which had been proclaimed at home on 1 January. The new Union Jack, in which St Patrick was made to tangle with St George and St Andrew, flew on 4 June, and royal mercy was extended to several Irish convicts.

When Lachlan Macquarie was governor, his aged convict laureate Michael Massey Robinson composed an ode for the king's birthday each year. Poetry had caused Robinson's transportation in 1796, when he was convicted of blackmail at the age of fifty-one after threatening to publish verses in which an alderman of the city of London was accused of having murdered his employer. Robinson's first king's birthday ode, for 1810, related the remote colony to its motherland:

> THO' far from ALBION's hallow'd Coast
> Ocean's first PRIDE, and NATURE's Boast . . .
> Still shall the Muse prefer her tribute Lay,
> And *Australasia* hail her GEORGE's Natal Day!
> Auspicious Morn! To BRITONS Dear:
> The Pride of each revolving Year.

Making Robinson his official poet was one of Macquarie's many gestures towards the prisoners, and on each king's birthday he encouraged them to look towards emancipation. The governor visited six hundred convicts on 4 June 1819 as they consumed the beef, plum pudding and punch he had put on for them in a handsome new barracks designed by Francis Greenway. He told them that the well-behaved could hope for further indulgence, and was given three cheers. Next year Robinson's ode described the advance of arts, science and agriculture in the colony and attributed it all to George III:

> Whence—but from ONE paternal Hand,
> Have these proud Trophies grac'd her Land?

It was an extravagantly loyal question to ask of a king who had been officially insane since 1810. Two months later news reached New South Wales that when Robinson recited his ode, George III had been dead for five months. Macquarie ordered a salute of eighty-two guns—one for each year of the king's life—and put the colony into mourning for George III and thanksgiving for George IV. Robinson's first ode to the new king, for 12 August 1821, was also a farewell tribute to Macquarie.

The monarch's birthday moved from 12 August to 21 August when George IV died in 1830 and his brother became William IV. Then on 24 May 1838 Australian colonists celebrated the nineteenth birthday of Queen Victoria. 'On the whole', the *Sydney Herald* wrote, 'we question if there was any part of her majesty's dominions in which the day was celebrated with more honours than in Sydney.' A new governor, Sir George Gipps, proposed the queen's health at a birthday ball. He had met her before leaving home, and could speak personally of her 'amiable disposition and extensive acquirements, which give promise of a reign that cannot fail to dispense happiness and prosperity among her subjects'. This queen was to reign so long that millions of her subjects everywhere came to think of her birthday as no more moveable a feast thanChristmas. She became in her own person an imperial symbol. John Bull, Britannia and the lion remained popular representations of England and empire in loyal verse, newspaper prose, pageants, transparencies and cartoons; but decade by decade the figure of the queen herself, the mother country incarnate, became more familiar to her colonial subjects. When governments issued postage stamps from 1850, she appeared on those of all but Western Australia. Unlike her predecessors in living memory, she was setting her people an example of respectable family life, and her husband Prince Albert acquired a sedate popularity in the colonies as at home. Salutes were fired each 26 August for his birthday. If a penal colony had been founded in the north-west of Australia in 1860, it might have been named Albert, and if people in the west of Victoria had formed a separate colony in 1861, they would have called it Princeland. Newspapers with black borders announced the prince consort's death in February 1862. The governor of New South Wales ordered nine days of mourning, the governor of South Australia six weeks. A bronze statue of him was unveiled in Hyde Park, Sydney, on St George's Day, 23 April 1866. It was a profoundly colonial tribute, for the statue was a copy of one in London which was known to have pleased the queen. More than ten thousand people subscribed to pay for it, and a great crowd described by a reporter as 'rich and poor, literate and unlearned', gathered to see the statue unveiled by the governor, Sir John Young, and to hear a choir sing 'God Save the Queen' and 'Des Deutschen Vaterland'. Compassion was added now to the esteem in which the queen was held. She never travelled to any of her colonies: Ireland took her as far from the centre of things as it was ever practicable for the monarch to go. But when she allowed her second son, Prince Alfred, Duke of Edinburgh, to visit Australia in 1867, he was welcomed everywhere with ardour. Passing through a township near Adelaide, the

GOVERNMENT HOUSE AND FORT MACQUARIE, SYDNEY

young prince read a chalked message which spoke for masses of colonists everywhere: 'We love you for your mother'.

There was no electorate in Australia for a popular movement to break away from the empire of which she was head. John Dunmore Lang, deeply impressed with the United States as a model, did his best over more than thirty years to generate such a movement, inviting Australians in 1870 to recognize that they were now adults and could leave home to fulfil their independent destiny as 'one of the mightiest Powers on earth . . . the only formidable rival to the United States out of Europe.' From time to time the rhetoric of republicanism momentarily attracted people who had particular grievances against the imperial government or one of its viceroys. But the crown's advisers always removed sufficient discontents to cool any campaign to cut the painter. In 1870 the job of the queen's advisers at the Colonial Office was so tranquil as to be almost tedious. Lord Granville, becoming secretary of state in 1868, opened all incoming letters himself and discovered that most needed no answer. If and when the elected representatives of Australian colonies advised the Colonial Office through the governors that their people wanted entire independence, that situation would be administered calmly and without grave concern whichever party was in office at home. The Victorian politician George Higinbotham judged it in 1869 the wish of ninety-nine out of every one hundred men and women in the colony that the imperial connexion should continue indefinitely. Their native children and grandchildren, he thought, might well have other desires; but the adults of the present generation were still so close to the mother country that nothing could shake their affection and respect for it. The thousands of miles between mother country and colonies could give the queen an enhanced significance to such people. 'Her Majesty', wrote a resident of Melbourne in 1861, 'has no truer or warmer hearts on her shores than amongst the exiled ones in distant lands, who, brimful of loyalty, delight in celebrating the Royal birthday with every honour.' For the homesick Briton, thinking of the queen might annihilate momentarily the ocean between the colony and motherland. 'I remember on the occasion of my first journey to the Bush,' a Presbyterian minister testified, 'when the feeling of separation and exile was heavy upon me, the delightful sensation I experienced when I reached a lonely hut, and read upon its lintel the two letters "V.R." It seemed as if distance had been suddenly obliterated; I felt that I was still a member of the great British family,—and a subject of the British Queen, whom she was caring for even at these ends of the earth, and would defend against all deadly.' A Protestant clergyman may have been likelier than other colonists to see the queen as a talisman against the perils of the bush, but it was not uncommon for newcomers to find the monarch a strengthening symbol of the civilization they were labouring to impose on the continent. The capital of the new Swan River colony was proclaimed on the king's birthday in 1829: twelve miles upstream from Fremantle, a ceremony combined the felling of a tree to christen the town with the volleys, cheers and feasting customary among British officers on the day. When an emigrant ship reached the colony in 1834, settlers hungry for news rowed out in boats calling up: 'How are you? How did you leave the King and the Royal Family?' Men far from settled society, prompted by no newspaper or invitation to ceremony, might think of Queen Victoria on her birthday. Ludwig Leichhardt's party, crossing the north of the continent in 1845, gave themselves a double allowance of fat cake on 24 May and drank the queen's health in sugared tea. On 24 May 1861 Robert O'Hara Burke's companion William John Wills, near Cooper's Creek and not far from death, recorded grimly in his diary that he had collected nardoo seeds 'to celebrate the Queen's birthday.' Young John Forrest, leading an expedition from Western Australia to Adelaide in 1870, flew the Union Jack from a gum tree on 24 May, ordered a twenty-one gun salute from rifles and pistols, and had his men sing 'God Save the Queen' and give her three cheers. 'I venture to record', Forrest wrote, 'that our vocal efforts were as sincerely and heartily made in the Australian wilderness as any which rang that day in any part of Her Majesty's wide dominions. We were all highly delighted—not only feeling that we had done our duty as loyal subjects, but other celebrations in more civilized places were forcibly recalled to memory.' Forrest was a native, not an emigrant with memories of another home. If his sentiment was shared widely by the Australian-born, the monarch's birthday was likely to remain a festival for a long time yet in these democratic colonies. In Sydney the *Empire* greeted 24 May 1870 as 'a national holiday', on which 'the strife of parties, the jealousies of emulation, the weariness of business are to give place to the exultant sentiments that become British subjects as they call to mind the memories associated with the name of Queen Victoria'. The paper noted with pleasure that as the sun rose earlier on her Australian subjects than on almost all others, they were among the first to welcome the anniversary, the New Zealanders alone being ahead. If staying away from work was the test, Australians were more loyal to the queen than people at the heart of the empire: in London most birthday festivities were held on the nearest Saturday, but in Sydney and her sister cities the day itself was a general holiday.

THE BEST PEOPLE

Governor Darling held a ball at Government House in Sydney for George IV's birthday in 1826. The *Sydney Gazette* reported the tailors and shoemakers busy and 'the belles and

QUEEN'S BIRTHDAY BALL, MELBOURNE
As the best people have become too numerous for Government House, the ball and the
levee are held in the Exhibition Building, whose exterior is shown on p. 147.

beaux of Australia . . . on the tiptoe of expectation'. They were not disappointed. 'It was
a grand entertainment' wrote Mrs Forbes, wife of the chief justice. Peter Cunningham
found it 'the most splendid and most numerously attended of any yet given in the colony—
two hundred individuals being present on this occasion, a considerable portion of whom
would be qualified by their wealth and respectability to move in genteel society in England.'
It was also the first ball in the colony at which the ladies were as numerous as the
gentlemen. New South Wales was becoming a proper society.

The elite of each colony was defined by the list of invitations to the governor's
levee and ball on the monarch's birthday. At first its limits were narrow. 'Society in
Sydney at this time', Mrs Forbes wrote of the 1820s, 'was composed almost entirely of the
families of the Government officials, the Military and Naval Officers and their wives,
and some few of the leading Colonists. The prejudice against trade, from a social standpoint,
was very pronounced'. The *Sydney Gazette* published 'The Clerk's Lament, on not being
invited to the Birth-day Ball at Government House.' In Sir Richard Bourke's time at
Sydney the elite became larger, not only because the free population was increasing but also
because Bourke took a broader view than Darling of who, in this society, the best people
were. The reception rooms became uncomfortably crowded. At Gipps's first ball in 1838,
not half the company could hear his words in praise of the new queen; for they had
increased from the two hundred of 1826 to eleven hundred, jammed into a house which
Macquarie had found inadequate before 1820. Sir Thomas Brisbane, denied permission to

enlarge it, lived instead at Parramatta house which Phillip began and Hunter and Macquarie enlarged. Finally the Colonial Office approved a residence fitter for the governor of a flourishing colony. It was designed at home in the Tudor Gothic fashion. The flag of St George floated over it on the queen's birthday in 1842, and its ballroom was used by Gipps for the first time on 24 May 1843. Thomas Braim, headmaster of Sydney College, described it minutely in his *A History of New South Wales* (1846), explaining that he did so from a desire to show that 'separated as we are by continents and oceans from our fatherland, we have yet the pride of the British-born to rear in their land such buildings as their sons may be proud to contemplate ... May the solidity, the splendour, and elegance, of this vice-royal mansion be an emblem of Australia's future history.' Comparably handsome messages to posterity were built by 1870 for the governors of all colonies except Victoria, which took a little longer to put up, in the 1870s, a palace whose vast ballroom could contain the largest elite in the continent.

Robert Lowe, campaigning furiously against Gipps and for responsible government, urged colonists in his paper the *Atlas* to boycott the levee at the new Government House on 24 May 1844 and leave the governor standing alone in his splendid drawingroom except for a few officials and sycophants. If the appeal had any effect it was to make the sick and infirm, who might otherwise have sent their excuses, determined to go along as a gesture of loyalty and disgust. 'The result', Lowe admitted, 'has greatly braced the somewhat shaken nerves of the Governor.' The guest list in 1847, Sir Charles FitzRoy's

QUEEN'S BIRTHDAY PLEASURES
Fireworks at Manly beach

first year, seemed to the *Sydney Morning Herald* unwholesomely long: 'persons of doubtful reputation' were being invited; and if that went on, the paper suggested, the only truly respectable citizens would be those people who were never seen there. But the list had to grow even faster now, as assisted emigrants and sons of convicts got themselves elected to the Legislative Council and then to the new Legislative Assembly. It was painful for guests who had been among the elect in Darling's time to have to put up now with such people as Henry and Clarinda Parkes dropping their aitches all over Government House. For the parvenu it could be an awesome experience to attend his first birthday levee and, with his wife, their first birthday ball, and to be saluted by a red-coated sentry, stared at by emus strutting on the lawns, and announced by a liveried servant in a powdered wig.

The queen's proxies were expected by their guests to put on a good spread. When Sir Charles Hotham, under orders to make economies, tried to reduce the bill for the birthday ball in Melbourne in 1855, he gave offence to those colonists within the circle of formal celebration. A governor had to watch out for other hazards. In Hobart the Catholic bishop declared that he would stay away from the birthday levee in 1864 because the list of guests violated the principle of religious equality by describing him as 'the Bishop of the Church of Rome' while the head of the Church of England appeared as simply 'the Bishop'. People of Nonconformist persuasion in Adelaide boycotted the birthday dinner in 1871 because the governor had put the two bishops, Church of England and Catholic, before all other clerical and lay guests.

For the mass of people not invited to Government House, the monarch's birthday was a day, weather permitting, to attend parades of soldiers or races between horses or men, go sailing, have picnics, and in the evening to attend plays or concerts, watch public displays of fireworks or let off their own. Thanks to the monarch and to the governor and his advisers most colonists were free on this imperial festival day to pursue the pleasures of their choice.

5 The Sabbath

SUNDAY MUSTER

The English Sunday came to New South Wales on 3 February 1788. A sergeant of the marines wrote on 26 January that the place was 'crisned this day'; but he spoke meta-phorically, for the ceremony on the day of landing at Sydney Cove had no ecclesiastical aspect. Judge William Burton, looking back from 1840 on that day, marvelled at its secularity. 'Was there then no act of contrition, no act of gratitude, which it had been becoming on such an occasion for Englishmen to offer to the God of their fathers, upon the erection of the national flag of England upon this distant land?' A few decades later there might well have been, once the leaven of evangelicalism had worked its way through the society; but that movement was young in 1788, and but for the intervention of its leader William Wilberforce the first fleet might not even have had a chaplain on board. Although the second day ashore was a Sunday, men went on unloading ships and pitching tents as if it were any other day. The worship of God as practised by the Church of England began on the second Sunday. Summoned by drums, the convicts and the marines gathered in the open air to hear the chaplain, Richard Johnson, preach the colony's first sermon. Of all the verses in the King James Bible, Johnson chose as text for his homily to the congregation of exiles Psalm 116, verse 12: 'What shall I render unto the Lord, for all his benefits towards me?' On that day too Johnson baptized for the first time a colonial-born child, the baby son of a marine and his wife. Three children, two of them born to convicts, were baptized on Sunday 10 February, and five couples offered themselves for Johnson to marry. The blessed sacrament was given and taken according to the rites of the Church of England, as required in Phillip's instructions, at divine worship on Sunday 24 February. The officer in whose tent the ceremony took place resolved to keep for the rest of his life the table on which the elements of bread and wine had stood, 'for it is the first table that ever the Lord's Supper was eat of in this country.' It was perhaps the earliest spontaneous gesture recorded in the settlement expressing a sense that events here would one day be regarded as a part of history.

The chaplain had other jobs from Monday to Saturday. It was on a Monday, 25 February, that he buried a child who had died of a fever; two days later he heard the confessions of three men sentenced to death for stealing food, two of whom were reprieved and one hanged. To people who could read he distributed tracts published by the Society for the Propagation of the Gospel. But Sunday was the day of which Richard Johnson had special custody. Convicts were not required to work on that day and were compelled to worship, or at any rate muster before the chaplain as he told them to pray, to avoid profanity, to live clean and honest lives, and to obey their superiors. The Sunday service was still being held in the open air when a Spanish priest happened to visit Sydney in 1793 and was amazed at the evident lack of regard for religious institutions. 'The first thought of colonists and of Government in our colonies', the Spaniard wrote, 'is to plant the cross and erect sacred edifices of religion.' It was not easy for a man from Catholic Christendom to understand that to English administrators the church was not so much an estate or a bearer of mystery as an auxiliary agent of morality and order, and for that purpose there was no pressing need to put up a sacred edifice. When a church was built later in 1793 it was at the chaplain's own expense.

Governors gave Johnson support by forcing convicts to be within earshot of his Sunday sermons. Phillip told them that their rations would be reduced if they did not go. Hunter ordered that any convict 'idling about' during divine worship was to be locked up. Such devices were necessary to assure a good attendance; for most of the English convicts were from a class not normally in the habit of going to church, and most other prisoners were Irish Catholics for whom Protestant worship was an abomination. Johnson's church was burned down in 1798. It was no accident, Hunter reported, but 'a designed thing'. Before Johnson sailed home with Hunter in 1800 he had come to despair of the adults under his charge and had begun a Sunday school to protect children against the corruption of their parents. Samuel Marsden, another evangelical, who came to help Johnson and remained as principal chaplain, was appalled by the ungodliness of the higher ranks as well as of the convicts. But he had at least the support of Macquarie whom he found attentive to the Sabbath day, compelling the convicts and exhorting everybody else to attend divine worship. 'I . . . used every means', Macquarie said at the end of his term, 'both by precept and example, as far as my influence extended, to inspire a religious feeling amongst all classes of the community; to excite sentiments of morality; and to inculcate habits of temperance and industry.' Only briefly had any of his predecessors allowed the Irish to worship according to the rites of the church to which nearly all of them belonged. In 1803 King appointed as chaplain James Dixon, a priest transported from Ireland for taking part in rebellion. The mass came to New South Wales, and the first Catholic marriage was celebrated on Sunday 15 May 1803; but the experiment ended when King became sure that the priest's assemblies for worship had been used for plotting insurrection (see pages 178–81). After March 1804, as before May 1803, all convicts including Catholics were ordered to attend services of the Church of England. Macquarie was nevertheless ready to allow Catholic worship if it could be arranged properly. He gave a courteous if wary reception to an Irish priest, Jeremiah O'Flynn, who turned up in 1817 calling himself prefect-apostolic of New Holland. But as no papers authorizing him arrived from either the Colonial Office or his own spiritual superiors, Macquarie sent O'Flynn away. Three years later two Irish priests, J. J. Therry and Philip Conolly, arrived with not only permission but also payment from an English government which was now disposed to sanction a general reduction of official intolerance against Catholics. Macquarie genially laid the first stone of a church in which Catholics could worship as they wished, and left it to their priests to teach Irish convicts the virtues of obedience and decency. It remained compulsory for convicts to worship somewhere. Darling treated habitual neglect of divine worship as a ground for not giving a prisoner a ticket-of-leave. It was necessary not merely to attend, but to behave properly and to stay awake: in Van Diemen's Land one convict was punished for throwing a missile during divine service, and another for sleeping.

By 1830 the colonies had not only clergymen of the Church of England and Catholic priests, but Presbyterian, Wesleyan and Nonconformist ministers at work in them. What were their rights out here? The question became more pressing as Australia attracted more and more free emigrants who had been accustomed at home to worshipping elsewhere than in the Church of England.

Whether the Church of England was in Australia, as at home, the church established by law, was a matter of mystery and controversy. Was the establishment of the church among those laws that British subjects were deemed to have carried with them when they settled New South Wales and Van Diemen's Land? Certainly all governors before Bourke behaved as if it were. The Church and Schools Corporation, set up in 1825 to provide revenue from land for activities of the Church of England, did not make sense unless it were. But the Colonial Office abolished the corporation before it had begun to work, and Bourke decided that in Australian conditions the principle of establishment could not be applied. It was one of John Dunmore Lang's early targets. Lang, the first thoroughly aggressive cleric outside the Church of England to live and work in Australia, declared in 1834: 'the greatest calamity that has hitherto befallen the Australian colonies, in regard to their moral and religious welfare, is the prevalence of a jealous, exclusive, and intolerant system of Episcopal domination.' He deplored the system that allowed chaplains of the Church of England to sit as magistrates, because it associated Christianity and secular punishment, and he declared that the free colonists from Scotland who formed his own congregation on Sundays had the right to be treated out here on a basis of utter equality with members of the Church of England. To Governor Bourke, coming himself from Ireland and appointed by a Whig government which had granted Catholic emancipation at home, it seemed evident that members of the Church of England had to be made to live on terms of civic equality not only with Presbyterians and other Protestants but also with Catholics, and indeed with Jews or any other body of colonists large enough to catch the eye of government. In 1836 the Legislative Council on Bourke's initiative passed an act which gave public money to religious denominations in proportion to the number of their adherents. Judge William Burton insisted that even now the Church of England was the church established by law, arguing in *The State of Religion and Education in New South Wales* (1840) that the money paid to other bodies was merely a mark of tolerance, not a recognition of equal status. Bishops went on demanding precedence over Catholics and others at public ceremonies such as queen's birthday levees, and sometimes being granted it. But Anglicans had to accept as a fact of Australian life that many of the principles and fictions which sustained the Church of England at home were inapplicable here. Even in England it was becoming harder for a sensible vicar to go on treating rival pastors in his parish as if they were mere interlopers; here, he had to recognize that they were participants with him for the time being in a situation of multiple establishment, and that before long—probably within his own working lifetime—public grants would be withdrawn from every church. South Australia led the way in 1851, Queensland followed in 1860, New South Wales in 1863, Tasmania in 1869 and Victoria in 1870. The Church of England thus became in Australia a voluntary association like any other church, its clergy paid not, as commonly at home, out of endowments which rendered them financially independent of their parishioners, but out of what they could induce colonists to offer them. When the clergyman at Stroud in New South Wales had

THE CHURCH OF ENGLAND: ST ANDREW'S CATHEDRAL, SYDNEY

the governor, the Earl of Belmore, lodge with him in 1870, he invited nobody to meet the eminent guest; for people who were not asked would have been offended, and under the voluntary system he could not afford to let that happen.

There was gain as well as loss for the Church of England in being placed on a level with others, for it helped to remove a popular notion that the main task of its clergy was to help the gaolers. In the years of free emigration the Church of England was in the colonies as at home the residual denomination, the body that appeared strongest when people were asked to state their religious affiliation. Among colonists who did not go to church on any particular Sunday between 1840 and 1870, most would have said if asked that it was the Church of England they were staying away from.

GOD AND MAMMON

It troubled John Dunmore Lang to see the Sabbath profaned in the Australian colonies by respectable free men as well as convicts, by new emigrants as well as old hands. A great drought which emaciated New South Wales in the late 1830s was caused in part, Lang argued, by God's displeasure at Sabbath-breaking. The Sabbath that Lang's God wanted colonists to observe was the version imposed on Scotland by the followers of John Calvin in the sixteenth century and carried by puritans into England, where it was eroded in the eighteenth century and renovated later by evangelicals. A man brought up to it would refuse to work on Sunday, or at least feel uneasy about it. At Perth in 1843 a postmaster caused an outrage by refusing to open the English mail when it arrived for the first time on a Sunday. Even for that purpose his principles would not allow him to work on the

Sabbath. When the Scottish surveyor-general Thomas Mitchell published his map of the nineteen counties of New South Wales, he explained that he had been obliged to do the actual drawing himself, 'and, but for such excuse, I ought to be ashamed to say, that I compiled and drew this map chiefly on Sundays, when I ought to have been at Church with my family.' There was no place in this Sabbath for secular recreation. Lang judged it an unholy contradiction to speak, as some members of the Legislative Council did in 1841, of 'the innocent pleasures and pastimes of the people on the Lord's day.' Godly young emigrants, Lang believed, were readily seduced by their betters into neglecting the Sabbath. He told the story in 1834 of a young clerk from Scotland who went to church for a few Sundays after landing. 'By and bye, however, he is invited to spend a Sunday with Mr. Whalebone the merchant, who prefers to drive to Parramatta or a water-excursion in the harbour to all the prayers and sermons in the colony . . . The progress to downright infidelity on the one hand, and to downright dissipation on the other, is short and rapid'.

Clergymen with a less austere view of the Sabbath than Lang could share his anxiety for its fate in Australia. Many from England were concerned especially about what would happen to Sunday in the bush, for out here the inhabitants of country districts, unlike those at home, were not the most diligent in their religious practice. In England the churches were finding it difficult to bring their ministry to bear on the towns, and the worst thing wrong with the country was that people were leaving it. The problem that colonial clergymen dwelt on most when they wrote of their work in the squatting age was how to reach the scattered and spreading rural population. William Grant Broughton reported soon after his consecration as bishop of Australia in 1836 that in outer pastoral districts of New South Wales there lived thousands of people among whom 'the observation of the Sabbath-day' was 'totally obliterated'. It was a strange experience for Englishmen to find people living fifty and even a hundred miles from a church, hearing no bells, seeing no spire or tower, remote from all those helps to devotion that could prompt a man to keep his religious habits. The squatter, according to an English observer in 1845, rarely tried to impress religion on his servants; 'he is himself, alas! but too often a total stranger to its Divine influences, and the consequence is that "like master like man", and the Sabbath is spent in some pursuit ill adapted to the day.' It seemed to another Englishman, writing in 1843, that Sunday was 'not, generally, a sacred day, a day of rest, in the bush . . . even the day of the week is forgotten.' Alexander Harris, who arrived in 1825, heard many people say: 'There is no Sunday in the bush.' In 1870 a Wesleyan minister in New South Wales found it a common remark that there was no God beyond the range. He meant the Liverpool Range, and was speaking of his time at Narrabri and Wee Waa, where he was appointed in 1868. Around Narrabri, some 250 miles north-west of Sydney, this minister learned that Sunday was much the same as any other day except that the pubs did better business and men put on a clean shirt.

It was a dark picture that many ministers painted of the spiritual condition of Australia, whether out in the bush or in the towns where most people lived. Painting dark pictures, however, had always been part of the preacher's job. The prophets of Israel were good at telling people how their religious behaviour had displeased Jehovah. Lang's Scottish clerk falling from Sabbath-breaking into infidelity and dissipation, though nominally a character in the history of New South Wales, really belonged to that awful art form, the Presbyterian sermon. The historian purported to follow the young man's remains to the grave and fancied his aged mother, 'sitting at the door of her cottage in some solitary Scottish glen' and weeping as she reminded her silent husband how long it was since they

SUNDAY ON THE GOLDFIELDS
Charles Perry, Bishop of Melbourne, preaches from a tree at Forest Creek (Castlemaine).

had heard from their boy. Moreover, behind many grim accounts of religion in Australia lay illusions about religion at home. 'The mass of the population here is vicious' wrote the continent's first archdeacon, Thomas Scott, soon after landing in 1825; 'all society, with few exceptions, is too bad and too horrid to have anything to do with.' Scott had come from, and would soon return to, a tranquil rustic parish in Northumberland. The workers whom Bishop Broughton met on sheep and cattle runs were no doubt sullen and secular compared with the people he had known as a curate in Hampshire and Surrey, but they might not have moved him to jeremiads about colonial religion if he had ever tried to work in the slums of London or Manchester or Leeds. Neglect of worship and decorum on Sundays was deplored by preachers at home just as vigorously as in the colonies. Not even the shortage of ministers and church buildings, which troubled leaders of all denominations, was peculiar to the colonial churches. Certainly it was difficult to persuade enough clergy to leave England, Scotland and Ireland for work in Australia. But it was no less difficult to get them at home to go into the cities where the population was increasing fast, and it was just as hard a struggle to put up churches in these areas as in the country towns and suburbs of the colonies.

　　Whether or not clergymen in Australia recognized it, they were in some respects better placed in 1870 than they had been forty years earlier. While it lasted, the system by which public money was applied to putting up buildings and paying ministers of several denominations helped to preserve the habit of religious worship among those who had brought it out with them. Churchgoers were more numerous among free emigrants than among convicts, and they were most numerous among the relatively affluent people who paid their own way, and who made up a suddenly enlarged proportion of all emigrants once gold was discovered.

Men of the churches were sure that the rush to gold would make colonial society still more ungodly. Judge William à Beckett, a devout Anglican, declared in 1852 that never before had Mammon gone forth with so vast and devoted a retinue as now marched beneath his banners in Victoria. The head of the Catholic church in Australia, Archbishop Polding feared that the abundance of gold would 'make more world-loving the souls of our people than they are even now.' But if Sabbath-keeping was a sign of spirituality, the people of the golden colonies in the 1850s were far from lost. Lang wrote more happily on the matter in 1852 than in 1834. Just after the first gold rushes he asserted that for Sunday observance 'the towns of New South Wales would not shrink from a comparison with the generality of towns in England.' He had visited the diggings at Turon on a Sunday and found 'the utmost decorum' there: 'to those who had witnessed the scenes of gambling and dissipation, of riot and violence, which were not unusual in California, the very different state of things at the Australian mines was equally gratifying and remarkable.' Observers of the great Victorian goldfields noticed, often with surprise, how generally the Sabbath was respected. It was partly a matter of prudence for all men to rest on the same day, so that none could infiltrate a neighbouring claim while its occupiers were idle; but there was often intense religious activity, as clergymen or lay preachers drew crowds of diggers into tents or around carts. The prophets had not realized that gold would increase the proportion of colonists for whom going to church or chapel on Sunday was a normal

SUNDAY ON THE GOLDFIELDS
Some people listen to a sermon, others jig to a fiddle.

part of the weekly round. Nor did they foresee how well the situation of the 1850s would suit the Methodists. Regions in which Methodists were strong at home contributed solidly to the emigration of the 1840s and 1850s. Their connexional polity, which had been devised in part to fit mining communities in England, provided a central direction of resources not present in either the Church of England, where the parish was an almost self-enclosed world, or those Protestant bodies in which the primary unit was the separate congregation. The colonies gained after 1850 many thousands of new citizens who would readily go on Sunday to one or other variety of Methodist worship—principally Wesleyan, Primitive or Bible Christian—if the means were not provided for them to attend whatever other form of Protestant worship they had been used to attending at home. The Methodists moved the minister around a circuit, preceded or supported him by local preachers, and extended their evangelistic and pastoral work with a cohesion, flexibility and enthusiasm which made them the only major church to have a number of adherents substantially higher than they gained by emigration and inherited attachment.

In the towns of all Australian colonies after 1850, Sunday was a time of quietness and public decency. People arrived at churches in carriages or on foot, the Protestants dressed in their Sunday best and the Catholics appearing to Protestants as if they cared less about clothes. As at home, it was generally agreed that only in Catholic churches were working-class worshippers prominent. 'I have heard it doubted', said the Anglican bishop of Sydney, Frederic Barker in 1860, 'whether any denomination of Protestants have hold of the working men of these Colonies, at least in the large towns.' Other people went off for the day to the country or the beach, and it was sometimes observed that the resort-goers were less wealthy than the church-goers: 'vast numbers of the small shopkeepers

SUNDAY PLEASURE: THE OMNIBUS

A ST. KILDA OMNIBUS ON SUNDAY.
Conductor.—"Jump up Sir—Lots o' room."

ST KILDA BEACH

and mechanics', William Kelly wrote of Melbourne, 'made it a point to take their
families into the country on Sundays'.

The sedate Sunday was secured by law. An early triumph of the evangelicals in
England had been the Act for Preventing Certain Abuses and Profanations of the Lord's
Day, Called Sunday, passed in 1781, which provided that any place of public entertainment or debate on Sunday to which people were admitted by paying money was
to be deemed disorderly. Some clergymen wanted the law to go further. Bishop Broughton
thought that men should be stopped from shooting, fishing and playing games on Sunday,
and an act of the Legislative Council in 1841 did prohibit shooting on Sunday for sport or
pleasure or profit. After 1850 Sabbatarian campaigns were mounted in several colonies
when news arrived from home that an alliance of evangelicals from different denominations
were sending petitions to Westminster for the prevention of both work and public pleasure
on Sunday. The New South Wales Society for Promoting the Observance of the Lord's
Day, founded in 1856 under the presidency of Bishop Barker and named after an English
body, noted with grief 'the multiplied ways by which the people are tempted to profane the
Day of the Lord, in their pursuit of sinful amusements and pleasures.' It had long been the
custom in Australia for foods hard to keep fresh in this climate, such as meat and bread
and fruit, to be sold on Sundays. Public houses had always been open on the Sabbath.
Among newer temptations were invitations to move about and to visit places of cultural
improvement. Cabs, omnibuses, steamers and railway trains were among the enemies
discerned now by the Sabbatarians. With the support of working men they tried to persuade
shopkeepers to shut on Sunday, and in the face of working-class and other hostility they
pressed governments to shut the pubs, leave the trains in their sheds and keep libraries and
galleries closed.

A zealous Sabbatarian was likely also to be an enemy of the Catholic church, seeing the profligacy of continental Europe on Sunday as a fruit of popery and believing it hypocritical or otherwise morally defective to take the Catholic view that innocent pleasures were licit on Sunday provided that a man first went to church. It seemed to Thomas Braim that desecration of the Sabbath was spreading from Europe to England and her colonies. In Sydney he noticed many people 'devoting the latter part of the Lord's Day to amusement and pleasure. Dinner parties, water or land excursions, and a thousand means are devised to "kill the time" of this sacred day, at least so soon as the morning service is closed . . . This is one of the evils which Englishmen, Protestant Englishmen, have but too readily copied from continental countries.' But Catholic as well as Protestant clergy could be anxious about the effect of Sunday temptations on 'thoughtless worldly-minded Christians', as Bishop Goold of Melbourne called them in 1862, who devoted the Sabbath 'to vain, idle, and criminal indulgence, often squandering in luxurious entertainments and dresses not over modest, the patrimony of the poor.' In 1870 the Australian Sunday was contested ground, over which campaigns were still to be fought between men of the churches and agents of freedom, secularity and pleasure.

RELIGION AND NATIONALITY

Sabbatarian controversy, like everything about Australian Christianity, travelled out from home. Most emigrants from England and their children counted themselves at least nominally attached to the Church of England, and the most respectable of them attended its Sunday services more or less often. Methodism became a little stronger, some forms of older Nonconformity a little weaker, than in England. The Presbyterian churches were Scottish and to a lesser extent Irish in membership and clergy. The Catholic church derived its character as a community from an overwhelmingly Irish laity. In the United States, Episcopalians dwindled and Baptists proliferated. No such large discrepancies between the strength of a denomination at home and abroad appeared here. Nor did new sects proliferate in Australia as they did so famously in the United States by 1850. Not for these loyal colonists were such universalist, utopian, millenarian movements, created to express the religious aspirations of a people which in the American way equated Europe with the evils of age and orthodoxy.

Nor did religion and nationality permeate each other here as in the United States. When the emigrants on the *Mayflower* reached Plymouth in 1620 they fell on their knees and thanked God; if any man knelt to thank God at Sydney Cove on 26 January 1788, nobody recorded it. 'God hath sifted a whole nation', said a governor of Massachusetts at the end of the seventeenth century, 'that he might send choice grain into this wilderness.' That could not be said with a straight face about the first settlers of Australia; and later arrivals, though not disreputable, rarely had a godly purpose. 'Our colonists', a missionary society in Van Diemen's Land reported wistfully in 1843, 'unlike the pilgrim fathers of America, have not emigrated to these shores as an asylum from persecution carrying with them their religious ordinances; they have for the most part quitted their native country principally intent on the acquisition of wealth, and with little thought, it is to be feared, of those durable riches, and of that better country, in comparison with which all the possessions of the world are a bauble.' When the Americans declared their independence they invoked the laws of nature and of nature's god and expressed a firm reliance on the protection of divine providence. Alexis De Tocqueville, visiting the United States in 1831, was struck first of all by the religious aspect of the country, noting an American prayer:

INDEPENDENT CHURCH, COLLINS AND RUSSELL STREETS, MELBOURNE
One of the grandest buildings put up in Australia during the 1860s

'Lord, turn not thy face from us, and grant that we may always be the most religious, as well as the freest, people of the earth.' That prayer would have been as unlikely in Australia as in Europe. As America's civil war approached, men on both sides reached for their bibles to prove that slavery was and was not Christian, and peacemakers looked to Christianity as a means of keeping the nation together. When the war ended, Abraham Lincoln spoke of it as a judgment of God. The colonists of Australia, not having contemplated revolution, had no need to invoke God against the motherland. Suffering no sectional conflicts grave enough to threaten bloodshed, they did not look seriously to their churches as agents of internal cohesion. The colonial churches helped to preserve sentiments of attachment to British homelands and to retard the appearance of a sense of Australian nationality, for some were governed directly from abroad and all had traditions of worship and fellowship exported from the United Kingdom and freshened from decade to decade by new emigration of clergy and laity.

The typical clergyman of 1870 was a new chum. To succeed out here, his seniors often told him, a man required more talents than in a long-settled society. The Anglican bishop of Melbourne, Charles Perry, gave in 1853 an awe-inspiring list of qualities necessary in the clergyman here. Apart from soundness of doctrine, personal piety, a well-instructed mind and a sincere zeal for God's glory, he must have 'a patient persevering energy, a cheerful and contented disposition, firmness, self-possession, a meek temper, a frank and conciliatory manner, and great natural good sense.' It would also help in the bush if he could ride a horse without falling off. A clergyman deputed by Perry to tour pastoral districts found a group of shearers hostile or surly until he swam his horse through a dangerously flooded river. 'This exploit', wrote the man whose sheep they were shearing, 'made a very favourable impression on the minds of the men on the station, for like most men of their class, they had a great admiration for pluck and daring. It was duly commented upon among them, and I have no doubt served greatly to enhance their respect for the clergyman and his ministrations.' The clergyman who took no more than ordinary qualities into his pulpit might be a bore in this secularizing age, this restless society, and this climate which made people want to be out of doors in daylight hours for much of the year. Alfred Deakin, son of William, recalled from his childhood in Melbourne during the 1860s 'the dreariness of Church and its endless service.'

The churches nevertheless retained at least the nominal adherence of almost the

THE HABIT OF WORSHIP
A bushman's hut on a Sunday morning

whole population. The great stone structures in the cities and the solid ecclesiastical buildings in every suburb, town and township were evidence that Australian colonists were willing to spend a good deal of money providing for varieties of Christian worship. About a third of the population went into one or other of these churches each Sunday. A large proportion of children attended Sunday schools. Whether or not they attended worship, most colonists had been baptized by a minister of religion out here or at home, and nearly all were married by one in a church and buried by one. In the civic cemeteries their bodies were laid alongside those of other adherents to the church whose Sunday services they had attended regularly or occasionally or never.

6 St Patrick's Day

ST PATRICK AND ST BENEDICT

An Irish immigrant described the feast of St Patrick as 'the sabbath of the Irishman's year'. It was a way of saying both that the weekly Sabbath was primarily a Protestant occasion and that, for people who looked back to Ireland as home, the day of her patron saint, 17 March, had a sacred character.

Emigrants from elsewhere in the United Kingdom had saints' days to use if they wanted them; but commemoration of St George on 23 April, St Andrew on 30 November or St David on 1 March was never so visible or audible as that of the man who was supposed to have carried Christianity to Ireland. Sometimes the day of St George was given formal recognition, such as a ball at Government House; but the English, reminded at every turn that they were living in colonies of their own homeland, felt little need to set aside one day in the year to express their nationality. The Scots did meet for conviviality in the name of St Andrew and the Welsh in the name of St David. On St David's Day in the 1850s Welsh miners at Ballarat introduced an eisteddfod which became an annual event in the cultural life of Victoria. But usually what the Scots and Welsh did on their days was done privately. St Patrick's Day was unique among national occasions. The great majority of Irish exiles and emigrants who were Catholics took saints more seriously than their Protestant fellow-colonists did, and they found more cause to stick together. In the towns of Australia, as in such other places as Boston and New York and Philadelphia, St Patrick's Day became a time for the Irish to affirm their communal solidarity and to talk of their achievements, hopes and grievances.

Governor Macquarie gave benign recognition to the anniversary in 1810 when he provided entertainment on 17 March for convicts employed by the government. It became the custom for a committee of the most reputable Irishmen—both Catholic and Protestant —to arrange a dinner for 17 March in a Sydney hotel. The governor attended or was represented, the first toast was to the king, and hopes were expressed for the continued entwining of the shamrock with the rose and the thistle. After 1830 Roger Therry, an Irish Catholic who was appointed Commissioner of the Court of Requests (small debts) in New South Wales in 1829, the year of Catholic emancipation, spoke regularly at these dinners. At the Royal Hotel in George Street on 17 March 1832, Therry proposed: 'The sons of England, Scotia and Erin, and may their affections and energies be ever united in support of the power and the glory of the British empire.' Many of the hundred men who stood and raised their glasses were Irish Catholic emancipists who had made good, and who were keen to make the dinner a display of loyalty and propriety. The dinner grew into a banquet, accompanied by a St Patrick's Society ball at which the carefully respectable Irish danced seemly quadrilles, played cards, drank tea or lemonade, and took an elegant supper with respectable colonists of English and Scottish origin. At the banquet, Irishmen who enjoyed civic eminence would affirm their kinship with the rest: convicts, sons of convicts, and assisted emigrants. When speakers moved the toast to 'the day we celebrate', it was common for them to contrast the misery of Irishmen at home with their progress abroad. Sometimes the company sang, in one of its numerous versions, the bitter ballad of 1798:

> O Paddy dear, an' did ye hear the news that's goin' round?
> The shamrock is by law forbid to grow on Irish ground!
> No more St. Patrick's Day we'll keep, his colour can't be seen,
> For there's a cruel law agin' the wearin' o' the Green!

ST PATRICK'S DAY DINNER, SYDNEY
J. H. Plunkett, attorney-general, presides, and Mr Justice Therry is the principal speaker.

In later years they might add this verse:

> But if at last our colour should be torn from Ireland's heart,
> Her sons with shame and sorrow from the dear old isle will part;
> I've heard a whisper of a country that lies beyond the sea,
> Where rich and poor stand equal in the light of freedom's day.

The composer meant America, but the contrast between Ireland and Australia was almost as great.

The vast majority of Irish emigrants and emancipists were Catholic and poor. The Protestants among them, and the Catholics from elsewhere than Ireland, were too few to prevent 'Mick' and 'Paddy' from becoming practically synonymous with 'Catholic' in Australian, as in American, speech. The eminence of J. H. Plunkett, who came to New South Wales as solicitor-general in 1832; of Roger Therry, who was made a judge of the Supreme Court in 1846; and of the rich pastoralist Terence Murray, son of an army officer, showed what an Irish Catholic might achieve out here. But the highest praise for such men on the lips of their countrymen was that they had not forgotten the mass of their humbler brothers. By the middle of the century, between a quarter and a third of the population of New South Wales was of Irish birth and Catholic faith—a proportion more than twice that of Catholics, both English and Irish, in England. In Victoria they were between a quarter and a fifth of the population, in Van Diemen's Land about a fifth, and in South Australia about a tenth. The depressed south-western province of Munster was supplying both Australia and America with more emigrants than any other region. They were people of peasant stock with little money, education or skill, forced off their land by poverty and after 1845 by starvation.

The poor emigrants and the Irish who had come out as prisoners offered St Patrick less inhibited tributes than their betters. The tradition began early. 'On the 17th', wrote David Collins in March 1795, 'St. Patrick found many votaries in the settlement. Some Cape brandy lately imported in the Britannia appeared to have arrived very seasonably; and libations to the saint were so plentifully poured, that at night the cells were full of prisoners.' On every anniversary Irishmen caroused in taverns and rampaged through streets, indulging in what their critics liked to call pat-*riot*-ism. 'Of all the days in the year for length', wrote the *Sydney Gazette* on 20 March 1832, 'commend us to St. Patrick . . . From twelve o'clock on Friday night till the same hour on that of Sunday did "the boys" celebrate its return with the usual honours festive and pugilistic.' For the Protestant press, a peaceful St Patrick's Day was news. 'Not a single head was broken, nor a shilelah was to be seen' reported the *Sydney Herald* in 1836. 'This year, we are happy to say,' wrote John Dunmore Lang's *Colonist* in 1837, 'St. Patrick's Day passed off very quietly, and there was less drunkenness than usual.' A year later the *Colonist* professed itself 'happy to hear that there were not many heads broken.' The *Hobart Town Courier* thought it worth reporting in 1849 that in Sydney, the anniversary had 'passed over in a manner highly creditable to the lower orders of the Irish population.'

It was a national rather than ecclesiastical occasion. The man at the head of the Catholic church in Australia, John Bede Polding, was an English Benedictine. The Irish priests who preceded him seemed in the judgment of Governor Darling to have exercised too much influence with their flock. When selecting a priest, Darling wrote in a remarkable sentence to the Colonial Office, 'it is most important that an Englishman should have the preference, the Catholics here being, I believe, nearly all Irish.' Polding came to Sydney as bishop in 1835 and was made archbishop of Sydney and metropolitan of Australia and Van Diemen's Land with the consent of the British authorities in 1842, eight years before the Catholic hierarchy was restored in England. Archbishop Polding wanted the church in Australia to be a Benedictine mission, and he went on hoping that it could be so even after it was plain that his order could not send out enough priests from England. Irish clergy had to be appointed. 'Unfortunately', one of them, the Reverend John McEncroe, wrote to Pope Pius IX in 1851: 'the Irish and English characters are very different in their nature, and when any difference takes place between an English bishop and an Irish priest, their national antipathies and mutual distrusts spring up . . . In my opinion very few Englishmen know how to guide or govern Irishmen, whether lay or ecclesiastical.' The diarist of the Benedictine community in Sydney recorded an ominous contrast between observance at St Mary's Cathedral of the feasts of St Patrick on 17 March 1851 and of St Benedict four days later. On 21 March he noted 'splendid singing in the choir, but very few persons in the church to listen to it. It is very evident from the differences in the attendance of the people . . . that Saint Patrick holds a place in their affections pre-eminently above that of Saint Benedict'.

Polding wished that the sentiment of attachment to Ireland, carried out to the colonies by so many laymen and priests and indulged so intensely on St Patrick's Day, would be discarded as quickly as possible. 'Before everything else we are Catholics', he wrote in a pastoral letter of 1856, 'and next, by a name swallowing up all distinctions of origin, we are Australians; from whatever land we or our parents have arrived hither, be it from Ireland, from France, from Scotland, from Germany, we are no longer Irishmen, and Frenchmen, and Englishmen, and Scotchmen, but Australians.' It was sound teaching no doubt, but it could be made palatable to most Australian Catholics only if it came from an Irishman. One by one, to Polding's disappointment, his English Benedictine clergy were replaced by Irishmen, and more often than not his requests to Rome for English bishops were rejected. Over the whole reign of Pius IX, from 1846 to 1878, twelve of seventeen bishops appointed to Australia were Irish. They did not like Polding telling them to forget their country. When he remarked at a meeting of bishops in 1859 that he disapproved of references to nationalities, almost every one of them dissented, 'wishing not to forget our Irish national history', Dr William Lanigan of Goulburn said, 'as being connected so closely with the Faith.' On this view, the continuing recollection of St Patrick in Australia was thoroughly wholesome.

Clergy and laity both wanted to hear about Ireland's present condition as well as its past. Efforts to establish a thoroughly popular Catholic newspaper in New South Wales did not succeed until the *Freeman's Journal*, modelled on the paper of that name in Dublin, was founded in 1850 by McEncroe. It gave a steady supply of information about Ireland, encouraged readers to preserve a sense of belonging to the old country, and was a source of irritation and even outrage to Polding and his fellow-Benedictines for its mistrust of Englishmen. In Melbourne the *Advocate*, launched by Charles Gavan Duffy and others in 1868, was directed at people whom it called 'Irish-Victorians'.

At the St Patrick's Day banquets in Sydney during the 1850s and 1860s, speakers dwelt on Ireland's modern wrongs as well as her ancient pains and glories. The most popular speaker was little Daniel Deniehy whose oratory could bring tears to the eyes of exiles even when it looked as if he would be too drunk to speak. One year, Deniehy had a place of honour at the banquet while he was under sentence of excommunication for disobedience to his English archbishop. Not only in colonial society at large but within the Catholic church itself, 17 March could be a day of difficulty in relations between wearers of the shamrock and the rose.

ORANGE AND GREEN

Mistrust of Catholics, whether they were English or Irish, travelled to Australia on convict transports and emigrant ships. Some Protestant zealots feared that the pope might be an even more devilish opponent out here than in Europe. The *Sentinel*, an anti-Catholic journal published in Sydney, detected by 1846 steady progress in Roman plans to capture the institutions of civil society. 'From Supreme Courts—through benches of magistracy— in halls of municipality—down to the constabulary forces of Sydney and the colony, Papacy lords and predominates beyond tolerance', the paper declared. Given the greater number of Catholics in such offices than in England, and given the normal limits of Protestant tolerance, that was perhaps true. Lang believed that strenuous efforts were needed 'to prevent our degenerating into a mere Irish Roman Catholic province.' He wanted more emigrants from Protestant countries, fewer from Ireland, and a vigilant awareness of Roman designs. Such fears may have been extravagant, but they were not wholly irrational. At home after 1850 members of the newly restored Catholic hierarchy thought hopefully about the conversion of England. In Australia the proportion of Catholics was higher, and their rights and needs were given public recognition. The Catholic vision, the Protestant nightmare, of a nation going over to Rome, was a little less far from reality here than in England. 'We only want priests to make this country Catholic', Polding wrote in 1836. Catholic ambition and Protestant bigotry both found plenty to nourish them in Australia.

The Irish contributed richly to both. Tribal contests between Protestant and Catholic Irishmen—Orange and Green—were a popular sport in these colonies. In some places St Patrick's Day became the occasion for an encounter, and return bouts were fought on 12 July, the day when Orangemen commemorated William III's victories over followers of the deposed Catholic king James II at Aughrim in 1690 and the river Boyne in 1691. In Melbourne on 12 July 1846 shots were fired into a crowd protesting against Orange banners hung from the windows of a hotel in which the William-worshippers— as Catholics called them—were celebrating their anniversary. 'The town looked as if in a state of siege', wrote Edmund Finn. Later in the year the Legislative Council of New South Wales passed a bill to prevent 'party processions' in the colony, which included Port Phillip. From 1843 to 1846 the St Patrick's Society had organized a procession through Melbourne each 17 March. That was now declared illegal. Similar troubles were in the air of other towns where Protestant and Catholic Irishmen met in these years of famine, anger and emigration; 17 March and 12 July could be dangerous days in Sydney, Liverpool and Philadelphia. Melbourne was an especially suitable ground for the encounter, for it was a small, raw community where party dispute was personal and rancorous and where members of the Protestant ascendancy could easily feel threatened by an influx of Catholics from the south and west of Ireland. It was in 1846 that assisted immigration had been resumed after being suspended for several years on account of commercial depression.

The Party Processions Act did not prevent less inflammable modes of celebration. On 17 March 1847 in Melbourne the main event was a ceremony at which men of goodwill tried to repair the damage done in 1846. The foundation stone of St Patrick's Hall was

ST PATRICK'S CATHEDRAL BEGINS TO RISE OVER MELBOURNE

laid, bearing the names of the queen, the governor of New South Wales, the superintendent of Port Phillip, and the office-bearers of the St Patrick's Society. In 1848 there was an orderly dinner. Opened in 1849, the hall was hired by the new government of Victoria in 1851 to accommodate the Legislative Council for a few years until the colony built its own houses of parliament. The greatest of all Australian memorials to St Patrick, the cathedral on Melbourne's Eastern Hill, had its first stone laid at a ceremony in 1850. Gold made it both necessary and possible to have a much grander cathedral than had been planned. Its design was entrusted to William Wardell, a pupil of the Gothic revivalist A. W. Pugin, who emigrated in 1858 to find a warmer climate than England's. Wardell designed a new St Mary's Cathedral in Sydney after the old one was destroyed by fire, and in Melbourne he created the most massive piece of neo-Gothic architecture in the continent. It was almost as grand as the St Patrick's Cathedral that Irish America was building in New York, and larger than any other Catholic church in the United States. Generations of the faithful would be canvassed by their priests to pay for it. When finished it would resemble a cathedral in thirteenth-century England, except for the Celtic cross at the top of the spire which rose high over Melbourne. The nave was ready for worshippers by 1870, and the cornerstone for the central tower was laid on St Patrick's Day in that year. It could seem

to an outsider 'a structure massive, isolated, and grand, like the communion it represents.' An Irish-Australian of the 1880s saw the cathedral rather as 'a monument of the undying faith and active piety of the exiled children of the Isle of Saints.' It was, indeed, a formidable symbol of the place the sons of St Patrick had gained for themselves in these colonies. As the Government Houses expressed British pride in the new land, St Patrick's Cathedral testified to Irish faith in it.

St Patrick's Days passed tranquilly in Adelaide, Hobart and Perth. When the Catholics of South Australia welcomed their first bishop, Francis Murphy, in 1844, they described themselves as few in numbers and humble in circumstances, but assured him that 'a friendly feeling subsists between the Catholics and the other religious denominations of the colony.' The fewer they were, the easier it seemed to be for Irish Catholics to live on terms of amity with their colonial neighbours. In New South Wales Roger Therry believed that relations between Catholics and Protestants had improved greatly between his arrival in 1829 and his departure—as Sir Roger—thirty years later. By 1859, he declared, 'all feelings of asperity' towards Catholics 'had ceased to exist, except in so small a fraction of society as to be of no moment.' Certainly in matters of civil and political liberty, Catholics were no persecuted minority by the early years of responsible government; and the complexities of society normally prevented sectarian animosity from being a powerful political force. But the old anti-popery of England had by no means died out in the colonies. It could become livelier in the emigrant's heart on the voyage out. 'The Papists had what they called prayers in the steerage as usual this morning', wrote a voyager in 1861, 'and were hardly off their knees till they had a hard box among themselves—a most infernal lot of Blackguards are the dirty Irish Papists. Never had such an opportunity of judging'. When they landed, the young men so numerous among the Irish contributed disproportionately to the colonies' criminal statistics, and especially to those of petty crime. The figures were cited with relish by some Protestant preachers, and could be wielded by politicians who hoped to benefit from anti-Irish and anti-Catholic sentiment among voters. Archibald Michie detected and lamented in the Melbourne of 1859 some surviving hostility between Orange and Green which impeded the movement towards nationhood. 'It may be very difficult—perhaps for a generation or two, impossible', Michie said, 'to secure a oneness in sentiment as well as interest amongst us. But if an Australian nation cannot spring up at our bidding, why are we to industriously import and cherish national prejudices, and so, of set purpose, with ingenious perverseness, retard such a growth?'

It was a cheering sign for colonists who wanted sectional prejudice to give way to feelings of Australian nationality that in some years, in some places, St Patrick's Day was a general holiday on which not merely the Irish celebrants but the whole community had a day off work. In Victoria it depended on whether or not Irish Catholics were in power: government offices and banks were shut on 17 March 1863 when John O'Shanassy, the tribal chieftain of the Irish Catholics, was premier, and open in 1864 when the ministry of James McCulloch, a Presbyterian, was in office. In New South Wales the day was becoming more widely celebrated irrespective of the ministry. 'For years past,' the *Sydney Morning Herald*, edited and owned by Congregationalists, said in 1868, 'the 17th of March has been set aside by the citizens—and by Irishmen especially—as a day of mirth and

ST PATRICK'S CATHEDRAL: BLESSING THE BELLS

AUSTRALIAN NATIVES WELCOME PRINCE ALFRED

pleasure, and social *reunion*.' It was the custom in the 1860s for the banks and commercial houses of Sydney to shut on 17 March. When organizers of the day in 1864 substituted a regatta on Port Jackson for the traditional banquet, the *Sydney Morning Herald* explained that the change was intended to 'extend the enjoyment of the day to thousands of both sexes in the community.' The government offices were closed on 17 March 1865, when the Anglican Charles Cowper was premier, and again in 1866, when the lapsed Catholic James Martin was premier and Henry Parkes was his deputy. No official decision about government work was required in 1867, when the day fell on a Sunday. Martin's ministry decided in 1868 that government offices would not shut on 17 March. As it turned out there was to be no public mirth or pleasure in Sydney on St Patrick's Day in 1868.

HENRY JAMES O'FARRELL

The second son of Queen Victoria, His Royal Highness Prince Alfred Ernest Albert, Duke of Edinburgh, aged twenty-three, landed in Adelaide on 31 October 1867 from the frigate H.M.S. *Galatea*, which he commanded, to begin a tour of the Australian colonies. His mother's subjects decorated their cities with triumphal arches and transparencies and gaslit illuminations, put on balls and banquets, presented him with golden trowels for laying the foundation stones of post offices and town halls, built carriages for him, and formed the greatest crowds ever assembled in the continent to see him drive by. There was talk of renaming the continent Alfreda or Alfredea. They gave him champagne down a coal mine, drove him across dusty plains until his eyes burned, and made him inspect pigs in a hot wind. They took him out to shoot an old Australian quarry, the kangaroo, and a new one, the rabbit. The latter, introduced only eight years earlier, was thriving so well on Australian grass that the prince and four companions shot with ease 203 in a day. At a free public banquet in Melbourne he was supposed to drink the first glass of wine from a golden goblet; but the feast attracted three times as many people as were expected and turned into a wild scramble from which the prince had to be rescued and escorted back to Government House. News of this and other mishaps and solecisms sailed back to London, leading *The Times* to reflect on the clumsy loyalty of the colonists: 'they do not seem quite up to the ceremonials . . . their ideas of precedence are hazy, and, for want of method they do a world of work which hardly makes a show'. Something more sinister than a mishap was rumoured to be threatening at a ball in Melbourne on 27 November. Fenians, it was whispered, were planning to shoot the prince.

They had been in the news all through 1867. The Fenian Brotherhood was a band of revolutionaries at home and abroad dedicated to seizing independence for Ireland. Some of them who had gained military experience in the American civil war crossed to

TRIUMPHAL ARCH FOR PRINCE ALFRED
IN COLLINS STREET, MELBOURNE

Ireland in 1865 and organized for insurrection, but they were betrayed by informers and thwarted by summary arrests. Uprisings in Ireland and Lancashire were defeated early in 1867, and the last convict ship to sail for Western Australia—leaving England on 12 October 1867—had sixty Fenians on board. Three Fenians arrested in Manchester for killing a policeman were sentenced to death. They were hanged on 23 November and became to their allies the Manchester martyrs. News of the uprisings and their suppression, though not of the death sentences, had reached Australia by the time of Melbourne's royal ball. The prince's hosts interpreted the rumoured threat not in the context of an international movement but as the result of a fracas in Melbourne earlier that evening which showed that the old hatred between Orange and Green was not yet extinct. Orangemen of the city had installed outside their Protestant Hall a huge transparency—a canvas lit from behind—showing William III crossing the Boyne with a figure of Britannia on one side and on the other the words 'THIS WE WILL MAINTAIN'. It was just such a provocation that had led to violence in Melbourne on 12 July 1846. To offer it now, during the visit of the queen's son, was taken as a great affront by Irish Catholics, an angry crowd of whom gathered outside the hall to shout abuse, throw stones at the device, and sing 'The Wearing of the Green'. Three people were wounded of whom one, a boy, later died. The threat to the prince, if it had been made at all, was readily put down to the fury aroused by the Orangemen. Nothing more was heard of any Fenian plot in Melbourne.

H.M.S. *GALATEA* ENTERS PORT JACKSON
UNDER THE COMMAND OF PRINCE ALFRED

The *Galatea* visited Tasmania and then headed for Sydney. She entered Port Jackson on 21 January 1868, surrounded by a flotilla which had come through the heads to meet her. At the Circular Quay the prince was greeted under a huge triumphal arch by the governor and the ministry. The governor, Somerset Richard Lowry-Corry, Earl of Belmore, was an Irish peer who had taken office only two weeks earlier and who had gratified arrangers of the coming St Patrick's Day regatta by consenting to be its patron. The ministry was led by James Martin and Henry Parkes, who despite the scorn of their political opponents had put on for this moment blue and gold court dress, swords and cocked hats. Charles Harpur, disgusted with his old radical friend Parkes, found it consoling to imagine the ministers tripping over their swords. Four bay horses drew the prince in a shining new carriage through streets packed with cheering people. Outside Parliament House in Macquarie Street he passed a transparency which showed a young female Australia demurely receiving a rudder from Britannia. He lodged at Government House, where Henry Parkes was invited to be presented on 23 January. 'I was the only member of Parliament or of the Government who was introduced to him personally', Parkes wrote to his sister in Birmingham next day. 'H.R.H. was alone and handed me a chair in a very pleasant way . . . Last night I and Mrs Parkes dined with his Royal Highness at Government House. The order of going into dinner was thus:

    The Prince and the Countess of Belmore.
    The Earl of Belmore and Mrs Parkes.
Poor Clarinda! Who would have dreamed when we were married at Edgbaston that she would live to dine with Princes and be led in by Earls.'

    The prince visited Queensland and country towns in New South Wales. On 12 March he attended a picnic at the harbour resort of Clontarf, seven miles from Sydney, which took its name from an ancient town in Ireland. A public holiday had been declared, and a large crowd of well-dressed people who had paid a pound a ticket, in aid of a sailors' home, turned up to be near the prince. Three hundred aborigines—the largest collection ever seen in Sydney by this generation of colonists—had been brought along so that the guest could see a corroboree ('a species of bestial *bal masqué*' as a recent author had defined it). As they were about to begin, a man walked up behind the prince, held a revolver close to his back, and fired. The man pulled his trigger again at the falling prince, but the revolver did not go off. As he fired again, his aim was spoiled by the first horrified bystander to move, and the bullet struck another man in the foot. The attacker was overpowered, stripped and battered by some of the colony's most respected gentlemen. Terence Murray, president of the Legislative Council, confessed later that he was one of the people, possessed by a terrible excitement, who tried to lynch the man. He was saved from immediate death by policemen and soldiers, and carried naked and bleeding to a boat and to Darlinghurst Gaol. The prince was lifted on to an improvised litter and taken back to Government House. A bullet was found two inches from his breast-bone, having slowed up when it hit the thickest part of his rubber braces, missed his spine by half an inch, and glanced off a rib. At hastily arranged services, Protestant and Catholic clergymen asked God to save the prince's life. As no vital organ was damaged and the patient was young and strong, the churches could soon hold services of thanksgiving. After twelve days he could walk a little, and by 4 April his hosts had him on the site of Sydney's new town hall with a golden trowel to lay a foundation stone. The *Galatea* sailed for home on 6 April, carrying emus and kangaroos for the royal palace of Sandringham and leaving behind a community in turmoil.

THE ASSASSIN STRIKES
Prince Alfred has fallen, and O'Farrell is being seized and battered.

When news of the attempt at assassination was flashed by telegraph through the
colonies, it set off a paroxysm of loyalty. Resolutions expressing grief, indignation and
allegiance were passed by meetings in cities and suburbs and country towns. Funds were
opened to establish memorials, and hospitals called Prince Alfred duly arose in Sydney
and Melbourne as appropriate monuments to the episode. Poems were published, including
two by Henry Kendall in the *Sydney Morning Herald* on 26 March. In one poem Kendall had
Australia, ashamed of the deed, strangling the fiend who committed it; the other
reassured colonists that the prince and his mother would not hold it against them. In
Melbourne the *Argus* was afraid that people at home, not knowing that the colonies were
separate from each other, would find Victoria guilty by association with New South Wales.
A politician in Sydney said that the name of New South Wales, scarcely exorcized from
the stigma of convictism, was now smirched with the foul stain of Fenianism. He urged a
new name for the colony at once. But the attacker, it turned out, had come from Victoria—

a 'foreign importation', as a Protestant minister in Sydney declared. His name was
Henry James O'Farrell.

St Patrick's Day, five days after O'Farrell shot the prince, was a grim occasion in
Sydney. The Earl of Belmore withdrew his patronage from the regatta, and the organizers
cancelled it. At an anniversary gathering of the St Patrick's Society in Melbourne, Charles
Gavan Duffy protested that the Irish community was being held responsible for the act
of a man who was probably a maniac. 'We can well imagine', said the *Freeman's Journal*,
'with what delight those who have always been hostile to Catholics and Irishmen seize
the opportunity to brand all assassins and murderers.' But in a leading article on St Patrick's
Day, the *Sydney Morning Herald* said that the Irish should not be surprised by accusations
of complicity when the *Freeman's Journal* itself had published treasonable and inflammatory
articles on the execution of Fenians in England. It was a terrible ordeal for old Archbishop
Polding, who decided to combine a rejoinder to such charges with an expression of joy
at the prince's recovery. 'The unhappy creature, who attempted the life of our Prince
and guest,' he wrote in a pastoral letter, 'professes to be a Catholic. Be it so. But will any
man of sense believe that his crime was Catholic?' Unable to bring himself to refer directly
to O'Farrell's national origin, Polding exhorted his people not to 'wantonly and wickedly
import miseries and enmities', and affirmed passionately his conviction that there was
only one nationality for Catholics in this country. 'Australians we should all be. We owe
it to each other, we owe it to duty, we owe it to Christianity. And I say, Australia for
Australians, our sole and sufficient nationality under the rule of our ever good and
gracious Queen, whom with her Royal Family may God in His infinite mercy long
preserve to us.' Australia for Australians: that was the slogan that came to the pen of an
agitated English Catholic archbishop admonishing an Irish laity in a British colony to
forget the pains of their homeland.

O'FARRELL AND NEW SOUTH WALES

NEW SOUTH WALES AND O'FARRELL

On the day after St Patrick's Day the New South Wales parliament passed through all stages a bill 'for the better security of the Crown and Government of the United Kingdom, and for the better suppression and punishment of seditious practices and attempts.' The Treason Felony Act, as it was called, provided among much else that any person using language disrespectful to the queen, or factiously avowing a determination not to join in any loyal toast or demonstration in honour of Her Majesty, or who expressed sympathy with or approval of any offence under the act, might be apprehended by any constable without a warrant, and on conviction be imprisoned for two years.

Was O'Farrell a solitary maniac or part of a conspiracy? Henry Parkes made it his business to find evidence that the man was a Fenian agent. The shooting at Clontarf produced, as Parkes wrote later, 'a strange lurid glare in the political atmosphere, and engendered feelings not simply acrimonious and bitter, but almost deadly in the depth and colour of their hatred.' Parkes himself did as much as any man except O'Farrell to engender that hatred, and more than anybody to keep it going, pumping the bellows of bigotry to keep the glare good and lurid. Whether Parkes himself tried to exploit other people's dislike of Catholicism at any given time was a matter of tactics; but his own, nurtured in Birmingham, was deep. 'The whole power of these people', he wrote of Catholics during his English tour in 1862, 'is used against the enlightened progress of the age.' In 1866, speaking of the Public Schools Bill, he had made menacing remarks which led many Catholic and some Anglican clergy to fear that he meant the state to interfere improperly with what they did in their own schools. Thomas Carlyle was delighted with a speech on the new schooling which his Australian admirer had sent him. 'I well enough understand the clamours of dark sectaries, Protestant and Catholic,' Carlyle wrote, 'especially of your Irish priests, the worst section of that miserable category'. Before the prince landed, Polding had been outraged by the manner in which Parkes equated Irish radicalism with Catholicism. 'He is a determined unscrupulous enemy to Catholics and to Irishmen', Polding wrote in October 1867. 'He purposely confounds the two, and makes the entire of us responsible for the indiscreet expression of a few.' Five months later Parkes set out to establish that Henry James O'Farrell was involved in a plot which had roots in the Irish-Australian community.

As minister in charge of the police, Parkes himself led the search for clues. He was one of a party which discovered a diary in the room where O'Farrell had lodged the night before he shot the prince. He talked with the accused man in gaol while, unknown to O'Farrell, a reporter from the *Sydney Morning Herald* listened outside the door of the cell. He offered a reward for information leading to the arrest of 'each and every accomplice.' A jury quickly found O'Farrell guilty of wounding with intent to murder. In New South Wales that was a capital offence, and the climate of public sentiment left no doubt, even despite a request for clemency from the prince, that O'Farrell would be executed. He was hanged on 21 April.

O'Farrell left behind few undisputed facts about his life and two contradictory accounts of his deed. His Irish parents had brought him from Liverpool to Melbourne as a child in 1840. He went to Europe, studied for the priesthood, returned to Victoria, sold corn and hay in Ballarat, speculated in gold mining shares, lost, and drank heavily. The diary found in his room spoke of avenging the Irish rebels of 1798 and the Fenians 'butchered at Manchester'. It cried out for warfare between Orange and Green in the colonies, which would harm English capitalists by causing depreciation of colonial debentures. It expressed the hope that every English ship in colonial ports would be

O'FARRELL IN DARLINGHURST GAOL

destroyed, and lamented that fate had denied the writer the opportunity of a more truly military attack on the accursed oligarchy of England. 'Oh, for a gallant cavalry charge, not such a thing as this!' Warders at Darlinghurst Gaol said that O'Farrell had described the crime to them in terms compatible with the diary. Ten members of a Fenian organization, according to the warders' version, had determined to kill both the prince and the Earl of Belmore; but when the governor announced his patronage of St Patrick's

Day the ten decided that he should not die. (If that were true, it might be said that St Patrick had saved Lord Belmore's life.) The assassin of the prince was then chosen by lot and the task fell to O'Farrell who, having heard that the heir to the throne, the prince of Wales, was drinking himself to death, believed that it was his destiny to deprive England of its next king.

At O'Farrell's trial the defending counsel brought witnesses, including his sister, to swear that O'Farrell was mad and took fits; and on the day before he died, the condemned man wrote a confession declaring that he had acted alone. He was not, he said now, 'other than in an indirect manner', connected with a Fenian organization and unless from mere hearsay had no foundation for asserting that there was such a body in New South Wales. 'From continually thinking and talking of what I may still be allowed to call "the wrongs of Ireland", I became excited and filled with enthusiasm on the subject, and it was when under the influence of those feelings that I attempted to perpetrate the deed for which I am now justly called upon to suffer.' Parkes said that this document had been composed at St Mary's Cathedral and dictated in the death cell by O'Farrell's confessor, the Reverend Michael John Dwyer, whom he dismissed as visiting chaplain to the gaol for insubordination in allowing the document to be made public.

The newspapers recorded a number of charges under the Treason Felony Act, but no convictions. On 23 March Bartholomew Toomey of Goulburn was committed for trial, accused of having said: 'It served the Prince right, he had no business in this country.' He was discharged after the crown declined to prosecute. In Cowra two men named Kelly and Noonan were charged with having said in a public house that 'there was no more harm in shooting the b—— Prince than a blackfellow of this country.' They too were discharged. Other men, some but not all of them bearing Irish names, many of them drunk, were apprehended under the act and either discharged or convicted of such minor offences as using obscene language. Those responsible for the preservation of order in New South Wales appeared not to believe that they were unearthing any Fenian conspiracy.

Parkes's belief in it was probably genuine. His determination to have it win him votes was certainly so. He made himself standard-bearer of Protestant loyalty, encouraging electors to believe that any Irish Catholic who denied the existence of a Fenian plot might well be implicated in it. 'Parkes and Martin have made great capital out of this most miserable affair', Polding wrote the day after O'Farrell was hanged. 'Of all hateful men, the first named is to the fore.' Speaking to constituents at Kiama, on the south coast, Parkes claimed to have affidavits proving not only that the assassination of the prince had been planned, 'but that some one who had a guilty knowledge of the secret, and whose fidelity was suspected, had been foully murdered.' Parkes resigned from the Martin ministry late in 1868 after quarrelling with his colleagues. The government fell, and a new ministry under John Robertson set up a select committee to inquire into what Parkes had alleged at Kiama. It found no evidence either that O'Farrell's crime was the result of a conspiracy or that any supposed confederate had been murdered. But the resilient Parkes moved successfully that the Legislative Assembly expunge the committee's report from its proceedings and resolve 'that the criminal O'Farrell was not alone and unaided . . . and that persons openly sympathised with the attempted assassination.' Parkes's motion ignored the murdered confederate, who had perhaps been put into his mind by a reference in O'Farrell's diary to a Judas whose horrible death would be a warning to others. No evidence about him was ever discovered. In the gibes of Parkes's opponents he was to live on as 'the Kiama ghost'.

The Protestant Political Association—a body whose object as Polding saw it was 'to keep Catholics out of every place of profit or honour'—responded to Parkes's triumph over the select committee by passing a resolution highly approving his conduct. William Bede Dalley, the native-born Catholic lawyer and politician who had defended O'Farrell at his trial, was appalled at Parkes's pandering to sectarian passion. 'It is practically affirmed', said Dalley, 'that no man can tolerate a catholic in public life and preserve his fidelity to the institutions under which we live.' Tens of thousands of people, Dalley told the electors of West Sydney, had been 'compelled to listen to the ravings, the insolence, the outrages of schemers and bigots, and have held their peace. I confess to you that I have marvelled at the patience . . . of the Irish Roman Catholics.' From Melbourne Charles Gavan Duffy wrote severely to Parkes: 'I and all the race from which I am sprung have good reason to complain bitterly of your conduct in office.' Perhaps he had gone too far ? 'So long as obstacles are opposed to our being one Australian people,' Parkes wrote in a conciliatory reply, 'we shall be a factious and senseless rabble.'

On the anniversary of the shooting, 12 March 1869, the prince and his *Galatea* reached Sydney again, for a visit which at the queen's request was defined as private. Five days later St Patrick's Day passed quietly in the city. Many loyal toasts were offered at a picnic at Balmoral, near Clontarf, presided over by the newly knighted Sir Terence Murray; but there was no regatta this year, and it was not a holiday in the public offices. The prince wore a shamrock for the day but did not attend the picnic. At Shoalhaven, on the south coast, the editor of the local newspaper wondered whether he had got the date wrong: 'the bank, shops and business places were in full life and vigour, not the colour of the "three-leaf shamrock" was to be seen, and only in one instance are we aware of a glass of "potheen" having been devoted to Ireland's patron saint. In fact, the day appeared to have been forgotton.'

Sydney's regatta was restored in 1870 under the patronage of the Earl of Belmore, who also attended the picnic at Clontarf and heard Sir Terence Murray affirm as president of the gathering that there was no other part of the world where the British crown and royal family were held in more reverence. The governments of Victoria and Queensland declared 17 March 1870 a holiday in the public offices. The government of New South Wales did not. When an excursion to Balmoral was announced for 17 March by a body known as Ireland's Patriotic Sons, the *Sydney Morning Herald* accused them of 'ostentatiously avowing their admiration and sympathy for those who have been declared outlaws or criminals'. O'Farrell's attempt to kill the prince, and Parkes's response, gave sectarian animosity in New South Wales a renewed vigour and made St Patrick's Day an occasion for wariness and suspicion. Elsewhere in Australia it was spent more convivially. The *Age*, controlled by a Scottish emigrant, described 17 March 1870 as a sort of semi-holiday in Melbourne: offices shut, shops open, the non-Hibernians benign bystanders as their Irish fellow-colonists worshipped in the morning and pursued pleasure through the afternoon and evening. 'With their national buoyancy of spirits,' the *Age* observed, 'those of our citizens who hailed from the Green Isle seemed determined to enjoy a high holiday in honour of St Patrick and Old Ireland'. Long after 1870, colonists of Irish birth and descent would be determined to honour their nation's saint on 17 March. The character of the day would vary from year to year and from place to place according to their relations with fellow-Australians of other national origins.

7 Christmas

THE GOOD OLD ENGLISH CUSTOM

On 25 December 1787, in the wind and swell of the Indian Ocean, Arthur Phillip and his officers did their best to follow what one of them called the good old English custom of eating a Christmas dinner. When Australia was first settled, the birthday of Jesus was in England a time for domestic conviviality: evergreen decorations, singing, exchanges of visits and sometimes gifts between family and friends, indoor games, and above all feasting. The comfortable classes sat for hours around family tables eating beef, turkey, plum pudding and mince pies. For many industrial workers, whether or not they could afford a weighty dinner, Christmas was the only day of the year except Sundays and Good Friday on which they were released from the factory. For them as for their country cousins and for people of higher rank, it was also a day for drinking. A figure named Father Christmas had a small place in the festival; but he did not come down chimneys or otherwise carry gifts to children, nor had he yet the American alias Santa Claus.

The ecclesiastical aspect of the season was less prominent in England than in Catholic countries. The puritans who vanquished Charles I had forbidden the traditional celebration of Christ's birthday both because it was popish and because it gave liberty to carnal delights. Two centuries later some English Protestants still had qualms about recognizing the festival. Millions of Englishmen at home and abroad did go to church on Christmas Day; but when in Victoria's reign they began to enrich celebration of the season, it did not occur to them to draw on symbols of their religion. The Christmas story that caught the imagination of England in the 1840s was not about a manger in Bethlehem. It was Charles Dickens's contemporary, sentimental and wholly untheological tale, *A Christmas Carol*, about petty commerce in England.

Wherever they went in the world, the English took their Christmas with them. Phillip and his officers dined heartily at Sydney on 25 December 1788. At Christmas 1789, when supplies were low, the governor was served a turtle from Lord Howe Island. The *Sydney Gazette* observed in its first Christmas issue, of 25 December 1803, that the season was one of solemnity, festivity and compliment. Solemnity was in the care of the clergy. Festivity was encouraged by acts of public benevolence, such as an extra ration of fresh beef, suet and raisins to everybody on the civil and military establishment and of salt pork and flour to prisoners. It was enhanced also by private enterprise: just before

CHRISTMAS AS SEASON OF EXILE
The man with the concertina is playing Home Sweet Home.

Christmas Day 1803 some pigs were reported missing in Sydney, and the *Sydney Gazette* prophesied that they would 'receive WARM invitations to a Christmas dinner'. Compliments were addressed by the paper to people engaged in agriculture, trade and commerce; to the ladies of the colony; and to the king.

It was paradoxical to be celebrating so domestic a festival so far from home. For an emigrant who felt himself an exile in Australia, Christmas could bring on the most intense yearning for the old land and the loved ones. 'I now conclude', a newcomer wrote from Adelaide on 1 January 1841, 'by wishing you a merry Christmas and a happy New-year, which are ever uppermost at this season, in an Englishman's bosom, wherever he may be, at *home*, surrounded by fond and kind friends, or *abroad*, mid arctic snows or in the torrid zone, where all around him are strangers to his name, and perhaps indifferent to his fate.' Some exiles did not even try to keep up the traditions of the season. 'In the upper classes it is not celebrated at all', Lieutenant-Colonel G. C. Mundy found in Sydney in 1848. 'It seems as though each felt it a mockery to talk of a "Merry Christmas", and a "Happy New Year", so far from the Home "where his forefathers sleep".' That was the judgment of an officer stationed in New South Wales for only five years, moving in the circle of a governor, FitzRoy, who stayed for eight. Less transient emigrants worked harder at reproducing the season. They ate dinners as similar as possible to the feasts they remembered. If sheep was the only fit meat within reach, a leg might be stuffed with sage and onions and called colonial goose. Beef was better. A settler at Geelong in the 1850s reported that Christmas was 'kept up in Australia in quite John Bull fashion, with hot roast beef and plum-pudding'. But he had to admit that 'the idea of any Christmas jollity apart from one's friends and relations and family gatherings,—with which in the English mind it is so intimately associated,—seemed to me somewhat melancholy.' For that sort of melancholy the best relief was mail from home. When letters and newspapers reached an early emigrant in Western Australia on 25 December he declared: 'This is a Christmas-box indeed'.

As in England, houses were decorated for the season with green foliage. In each colony a native plant was named Christmas bush and gathered as a substitute for the holly and other evergreens of Europe. Aborigines who had come to know the rituals of the newcomers used to stroll through the streets of Sydney in the 1830s offering Christmas bush to householders. Mrs Charles Meredith, experiencing her first Christmas in Sydney, noticed carts heaped with green boughs and children running beside them laughing and shouting in proper seasonal jollity. 'I liked to see this attempt at the perpetuation of some of our ancient homely poetry of life', she wrote, 'in this new and generally too prosaic Colony, where the cabalistic letters £.s.d. and R U M appear too frequently the alphabet of existence.' Christmas trees, following recent English fashion, were becoming familiar in the colonies by 1850. But it was difficult, in most parts of Australia, to keep foliage fresh in December.

THE HEAT

'How curious a hot Christmas day must seem!' a lady in Devon wrote to her brother and sister in New South Wales. It seemed just as curious to American visitors as to the English, for although they or their ancestors had crossed thousands of miles of ocean they remained in a world where June was midsummer and December midwinter. 'We could hardly become familiar with windows and doors entirely open at Christmas time', wrote an American visitor to Sydney in 1839.

Emigrants shut their eyes to remember the crisp Decembers of the north and performed the old ceremonies as best they could. Mrs Meredith found the Christmas dinner 'a most odd and anomalous affair'. Instead of working up an appetite for it by a brisk walk over the snow, she lay on a sofa feeling half-dead with heat, in her coolest muslin dress, sipping lemonade and trying to recall what it was like to touch a lump of ice or grasp a snowball. 'It is too hot to be affectionate!' exclaimed Mundy. It was also too hot, he observed, for the Old English games and drinks. 'Only picture to yourself, middle-aged reader, a round of snap-dragon, a cup of hot spiced claret, or a plunge down fifty couple to the tune of "Merrily danced the Quaker's wife", with the thermometer steady at 95°!' Snap-dragon was a severe test of the emigrant's determination to ignore the heat, the game being to pluck raisins from a bowl in which they were covered with burning brandy and pop them into one's mouth. The Denisons, who moved into Sydney's Government House in 1855, made more of Christmas than their predecessors the FitzRoys. Lady Denison wrote home to describe a Christmas so oppressive that the household sat still all day except to join the congregation fanning itself in Church. 'You will laugh to hear that, after all this heat, we went in doors, and played at snap-dragon! I really believe the children would hardly think it was Christmas Day without this game.'

Emigrants recorded in their journals and letters heroic feats of celebration. At Adelaide's first Christmas, in 1836, Mrs Mary Thomas and her family, six weeks resident in the colony, 'kept up the old custom of Christmas as far as having a plum pudding for dinner, likewise a ham and a parrot pie'; and thanks to the accidental death of a cow which had travelled out with them, some of the party had beef. Divine service was held in a hut, but the thermometer stood at one hundred degrees and most of the congregation found it less unbearable to stand outside. 'It was on this occasion', Mary Thomas wrote soberly, 'that my son William, whose eyes had been for some time affected, became totally blind and was led back to our tent at the conclusion of the service.' Next day, she learned it was 120 degrees in the shade and 150 in the sun. A lady in Melbourne noted that on 25 December 1852 the sun blazed, a wind like the breath of a furnace scorched the flowers and shrubs, and all nature wore an air of suffering. Nevertheless she and her family piled their breakfast table high with gifts, rowed down the Yarra to church, 'and in the evening some friends joined us in endeavouring, by the help of roast beef, plum pudding, and mince pies, to cheat ourselves into the belief that it was Christmas day, while the heat of the atmosphere compelled us to put our handkerchiefs to our faces continually in a very unaristocratic fashion.' The hand of William Howitt was sweating the same day as he sat in his tent at the Ovens diggings and wrote: 'Christmas-day! which we are going to celebrate with the good old orthodox roast-beef and plum pudding. We have invited two young gentlemen diggers . . . to dine with us; and shall drink a Merry Christmas to all our friends in Old England, in a tumbler of brandy and water. We shall *try* to believe it Christmas, spite of the thermometer at 120°, of diggers' tents in the distance, and the bush around us.' The novelist Henry Handel Richardson made Christmas in the Ballarat of the 1850s a grim rite for her doomed emigrant hero Richard Mahony. The dinner was prepared in tiny kitchens almost as hot as their ovens. Mahony's wife cooked a goose. 'Towards four o'clock on Christmas Day they drew their chairs to the table, and with loosened collars set about enjoying the good things. Or pretending to enjoy them. This was Mahony's case; for the day was no holiday for him; and his head ached from the sun.'

In the years of the gold rushes, some people moderated the heat of midsummer a little by the use of ice. Cut from ponds in Massachusetts, stored in ice-houses and packed in straw or sawdust aboard ship in Boston, American ice dispatched by American ingenuity cooled Christmas drinks in Melbourne and Sydney and even as far inland as Beechworth before it melted. After 1860 ice was made in the colonies by machines using ammonia, and sold in blocks at threepence a pound. At that price it could be used by many colonial households not only in drinks but in ice-boxes to keep food and drink cool.

For the homesick emigrant it might give momentary consolation to touch a lump of ice at Christmas, but the only sure way for him to enjoy the season in this country was to learn to live with heat and to accept that it was not unnatural for December. Some taught themselves more quickly than others. Edward Millett, a clergyman, came with his wife to Western Australia in 1863. By 1868, Mrs Millett testified, 'we had learned to think an excessive degree of heat at Christmas was quite as correct as an equal amount of cold would have been at home'. Ideas of a *merry* Christmas, she confessed, were not so easily shifted: 'these require the contrast of sharp weather out of doors with light and warmth within, beside which mirth is so inseparable from activity that the sun-heat in repressing the last goes far to extinguish the first.' A visitor to Melbourne in the early 1870s observed that although a person could not at first reconcile Christmas with a blazing sun and a bright blue sky, 'in a short time he ceases to wonder, and enjoys his smoking roast-beef and plum-pudding all the same'. The traveller added, however, that 'the Australian in this respect is entitled to more credit than the Englishman, who has all the appetising influences of cold weather to give zest to his enthusiasm.' It was an act of virtue, a pleasure spiritual rather than bodily, to eat in this climate the good old English Christmas dinner. Francis Augustus Hare described his Christmas dinner of 1852 on the Victorian diggings as if it were not merely a meal but a sacrament. Like many diggers and other men in this land where women were scarce, he had to cook it himself. 'I bought the materials for a plum pudding; for a dozen of eggs I gave £1. I forget the price of the raisins, &c., but I shall never forget the pudding! We boiled it for twenty-four hours!—it took us a week to digest'.

Sentiment triumphed over environment whenever Australian colonists had plum pudding for Christmas, for it was a dish created by Europeans to be eaten in the months when no fresh fruit was to be had. Sensible people sometimes thought of abandoning it. Charles Dilke noted with interest in 1867 that at Hobart the Christmas dessert consisted often of fresh fruits. But how far could a colonist go in shedding the symbols of English celebration and still retain his sense of kinship with people at home? The case for and against plum pudding was much discussed. 'It would be a desirable innovation', wrote a resident of Victoria in 1872, 'could the hot and heavy plum-pudding of the United Kingdom be replaced by some cooler and more seasonable dainty dish; but long-cherished associations cast a "glamour" over the luscious compound, with its blue ghostly flame, which will not readily be effaced.' It was a canny prediction. Some Australians were to do without the blue flame either because they had a conscientious objection to taking alcohol or because they thought it a waste of good brandy. But it would long be an Australian tradition to enjoy both the heavy Christmas dinner and the absurdity of it.

Eating it need not mean that one still craved a cold December. 'Perhaps those of us who spent their early life in England, where Christmas falls in winter', said the Adelaide *Advertiser* on 24 December 1880, 'find it at first difficult to believe in the possibility of Christmas-keeping under a fierce sun like ours. But it is astonishing how soon they adjust themselves to the new conditions of the climate. The brightness, the warmth, the transparency of air and sky, at length seem to them more fit emblems of the season than the devices of England for battling it out bravely with the nipping frost and biting cold. Nature seems to be keeping holiday.' In that activity Australians liked to collaborate with nature.

THE HOLIDAYS

The less happy an emigrant's memories of home, the more readily could he enjoy Christmas as it was celebrated in this country. For the native-born, knowing no other climate or society, it was easier still. James Martin, brought to New South Wales so young that he thought of himself as a native, composed a cheery account of Christmas in New South Wales for *The Australian Sketch Book* which he published at the age of eighteen in 1838. 'During the week immediately preceding the twenty-fifth of December,' he wrote, 'every family in the whole colony appears to be thrown into a state of bustle and activity. The farmer hurries to the metropolis with his eggs, his poultry, and the produce of his lands, and purchases an ample supply of Christmas dainties for the celebration of the approaching holidays. Plums, currants, wines, spirits, and a large variety of other niceties . . . are obtained by the active housewife to adorn and set off the Christmas dinner. Everyone

THE CHRISTMAS HOLIDAYS
A gathering on Christmas Eve

is employed in providing for the eventful day, and the ordinary avocations of society seem to be almost forgotten.' Nurtured in the colony, Martin was perceiving not an exotic institution transplanted but a round of activities performed spontaneously by Australians.

Among the activities was drinking, as Martin reported. 'Some there are among the lower orders, who, instead of indulging in innocent and harmless festivity, give way to riot and intemperance . . . But this will not be surprising when it comes to be understood that drunkenness is the prevailing crime among us.' It was a bother for pastoralists and other employers who had work to be done at Christmas. Flocks wandered freely on Christmas Day as shepherds lay stupefied under the trees. Servants were notoriously unreliable out here in any season, but they were so likely to be drunk at Christmas that it could be difficult for respectable citizens to celebrate at all. 'I have heard', wrote Mrs Meredith in Sydney, 'of a Christmas-day party being assembled, and awaiting the announcement of dinner as long as patience could endure; then ringing the bell, but without reply; and on the hostess proceeding to the kitchen, finding every servant either gone out or rendered incapable of moving, the intended feast being meanwhile burned to ashes.' The Reverend J. D. Mereweather, arriving to take a Church of England service near Bendigo on the morning of 25 December 1850, found the schoolmaster who was supposed to act as his clerk so drunk that he was obliged to turn him out of the church. It was not, he said, an unusual experience. 'Christmas time is quite a saturnalia here, and drunkenness abounds.' There was a thoroughly saturnalian aspect to the next Christmas in Victoria, as men who had tramped soberly to the diggings roared back into Melbourne to spend their gold.

By 1870 Christmas was for city dwellers a time to get away from town. 'The excursion train, the steamboat, and public conveyances of all sorts,' wrote the *Sydney Morning Herald* on 25 December 1869, 'will thin the streets, and carry numbers into the country to enjoy the fresh air. Not long ago the utmost possible range of the mechanic or labourer of Sydney was within a few miles of rather barren country. The railroad, however, has opened a far more extended space'. Most people could count on having

THE CHRISTMAS HOLIDAYS
Shopping at Belmore Markets, Sydney, on Christmas Eve

THE CHRISTMAS HOLIDAYS
Manly beach

26 December free to continue or get over whatever they had been doing on Christmas Day, for Boxing Day—St Stephen's Day in the church calendar—was embraced as a holiday in Australia. The English custom of making gifts to servants on this day did not take hold out here, and few colonists knew what 'Boxing' meant. They nevertheless enjoyed a holiday on 26 December while other English-speaking people worked: in the United States the day was not observed at all, and in the United Kingdom it was commonly a working day until the Bank Holiday Act of 1871 made it a public holiday. Out here the banks and offices and most shops were closed. In Sydney on 26 December 1870 the *Empire* reported people 'flying from the town as though an enemy were invading it, and the water, or the hills, were the only places of safety.' Thirty thousand people bought railway tickets at the Flinders Street station in Melbourne that day. The beaches were crowded, boats sailed on the bay, and the river Yarra was a highway of pleasure. Boxing Day was a popular occasion for friendly societies, trade associations, and churches to hold fetes and picnics and sporting contests, and in the evening theatres and music halls had full houses. It was second only to St Patrick's Day for festivity among Irish-Australians, of whom about ten thousand attended a Hibernian fete in Melbourne on

26 December 1870. 'Good order was kept in the paddock during the day', reported the *Age*, 'the only notable deviation from propriety being an ineffectual attempt by three or four fellows to stop the playing of God Save the Queen at the termination of the sports.'

The turn of the year was connected with Christmas as a time for holiday and compliment. Here as at home the new year was welcomed with church bells, and people resolved to do and be better for the next twelve months. Governors held levees. Citizens played or watched games, went for picnics, listened to bands. From the first years of settlement it was customary for men in towns to stay out late carousing and larking, lighting bonfires and fireworks. On the morning of 1 January the laundry's sign 'Mangling done here' might be found at the gate of a surgeon. Occasionally these acts of homage to the god of misrule got out of hand. In the early hours of 1 January 1850 the police force of Sydney could not stop a riotous crowd from smashing and looting. But by 1870 the

THE CHRISTMAS HOLIDAYS

A picnic in Studley Park, Melbourne. 'It comes to us in the full flush of midsummer, and it is celebrated—like many of the religious festivals of ancient Greece—in the open air. It is a prolonged merry-making, for there is a suspension of all business from Christmas Eve until the morrow of New Year's Day ... We have not lost the capacity for hard work which distinguishes our countrymen at home; but as the earnings of all classes of society are sufficient to provide for something more than the satisfaction of our daily wants, we can afford to make holiday at Christmas, and to do so in a genial, generous, and ungrudging spirit.'

THE CHRISTMAS HOLIDAYS
A steamboat excursion on Port Phillip Bay

disorders of the night were usually amiable and licensed. 'In every part of the city,' the *Sydney Morning Herald* reported on 1 January 1870, 'the youngsters especially were in their glory, producing the most discordant noises by their ringing of bells, their performance upon whistles and other toy musical instruments, and their thumping with sticks upon castaway kettles and sundry other kitchen utensils.' In the morning, people on their way to public holiday pleasures found shutters, doors, verandah posts and walls chalked '1870'.

For colonists from puritan Scotland and parts of northern England the new year was more important than Christmas. 'The commencement of a New Year is universally hailed throughout Scotland with demonstrations of joy', John Dunmore Lang explained in 1826 to colonists from elsewhere. 'Warm gratulations and kindly wishes are mutually interchanged by people of all ranks; while enthusiasts for the customs of the olden times circulate the juice of the Scottish grape much more freely than is deemed convenient at other seasons.' After gathering on New Year's Eve, which they called Hogmanay, to play bagpipes, eat haggis and drink whisky, Scottish emigrants in Australia were generally believed to contribute more than their share to the noises and sights of the night.

Were the Scots also responsible for making Christmas a less solidly domestic occasion than in England? 'Christmas among us is more a general holiday than an occasion of family *reunions*', said the *Illustrated Melbourne Post* on 20 December 1862. Two visitors to Melbourne a decade later, noticing that 'the proportion of family groups was smaller than on Christmas Day in England', suggested as an explanation the Scottish disregard for Christmas as a family festival. But people of Scottish birth and parentage were too few—not much more than 10 per cent of the population—to set the style of Christmas celebration, and their children usually came to spend it as other Australians did. The main reason why people in this emigrants' country were less apt than people at home to cluster in families at Christmas was simply that they had fewer relatives within visiting distance.

Another peculiarity of the Australian Christmas was discerned by 1870. Late in December the year could be felt to be running down, in a manner unfamiliar to contemporaries in England or America. 'We know how difficult it is to do anything in the way of public business when the Christmas holidays approach', said a member of the

NEW YEAR'S DAY
Morning on the St Kilda Road. '... we venture to indicate Melbourne as the picnickiest point of this southern hemisphere ... What between Melbourne visiting the country, and the country returning the compliments of the season, the steam of the Railway department had nothing to spare; and the highways, especially in the neighbourhood of towns, were crowded by all sorts of turn outs.'

Victorian parliament in 1870. Falling in the middle of summer, Christmas was well placed to become the nucleus of an extended period away from work. A reporter in Melbourne observed that Monday 27 December 1869 had been 'given up to holiday-making', and declared proudly: 'there is not another city in the world perhaps where any holiday would be so universally kept as was Monday by the citizens of Melbourne.' He was writing on Wednesday 29 December. 'The resumption of business yesterday morning', he went on, 'was but a half-hearted attempt, and the normal state of Collins-street will not be restored for another week to come'. Native Australians, used to having a season of leisure from Christmas to New Year, could be surprised when they visited England to discover how briefly most people there stopped work.

To English eyes it was a sign of the colonists' democracy that rich and poor took holidays at the same time, and a sign of their prosperity and taste for leisure that they did it so often. 'A stranger, accustomed only to the few and rare occasions when the whole British nation can unite in enjoyment', wrote an observer in 1872, 'is astonished and amused at the frequent and widespread holiday-keeping of their colonial countrymen.' Not only at Christmas but also at Easter, Australians were stopping work longer than people at home. In Victoria both Good Friday and the following Monday were, by 1856, holidays in the public offices, and people spoke of 'the Easter holidays'. On Good Friday itself, Catholic and Church of England services drew crowds of worshippers. Presbyterians, Methodists and other inheritors of the puritan tradition were less disposed to make Easter a special occasion. They tended to mingle with people not in the habit of worshipping anywhere who dressed up and took off in a carriage, an omnibus or an excursion train to the country or the seaside. On Monday people of all faiths pursued pleasure, 'the denizens of the country rushing into town', as the *Sydney Morning Herald* observed on 19 April 1870, and 'the residents of the town making for the country, each crossing the track of the other in the search for change'.

In England Sir John Lubbock's Bank Holiday Act of 1871 enlarged the amount of leisure enjoyed by millions of people when it guaranteed them, apart from Sundays, four public holidays a year: Easter Monday, Whit Monday seven weeks later, the first Monday in August—St Lubbock's Day—and Boxing Day. The work-shirking folks of Sydney, said a writer in the *Sydney Morning Herald*, could barely appreciate what Lubbock's act had done for the workers of England. The number of holidays enjoyed by an Australian in 1870 depended on what his job was and where he lived, but it would not be unusual for him to have the queen's birthday, Christmas Day, Boxing Day and New Year's Day, Good Friday and the following Saturday and Monday, and a day to celebrate the birth of his colony. He might also have St Patrick's Day and the days between Boxing Day and New Year. If he lived in Victoria he might enjoy two further days of leisure unknown elsewhere.

8 New Festivals of Leisure

THE SACRED GIFT OF TIME

The movement for an eight-hour day was a crusade by emigrant artisans of the 1850s who were determined that no man would treat them as if they were convicts or paupers. James Galloway, a stonemason who came from England in 1855 at the age of 27, spoke for men like himself a solemn declaration of rights: 'We have come 16,000 miles to better our condition, and not to act the mere part of machinery; and it is neither right nor just that we should cross the trackless regions of immensity between us and our fatherland, to be rewarded with excessive toil, a bare existence, and premature grave.' Like most ambitious working men who left England for Australia in that decade, Galloway had chosen to go to Victoria. Melbourne's population had just passed Sydney's when he landed. Men like himself, builders of the city in the years of gold, were paid better wages than at home. But costs were higher too, and hours were no shorter: on building sites here as in England men normally worked ten hours a day.

Reduced working hours had become an aspiration of radicals in England on behalf of men, women and children for whom the rhythms of rural labour had been replaced by the more rigid disciplines of industry. In the rhetoric of some reformers, division of man's day into eight hours of work, eight hours of recreation and eight hours of rest was proclaimed as a natural right. It was to be among the hopes generated in England which proved easier to realize in Australia.

At home a Ten Hours Act was applied to textile trades in 1847. Building workers in London went on strike in 1853 for a nine-hour day, but they did not get it. Stonemasons in Melbourne resolved early in 1856 not to work more than eight hours a day, six days a week. They were well placed to be pioneers of industrial solidarity. Moving from job to job together, as a carpenter observed, stonemasons 'could get in closer touch with each other, reason out differences, and come to fixed conclusions and permanent understandings.' They were also working for employers most of whom had been artisans themselves, and who could pass on costs fairly easily to clients. Galloway had become secretary of the Operative Stonemasons' Society within months of reaching Melbourne. His president was James Stephens, a Welshman aged thirty-four who was unusual among the campaigners for eight hours in having been a prominent agitator at home: he was dismissed from a job on Windsor Castle for being a chartist, he helped carry the chartists' petition to Westminster in 1848, and he held senior office in a society of stonemasons before coming out as an assisted emigrant with his wife and two sons in 1853. Galloway, Stephens and their workmates offered to serve employers from seven o'clock to five in winter and from six to four in summer, taking an hour off for breakfast and an hour for dinner. Most contractors in the city agreed. Two did not: W. C. Cornish, whose men were building the new houses of parliament, and Holmes, who had the contract for a market. Stephens was at work on the new university. On the morning of 21 April 1856 he called on stonemasons there to stop work and protest against the two contractors who refused to shorten working hours. They put down their tools and marched to Eastern Hill, joined on the way by others until about seven hundred men were marching. Galloway was chairman of a meeting which resolved not to work for any employer who held out, and appointed a deputation to wait on Cornish and Holmes. Like the chartists in England the stonemasons were uncertain how hard to press employers. Some were prepared for physical force if necessary, but Galloway wrote to the *Argus* assuring the community that the movement was moderate and reasonable.

One argument used in favour of the eight-hour day was that in the heat of Australia a man needed more rest than under the gentle skies of England. It was a common belief among emigrants. Alexander Harris found that after a year or so of exertion an 'invincible lassitude takes possession of the whole frame; and without anything like illness one feels destitute of all that alacrity that is usually associated with health.' (Brain as well as body was thought to be affected by colonial weather: the Reverend W. B. Clarke, declining an offer from the University of Sydney in 1853 to profess both geology and mineralogy, observed to Sir Charles Nicholson 'that people can not work here even as hard as they do at home owing to the influences of climate.') When James Stephens spoke many years later of the historic morning on which he and his brothers had stood up against the employers, he thought of the Australian sun. 'It was a burning hot day,' he recalled, 'and I thought the occasion a good one'. The old agitator's memory had deceived him: 21 April 1856 was a normal autumn day in Melbourne with a cloudy sky and a temperature that never reached sixty degrees Fahrenheit; but in the preceding months he had sometimes worked in temperatures more than forty degrees higher than that. In any case, the stonemasons argued that whatever the climate, a man living in an age when knowledge was increasing rapidly needed more leisure in order to acquire it. That approach appealed more to men who worked indoors. 'It was nothing to the purpose to say that they had not to work in the sun', a group of men in manufacturing trades declared. 'What they wanted was the sacred gift of time, to employ it to the advantage of their intellect as well as in the repose of their physical energies.'

Of the two contractors, Holmes gave in at once. Cornish proposed at first to grant eight hours but to reduce wages, from fifteen to thirteen shillings a day. The stonemasons refused. Then he offered fourteen shillings a day, and they went back to work—prepared, after all, to give up a little money in order to gain time. But within a few weeks nearly all workers in building trades won the eight-hour day without any loss of wages, and it was extended to several other occupations, including quarrymen, saddlers and harness-makers. On 12 May the men who had obtained 'the boon', as they called it, met to celebrate their victory. They marched through the city to the music of a band behind a red, white and blue banner made in the workers' suburb of Collingwood by the wife of a stonemason from Scotland. It bore the inscription:

8 HOURS LABOUR
8 HOURS RECREATION
8 HOURS REST.

The procession passed the houses of parliament on its way to a dinner and fete at the Cremorne Gardens, a pleasure ground on the Yarra. The festivity was not merely sectional: 'every working man and the public at large' were invited; and it was under the patronage of the mayor and the committee of two civic institutions, the Melbourne Hospital and the Benevolent Asylum, which were to profit from the day's revels.

Having won the day, the emigrant craftsmen could look back with pity on their brothers who had not dared the trackless regions of immensity. In 1859 the chairman of a ceremony to open a trades hall in Melbourne asked why this was the first hall in the world erected for working men. Because, he answered, 'in other countries, although working-men had struggled to obtain the boon of eight hours' labor, they had never been able to obtain it. The poor docile working-classes of England had been content to labor on and permit the upper classes to think and act for them.' There was no disloyalty in this swaggering talk on behalf of colonial artisans. Indeed, the day chosen to open the Trades Hall was the queen's birthday. They were rather affirming that men such as themselves were the best of Britons.

The case against as well as for the eight-hour day travelled out from England. The day after the meeting on Eastern Hill in 1856, the Melbourne *Herald* declared that the innovation would set off a rush of masons and carpenters from home who would force wages down. 'Who will go on toiling ten or twelve hours a day, at the Parliament Houses in Westminster, when he can come out and enjoy life so much more pleasantly, in building up the Legislative halls at the top of Bourke Street?' The paper misjudged both the mobility of English labour and the demand for skilled workers here. Most of the time there would be jobs enough for the men who gained the eight-hour day, though in periods of depression some workers saved it only by accepting lower wages. There was much public building to be done in Melbourne, and the suburbs and country towns were waiting for villas and cottages and terraces, halls and post offices and banks and churches. The boon travelled from trade to trade and place to place. 'The eight hours' system', said the *Age* on 17 October 1859, 'has now become a great public fact . . . too vast in dimensions, too national in character, to be retarded by temporary opposition.' But it would take a long while to reach all workers. In 1859 C. J. Don, a mason's labourer who had been a chartist in Glasgow and more recently a digger, was elected to the Victorian parliament. At a meeting of the Eight Hours League he declared the right of the man who put up the public buildings and mansions of the colony to better housing of his own. 'He builds the homes, aye, and the cloud capped towers, and the gorgeous palaces that crown the cities of the world, and he goes home to live, nay, rather to sleep, in the mud flats of Collingwood and Richmond.' Don had been elected by votes from Collingwood and introduced himself to parliament as 'a new fact in the British Empire—an actual working artisan in a Legislative Assembly to speak and vote for his class.' In his own vision of society the eight-hour day was a panacea for poverty. 'Look upon the toiling millions of the world', he declaimed, 'who lay the foundations of all physical, intellectual and moral prosperity. What scheme should be left untried to raise up the industrial masses of this and every other country? And what scheme stands so great a chance of success as the Eight Hours' Movement?' His first motion in the Legislative Assembly was for the legal enactment of an eight-hour day for all workers. It was defeated, and so were similar motions in the next

EIGHT HOURS DAY
The anniversary committee, Melbourne, 1858

ten years, by a parliament which was more responsive to the interests of employers than of workers.

In New South Wales as in Victoria, emigrants engaged in building the capital city took the lead in demanding eight hours. In 1855 some stonemasons in Sydney struck for an eight-hour day and got it. Thus, wrote a colonial patriot, E. W. O'Sullivan, 'the beauteous tree of the eight-hour system was fairly planted in the soil of New South Wales, a year before the seed was sown in the more democratic colony of Victoria.' But it was tended more cautiously. When an Operative Stonemasons' Society sought a general reduction from ten hours to eight in 1856, its leaders assured employers that they were willing to have wages lowered from fifteen shillings a day to twelve shillings and sixpence, and on that understanding they were given the eight-hour day. By 1862 members of the societies of carpenters and joiners, bricklayers and plasterers had also gained it by taking lower wages; artisans in these trades who did not belong to the societies worked longer hours. The carpenters and joiners celebrated at a picnic in Sydney each year, which was joined by other tradesmen and acquired by 1868 the character of a general demonstration seeking the eight-hour day for all workers. An Eight Hour Extension League began in 1869 to organize the picnic and demonstration and to urge that parliament should compel all employers to grant the eight-hour day. Once, in 1856, Henry Parkes had presided at an eight-hour meeting called by carpenters and stonemasons. He had told them that the interests of themselves and their employers were inseparable, that labour was honourable, that he himself had never been happier, better or prouder than in the days when he was a journeyman tradesman, and that men had the right to reduced hours in order to be thinkers as well as workers. 'He was a great sympathiser at that time', one of the pioneers recalled, 'but he never bothered much about it when he had the power.' As in Victoria, the politicians were reluctant to legislate for the boon.

The stonemasons of Brisbane won an eight-hour day in 1865, and on 1 March in that year societies of masons and plasterers arranged a march of five hundred men through the streets in the cause of urging others to agitate. In Adelaide in 1865, at a time when artisans generally worked nine hours a day, six days a week, stonemasons and bricklayers formed a society which had among its objects the eight-hour day; but they settled for a half-holiday on Saturday. Sydney had by 1870 a Saturday Half-Holiday Association which published the names of shops whose proprietors had agreed to close at one o'clock on Saturday and exhorted the public to buy nothing after that time. The drapery stores of Farmers and David Jones were among establishments that gave their employees Saturday afternoon.

In Melbourne the anniversary of the demonstration in 1856 was celebrated as a grand festival of labour. For working men modest in their hopes of social change and robust in pursuing them, the day was a fine occasion for mutual congratulation, inspiration and pleasure. 'The Eight Hours' system', ran the toast: 'may its physical, intellectual, moral, and social advantages be extended to every member of the human family.' For days before 21 April, old banners were unfolded in the Trades Hall and new banners, costing between a hundred and two hundred pounds each, were created for the felt hatters, or the cutters and thinners, or the cigar makers, or whichever society had gained the boon since the last procession. On the day itself, crowds gathered from early

EIGHT HOURS DAY
A procession in Sydney

morning outside the Trades Hall, which was decorated with flowers and greenery, to watch marshals assemble the various societies with their floats and banners and bands. At ten o'clock the anniversary committee stepped off under the old red, white and blue banner which had been carried in 1856. The marchers made a splendid and orderly procession. James Galloway was not among them, for in 1860, at the age of thirty-two, he had gone after all to a premature grave in the Melbourne General Cemetery. Near the houses of parliament the procession halted and stood at attention while bands played 'God Save the Queen'. The demonstrators cheered the governor and moved on to enjoy themselves at the fete with foot-racing, side-shows and merry-go-rounds. In Sydney a procession like Melbourne's began in 1871.

The procession in Melbourne was open only to members of associations that worked by the eight hours system. That was an incentive for workers outside the circle of celebration to win the boon and come in. But the fete was public, and so was the theatrical performance later in the day whose takings went to the hospital. Here each year an ode was recited from the stage. For the twentieth anniversary, in 1876, the laureate was Marcus Clarke. Having written of the bad old days in *His Natural Life*, which had lately been published in book form, Clarke was now asked to compose an anthem for the free and proud artisans of a new age. He called it "An Australian Paean" and declared that, although April here bore no promises of spring, yet:

> Our children's tend'rest memories
>   Round Austral April grow;
> 'Twas the month we won their freedom, boys,
>   Just twenty years ago.
>
> Liberty! name of warning!
>   Did'st thou feel our pulses beat
> As we marching, moved this morning
>   All adown the cheering street?
> In our federated freedom,
>   In our manliness allied,
> While the badges of our labour
>   Were the banners of our pride.
>
> But never let our sons forget,
>   Till mem'ry's self be dead,
> If Britain gave us birth, my lads,
>   Australia gave us bread!
> Then cheer for young Australia,
>   The empire of the Free,
> Where yet a Greater Britain
>   The Southern Cross shall see!

Newcomers saw that working men in Australia were doing better than those in England at gaining both money and time. Charles Thatcher, an English emigrant to the Victorian goldfields who composed and sang popular songs to colonial audiences, invited them to imagine English visitors disapproving of the Australian labouring man's achievement and demeanour.

No workhouse have we here,
　No poor law coves so cruel,
No bullying overseer,
　No paltry water gruel,
No masters to oppress
　A wretched starving devil,
But here, I rather guess
　We're all upon a level.

When great folks come, they find
　That labour's in the ascendant;
No cringing beggars, mind,
　But all are independent:
Their pride receives a blow,
　Their greatness is a failure;
And to England back they go,
　And run down *poor* Australia.

Perhaps Thatcher knew of such nasty people, or perhaps he was making them up to delight the independent working men who were spending some of their wages and leisure to hear him. The English visitor whose words were most widely read, Anthony Trollope, offered a very different judgment. As a hard-working professional man and the father of an emigrant, Trollope was keen to compare the conditions of life here and at home for the various classes. For the well-to-do, he concluded, no land could beat England; for the bulk of the working population Australia was the place. 'There is perhaps no town in the world', he wrote, 'in which an ordinary working man can do better for himself and for his family with his work than he can at Melbourne.' In the last paragraph of his two volumes on Australia and New Zealand, Trollope told English readers that for men who could and would work with their hands and for women who could cook and be useful about a household 'these colonies are a paradise. They will find the whole condition of life changed for them. The slight estimation in which labour is held here will be changed for a general respect. The humbleness, the hat-touching, the servility which is still incidental to such work as theirs in this old country, and which is hardly compatible with exalted manhood, has found no footing there. I regard such manhood among the masses of the people as the highest sign of prosperity which a country can give.' Working-class emigrants could expect still more prosperity for their children, Trollope believed; for the labourer born in the colonies 'is better fed than the labourer at home, better housed, better clothed, and is therefore more of a man.' Food was something Trollope always noticed. It struck him as a fundamental difference between life for the masses of men and women in England and in these colonies that at home many did not get enough to eat and many more were doomed so to work that they could think of nothing but a sufficiency of food; but out here, 'if a man will work the food comes easily, and he can turn his mind elsewhere.'

Where did the working men's minds turn? What were they doing in the hours they had won from labour for recreation and rest? Boozing and betting, some said. The campaigners denied it. People who saw the boon as an extension of drinking time, declared an eight-hour man in Sydney, 'were liable to the charge of measuring others' corn by their measure.' Another said that men would use the time gained to elevate themselves to the place on the social scale 'which the artificer, the mechanic and the labouring man ought . . . to hold in all parts of the globe'. They could if they wished read books and newspapers. The ability to read and write was more widely diffused in these colonies, especially Victoria, than at home. The Trades Hall built in Melbourne in 1859 was also a Literary Institute. In all the colonial cities, books could be borrowed from a mechanics' institute or school of arts, bought new or second-hand from booksellers—Sydney had thirty by 1860 —or read free at public libraries. Of the latter, Melbourne had the best. Its foundation stone and that of the university were laid on the same day in 1854, to the great satisfaction of Redmond Barry, a judge of the Supreme Court of Victoria, who had done more than any other colonist to found both institutions. The great reading room of the Melbourne public library, modelled on that of the Library of Congress, was opened in 1856. Its collection was available to self-improving readers from Monday to Saturday until ten o'clock at night.

Among newspapers, the *Age* in Melbourne and the *Empire* in Sydney were sympathetic to popular aspiration. The *Age*, under David Syme, was for the working man in the sense that it advocated policies, especially the protection of colonial manufactures, which its proprietor believed were in their interests; but it was made to be read by only the most serious-minded and learned among them. Its circulation was higher than that of any other paper in Australia, and it was rising, from some 15 000 a day in 1868 to more

MELBOURNE PUBLIC LIBRARY

than 20 000 a day in 1874. Some of those copies found many readers; but most wage-earners did not regularly see newspapers or buy books or frequent libraries.

The *Argus*, friendly to the eight-hour campaigners of 1856—though soon to turn conservative—thought that the artisan would spend the hours gained from work neither in idleness nor in education but in 'the peaceful pleasures of home . . . digging in his garden, feeding his poultry, milking his cow, teaching his children'. For the cow he would need grass nearby in a paddock, as any empty suburban block in Australia came to be called; and here, as well as in his own backyard, he might grow fruit and vegetables. He might also build a house. W. S. Jevons, a young Englishman employed for a while as an assayer at the mint in Sydney, observed in new suburbs of the late 1850s thousands of 'frail and small habitations . . . in many or most cases belonging to and built by those who inhabit them. Almost every labourer or mechanic here has his own residence . . . and unpretending as it is to any convenience or beauties, it yet satisfies him better than the brick built, closely packed and rented houses of English towns . . . In a great majority of cases the first plan only includes two small rooms, to which others are sometimes added afterwards'. Many men putting up brick and stone structures for other people eight hours a day worked for themselves in their own time at building cottages for their families.

Charles Dickens believed that the masses of his countrymen had to work too hard. 'I entertain a weak idea', he wrote in *Hard Times* (1854), 'that the English people are as hard-worked as any people upon whom the sun shines. I acknowledge to this ridiculous idiosyncrasy, as a reason why I should give them a little more play.' Those who went to the towns of Australia tended both to work less and to play more. Charles Dilke detected in 1867 that 'a national character is being grafted upon the good English stock'. Among its elements, he suggested with condescension, were 'an admirable love of simple mirth, and a serious distaste for prolonged labour in one direction'. It was perhaps evidence of both these predilections that, by 1870, people in the largest of Australian cities had holidays in honour of both the eight-hour movement and the Melbourne Cup.

CUP DAY

Eight hours work, eight hours recreation, eight hours rest, the campaigners said. They meant not that each day was to be divided into three precisely equal parts, but that a man had a right to plenty of sleep and that his waking hours belonged to him as much as to his employer. In general usage, recreation meant above all sport; and sport came earlier in the colonies than at home to mean not primarily hunting animals or shooting birds or catching fish, but playing games. Sport appeared to be the main occupation of the whole people on public holidays; of those who did not have to work, on Saturday afternoons; and of boys whenever they had an opportunity. Archibald Michie observed after living for many years in Sydney and Melbourne that, in the view of 'more serious' people, 'Australians give an undue portion of their lives to sport and pleasure'.

Whatever games people played or watched at home were transported to the colonies. Some traditional diversions such as cock-fighting, rat-fighting and bull-baiting were popular in the early decades of New South Wales but declined there, as at home, in favour of gentler pursuits. After 1850 emigrants were coming from an England in which outdoor games had a new popularity and social purpose. Two conditions making them flourish at home—concentration of people in towns and increasing provision of schools—were also present in Australia. Here, indeed, the urban population was proportionately greater; and in the 'public' schools formed in imitation of those lately transformed or created in England, nothing was copied more ardently than the system of manly and compulsory games. For boys at other schools or none, it was easier than in urban England to find open spaces for games; and for rich and poor, young and old, the weather was a constant invitation to play. Most Victorian boys, the *Argus* observed in 1860, 'excel in out-door exercises and make the most of a climate so well adapted for the development of "muscular Christianity" '.

Sailing and rowing, walking and running, prize-fighting, cricket, football and horse-racing were popular sports in the colonies. Sailing boats raced regularly on Port Jackson by 1840. Rowing began on the quieter reaches of the harbour, was taken up in the schools of all colonies, and became in the 1860s a sport in which teams representing colonies raced against each other. Swimming was not a common pastime or skill among Englishmen. Out here the weather and the proximity to water encouraged it and the fear of attack by sharks was a deterrent. A son of Robert Howe of the *Sydney Gazette*, Alfred Australia Howe—perhaps the first child ever named after the continent—was taken by a shark while swimming at the mouth of the Macleay River in 1837. Swimming was to become more popular in the colonies than at home, but by 1870 most people who went to the seaside merely sat or strolled on the beach. On holidays they made for it in thousands, living as most of them did within fairly easy reach of the sea and knowing that it would rarely be too cold to enjoy the outing. On a sunny day in Sydney, steamers from the Circular Quay were full of pleasure-seekers off to paddle or bathe in the calm water of harbour beaches, or to fill their lungs with ocean air as they watched the great surf roll in. The popularity of prize-fighting was registered in the name of Bendigo, which came from a pugnacious shepherd of the neighbourhood who had in turn been nicknamed after William 'Bendigo' Thompson, a famous English boxer of the 1840s. But pugilism attracted fewer colonists than walking and running, or 'pedestrianism'. William Francis King, who sold pies from a tray in the streets of Sydney, was famous as 'the flying pieman' for his pedestrian feats in the 1840s, such as winning a race against a coach from Brisbane to Ipswich while carrying a pole weighing a hundred pounds. Much money changed hands on Saturdays and holidays in the 1850s and 1860s after walking and running races. On Easter Monday 1870 about fifteen thousand people filled Sydney's Albert Ground (named in honour of the late prince consort) to watch three Englishmen—Frank Hewitt, the champion quarter-mile runner of the world, Albert Bird, the champion mile runner, and George Topley, the champion walker of England and America—compete in handicap races against local pedestrians.

Cricket was probably the first game to be played in the colonies between teams. From the earliest days in Sydney and Melbourne the teams that met each summer were not mere collections of individual players who had joined together for recreation, but representatives of groups testing their skill against each other. Soldiers took on civilians. Currency took on sterling. The first contest between teams representing New South Wales and Victoria, at Melbourne in 1856, was also virtually an encounter between natives and immigrants, for ten of the visiting team were of colonial birth and all the Victorians were born in the United Kingdom. The men from Sydney won. For the return game at Sydney in January 1857, which was billed as a Grand National Cricket Match, the Victorians had a new player who was not only a native but, like very few Victorians, the son of a native. He was Thomas Wentworth Wills, whose father Horatio, now a solidly established squatter, had lately become one of three Australian-born members of the first Legislative Assembly. At the English public school to which Horatio Wills sent his son in 1852 for the best education the empire had to offer, games were on the way to gaining an almost religious stature. Thomas Arnold would not have approved; but Arnold had died before young Wills arrived, and his successors believed in manly games as educators of body and spirit. The second-generation currency lad became captain of cricket and football at Rugby; and at Cambridge, where he went to play in 1856 though not to study, he was thought to be one of the most promising cricketers in the kingdom. Against New South Wales at Sydney in January 1857, he took ten wickets in two innings; but the Victorians were still beaten. A year later in Melbourne his batting and bowling helped Victoria to win. Under Tom Wills's captaincy the Victorians won four games in a row. The encounter in January 1859 was the first to be reported by intercolonial telegraph, news of each day's play in Sydney being read at breakfast next morning in Melbourne. As the third and last day of the game began, people in Melbourne knew that the odds were heavily against their men. But they rallied and won. It was 'a brilliant victory for the Victorians', said the *Age* on 25 January. When Wills and his men sailed home the Melbourne *Herald* greeted them as 'laurelled warriors'.

A team from England toured the colonies in 1862. Two emigrants who ran a restaurant in Melbourne, Spiers and Pond, tried to engage Charles Dickens, offering him ten thousand pounds to give colonial audiences the readings from his works which had been vastly popular at home since they began in 1858. When the novelist declined, the two investors turned to cricketers, judging that Australians had enough money, enthusiasm for the game, and interest in an encounter between Englishmen and colonists, to make the venture profitable. They were right. On Christmas Eve 1861 the people of Melbourne gave the players when they disembarked from the *Great Britain* a welcome more ardent than was offered any other visitor of the age except the queen's son in 1867. But there was strain as well as delight in the air. One would imagine, said the *Argus*, 'that some tremendous crisis was at hand, or that some trial which is to make or mar us for ever is approaching'. The Englishmen were amazed to find in Melbourne a cricket ground as impressive as the best ground in England—Kennington Oval—with a fine water supply, a grandstand for six thousand spectators and banked seats for thousands more. It had all been brought to perfection just in time by an architect and surveyor named R. C. Bagot. On the public holiday for New Year's Day in 1862, more than twenty-five thousand people made their way to the ground and paid from one to five shillings to see the first day of play. They made possibly the largest crowd to have watched a cricket match anywhere in the world, and although 2 January was not a public holiday the crowd on the second day was very nearly as great.

The spectators saw eighteen Victorians, most of them emigrants, play against eleven Englishmen. The rules and conventions of cricket, as of other games, had yet to be fixed, and the number of players on each side was normally a matter for negotiation. It was the custom for teams of leading English players to handicap themselves by allowing their opponents more men. In 1859 an eleven touring North America had played against teams of twenty-two. A similar ratio was anticipated in Australia; but on the eve of the first match the English captain, H. H. Stephenson, refused to allow more than eighteen in the local side because his men were going on to the field stiff from their few days' practice after two months at sea. Many colonists thought that their own side was too small for equity. 'Are the cricketers in Victoria so much superior', asked the *Herald*, 'that the Eleven of England cannot play 22 of them?' But Stephenson insisted; and his men won easily. The game began with 'God Save the Queen' and ended with the ascent of a

MELBOURNE WELCOMES THE ALL-ENGLAND ELEVEN
The Cafe de Paris was owned by the entrepreneurs who brought out the team, Spiers and Pond.

manned balloon, the first seen in the colony, named 'All England' and bearing pictures of the queen and the English cricketers. For all other games in Victoria, New South Wales and Tasmania the hosts were allowed twenty-two men. The exception was at Beechworth, where a single Englishman played eleven colonists and beat them by five runs to one. The visitors won eight encounters, drew two, and lost two: one in the mining centre of Castlemaine, and one in Sydney to a team representing both New South Wales and Victoria which was perhaps the first formal combination of men from the two colonies for any purpose.

Colonists made every match a big event. The game between England and New South Wales aroused a public interest which led the *Sydney Morning Herald* to compare it with the Crimean War. The two promoters made eleven thousand pounds out of the tour—enough to return home and set up as restaurateurs in the west end of London. One of the

Englishmen, questioned at home about the colonial cricketers, offered a judgment which became a legend: 'Well, I don't think much of their play, but they are a wonderful lot of drinking men.' To improve their play one of the visitors, Charles Lawrence, stayed behind as coach to Sydney's Albert Club. Another twelve English cricketers toured the colonies in 1863–4, paying their own way, making seven thousand pounds between them, and winning all their games. They came close to defeat only once, by twenty-two men representing New South Wales. From this tour William Caffyn remained, to teach young men in Sydney and Melbourne skills with bat and ball which might enable them one day to compete with the best of the mother country on terms of parity. A match between eleven men from England and eleven from Australia might then be called a test.

Tom Wills had been unable to play against Stephenson's eleven in 1862. His father Horatio had decided to lead an exodus of family, servants and sheep up to the new colony of Queensland. The Wills caravan travelled overland for ten months of 1861 as far as Cullinlaringo, in the Maryborough district, where on 17 October 1861 aborigines pounced on their canvas settlement and killed all nineteen white occupants. Tom Wills survived, a broken dray having kept him away from the camp. He returned to Victoria, played against the English visitors of 1863–4, and gave coaching to many young colonists as well as to a group of aborigines who began to play cricket at Edenhope in western Victoria.

On Boxing Day 1866 Wills led a team of aborigines to play before ten thousand people on the Melbourne ground against a team from the Melbourne Cricket Club. They visited Sydney, three of them dying on the tour or soon after it. Early in 1868 a team of thirteen aborigines said by a country newspaper to have in it 'the best of those who were left alive after the last tour and some other darkies', set off for England under Charles Lawrence, the professional who had stayed on in 1862. They played first a number of games in Victoria and New South Wales. Among the transparencies greeting the duke of Edinburgh in Sydney was a picture showing the progress of aborigines under British rule from barbarism to cricket. On 4 and 5 February 1868 the prince watched the blacks play a drawn game against an army and navy team which included William Caffyn.

'Nothing of interest comes from Australia except gold nuggets and black cricketers', wrote the London *Daily Telegraph* after the team disembarked from a clipper on 13 May 1868. *The Times* welcomed them with a magisterial indifference to facts about the colonies, announcing that they represented 'the colonies of Victoria, Queenstown, South Australia and New Zealand.' The aborigines played against teams from counties, towns, and the Marylebone Cricket Club, and won as many games as they lost. Australian colonists in England turned out to watch. In their first game, against Surrey at the Oval, a digger back from Victoria called 'Coo-ee!' at the luncheon adjournment, and the blacks came running to him. One player died in England, of tuberculosis. Lawrence and his fellow-sponsors lost a little money on the tour. In some English minds the visit confirmed the idea that all Australians were blackfellows. When the first white cricketers from the colonies reached the old country in 1878, somebody said to a member of the English team which was to meet them at Lord's: 'I hear you are going to play against the niggers on Monday.'

Varieties of football, like cricket, had been played early by soldiers of the imperial regiments, but it was not until Tom Wills returned from Rugby that organized football began. In the winter of 1858, when he was secretary of the Melbourne Cricket Club, Wills wrote to a sporting newspaper, *Bell's Life in Victoria*, suggesting that young men who had put their bats away for the season should keep themselves from getting stiff and stout by forming a football club, or perhaps a rifle club. Wills's cousin, H. C. A. Harrison, and two other cricketers responded by drawing up a set of rules for a football club. From Wills they knew the game he had played at Rugby, but he advised that the Rugby tackle was too dangerous for grown men on the hard ground of Melbourne. There was no other formal model for them yet to consider. The age of regulated sport was just beginning, and these men were pioneers of it: the Football Association, proprietor of the code that came to be known as soccer, was not formed in England until 1863. Boys in Melbourne schools who already were playing cricket against each other were keen to take up a winter game, and teams of forty a side from Scotch College and the Church of England Grammar School met at football in 1858. The game caught on. By 1859 people were debating how far the colonial passion for sport could be attributed to the publication in 1857 of Thomas Hughes's novel about Rugby. 'Whether that manly and healthy book *Tom Brown's Schooldays* has produced a love for violent exercise', said a newspaper, 'it matters not to enquire . . . Football, like cricket, has become an institution in and around the metropolis, and it would not be surprising if the epidemic spread wider.' Clubs at Melbourne, Richmond, South Yarra, Carlton, Geelong and elsewhere challenged each other to contests on Saturday afternoons. Rules and conventions were fluid, and umpires were not introduced until 1872. A single game might go on for several Saturdays, or it might not begin at all if something more urgent had to be done; 'owing . . . to the almost universal occupation of letter writing previous to the departure of an English mail,' it was announced on one occasion, 'there was no football.' The game was known by 1870 as Victorian Rules. In New South Wales, schoolmasters from England introduced the Rugby game, a Rugby Union club being formed at the University of Sydney in 1864.

Among players and spectators, football was not yet as popular as cricket. Its eventual spread may appear to be a striking exception to Edward Gibbon Wakefield's dictum in *A Letter from Sydney* (1829) that while in old countries modes and manners flow downwards from the higher classes, they must, in new countries, ascend from the lowest class. For football came to the colonies from Rugby and was taken up in the schools of the well-to-do and in the universities before being embraced by young men at large. But the Victorian game did have a thoroughly Australian origin in so far as its creator, or at least its John the Baptist, was the grandson of a convict, son of the colonial patriot who named him for William Charles Wentworth. 'Rise, Australia!' Horatio Wills' *Currency Lad* had exhorted readers each week. In the variety of football provoked into existence by Tom Wills's letter to *Bell's Life in Victoria*, one distinguishing rule encouraged players to rise higher in the Australian air than those of any other code. Men in Victoria would name it eventually Australian Rules; but in Sydney, where Rugby was the people's game, that sounded like blowing. As Rugby was not commonly played in Melbourne and the Victorian Rules were rarely followed in Sydney, there could be no football matches between representative teams from the two colonies.

The most nearly national sport in Australia by 1870 was horse-racing. John Dunmore Lang had declared in 1834 that the three accompaniments of advancing civilization in New South Wales were a racecourse, a public house and a gaol. It seemed to him that the first two evils led men to the third. He blamed Governor Brisbane for allowing the racing of horses to become popular and respectable. 'When I ask, *what memorial he left behind him to endear his memory to the country and to perpetuate his fame*; a hundred fingers point to the *Brisbane Cup*, and I am told to listen to the song of the drunkard, as he tosses up in the air a hat bereft of three-fourths of its brim, and hiccups out *Sir—*

Thomas—Brisbane—for ever! at the half-yearly races of Sydney and Parramatta.' In the time of which Lang wrote, the spirit of faction affected horse-racing as it did so much else in the colony. Two popular gallopers were named Currency Lass and Emancipation. The Sydney Turf Club, founded in 1825 under Brisbane's patronage, became after he left a base for opponents of his successor Darling. Supporters of Darling formed in 1828 the Australian Racing and Jockey Club, known as the Governor's Club. Horses raced under its auspices for the Governor's Cup; at the Sydney Turf Club they competed for the Brisbane Cup and the Wentworth Purse.

Racecourses were early amenities in every other colony. 'There is hardly a town to be called a town which has not its racecourse,' Trollope noticed, 'and there are many racecourses where there are no towns.' Before 1850 horses were being brought across Bass Strait and down from Sydney to Melbourne for meetings at a course on the banks of the Saltwater River, a few miles from town, known as Flemington. Here, on Thursday 7 November 1861, at the spring meeting of the Victoria Turf Club, seventeen horses raced for the first Melbourne Cup. It was a handicap event, over two miles, for horses three years and older. The winning owner took a sweepstake of twenty sovereigns and another two hundred sovereigns added by the club. The race was run in a week when many people in Melbourne were distracted by disasters: the massacre of Horatio Wills and his party in Queensland, and the death of his namesake William John Wills and Robert O'Hara Burke at Cooper's Creek. Nevertheless some four thousand people— the largest gathering at Flemington for two years—saw a horse named Archer win the new race by six lengths. Archer, owned by a squatter in New South Wales, had been walked five hundred miles from Braidwood in easy stages for the occasion. The spectators had travelled by train, river and road. They had paid a shilling and upwards to get in, and were sold food and drink between races by Spiers and Pond. Seven thousand people watched Archer win again in 1862. Until now two bodies, the Victoria Turf Club and the Victoria Jockey Club, had shared Flemington. They merged; and from 1864 the Melbourne Cup was an enterprise of the Victoria Racing Club.

The Thursday in November on which the race was run soon became a festive time in Melbourne. By 1865, when thirteen thousand people attended, the day was observed as a half holiday by public offices and banks. In 1869 members of the Legislative Assembly stopped debating an eight-hours bill and adjourned so that members could be among the twenty-five thousand spectators. In 1870 the attendance was up to thirty thousand, a figure equivalent to about one in six of Melbourne's population. By 1872 the University of Melbourne was being accused of perversity for holding examinations on the day of the race; a correspondent in the *Daily Telegraph*, signing himself 'Pleasure', argued that the hard-working young gentlemen should be able to enjoy themselves with every other class in the city on the Melbourne Cup day. Alone among public institutions in Melbourne, the university went on ignoring the Cup and imposing a hard decision on its members.

The best horses and the most distinguished people in the continent converged on Melbourne each November for the event. Pastoral families from the Western District of Victoria, the Riverina and beyond came to town for it. Governors sailed from other colonies, and as they entered the grandstand the crowd stood bare-headed for 'God Save the Queen'. Warships of the Royal Navy found it necessary to moor in Port Phillip early in November. Men spoke in the 1870s of a 'Cup fever' which seized Melbourne at this season. The telegraph and the newspapers carried news of candidates' form and prospects to country districts and other colonies for weeks before each Cup, and gave the result quickly to most of the population. 'Within the circle of our telegraphic radii,' wrote the *Argus* in 1867, 'from Bowen in Queensland to Adelaide in South Australia, the hearts of men have been leaping within them for months as they speculated on the chances of each of the twenty-nine horses entered for yesterday's great race.' The papers put their best men on to reporting the event, this *Argus* account being by Marcus Clarke, aged twenty-one: a perfect stranger 'would have thought that something of the deepest importance to the human race was at stake, so utter was the anxiety expressed on every feature of the spectators'. Six years later Clarke published in the *Herald* an imaginary report in which he pretended to have watched the race through a camera obscura on the roof of the office, in order that 'an account of a race run at Flemington at four should be in print in Melbourne at half-past 5.'

Poets as well as journalists recreated the Cup, as in John Whiteman's description of the race in 1865:

> Old Toryboy wins! Yes, the neat little grey
> Has shown them his heels for the rest of the way;
> Close followed by Panic—his number goes up,
> And three forty-four was the time for the Cup.

OLD TORYBOY WINS!
The finish of the Melbourne Cup, 1865

One of Adam Lindsay Gordon's first published works was a narrative poem about the Cup in 1866:

> The bell has rung. With their riders up
>   At the starting post they muster,
> The racers stripped for the 'Melbourne Cup',
>   All gloss and polish and lustre;
> And the course is seen, with its emerald sheen,
>   By the bright spring-tide renew'd,
> Like a ribbon of green, stretched out between
>   The ranks of the multitude.

Five galloping stanzas later, Tim Whiffler wins by a neck. In fact Tim Whiffler ran sixth. Gordon's rhymes had been written before the race for *Bell's Life in Victoria*, in which it was the custom for prophets to publish their forecasts in verse. Gordon himself rode in steeplechases at Flemington. Three weeks before the Cup in 1868 he rode Babbler, Viking and Cadger to victory in a single afternoon. When he and Viking won a race two days after the Cup, the *Argus* noticed that many winning betters had been backing the rider rather than the horse. Oscar Wilde, reviewing Gordon's verse in 1889, was amused at the relation between life and art in Australia. Only after his victory on Babbler, Wilde declared, did Gordon become really popular, 'and probably there were many who felt that to steer Babbler to the winning-post was a finer achievement than "to babble o'er green fields."' Gordon lived through only one more Cup season. The horseman and poet had his *Bush Ballads and Galloping Rhymes* published on 23 June 1870 and shot himself dead next day.

As the telegraph wires stretched farther out, more and more colonists could gossip and bet on the race. It became a staple of conversation among rich and poor across the continent. Men counted the years by Cup winners. Tales were told of people who divined the winner by other than secular methods. Before the Cup of 1870 Walter Craig of Bendigo, owner of Nimblefoot, dreamed that a horse wearing his colours would win, ridden by a jockey with a black armband. Craig deduced that he himself would not live to see the event, told friends of the dream, and died. The *Age* told the story on 9 November. 'Whether Nimblefoot will win the Melbourne Cup is another matter,' it observed, 'but should that be the case it will be somewhat startling.' Next day Nimblefoot, his jockey wearing a black armband, won the race by inches at twelve to one. A year later, a farmer in New Zealand who had saved the life of a Maori chief's grandson was said to have had his fortune told in gratitude by a tribal oracle. The farmer interpreted the message as prophecy that a horse named The Pearl would win the Melbourne Cup. He put fifty pounds on it, and the horse finished two lengths clear of the field at a hundred to one. However encrusted with legend, the story showed that the race was followed on the other side of the Tasman even before Australia and New Zealand were connected by cable in 1876.

A larger mystery attached to the Cup. How had it come to be the most truly national event of the Australian year? Visitors and residents speculated seriously or facetiously on the matter for decades. The place of the horse in this society was often mentioned. In the Great Britain of 1870, there was one horse to every twelve people. Australia had one horse to every two and a half colonists. 'It is natural', a visitor reflected, 'that in a young colony, where horsemanship is necessarily more of a habit than an accomplishment,

THE HALF-GUINEA FOLK
The lawn in front of the grandstand, Flemington

racing should occupy a foremost place in the list of its sports.' The gods, it was suggested, had fashioned at Flemington an amphitheatre fit for a great festival. One observer fancied that at the creation of Australia 'Nature, anticipating the coming of the white man, determined, at least, that there should be one memorial which science and the arts could not lay claim to; she accordingly formed a race-course, and such a race-course!... No course in the world gives such wonderful facilities to spectators, there is no need of neck straining, elbowing, toe-mangling, and climbing.' The great designer had foreseen that these white men would bring democracy. 'The hill behind the stand', another observer wrote, 'would appear to have been made by nature in order to allow the half-crown public to see the finish, as well as the half-guinea folk in the stand'. Australian natives who visited Epsom or Chantilly were amused or outraged to find how undemocratic these famous courses were, giving only the rich a continuous view of any race. This was unlike courses in Australia, and above all unlike Flemington, where the working man could see it all. What nature had given at Flemington, man improved. The grandstand impressed visitors who knew the best courses in Europe. The lawn in front of it was a glory. The Victorian Railways ran frequent trains from the city right to the course, selling patrons a single

ticket for the journey and the meeting. That arrangement, and many other attractions
of Flemington, owed much to a well-chosen official, R. C. Bagot, son of an Anglican
clergyman in Ireland, an emigrant of the 1840s who was appointed secretary of the Victoria
Racing Club in 1864 after he had planned the amenities of the Melbourne Cricket Ground.
In the 1870s he used to ride around the course an old hack named Badger which had
once been a celebrated steeplechaser and had belonged to Adam Lindsay Gordon. Bagot
was a fine administrator: he had no interest in horse-racing, but his ambition was to make
Flemington the finest course in the world, and he lived to see it attract more than a hundred
thousand people to a Melbourne Cup.

Cup fever was not necessarily connected with horsemanship, nor was it confined to
people who actually attended the race. 'The popularity of the Melbourne Cup', wrote a
student of the subject in the 1880s, 'is largely due to its being the great gambling
event of the year ... Everybody backs his fancy, if only because, unless he is a strict
Methodist, it would be peculiar not to do so.' Strict Methodists, lamenting the festival,
were apt to observe that Victoria had been affected more deeply than any other colony
by the great gamble for gold. Was it an accident that the one city virtually abandoned by
its inhabitants in the rush to the goldfields became the setting for the horse-race on which
the whole continent gambled? The betting, moreover, like the topography of Flemington,
catered for the working man. In England the classic races were for three-year-old horses all
carrying the same weight. The odds were never such as to give a poor man the hope of
making much money. The winner of a handicap race such as the Melbourne Cup, run by
horses of various ages carrying different weights, was harder for anybody including the
bookmaker to pick. The favourite came home only once in every four races, and the odds

THE HALF-CROWN PUBLIC
The hill behind the grandstand, Flemington

could be long enough to encourage dreams of affluent leisure, especially among people of Irish origin who were prominent in the racing industry and famous as punters.

To many of her citizens it was no puzzle why Melbourne should be the home of any national festival. In the years when Cup Day was made, their city was the greatest in Australia and the second most populous (to Rio de Janeiro) in that abstraction invoked by blowing colonists and kindly visitors—the southern hemisphere. Dilke made firm comparisons in 1867. 'Victoria has grander public buildings in her capital, larger and more costly railroads, a greater income, and a heavier debt than any other colony, and she pays her Governor £10,000 a year, or one-fourth more than even New South Wales.' What more natural than that the great sporting event of the year should take place in Melbourne?

People compared Cup Day with the Americans' fourth of July. In one respect the comparison was precise: it was the one day of the year when people throughout the continent concentrated on a single event. In other ways it was not satisfying, and even embarrassing. As an occasion for communal celebration Cup Day had the disadvantage that it excluded the part of the population loosely called Methodist. There had always to be a defensive note in the rhetoric celebrating it. Horse-racing, it was said, 'holds the premier position in public favour, let the preacher declaim never so strenuously against the evils that beset the paths of those who frequent the racecourse.' Yet even a moralist only lightly touched by puritanism could have qualms about Cup Day as a festival of nationality. 'If the cup of pleasure, of which we have lately drunk so deeply,' said a preacher at the time of the Cup in 1877, 'indisposes and unfits us for the serious business of life . . . it is surely a sign that we have drunk of it too deeply.' It would hardly do for Australians to have a national day that celebrated the indulgence of a vice, or even a pleasure. But did any other day express their character more aptly?

9 Anniversary Day

THE LAND, BOYS, WE LIVE IN

The people of New South Wales had one holiday of their own. They called 26 January Anniversary Day, and remembered on it the beginning of their history that day in 1788 when Arthur Phillip had the Union Jack raised at Sydney Cove. By Governor King's time it was an occasion for spontaneous drinking and dining, especially among men who had come out as convicts and prospered in freedom. Governor Macquarie, characteristically, blessed the festivity. For 26 January 1818 he declared a public holiday and had a salute of thirty guns fired, one for each year of British civilization. He put on a military review, a dinner, and a ball at which the central decoration was a portrait of Phillip created by Francis Greenway and inscribed to honour the first governor as the man chiefly responsible for the prosperous state of the colony. Convicts were encouraged to think amiably of the anniversary by getting the day off work and a pound of fresh meat.

The formal recognition conferred by Macquarie was continued by his successors. On 26 January everybody within earshot of the guns was invited to count the years since 1788. The *Sydney Gazette* gazed loyally around Australia as the anniversary came up in 1827 and blew what it saw into 'smiling villages, crowded towns, growing cities, extending settlements, infant Colonies, and thousands upon thousands of the human family who are ramifying themselves in all directions, and attract, by their unparalleled exertions, the notice and admiration of Europe.' But the main event of the day was an unofficial and sometimes even anti-official dinner in a Sydney hotel. The price of admission—eighteen shillings one year, twenty-five shillings another—guaranteed that the celebrants would be men of substance; but most of them had also in common that they had been prisoners, and the rest were men who embraced the former convicts' cause. It was an emancipists' festival, at which the diners affirmed that they belonged not to the country from which they or their fathers and other men had been sent in shame, but here. The former convict Michael Massey Robinson presented odes. At the dinner of 26 January 1820 his stanzas proposed toasts to old England, the king, the prince regent, Australia and Macquarie. In 1822 the dinner was postponed to 31 January so that it could be eaten on the birthday of Macquarie, who left the colony twelve days later. Robinson wove into the anniversary ode an emancipist's tribute to his old patron. William Charles Wentworth was back in his homeland to take the chair for the dinner of 1825, and rose with his fellows for

Robinson's toast: 'The land, boys, we live in'. Quaffing toast after toast was among the pleasures of the anniversary dinner—to trial by jury, a house of assembly, liberty of the press, the fleece, the plough, the trade and commerce of the colony, the currency lasses and other good causes. Robinson's ode of 1826 was in large part an apology for festive drinking. Its verses rolled on from pun to pun in praise of intoxication:

> Then true to the sport,
> My boys, let us *sup port*,
>   And relish the boon we inherit,
> Ever proud to proclaim
> We are Britons by name,
>   Let us prove ourselves Britons in *spirit*.

At the end, though straining for rhyme, he worked in the newly fashionable phrase 'Advance Australia' as he sang of the coming nation:

> "ADVANCE" THEN, "AUSTRALIA",
> Be this thy proud gala,
>   Which no party *spirit* can sever;
> May thy stores and thy plains,
> Echo loyalty's strains,
>   And thy watch-word be "FREEDOM FOR EVER!"

'Hail to Australia!' cried Wentworth and his companions. It was Robinson's last ode, for he died that year at the age of eighty-one.

The anniversary diners in Governor Darling's time, from 1826 to 1831, drank to the memory of Phillip and of Macquarie, whom they called the father of Australia and from whom some of them had received pardons. Darling they toasted with cold propriety, thinking of him as the obstacle when they drank to the various liberties of Englishmen. They differed among themselves about whether it was in order to pursue at the dinner the emancipists' conflict with the governor. Robert Nichols, aged twenty-one, son of a convict who had been host at anniversary dinners in Macquarie's time, denounced Darling as a tyrant when moving the toast to the natives of the colony at a gathering of 130 men in the Crown and Anchor Tavern on 26 January 1831. Some of the company objected, others applauded, and one man who called for Nichols to stop was hit by another. The president, Samuel Terry, transported in 1800 for stealing four hundred pairs of stockings but known these days as the Botany Bay Rothschild, left the chair after trying in vain to divert Nichols from the despotism of the governor to the promotion of Australian produce. But there was no dissent among the cheers when Nichols proposed the health of 'William Charles Wentworth, the patriot of Australia'. By 26 January 1832 Darling had gone. Wentworth presided over a tranquil anniversary dinner at which Sir Richard Bourke was welcomed as governor, Phillip and Macquarie and Sir Thomas Brisbane were toasted, and Darling was not mentioned.

The next anniversary, 26 January 1833, was made the occasion for a public meeting to demand a larger measure of liberty than had been given to colonists by the Constitution Act of 1828. Wentworth was at his most popular and choleric. As the meeting was in the court house, the sheriff was formally in the chair. Wentworth threatened to have the meeting remove him from it if he interrupted. James Macarthur turned up to put the exclusives' view, but a petition expressing the grievances of emancipists was adopted. It was a fine Anniversary Day ceremony.

Wentworth himself became a subject of controversy at the anniversary dinner of 1837. Early in January a 'General Meeting of Australians' resolved 'that the Anniversary of the Foundation of the Colony should be celebrated as a National Dinner amongst themselves'. The anniversary was to be annexed by natives. It was announced that Wentworth would be in the chair; but when 159 men sat down at the Royal Hotel on 26 January he was not among them, for he disapproved the decision to invite only the colonial-born. His absence, said the *Sydney Gazette*, 'gave considerable dissatisfaction'. So did his whole demeanour these days, to those who saw him moving closer towards the old exclusives, but the words 'Australian' and 'Patriot' stuck to him, and it was a rare democrat who could feel wholly antagonistic to the man who had drunk on 26 January to 'The land, boys, we live in'.

He was guest of honour at the dinner of 26 January 1846, though he disappointed radical reformers among the 250 men gathered in the hall of Sydney College by avoiding the great issue of self-government and speaking only of squatting. Even when he became an old absentee colonist in England, living the life and thinking the thoughts of a Whig aristocrat, he was not forgotten at the dinners. Richard Driver, whose father had been host at the dinner in 1837, spoke warmly of Wentworth at an Anniversary Day ceremony in 1867, praising him on behalf of 'every native-born Australian' as 'one of their greatest fellow-countrymen'.

To the population at large, 26 January was not for politics but for enjoyment. 'It was a day entirely devoted to pleasure', the *Sydney Gazette* reported in 1837. A correspondent of John Dunmore Lang's *Colonist* observed that the day was given over to feasting and intemperance. When he urged that it be devoted instead to repentance, abstinence from drink, and chastity, the *Colonist* commended the writer's piety but added that 'as a great Public Anniversary, we esteem it also as an occasion eminently calculated to call forth joyous emotions' which need not be inconsistent with religion. Intemperance was always apparent around Sydney on the day, and whether or not consistent with religion it was apt to be treated indulgently by the law. A man charged with making a disturbance in George Street on 26 January 1837 was given only three hours in the stocks after pleading 'anniversary, your honour, anniversary'.

The most spectacular pleasure was a regatta on the harbour, arranged for the first time in 1837 and so popular that it became an annual event. In Sydney's climate Anniversary Day was likely to be a better time than the queen's birthday, 24 May, for outdoor activity. The queen's birthday regattas were often spoiled by cold and rain. On 26 January more than on any other holiday except perhaps Boxing Day, the people of Sydney enjoyed the delights of sun and sea. Happy parents with shouting children making for the water, youths with smiling girls on their arms, picnics on the Domain, fruit stalls around the Circular Quay, decorated boats on the harbour: it was such outdoor scenes that the *Sydney Gazette* had in mind when it said that 26 January 1842 was 'celebrated in a manner that speaks plainly the wish, on the part of all, to make this day the grand festival of our adopted country.' Unlike Christmas, this festival provoked in the emigrant no distracting or saddening memories of home. It was made by people who by birth or disposition were Australians; and it became traditional for authors of anniversary paeans in Sydney to blend praise of their climate, their harbour and their summer way of life.

ANNIVERSARY DAY
The water jump in the Grand Bicycle Steeplechase at the Albert Ground, Sydney, 1870

'What can be brighter than an Australian sky', asked the *Sydney Morning Herald* on 26 January 1867, 'or fresher than an Australian breeze, or more luxuriant than Australian flowers; or what gayer scene than the bosom of the waters when animated by gala signals and aquatic sports?'

26 January 1838 seemed to the *Sydney Gazette* 'as lovely a day as ever the sun shone upon.' The guns boomed fifty times, for this was 'the Australian Jubilee'. Sydney glowed proudly that evening as residents illuminated their houses and fireworks exploded over the water. The *Sydney Gazette*, which had lived through more than thirty of these fifty years, saw the jubilee as the beginning of a new era in which a community once the mere receptacle of Great Britain's outcasts would assume a new character. Australian and imperial sentiments mixed easily in the rhetoric of the occasion. Toasts at the dinner in the Pulteney Hotel, where Robert Nichols presided, began with the new monarch and the royal family and the governor, and the band of the regiment played 'God Save the Queen' and 'Rule Britannia' before it struck up the air 'Hail Australia' for the toast to this land.

As New South Wales entered a second half-century of history and colonial society was transformed by the end of convictism and the flow of free emigration, some of its leaders wanted to make 26 January an occasion for marking the disappearance of old divisions and the affirmation of a new civic unity; 'these anniversaries', the *Australian* wrote in 1842, 'are worthy of the approval of the wise and the good . . . and tend to mitigate the rancour of party.' Governor Gipps, not realizing at first that the anniversary regatta was more than a sporting event, had drawn the censure of colonial patriots by declining to be its patron in 1839. After that mistake Gipps made himself plainly visible at the regatta each year, held an anniversary levee, and marked the day in 1842 by a gesture which reminded citizens that their colony would soon be older than any of its pioneers. 'First Fleeters'—survivors of 1788—were granted a pension of a shilling a day. 'We are glad', said the *Sydney Gazette*, 'that the Government have commemorated the auspicious day of our anniversary in so handsome a manner.' The pension did not violate Gipps's instruction from the Colonial Office to spend money sparingly, for by 26 January 1842 only three surviving First Fleeters could be found.

An effort was made in 1842 to broaden the character of the anniversary dinner. Robert Nichols was vice-president, but the president was a most unusual native. Captain Maurice O'Connell was the grandson of Governor Bligh and the son of the officer who now, as General Sir Maurice O'Connell, commanded the imperial military forces in Australia. They were kinsmen of Ireland's national hero Daniel. Maurice O'Connell had left the colony with his father in 1814 at the age of two and returned in 1838 as his military secretary. He and the son of a convict appeared an appropriate pair to preside

ANNIVERSARY DAY
The regatta: the flagship at Circular Quay, 1866

over a festival of harmony. Nichols, proposing a toast to General O'Connell, described the gathering as the first *great* anniversary dinner, held at last in a spirit free from all faction. But it proved impossible to avoid divisive issues. For one thing, the colony was sunk in a commercial depression; and James Martin, responding to the toast to civil and religious liberties, alleged that the economic difficulties were 'in a great measure if not entirely owing to our want of self-government—to our being subject to the foolish dictates of men such as Lord John Russell'. The president, moreover, chose to express an opinion on the most inflammable of all political questions. Proposing 'Australia the Land we live in', O'Connell said that he would like to see the transportation of convicts 'continued to a sufficient extent to meet the demand for labour on public works'. Nichols could not let that go. Who were the men, he asked, that desired a return to the system? 'They were those who had grown rich by it, and who desired it again to add still more to their heaps of ill-earned wealth.' Old emancipists cheered. Somebody shouted: 'A most scandalous imputation!' Supporters of Nichols demanded to have the interjector removed. Captain O'Connell called for order. Even at the anniversary dinner, the colonists of New South Wales in the 1840s could not stay off the terrible subject of convicts. When that issue died, the regatta came to the centre of formal ceremony on the day and the oratory was attached to it, the regatta committee acting as hosts on board their flagship to the governor and the ministry. Henry Parkes's *Empire* said in 1856 that the day was now regarded by unanimous consent as 'the national holiday'. In 1867 Parkes as colonial secretary attended the anniversary luncheon in the saloon of the *Great Pacific* and proposed the toast to 'the day

ANNIVERSARY DAY
The regatta: the finish of the Ministerial Plate, 1867

we celebrate.' He declared that in seventy-nine years, a great country had grown up. 'We had peopled great cities; we had converted wild forests into fruitful districts; we had constructed iron roads and built a University; and we had around us all the elements of civilisation'. The toast to 26 January, Parkes said, meant 'all the noble and sacred feelings of a people in their aspirations for nationality.'

A NATIONAL HOLIDAY?

Only if New South Wales was a nation could 26 January be called a national holiday. It might puzzle an American to hear language appropriate to the fourth of July used of the day by Henry Parkes, a contented subject of the British monarch. People elsewhere in Australia would think it presumptuous of Parkes to speak as if the day meant anything to them. To celebrate 26 January outside New South Wales would have been to recognize a continuity from the penal days to the present, and to admit that New South Wales had some kind of seniority. Patriots in Tasmania, Victoria and Queensland chose to think of New South Wales as a former guardian rather than a parent, and to remember the dates of their own separation from New South Wales. In Western and South Australia they celebrated their own independent foundation. Tasmanians, having the greatest incentive to forget the convict system, liked to think not only of the day in 1825 when Van Diemen's Land was proclaimed a separate colony but also of the day in 1642 when free men from Europe visited their island. As Tasman had anchored off their shore on 2 December 1642 and Darling declared the colony released from New South Wales on 3 December 1825, both events could happily be celebrated together. Separation Day in Victoria might have become an occasion for serious passion if the imperial authorities had been slower to cut the cord from Sydney. John Dunmore Lang composed a spirited imitation of the American declaration of independence for the people of Port Phillip, and at a Grand Separation Festival in 1846 the mayor of Melbourne said: 'We have with voices deep, loud and unanimous, remonstrated against being any longer continued the *dependency of a dependency*.' They had not long to wait. The movement to separate had time to arouse no more fierce emotion than impatience. After a bout of processions, sports, bonfires, illuminations and feasts when the news of it reached Melbourne, the anniversary of formal separation on 1 July 1851 could be recalled sedately and 26 January ignored. In Moreton Bay, the Brisbane Anniversary Regatta was held on 26 January when the district was part of New South Wales, but it moved after separation to 10 December, the day the first governor arrived in 1859. In Western Australia 1 June was remembered as the Foundation Day of settlement at Swan River in 1829. South Australians celebrated the proclamation of their colony in Holdfast Bay, near Adelaide, on 28 December 1836. On the tenth anniversary, five hundred guests of Governor Robe danced until daybreak. It became a general holiday, with aquatic sports at Port Adelaide and Glenelg, picnics, and demonstrations to recall the landing of the pioneers. Of all the Australian anniversaries except 26 January this one evoked the most enthusiasm. Only in South Australia could colonists affirm that convicts had no part in their history, and people in Adelaide found Proclamation Day a seemly time to declare their communal purity.

Each colony in 1870 had its own flag, which flew near the Union Jack for public festivities and was often called the national flag. A united Australian nation did not appear imminent, though it had been talked about a good deal over the past twenty years. When Earl Grey announced separation for Port Phillip, he proposed that the Australian

VAN DIEMEN'S LAND'S OWN ANNIVERSARY DAY
A race for whaleboats in the regatta held on 2 December 1838 (?)

legislatures should co-operate for certain purposes of a more than local but less than imperial character, such as communications and tariffs. But his idea of a 'general assembly' for such matters was not popular in the colonies. Politicians in Melbourne eager to be free from Sydney were in no mood to take on new responsibilities towards the old master. If there were to be one government supreme over Australia, then it seemed to the Legislative Council of Victoria in 1852 that Melbourne should be its seat; for Victoria, under divine providence, had 'attained a degree of prosperity unexampled in the history of colonization'. In New South Wales such talk sounded like the arrogance of a suddenly enriched youth. Politicians in Sydney disliked in Earl Grey's scheme the idea of giving Van Diemen's Land and South Australia, colonies inferior in wealth and population, equal representation with their own. Politicians in Adelaide and Hobart feared rather that the two larger colonies would overwhelm the smaller. In Adelaide after 1850 it could appear wise to keep a sanitary distance not only from Botany Bay and the Vandemonians but also from the polyglot hordes lured lately to Victoria. 'We have escaped . . . the contagious abominations of a gold thirsty and gold inflated populace', said a writer in the

South Australian Register in 1853. 'The true Anglo-Saxon spirit—energy, industry, honest contentment and wholesome enterprise are rife amongst us.'

Australian Federation did have advocates in the 1850s, among them Wentworth in Sydney, Duffy in Melbourne, West in Launceston and Sydney, and Lang wherever men would read his *Freedom and Independence for the Golden Lands of Australia* (1852). Their visions of a federated nation were diverse. Lang saw it as a republic. West declared: 'To strengthen the authority of the British crown no measure would be more effectual than a federal union of these colonies.' Radical and conservative, they had yet no large following, no sustaining issues. Anti-transportation did become a 'national movement', as Parkes said; but victory dissolved it quickly. Adjoining states, Duffy argued to his colleagues of the Victorian parliament in 1857, must become confederates or enemies. In the long run, perhaps; but for a while the people of these colonies could simply remain neighbouring kin, living in moderate amity interrupted by family squabbles, and their politicians debated for the most part domestic matters such as how to distribute the land and how to educate the children. They could even treat as domestic the issue of rail gauges, lines of different width being laid down in Victoria and New South Wales. Their posterity would blame the men of the 1850s for letting that happen, but so long as railways ran only from each capital city to the interior the difference caused no inconvenience. 'The continental theory is undreamt of by Australians,' Charles Dilke observed, 'owing to their having always been inhabitants of comparatively small states, and not, like dwellers in the organized territories of America, potentially citizens of a vast and homogeneous empire.'

Prophets of federation spoke sometimes of Australia, sometimes of Australasia. By 1870 Australasia could mean the mainland alone, as in *The Emigrant's Guide to Australasia, Tasmania and New Zealand* (1867); or the mainland and Tasmania; or all the Australian colonies and New Zealand. From afar in England, where the British settlements of the region might be lumped together as 'our antipodes'—meaning that they were at the other end of an imaginary diameter drawn through the globe from home—it was easy to suppose that they were closer to each other in geography and spirit than was evident on the spot. Dilke, visiting in 1866–7, heard Australasia spoken of less commonly out here than at home, and more narrowly—to include Tasmania but not New Zealand. New Zealand and Australia, he informed English readers, 'are as completely separated as Great Britain and Massachusetts.' He found scarcely a reference to either in the newspapers of the other. But only a rash prophet would have pronounced firmly in 1870 on whether or not New Zealand would be a partner in any future Australian federation. Western Australia, after all, was connected with the rest of the continent only by shipping; and it was a longer journey from Sydney to Perth than to Wellington. The rashest of all prophets, Lang, omitted both Western Australia and New Zealand from his republic, but believed that once the United Provinces of Australia were established, New Zealand would petition to join.

The electric telegraph line constructed from Adelaide to Sydney by way of Melbourne in 1858 required intercolonial planning and brought the three principal cities of Australia suddenly closer to each other. 'I rejoice at the shortening of the distance between us', Sir William Denison said by wire to his two fellow-governors on opening day. The newspapers of each city began to publish a few inches daily of telegraphic intelligence about the others, including the weather, the business of parliament, the movement of ships and the price of goods, and seasonally news of racing and cricket. One game, chess, was actually played between colonies by telegraph. Tasmania and the mainland were joined in 1859 by the great mechanical artery, as a Victorian writer called it; but the submarine cable proved as faulty as those first laid under the Red Sea and the Atlantic until a new one was laid in 1869. Electrically at least, Australia was now on the way to becoming a federation. The high cost of messages, however, kept them starkly short and deterred all but the rich from using the wires for private purposes. Nor did the telegraph necessarily enhance amity between neighbours. As Europeans discovered, an ultimatum or an order to mobilize could speed along the wires as easily as any message of goodwill, and perhaps more easily. In 1864 a Victorian police officer skirmishing with a customs man from New South Wales at Echuca, on the Murray, wired back to Melbourne for orders and was told: 'So far all right. If Customs Officer interferes further put him in the lock-up.'

Customs policy, mails, shipping and other matters were discussed when representatives of several colonies met at Melbourne in 1863, 1867 and 1870. They dined well and made large speeches to each other. At Scott's Hotel on 16 March 1867 Henry Parkes as colonial secretary of New South Wales offered a picturesque forecast that the present meeting would lead to a more permanent federal understanding, though not in a hurry. 'I do not mean to say that when you leave this room to-night you will see a new constellation of six stars in the heavens; I do not startle your imagination by asking you to look for the footprints of six giants in the morning dew, when the night rolls away; but this I feel certain of, that the mother-country will regard this congress of the colonies just in the same light as a father and mother may view the conduct of their children, when they first observe those children beginning to look out for homes and connexions for themselves.' Parkes sailed back to Sydney and persuaded his parliament to pass a bill for a Federal Council of the Australasian Colonies; but neither in New South Wales nor in any other colony was his rhetoric taken very seriously.

Tariffs were a rich source of consultation and conflict between colonies once the imperial government allowed them in 1850 to impose their own duties. Customs houses appeared on the Murray in 1855 because so many people in the southern districts of New South Wales were importing duty-free goods from Victoria. Later that year the two governments agreed to abolish the customs houses and to share the proceeds from duties collected on goods travelling up the river from South Australia. That arrangement came unstuck in 1857 when politicians in Sydney concluded that they were losing by it. At Melbourne in 1863 delegates from Tasmania and the three colonies that shared the Murray River tried to agree on a uniform tariff, and failed. The *Argus* was not surprised. 'The half-developed, unconsolidated communities of the continent', it said, 'are wholly unfit for anything like a systematic consolidated policy'. A single policy became still more unlikely when politicians in Victoria, stirred by the evangelism of David Syme in the *Age*, began in 1864 to use the tariff not merely to raise revenue but to incubate manufactures. In Victorian theory, protection of local factories would provide work for those emigrants who had come for gold and were now in danger of drifting elsewhere, and it would help to make everybody else in the colony more prosperous. The Intercolonial Conference at Melbourne in 1870 became a dogmatic exchange between Victorian protectionists and New South Wales free-traders. 'Both parties being immovable,' one of the three South Australian representatives reported, 'the co-operation of the two leading colonies was out of the question.'

There were aspects of both co-operation and competition in exhibitions of colonial products held in the capital cities. The government of Victoria began the practice in 1854 when it put up a modest version of the Crystal Palace which had housed the Great Exhibition of 1851. Displayed in it for a month were bales of wool, gold nuggets, blocks of coal and other goods which were to represent the colony at the Paris Exhibition of 1855. Similar previews of entries to exhibitions in Europe were offered from time to time in Sydney and Melbourne. Before the Paris Exhibition of 1867, Victoria 'challenged comparisons', as a Victorian author put it, 'by inviting all the other Colonies to take part'. Nearly three thousand exhibitors responded, and attendances of more than 250 000 were reported at an annex built on to the public library for the 'Intercolonial Exhibition'. The Agricultural Society of New South Wales planned a more splendid display for 1870 in Sydney, calling it the 'Metropolitan Intercolonial Exhibition' and planning an elegant new building to house it. The *Sydney Morning Herald* celebrated it with a careful superlative as 'one of the

EXHIBITION BUILDING, MELBOURNE, 1854

grandest sights ever witnessed South of the Equator'. Reporting a festival of music which was part of the exhibition, the paper noted proudly that it was a 'colonial production', meaning that it was the work of New South Wales: the organ was built in the colony, the principal singers were either natives or long residents, and 'in no other colony has there ever been such a large number of vocalists brought together and so well drilled in a short time.' Victoria was represented at the opening by the governor, Lord Canterbury, and John O'Shanassy, who both spoke fraternally; but the *Sydney Morning Herald* could not describe the occasion without having a dig at Melbourne. Sydney, it said, was the right site for this exhibition as 'the capital of the oldest of the Australian sisterhood' and 'if not the "fastest" and most self-asserting may yet claim to be the most highly favoured and stable of the group.' Like sporting contests, exhibitions provided a means for some people to become a little better acquainted with their neighbours and an opportunity for blowing at them. The sentiment they expressed was more provincial than federal.

Of particular obstacles to federation in 1870 the tariff question was the largest; but obstacles apart, there was no strong popular will to reach it. 'The idea of Australian Federation', wrote the *Freeman's Journal* in 1866, 'which we hear of occasionally, as in England they talk sometimes of the Parliament of the world, or of the Millennium, is not likely we are afraid to be very speedily realized.' The Americans at Philadelphia in 1787 had resolved larger differences than the tariff because they feared that the con-federation thrown together at the end of the revolutionary war in 1783 was too feeble to survive. In Canada a large impediment, the division of British and French nationalities, was overcome in 1867; but the Canadians had a common border with a great and turbulent foreign country to impel them towards federal union. The Australians were surrounded by oceans.

Evangelists of Australian federation encouraged colonists to see themselves not as inhabiting settlements remote from the rest of the world but as a people of the Pacific, menaced by whatever designs the governments of Europe had on that ocean and capable themselves of being its masters. In the early years of New South Wales men hoping to make their fortune had looked out to sea rather than inland. Pork from Tahiti, sandalwood from Fiji, whales and seals from the sea itself, were commodities to pursue from a port which appeared to have cultivable land only between the coast and the Blue Mountains; and even after men and animals spread across the plains, the maritime frontier attracted enterprise from Sydney. John Macarthur remained a Pacific trader long after he began to experiment with sheep. Wentworth tried in 1840 to buy a third of New Zealand. It was one of Lang's favourite themes that Australians should be not merely traders but rulers in the region. His 'Australian Anthem' of 1826 declared it the colonists' destiny to take true religion and freedom to the peoples around them:

> 'Till Christian liberty,
> Wide o'er the Southern Sea,
> Triumphant reign!

By 1870 Lang saw the future Australian empire, as he called it, ruling not only Fiji and the New Hebrides but also Tahiti and New Caledonia, taken in 1843 and 1853 by the French, who had 'neither the tact nor the spirit for the heroic work of colonization.' Lang's vision was Protestant as well as imperial; but the Irish Catholic patriot Charles Gavan Duffy had a similar, and even grander, idea of Australia's destiny, foreseeing in 1856 'a new empire, which some day would claim as its inheritance the thousand teeming islands of the Pacific, which would carry our Christian civilization into the swarming hives of China, and in the fulness of time grasp the sceptre of India.' Wentworth closed a farewell speech to his native land in 1854 by looking forward to 'its rapid expansion into a nation, which shall rule supreme in the southern world.' Perhaps Australia would be a new Britannia in the south even while the old Britannia was a great power in the north?

'Westward the Course of Empire takes its Way', George Berkeley had written of America in 1726. Lang and other Pacific imperialists liked to quote the lines and infer that Australia's turn would be next. 'History has gradually changed its theatre from the west, from Assyria and Palestine, to Greece, Italy, and Britain', the *Argus* reflected in 1853. 'Thence it has moved still westward, over the American Continent; and it was not till America reached the Pacific that history held out her hand to Australia. The once busy Euphrates is now a swamp; the Mediterranean has dwindled into a "French lake", and the Atlantic will remain an Anglo-American ferry; and the real highway of the nations will be found in the Pacific.' On 4 July 1858, the Americans' independence day, a contributor to the *Sydney Morning Herald* cried: ' "*En avant*, Australia!" ' . . . The tide of power and civilisation, now slowly drifting westward, may settle on your shores, and America and Australia one day stand side by side sister queens of the earth.' The mystical notion did not convince Dilke when he arrived in 1867 after seeing America: 'it may be doubted', he wrote, 'whether we have not become so used to trace the march of empire on a westward course, through Persia and Assyria, Greece and Rome, then by Germany to England and America, that we are too readily prepared to accept the probability of its onward course to the Pacific.' Dilke thought it unlikely that a continent whose best land was already occupied could ever support a population dense enough to inherit the mantle of empire.

The Australian Pacific empire was a dream, not a policy. The Germans or the French or somebody else would have to become more aggressively interested in the region before many colonists could be persuaded that Australia's geographical situation compelled a continental union. New Caledonia and New Guinea were very remote places in 1870, when as Duffy said 'we scarcely know what is happening beyond our own borders; we know most imperfectly who are the men of intellect and action beyond Cape Howe and the Murray.' He was citing this ignorance as an argument in favour of federation, which would 'result in the creation of a national spirit—that spirit which has inspired some of the greatest actions in history.' But could federation be achieved unless the national spirit was already there?

In 1870 it could seem more plausible to imagine each colony being nudged by Great Britain into a nationhood of its own. Charles Cowper, premier of New South Wales, proposing 'The Day We Celebrate' at the regatta luncheon on 26 January 1870, observed that the colonies' relations with the imperial government 'were rapidly approaching to those of independent states.' Trollope remarked on 'the intensity of the feeling of separate interest dividing the various colonies. 'Australia', he found ,'is a term that finds no response in the patriotic feeling of any Australian.' He was nevertheless certain that when colonial-born politicians took over from emigrants there would 'rise up among them a feeling of Australian patriotism,—rivalling, and at last exceeding, that British patriotism which is at present felt as a passion among the people.'

It was not yet easy to foresee a day on which people throughout Australia would celebrate their common nationality as Americans had long celebrated theirs on the anniversary of 4 July 1776, or as the French were to celebrate theirs, in the years after their humiliation by the Prussians in 1870, on the anniversary of the storming of the Bastille on 14 July 1789. If federation were achieved in due course, it seemed likely to come too soberly to be the object of passionate commemoration. *Marchons, marchons*, sang the French, *qu'un sang impur abreuve nos sillons*. 'The 4th of July!' wrote an American resident in London in 1827. 'What magical sounds to an American ear! What associations do they not awaken of hard fought battle-days and nights of danger, toil, privation!' The furrows of Australia were stained with no invaders' blood, and with little domestic blood by the measure of other lands. If providence went on guarding Australians against the experience of warfare, they might never have a national day. For the time being they could afford to spend their anniversary and separation days, their festivals of empire and church, and whatever other days they could win from work, in the spirit observed benignly by a widely-travelled journalist in Sydney on 26 January 1878: 'I dare say', wrote 'the Vagabond', 'a large proportion of freeborn white Australian citizens, who awoke on Saturday morning with a full intention of going in for a day's enjoyment, recked little of the occasion so long as they got their holiday. And why should they? The past affects us slightly. The real history of Australia is beginning; it behoves us to be careful how it is made. For the present, let us make the most of our holiday!'

War and Peace

War and colonies went together in imperial minds. For half a century the minister to whom governors in Australia addressed their dispatches was entitled the secretary of state for war and the colonies. To the rulers of a maritime empire the conjunction of offices made good sense. Colonies might be founded to thwart actual or possible enemies; they might be strategically valuable or dangerous; they might change hands in the course of a war; they might rebel; they had always to be guarded.

From 1793 to 1815 it was reasonable for people in New South Wales and Van Diemen's Land to believe that the ships on which the colonial settlements depended were in danger of attack by French men-of-war somewhere between England and Sydney, and it was not absurd to fear a French (and from 1812 to 1815 American) bombardment or landing on their shores. The pattern of settlement around the coast of Australia was determined in large part, before and after 1815, by apprehensions about the French. The style of government and the texture of colonial society were affected profoundly by the veterans of the war who came out as governors, officials and settlers.

Military skills and virtues were exercised by explorers, for many of whom the conquest of nature in Australia was a substitute for war. Other colonists had to struggle against the elements in ways unfamiliar to people at home. The very crossing of the seas was a perilous enterprise. No ship carrying passengers or goods or mails was sunk by the French, as it turned out, but many went down in the years of peace. Flood and fire were intermittent enemies of settlement, and drought was a constant menace over large parts of the continent. The elements gave some help to those older inhabitants who tried to repel or hold back the intruders. The aborigines were bound to be defeated; but they put up a more sustained and damaging resistance than later generations of white and black Australians were to recognize.

Among the newcomers themselves, convicts were always a possible source of riot and insurrection. Escaped convicts and other bandits from time to time endangered other people's lives and property; and once, in 1804, convicts rebelled on a scale that provoked the governor to call on all the soldiers at his command. A governor was deposed by military officers in 1808, when a quarrel at the summit of the little world of Sydney erupted into rebellion. In later decades some men used more or less seriously the vocabulary of revolution; and in 1854, on a Victorian goldfield, a band of colonists engaged in battle with British soldiers and colonial policemen. Violence less bloody but more persistent occurred on other goldfields between European and Chinese miners.

Remote from their motherland, scattered around a continent, having to rely on information months old about the state of the world, Australian colonists were ready prey for rumours about any war that might imperil them. As it happened, England was involved in only one major conflict between 1815 and 1870. Australian colonists responded to the Crimean War with an ardent loyalty from which there was little audible dissent. British regiments and warships guarded Australian shores from 1788 to 1870. Once the colonies were self-governing, the regiments were bound to withdraw before long, leaving the colonists with dilemmas about self-defence which they did not need to resolve in a hurry so long as history went on giving such immunity from attack as they had enjoyed so far.

10 Natural Enemies

THE ELEMENTS

Whether a colonist found nature in Australia hospitable or malignant depended on his location and experience and temperament; but to get there at all he had to endure a dangerous battle with water and wind. Shipwreck was a hazard faced by all the people who took part willingly and unwillingly in the migration from Europe to its new worlds; but the encounter with the elements lasted longer for voyagers to Australia and New Zealand than to any other land of European settlement. Bond or free, the traveller could never be sure until the moment he entered the calm waters of his last southern port that he would not perish at sea. The schoolmaster Thomas Braim recalled in 1846 'the thrill of rapture' as the scenery of Port Jackson burst upon him 'on a fine Australian autumn day, and that too after a long baffling with waves, buffeting with storms, patient endurance of calms, and all the monotony of a sea voyage, interrupted only by the shock of a tempest'. Richard Horne, a passenger in 1852 on the sailing ship *Kent*, told readers of Dickens's paper *Household Words* what it was like for emigrants to think that the end was coming. Somewhere in the Indian Ocean a storm struck in the middle of the night, sending water through the cabins, making the ship roll so heavily that Horne thought it must go clean over, and bringing down an avalanche of crockery, boxes, tubs and furniture. It seemed, Horne wrote, 'like the total destruction and end of all things.' Horne and his fellow-travellers were relieved to see Cape Otway, one of the most southerly points on the Australian mainland; but sometimes the end of the run to Port Phillip or Port Jackson was the most perilous part of the thirteen thousand or so miles at sea. King Island in Bass Strait was a place of terrible danger. When the *Neva*, a convict ship from Ireland, hit a reef near the island in 1835, 218 people drowned, and of the twenty-two who got ashore seven died of starvation. Ten years later the emigrant ship *Cataraqui*, from Liverpool, was wrecked there and 406 people died. In thirty years nineteen ships were wrecked off King Island, and many more ran on to rocks as they tried to enter Port Phillip. When the *Dunbar* ran against cliffs just outside Port Jackson at the end of a voyage from England one dark night in 1857, sixty-three passengers and all but one of the fifty-nine crew died, and Sydney went into mourning for them. The rich and eminent, having means and occasion to cross the sea more than once, ran greater risks than the convict or the humble emigrant who sailed out and stayed for life. The principal of the University of Sydney, John Woolley, and a leading Methodist minister, Daniel James Draper, were among 231 people who went down in the *London* en route from Plymouth to Australia in 1866. Travelling by sea from one colony to another could also be fatal. John Dunmore Lang's father was in a ship of fifteen tons which disappeared between Newcastle and Sydney in 1830. The *Admella*, a steamship of 395 tons, was wrecked between Adelaide and Melbourne in 1859 with the loss of eighty-nine lives. Adam Lindsay Gordon saw it happen and wrote a vivid poem, 'From the Wreck', about this disaster.

Water was an intermittent enemy to settlers along rivers. James Ruse, the first freed convict to go in for farming, had his crops washed away in a great flooding of the Hawkesbury River in 1806 which brought the whole colony close to starvation. Bigge censured in 1822 those emancipist farmers on the Hawkesbury and the Nepean Rivers who 'persisted in exposing themselves and their property' to the ravages of flooding, 'that they might indolently reap the benefits of the fertility that it left behind.' A flood on the Hunter drowned six people in 1832. The Murrumbidgee swept away the town of Gundagai in 1852, drowning 89 of its 250 inhabitants. Charles Harpur, farming on the Hunter, was lucky to save his house in 1857 from a flood which he believed was the worst ever seen on the river by white men. Harpur the farmer drove his sheep to high ground, from which Harpur the poet looked down at the flooded valley. 'Much of the water covering the flats, the back water', he wrote, 'is apparently as still as that of a mountain lake; but far away, through the tops of the trees, you can trace the mid-current of the river as it goes raging and boiling along in a rough, heaping line or ridge, with the countless sprays tossing and foaming and flashing out of its whole length, like the manes of ten thousand horses (I can liken them to nothing else so truly) charging in column!' In February 1860 cattle, crops and the wreckages of houses were carried out to sea by the Shoalhaven and Araluen Rivers. Ten men died when the Macleay River flooded in 1863. On sheep runs along the Darling, thousands of sheep could be washed away by a sudden torrent. Even inhabitants of cities were occasionally threatened by water, from the Yarra and Saltwater Rivers in Victoria, the Derwent in Tasmania, the Torrens in South Australia, the Swan in Western Australia and the Brisbane in Queensland.

More commonly nature gave Australians not too much water but too little. 'Our greatest enemy is the drought', a prospective emigrant was warned in 1831, 'which burns up the land in the interior, frequently destroying both crops and stock.' The rainless summer of 1812–13, drying up the plains around Sydney, gave Wentworth and his companions a powerful incentive to look for new grass on the other side of the mountains. The drought lasted another year, killing stock and reducing the harvests of wheat and corn. Charles Sturt described starkly the condition of the land through which he moved in 1828 under perpetually cloudless skies, and noted its effect on the spirits of the newcomers. 'The surface of the earth became so parched up that minor vegetation ceased upon it. Culinary herbs were raised with difficulty, and crops failed even in the most favourable situations. Settlers drove their flocks and herds to distant tracts for pasture and water, neither remaining for them in the located districts. The interior suffered equally with the coast, and men, at length, began to despond under so alarming a visitation.' When that drought broke after three years, Governor Darling ordered 12 November 1829 to be observed as a day of thanksgiving to God.

Governor Gipps declared 2 November 1838 a day of fast and humiliation in the hope that prayer and penitence might induce God to send rain to a colony which had been gravely short of it for three years. It was this drought which Lang interpreted as a message from God about Sabbath-breaking. The clergy of the Church of England were

FLOOD
The River Torrens at Port Adelaide

instructed to read these words at morning prayer: 'Consider our contrition; accept our prayers; assuage our sufferings, as shall seem to thee most expedient to us, by sending to us in our necessity, such moderate rain and showers, that we may receive the fruits of the earth to our comfort.' At Maitland a clergyman speculated in a sermon on the day of fast that God might be depriving his people of water in order to let them increase their taste for alcohol, so that in the end he might 'execute on us that signal vengeance which our incorrigible iniquity will then deserve and loudly demand.' An inscrutable providence allowed this prophet to be drowned ten years later in a waterhole near Brisbane. Days of fast and humiliation were a custom imported from England, where they were held for such occasions as wars and outbreaks of cholera. At home they went out of fashion when the queen and her advisers grew doubtful about their theological propriety. They lasted longer in Australia. When Bishop Barker of Sydney persuaded Governor Young to hold one during a severe drought in 1866, rain began to fall on the very day of contrition. A day of humiliation proclaimed by the Earl of Belmore for a drought in 1870 was followed by rains so immoderate that the rivers flooded. A reader of the *Empire* suggested that the governor be now petitioned 'to cause a day to be set aside as a day of humiliation and prayer to the Great Ruler of all things to grant a cessation of this dreadful weather, which in its ruinous and disastrous effects is unparalleled in the annals of New South Wales.'

FIRE
The bush ablaze on the railway line to Echuca, Victoria

In dry times settlers had to watch out for the most frightening visitation of all. Grass fires were liable to occur all over the continent, and in times of low rainfall they could spread into the forests. Bushfires could even threaten to destroy towns. 'To traverse the streets was truly dreadful', the *Sydney Gazette* said on 29 November 1826 of a fire which roared through the hills on a north-west wind. 'Sydney was more like the mouth of Vesuvius than any thing else.' The phenomenon attracted colonial poets. Lang composed a 'Sonnet, on the conflagration of the forest around Sydney, November 25th, 1826', in which he compared the spectacle not with Vesuvius but with hell. Charles Harpur tried over four pages of blank verse to convey the 'lurid splendour' of a bushfire, then gave up:

> But enough!
> Where are the words to paint the million shapes
> And unimaginable freaks of Fire,
> When holding thus its monster carnival
> In the primeval forest all night long?

Henry Kendall described the movement of a bushfire on a windy night, when

> with fourfold speed,
> A harsh gigantic growth of smoke and fire
> Would roar along the bottoms, in the wake
> Of fainting flocks of parrots, wallaroos,
> and 'wildered wild things, scattering right and left,
> for safety vague, throughout the general gloom.
>
> Anon, the nearer hill-side growing trees
> Would take the surges; thus, from bough to bough,
> Was borne the flaming terror! Bole and spire,
> Rank after rank, now pillared, ringed, and rolled
> In blinding blaze, stood out against the dead
> Down-smothered dark, for fifty leagues away.

An artist was inspired by a bushfire which devastated parts of Victoria on Thursday 6 February 1851, the worst day of fire ever seen in any colony. Burning leaves fell in showers on the decks of ships out in Bass Strait, and the sky was dark not only over Melbourne and Geelong but as far as north-western Tasmania. 'Many timid persons flying from the fires of Black Thursday,' a resident wrote, 'believed that the end of all things was at hand, and that the Great Day of Wrath was come.' At least ten people died, and survivors talked about the experience for the rest of their lives. 'The old colonists still repeat the most terrible stories of "Black Thursday"', a clergyman wrote nearly forty years later, 'when the whole country seemed to be on fire. The flames leaped from tree to tree, across creeks, hills, and gullies, and swept everything away. Teams of bullocks in the yoke, mobs of cattle and horses, and even whole families of human beings in their bush huts were completely destroyed, and the charred bones alone found after the wind and fire had subsided.' A young English painter who had reached Victoria in 1850, William Strutt, sketched scenes of the fire, and after returning home in 1861 made it the subject of a painting more than eleven feet wide which was exhibited at the Royal Academy and the Crystal Palace before touring the cities of Australia and being hung permanently in Melbourne.

FIRE: *BLACK THURSDAY*

It showed men, women, children and animals fleeing like a routed army. Strutt's 'Black Thursday' helped to impress on some English and many colonial minds the hostile aspect of nature in Australia.

Melbourne had only one Black Thursday. As a hazard of life for urban colonists, bushfires, like floods, were unusual. Drought was more pervasive, withering the flowers in their gardens and the fruit and vegetables in backyards, depressing the economy and thus encouraging workmen to feel hostility towards assisted emigration. It raised the price of food. 'A severe drought had just passed over the country', Henry Parkes recalled of his own arrival in July 1839; 'the price of bread rose as high as 2s. 8d. for the 4 lb. loaf, and the other necessaries of life were correspondingly dear.' But fighting the elements was not for men of the towns, as it was for squatter and farmer and rural worker, a large part of ordinary life.

For the man in the front line of settlement, the explorer, discovery could seem rather like warfare. Some explorers were actually professional soldiers deprived of war by the European settlement of 1815. Thomas Mitchell, who had served in Spain, decided in 1827 that being a surveyor in New South Wales would offer better prospects than staying in the army. Another army officer, Charles Sturt, had served in Canada, France and Ireland before coming to Sydney. 'The field of Ambition, professionally speaking,' he reflected, 'is closed upon the soldier during the period of his service in New South Wales. Had it been otherwise, however, no more honourable a one could have been open to me, when I landed on its shores in 1826, than the field of Discovery.' George Grey resigned a commission in 1839 to lead an expedition in the north-west of Australia. Edward John Eyre had planned to go into the army but used the purchase money to emigrate and buy sheep. John McDouall Stuart was the son of a soldier who intended him for the army but decided that he was too small to make a leader. Robert O'Hara Burke had served in the Austrian cavalry and the Royal Irish Constabulary before emigrating to Victoria and joining the police force. Burke's last words were to ask that a pistol should be put in his right hand and that he be left unburied; 'the picture of a fallen warrior upon the battlefield', said the governor of Victoria after his death, 'was vivid in his imagination'.

Some exploring parties had an actual and not merely metaphorical enemy, the aborigines, who collaborated with the elements to resist the white invaders. They could exploit shipwreck. After the *Maria* was wrecked off South Australia in 1840 at least nine

DROUGHT
An outstation in the far north of South Australia

men, women and children were killed by blacks and none of the other seventeen people on board was ever found. In the north of Queensland in 1872 aborigines attacked survivors from the wreck of another *Maria* and killed eleven. Aborigines used fire as a weapon, lighting homesteads with firesticks and setting fire to grass in which sheep were grazing. Settlers suspected the blacks of having lit any fire in the bush whose origin was otherwise unknown.

ABORIGINES

The first shots in the encounter between the aborigines and the intruders were fired by James Cook on 29 April 1770. When two men at Botany Bay behaved as if they did not want Cook and his companions to come ashore from a small boat, Cook fired a warning shot from a musket. One of the men replied by throwing a stone. Cook fired a second musket loaded with small shot, some of which hit the man. He and his comrades picked up spears and threw them at Cook's party. So Cook fired a third time, the two men made off, and the advance agents of empire landed unopposed. Henry Kendall, reading a century later Cook's humane account of the meeting, compared the two defenders with ancient Britons resisting the legions of Caesar.

Phillip, commissioned both to conciliate and protect the natives (as they were called in the early days) and to secure his own people from attack by them, found cause at first to hope that relations would be quite peaceful. As he entered Port Jackson on 21 January 1788, Phillip noticed a group of aborigines standing on the shore just inside the northern head of the harbour. Twenty of them waded into the water, accepted gifts, examined his boats, and carried themselves in a manner which moved the standard-bearer of British civilization to call the place Manly Cove. But soon the aborigines around Sydney became a nuisance, throwing stones, stealing food and tools. On 29 May 1788 at Rushcutters Bay two convicts were speared to death. Phillip searched hard for the killers, though in vain; and he tried to find out whether convicts had done anything to provoke aggression. Phillip himself was speared in the shoulder by a native when he was out at Manly Cove trying to persuade a black protegé named Bennelong to return with him to Sydney.

It became public policy under Phillip's successors to keep natives away from the settlements. They remained a hazard on the outskirts, skirmishing with soldiers and killed in unknown numbers by the private weapons of individual settlers. Not all learned as quickly as Cook's momentary antagonists that their spears and sticks and stones were no match for gunpowder. In 1816 at Airds, thirty miles from Sydney, a military detachment could not stop a large band of blackfellows from throwing spears until fourteen of them had been shot dead, many wounded and others taken prisoner. Like Phillip before him, Macquarie had begun with high hopes which were disappointed by experience. 'I begin to entertain a fear', he confessed in 1816, 'that I shall have a more arduous task than I imagined, tho' I am still determined to persevere in my original plan of endeavouring to domesticate and civilise these wild rude people.' When they attacked white men, however, he believed it necessary to inflict exemplary punishment by shooting aborigines dead and hanging their bodies from trees.

All the inland explorers were invaders of tribal territory, whether they knew it or not. Some had better luck than others with aborigines, moving across the land or along the rivers without being attacked. Charles Sturt was proud of his impeccable treatment of the blacks. Hamilton Hume regarded peaceable dealings with them as one of the explorer's skills. Ludwig Leichhardt's party was attacked by aborigines of the far north in 1845 and John Gilbert was killed; but Leichhardt knew that the aggressors had been provoked by two aborigines with the expedition who had molested their women. Thomas Mitchell's experience was bloody. On his first expedition, in 1831–2, blacks killed two of his men and plundered the stores. On the second, in 1835, they killed the superintendent of the Botanic Gardens in Sydney, Richard Cunningham. Mitchell decided to return home after a fight on the Darling in which several aborigines were killed. They had shown themselves, he reported, 'implacably hostile and shamelessly dishonest.' Mitchell described his party of 1836 as 'the army with which I was to traverse unexplored regions, peopled, as far as we knew, by hostile tribes.' When his army met a body of aborigines whom he thought he recognized as the trouble-makers of 1835, Mitchell set an ambush in which seven were shot dead and the rest fled. After an official enquiry into this episode Governor Bourke's executive council expressed regret that Mitchell had not been more conciliatory; but in view of the aborigines' numbers and threatening aspect, it could not blame Mitchell severely. His knighthood was held up while the Colonial Office investigated the affair, and it was duly granted in 1839. Sir Thomas Mitchell's fourth expedition, of 1845–6, turned back on the Barcoo when short of supplies and threatened by aborigines. When John McDouall Stuart raised the Union Jack at the very centre of the continent on 22 April 1860 he gave three cheers, so he wrote in his diary, 'as a sign to the natives that the dawn of liberty, civilization and Christianity was about to break on them.' The name Attack Creek recorded how some of the natives responded two days later, throwing boomerangs and setting fire to the grass.

Until the natives were exterminated or tamed or driven to regions unwanted by newcomers, the advance of white settlement was bound to lead to the shedding of blood, most of it aboriginal. Black and white endured on the frontier a relationship of wariness and tension punctuated by what the whites called outrages, affrays and incidents, and on occasions flaring into engagements which they described in the language of warfare. Outrages were committed by aborigines because their women had been kidnapped or their waterholes taken or for some less apparent reason. Outrages were committed by settlers because their grass was burned or their animals were speared or because they believed it necessary to force the aborigines back. Outrages were committed on each side in retaliation for outrages by the other. Gipps wrote in 1838 of 'the extreme difficulty of devising any measure, that shall effectually check the outrages which, I regret to state, are now of frequent occurrence beyond the boundaries of location.' Although the ultimate outcome was inevitable, the doomed defenders could inflict substantial casualties and could even win particular engagements if they had the numbers and the stealth. Captain Patrick Logan, commander of the new convict settlement at Moreton Bay, was killed by natives in 1830. They were perhaps the only aborigines ever celebrated in a popular ballad. As a convict poet saw the tyrant's death:

> Like the Egyptians and ancient Hebrews,
>   We were oppressed under Logan's yoke,
> Till kind Providence came to our assistance,
>   And gave this tyrant his mortal stroke.

Eight drovers taking sheep and cattle south to Port Phillip were killed in 1838. Colonists

ABORIGINES AT WAR
Port Lincoln, South Australia, 1864

around Port Fairy declared that in two months of 1842 the aborigines had killed four whites
and wounded six others, and stolen or maimed nearly four thousand sheep. The blacks
struck often enough for thousands of white men, women and children in pastoral districts
to live in fear of their lives. The horror of such a raid was articulated by Charles Harpur
in a long poem in blank verse which he published in 1853. 'The Creek of the Four Graves'
is about a settler and four of his men, out searching for fresh grass, who are attacked by
painted savages as they sleep. The four men are clubbed to death; the master shoots one
black and escapes. The killers are perceived as merciless and incomprehensible fiends.

Colonists demanded protection and vengeance against black aggression. In the plains
beyond the Blue Mountains, Governor Brisbane ordered military intervention in 1824
after a number of stockmen and many animals had been killed and graziers demanded
'prompt and effective' action. Martial law was proclaimed, and soldiers were sent to the
district. In Van Diemen's Land Governor Arthur, a man experienced in both warfare
and colonial administration, decided that the problem of friction between black and white
required a military solution. On 15 April 1828 he issued a proclamation forbidding all
natives to enter the settled districts, and on 1 November declared martial law in those
areas. White settlers were now free to behave as if they were in a state of war with the blacks.

Two years later Arthur declared the whole colony under martial law, and five thousand men under his personal direction, including hundreds of convicts, tried to drive all the aborigines in the colony—perhaps a thousand men, women and children—towards Tasman's Peninsula in the south-east of the island. A 'black line' of sentinels was formed across a front of thirty miles. But the blacks slipped through it, some of them attacking settlers in its rear. A young woman was speared in the breast; a settler who had sent all his men to the line was killed by blacks who plundered his house. 'This man was at the battle of Trafalgar,' wrote John West, 'and present when Nelson fell—himself reserved to perish in Tasmania, by savage hands.' In a month of operations two aborigines were caught, at a cost of nearly thirty thousand pounds. West, who came to Van Diemen's Land in 1838, described the engagement in mock-heroic prose. 'The settler soldiers returned to their homes, their shoes worn out, their garments tattered, thier hair long and shaggy, with beards unshaven, their arms tarnished; but neither blood-stained nor disgraced. They had seen much and dreaded more; but, in general, they met no other enemies than scrub and thorns, and they sat down on their own hearths, happy in having escaped the ramrods of their friends . . . Yet though not very glorious, perhaps no evening in the year passes, but some settler's fireside is enlivened by a story of the fatigues and frolics of the Black War.' Many of the aborigines who eluded Arthur's soldiers died in the next few years of diseases, and by 1835 most of the rest were caught by peaceful conciliation and put into an evangelical prisoner-of-war camp on an island named after Matthew Flinders.

In Western Australia as in Van Diemen's Land a governor took charge of a military operation against aborigines. A number of the first white residents were speared. 'No person should move without a gun', James Henty advised in 1831; 'although they appear at times very friendly they are treacherous and never to be depended upon.' The contingent of British soldiers available to the governor, Captain James Stirling R.N., seemed to Henty a tiny force for the situation. The governor, he wrote, had 'distributed our *Army* (50 Men)' in small parties to five centres between Perth and King George Sound. In 1834 a punitive expedition of soldiers, police and settlers set out under Stirling's command to a place called Pinjarra. On 28 October the force met seventy or eighty blacks. Between fifteen and twenty of them were shot dead, and the superintendent of police died of spear wounds. The engagement entered Western Australian history as the Battle of Pinjarra. A settler who had expressed admiration for the natives until they began burning grass and destroying stock reflected in his diary that the treatment dealt out at Pinjarra was likely to be the most humane policy in the end.

More aborigines were killed by private enterprise than by official expeditions. How many, nobody knew. Heaps of bones which had been aborigines were no unusual sight in squatting country. They were killed not only for what they had done and for what they might do, but even for sport, like kangaroos or emus. A civilized man could take potshots at aborigines with a clearer conscience if he genuinely believed them to be more animal than human. 'The face of the emu', wrote an observer in 1846, 'bears a most remarkable likeness to that of the aborigines of New South Wales.' To regret their disappearance, said a colonist of Port Phillip in 1847, was 'hardly more reasonable than it would be to complain of the drainage of marshes or of the disappearance of wild animals.' Anticipating the early extinction of the original inhabitants made it all the easier for colonists to use the word 'native' as if it belonged unambiguously to whites born in Australia.

Governors sometimes used British soldiers to deter outrages by aborigines because they knew that the alternative, leaving it to citizens, would be bloodier. Gipps rejected a request from settlers of Port Phillip in 1838 that they be allowed to 'levy war against the Blacks', and proposed instead to establish military posts between Sydney and the south. His successor FitzRoy, telling London in 1847 why a detachment of troops was necessary at Moreton Bay, argued that it was better to check the aborigines by a small military force 'than to run the chance of a collision between these people and the Settlers, and the consequent retaliatory proceedings which would ensue.' Whenever an official wrote in that vein in the 1840s, Myall Creek was not far from his mind.

Myall, as Mitchell wrote in his journal, was a name which natives close to civilization 'apply in terror and abhorrence to the "wild blackfellows", to whom they usually attribute the most savage propensities.' But it was not the blackfellows who displayed savagery at the Myall Creek station in northern New South Wales in 1838. Here on Sunday 10 June twelve stockmen, eleven of them convicts and one a native of the colony, killed at least twenty-eight aborigines. They did it easily, for they had guns and their quarry were unarmed and unsuspecting; some were women and children. Seven of the stockmen were condemned to death. If the sentences were carried out they would be the first men executed in Australia for murdering aborigines; 'they all stated', Gipps wrote, 'that they thought it extremely hard that white men should be put to death for killing Blacks.' The governor was unmoved by widespread appeals, even demands, for clemency, and the seven men were hanged in December. The decision was approved in London, for the Aborigines' Protection Society had lately aroused much concern at home about what the colonists of Australia were doing to the native inhabitants. In New South Wales the verdict and sentence were denounced indignantly. 'We say, protect the whites as well as the blacks', declared the *Sydney Morning Herald*. 'Protect the white settler, his wife, and children, in remote places, from the filthy, brutal cannibals of New Holland.' But Gipps had some support in the colony, especially from clergymen. 'If the native black be but an inferior animal', one said in a sermon, 'he is at least entitled to brotherly love, and as a fellow creature he is entitled to justice.' The hangings were thoroughly approved by Charles Harpur, who saw them carried out in Sydney. The poet's imagination could move him to feel as deeply for black victims of white massacre as for white victims of black. Nearly ten years later he thought of a woman and child who had survived the slaughter at Myall Creek and composed 'An Aboriginal Mother's Lament'; and in 1858 he wrote again of the episode as a stage in the extinction of the race.

Gipps was instructed in 1838 to reserve certain lands for aborigines and appoint protectors to educate them, make them Christians, and defend them against settlers. The scheme foundered, so it seemed to James Stephen of the Colonial Office, on 'the hatred with which the white man regards the black.' Alexander Harris put it differently. When aborigines heard that they were to be 'protected', he wrote, they assumed that they could do no wrong. 'The blacks cannot be conciliated unless by giving up their country. If they are to be intimidated, it must be by something that is more prompt and effective than their own spear, and less dilatory than our law.' There was no protection for aborigines on the border of Port Phillip and South Australia when settlers resolved to give them the only sort of education that public opinion in the area believed appropriate. A settler named Brown had been murdered. His neighbours, wrote a colonist who heard about it later, 'decided to take the law into their own hands . . . a call to arms was made . . . It was a bad day for the ill-fated darkies. The horsemen came up with them in the ranges behind Narracoorte, and saw one fellow carrying poor Brown's gun, and a lubra wearing a coat. They opened fire and many of the blacks went under. They made no show of resistance . . . The lesson given to the blacks that day made them understand that they must respect the lives of white men.'

Some aborigines threw in their lot with the newcomers. In the first weeks of settlement at Melbourne, a blackfellow saved the lives of white men and their families in circumstances inscribed over his grave in the Melbourne General Cemetery thirty years later: 'This stone was erected by a few colonists to commemorate the noble act of the native chief Derrimut who by timely information given October 1835 to the first colonists Messrs Fawkner, Lancey, Evans, Henry Batman and their dependants, saved them from massacre, planned by some of the up-country tribes of aborigines.' A guide named Jackey Jackey stuck by the explorer Edmund Kennedy when he was attacked and killed by blacks on Cape York peninsula in 1848, buried his master's body, and led an expedition to find it next year. He was rewarded by FitzRoy with a brass breast-plate and a gratuity, and died in 1854 when he fell drunk into a camp fire. Native police were recruited and trained to pursue and apprehend blacks. The white commandant of native police in Port Phillip reported proudly in 1845 on their coolness and determination in an encounter with aborigines who had stolen sheep from a station. But they were apt everywhere to take to drink, and they were sometimes suspected of spying for their own tribes. It was the custom of their white officers to travel behind them rather than ahead, in case of mishap or treachery. Where they were still employed by 1870 it was mainly for their uncanny skill at following tracks. 'The native police, or "black trackers," as they are sometimes called', said a guide to Australia in 1867, 'are . . . a very clever expedient for coping with the difficulty . . . of hunting down and discovering murderous blacks, and others guilty of spearing cattle and breaking into huts'.

Native police were kept busy in the Moreton Bay District—from 1859 the colony of Queensland—as the pastoral frontier moved north. A massacre at Hornet Bank on the Dawson River in 1857, when a black servant of the Fraser family led a band of comrades to kill Mrs Fraser, seven of her eight children, and six other people, was followed by the slaughter of about sixty aborigines. The killing of Horatio Wills and eighteen other people at Cullinlaring in 1861 was avenged by the death of perhaps 170 blacks, some shot by native police and others by settlers imposing what seemed to them natural justice. The Jardine brothers, travelling north in 1864–5 to settle at Cape York, were harassed by blacks for more than five hundred miles. 'We shot our way through', they said. On 18 December 1864 they fought what came to be known as the Battle of the Mitchell River, in which hundreds of myalls charged the white men, hurling spears, to be shot down by carbines. The Jardines' party suffered no casualties; but over the whole of north Queensland, it was once estimated, more than one in every ten white men was killed by aborigines during the 1860s. The blacks who were shot dead probably numbered thousands. Life was never safe, said the manager of one station, 'and the only wise thing to do on seeing a black was to shoot and shoot straight, otherwise he would certainly spear you.' Charles Dilke visited the region during his tour of 1867, and reflected: 'We live in an age of mild humanity, we are often told; but, whatever the polish of manner and of minds in the old country, in outlying portions of the empire there is no lack of the old savagery of our race.' The gentler class of settlers in Queensland had sometimes to restrain 'station blacks', eager to please their new masters, who had learned that the remedy for thefts by the myalls was to shoot them.

ABORIGINES AT PEACE
George Street, Sydney, in the 1820s

Aborigines became an unfamiliar sight in the densely settled regions of the continent. What gunfire began, quieter agencies continued. They were an oddity in the part of New South Wales—from Sydney to Bathurst—visited by Charles Darwin in 1836. Darwin noted alcohol, disease and famine as causes of their decline in numbers, but sensed also 'some more mysterious agency at work . . . The varieties of man seem to act on each other in the same way as different species of animals—the stronger always extirpating the weaker.' One day people would attribute that theory to Darwin himself; but it appeared as mere common sense to the colonists of Australia in 1836, as to Europeans elsewhere in contact with primitive societies. In Victoria, where the aboriginal population fell from perhaps 11 500 at the beginning of pastoral settlement to about 2000 thirty years later, David Syme's *Age* declared in 1858—a year before *The Origin of Species*—that the aborigines of the colony were destined for extermination, and that his readers could do no more than 'smooth the pillow of a dying race'. A Russian who visited Sydney in 1863, driving back by coach from an outing to Manly, came across a crippled brown figure by the road, grunting for alms. This stupid and hopeless figure, he learned, was Ricketty Dick, the last survivor in the district of the people whose manliness had impressed Phillip. The visitor was not indignant, but puzzled. Was the law of nature *right*, he wondered, which condemned this pitiful race to extinction? He threw a shilling down to Ricketty Dick and had the coach drive on.

The defenders did not use the white man's firearms against him; for unlike natives of agricultural societies, these people had nothing to offer in exchange to the traders who might have sold them weapons. When one side had guns and the other had spears and axes and fire-sticks, a battle was so uneven that there was always an element of extravagance or irony in calling their contest a war. Certainly it seemed less than war to Americans who compared the long encounter with Indians in their own continent. 'They do not carry on any systematic attacks', an American visitor to Sydney wrote of the aborigines in 1839, 'and their fears of the whites are so great, that large companies of them have been dispersed by small exploring parties and a few resolute Stockmen.' Nor did the aborigines compare favourably as warriors with the natives of New Zealand. The Maoris' ability to resist so long, fighting with the invader's own weapons and exhibiting military qualities similar to his own, earned them some indulgence and much praise, including the title 'Britons of the south'. George Higinbotham called the Maoris in 1869, just before their subjugation was complete, 'the noblest race of uncivilized men known in the world'. At a ceremony in Sydney in 1864 the governor, Sir John Young, pinned a Victoria Cross on the chest of a marine who had fought in New Zealand. It was a new and precious award, introduced by the queen in 1856 to recognize the individual gallantry of ordinary soldiers and sailors. Conferring it on a marine for valour in New Zealand was a tribute both to him and to the Maoris. Nobody ever thought of describing as valorous any deeds performed against aborigines in Australia. The black wars of this continent would never enter comfortably into national memory. Towards the defeated Maoris the victors could feel respect and affection; they might speak of the encounter as a kind of blooding. The dispersed and dwindling aborigines could more easily inspire pity and shame. In 1870 James Bonwick ended his book *The Last of the Tasmanians; or, the Black War of Van Diemen's Land* by reporting that all the aboriginal inhabitants of the island were now dead. 'We cover our faces', he wrote, 'while the deep and solemn voice of our common Father echoes through the soul, "Where is thy brother?"'

Poets and historians and politicians could describe Australia as a land free of strife, as if the occupiers of the land had never resisted the European intrusion. A sense of guilt must have pushed from many Australian minds the knowledge that thousands of blacks had been killed by whites; but they tended also to forget the hundreds of white settlers killed by blacks, as if there was no pride or comfort or useful lesson to be had from contemplating the dead on either side.

11 Bushrangers

BOLTERS

The most persistent disturbers of the peace in Australia were the bushrangers. Their activities caused that name to be coined in the first generation of settlement. Decade after decade they robbed and shot and threatened other colonists, aroused terror and admiration, bothered local agents of law and order and worried colonial governments. Their normal fate was to be killed or captured; but it was not certain that they were extinct in 1870.

The *Sydney Gazette* had news of two on 24 August 1806: '*Fitzgerald*, the bushranger last week advertised as having escaped from the county gaol, is again in custody. The unaccountable hardihood of this extraordinary delinquent was never more extravagantly displayed than upon his re-apprehension . . . *Murphy*, the bush ranger, was last week in custody for a short time near Parramatta; but craftily conducting himself with apparent submission to his captors until an occasion offered, he tripped up the heels of his unsuspecting *guards*, and arming himself with a reap hook, made off without further interruption.' Fitzgerald and Murphy were early members of a long line: wild men, makers of vivid news, having prodigies of strength and daring attributed to them; and like many of their successors they had Irish names. Sometimes in the penal days they were called bolters, to describe how they came to be living in the countryside; or banditti; but bushrangers became the most common description. They resembled the highwaymen of England; and one of the most notorious, Michael Howe, had actually been transported to Van Diemen's Land for highway robbery. But out here they worked on roads not fit to be called highways, and the bush was their element. They pounced out of it, vanished into it, and stayed free by knowing it better than their pursuers.

What made a man a bushranger? Governor Macquarie believed that many convicts assigned to work for settlers were provoked to bolt by brutal treatment. Judge Therry observed that all the bushrangers he knew were men who had been whipped first. There was certainly more whipping of prisoners here than at home. Matthew Brady suffered 350 lashes in four years before he escaped from a penal settlement in 1824 and went into the bush of Van Diemen's Land. Frank Melville, a bushranger in Victoria from 1851 to 1854, had been flogged frequently in his ten years of imprisonment at Port Arthur. Experience of the lash perhaps disposed bushrangers to display the bravado for which they were famous: the scourger's clients, an army officer in Sydney remarked in 1836, were made more reckless by flagellation. Some men behaved, however, as if they were not merely driven to bushranging, but drawn to it. 'The vanity of being talked of, I verily believe, leads many foolish fellows to join in this kind of life', wrote Peter Cunningham. People did indeed talk, and write, and sing, about them. No law-abiding settler of Van Diemen's Land was better known than Matthew Brady or Michael Howe. In New South Wales the name of Jack Donohoe (or Donahoe or Donahue) became a legend within the five years of his colonial lifetime. Donohoe was an Irishman who arrived as a convict in 1825, was sentenced to death in 1828 for robbing bullock drays on the road to Windsor, bolted, and for more than two years was one of a gang of ten or twelve young men who ranged the bush from Bathurst to Yass, from the Hunter to the Illawarra. He was killed in a gun battle on 1 September 1830 at the age of 23 and remembered in story, verse and song.

Apart from fame, what were bushrangers hoping to achieve? Permanent escape? Many of the Irish, a people notorious among their neighbours for credulity and ignorance, were said to believe that a colony of white people lay within four hundred miles' walk of Sydney, where the comforts of life could be had without work; or that there was land all the way to China, or even to Ireland. Donohoe, who knew more geography than that, told some victims in 1829 that he would have gone to Sydney, fenced his swag, and left the country, were it not for the large reward on his head. 'I would rather meet my death by a ball than the gallows', he said. The Donohoe who entered legend was a man determined to roam the bush in freedom instead of living as a slave of the government.

Sometimes a bushranger used what sounded like the language of insurgency. John Jenkins, sentenced to death for murdering the lawyer and editor Robert Wardell on his estate at Petersham, told the crowd at his scaffold in 1834 that he had shot Wardell not for gain but because he was a tyrant towards other convicts. 'I have one thing to recommend you as a friend', he went on, 'if any of you take the bush, *shoot every tyrant* you come across, and there are several now in the yard who ought to be served so.' No sane bushranger imagined that he and men like him could overthrow a colonial government; but he could well think of the bush as his own domain, a land from which he could make raids across the frontier of settlement and to which he could then withdraw. Macquarie admitted the virtual impossibility of catching bushrangers in their own element when he offered a free pardon in 1814 to all, except murderers, who gave themselves up by the end of the year. Some did so, including accomplices of Michael Howe in Van Diemen's Land; but Howe found new recruits among bolting convicts and deserting soldiers, with whom he looted and burned in March 1815 the property of a magistrate hated for his severe punishments, and ransacked the settlements of New Norfolk, killing one settler and wounding others. The lieutenant-governor, Colonel Thomas Davey, did Howe's gang the honour of declaring martial law against them. Before long Howe was treating his men as subjects bound by an oath of obedience and addressing the authorities in Hobart Town as if bush and town were neighbouring states at war. 'Lieutenant-Governor of the Woods', Howe signed himself in letters to Government House. Matthew Brady's gang captured the town of Sorell for a night after disarming and locking up a band of soldiers who were out searching for them. Colonel George Arthur's secretary issued a proclamation which began: 'Government House, April 14th, 1825. It has occasioned the Lieutenant-Governor much concern that the continued outrages of the two prisoners, McCabe and Brady, have led to the death of another settler. His Honour has directed that a reward of £25 shall be given for the apprehension of either of these men'. A few days after this message was circulated, a notice signed by Brady was stuck on the door of an inn: 'Mountain Home, April 20th,

1825. It has caused Matthew Brady much concern that such a person known as Sir George Arthur is at large. Twenty gallons of rum will be given to any person that will deliver his person unto me.' Brady's gang threatened to attack the town of Launceston early in 1826. They were driven off, and their leader taken, only after the commander of the imperial military forces in the colony had mounted a serious campaign against them. Such men were going in for effrontery rather than rebellion, filling their months of freedom with actions expressing an affinity with the legendary outlaws of the old world. In the long run they were bound to surrender, be captured or be killed.

They were pursued by soldiers and by settlers formed into bodies of volunteers. Black trackers were engaged to hunt for hidden camps; but in Van Diemen's Land one of them, named Mosquito by his employers, himself took to the bush. Mosquito was both an aboriginal and a transported convict, having been sent from New South Wales for murdering a woman. Now he led a band of aborigines who murdered isolated settlers before being flushed in turn by a native tracker and taken to Hobart Town, where Mosquito the black bushranger was executed in February 1825. After 1825 the bushrangers of New South Wales were also pursued by mounted troopers. From Bathurst in August 1825 the commandant reported to Sir Thomas Brisbane 'an extensive confederation among certain runaway Convicts, commonly called Bushrangers, for the purposes of Robbery and Murder'. Colonel William Stewart, commanding officer of the military forces, arranged for a contingent of mounted police to be formed by taking horses from the shafts of government carts and having soldiers ride them over the mountains to Bathurst, where they put themselves at the disposal of the civil authorities. Tranquillity was soon reported from the Bathurst district, and the mounted police became a regular force in New South Wales. Regiments leaving home would recruit fifty men more than their strength, to supply men for mounted police work. They wore uniforms similar to those of British dragoons, and they carried the carbines, pistols and swords used in cavalry regiments. Their military style was like that of the Royal Irish Constabulary, formed between 1814 and 1836, which became a model for police forces in various parts of the empire. They were similarly unpopular among many of the people they were supposed to be protecting. Having to be as fast and as tough as their quarry, the mounted troopers were inclined to treat prisoners in a manner that attracted criticism, such as handcuffing a captive to a stirrup and setting the horse at a smart pace. The troopers, as they came to be known, were kept busy. It was a trooper who shot Donohoe in 1830. In the first five months of 1835 alone, mounted policemen in New South Wales apprehended 220 bushrangers and runaways.

The law itself was hardened in 1830 when the Legislative Council passed a measure known informally as the Bushranging Act, permitting anybody to arrest without warrant a person suspected of being 'a transported felon unlawfully at large' and making him prove that he was not. The act allowed justices of the peace to sentence men to three hundred lashes, two years in a chain gang or three years in prison. Cases of perverse and otherwise unjust arrest were the talk of the colony, especially of currency lads. An emigrant or an emancipist could normally produce a document proving that he had arrived in the colony free or been granted his freedom; but the native-born colonist might have no way to identify himself. One lad told Alexander Harris that he had 'passed seven weeks out of three months marching in handcuffs' under groundless suspicion of being a bushranger. Governor Bourke agreed with judicial opinion that the act was contrary to the spirit of the laws of England, but believed that 'it would occasion very great dissatisfaction amongst

the free People of the Colony to deprive them of the protection which this law affords.'
It helped the courts of the colony to achieve a statistic which seemed remarkable to the
House of Commons committee on transportation in 1837; 'in proportion to the respective
population of the two countries', the committee found, 'the number of convictions for
highway robbery (including bushranging) in New South Wales, exceeds the total number
of convictions for all offences in England'.

Despite the Bushranging Act and the mounted police, bushrangers went on
menacing the property and life of settlers, especially in outlying areas. Fifty outrages were
reported from the Bathurst district in a few months of 1840. The cry of 'Bail up!' became
familiar to travellers on all the main roads. Authors explained the term for English readers.
'The bushrangers', wrote Mrs Charles Meredith in 1844, '"bail up," i.e. bind with cords,
or otherwise secure, the male portion'. Alexander Marjoribanks interpreted it in 1847 as
'the colonial phrase for those who are attacked, who are afterwards all put together, and
guarded by one of the party of the bushrangers when the others are plundering.' The cry
became more familiar still in the 1850s, when bushrangers were provided with the perfect
commodity to plunder.

GOLD ROBBERS

From 1851 the main object of bushrangers was to steal gold as it travelled along the roads
from the diggings to Sydney and Melbourne. In Victoria the most familiar marauder on
these routes was Frank Melville, whose gang stole much gold from travellers in the three
years between his arrival from Van Diemen's Land late in 1851 and his capture at Geelong.
Some of the gold robbers, like Melville, were convicts; but the transported population was
growing too old now to provide many recruits for such a vigorous life. Free immigrants
were numerous among the bushrangers of the 1850s, and in the 1860s the occupation was
largely taken over by young native-born men, some of whom had convict parents. They
were sometimes said to be disappointed diggers; but in fact the bushrangers were rarely
men who sought gold by the pick and shovel and the cradle before they began taking it with
guns. Many had Irish names. Most who were arrested gave their religion as Roman
Catholic; but that did not make them active worshippers. They were boys of the bush,
untamed by the teachings of priest or parent or schoolmaster. Frank Melville was one of
several bushrangers who emigrated from Tasmania to Victoria in search of richer
opportunities; after 1860 the occupation disappeared from the island. In South Australia,
which had neither convicts nor goldfields, bushrangers were few before and after 1851,
and were apt to be described as visitors from the penal colonies.

Among the new generation of bushrangers were men at home in more than one
colony. Daniel Morgan, a solitary and murderous man, left New South Wales in April
1865 to bail up people in Victoria. The police there had boasted that he dared not cross
the Murray; but they were no more able to catch him than police north of the border, and
it was a station hand, not a policeman, who shot Morgan dead near Wangaratta. Frank
Gardiner, alias Christie, alias Clarke, alias The Darkie, born near Goulburn in 1830 to a
Scottish father and a part-Irish, part-aboriginal mother, had his first conviction for
horse-stealing at Geelong in 1850 and his second at Goulburn in 1854. During 1862
Gardiner, John Gilbert, Ben Hall and other associates defied the police of New South
Wales, robbing mail coaches and bailing up scores of travellers. On 15 June Gardiner's
gang held up an armed gold escort at Eugowra, between Forbes and Bathurst, and got

BUSHRANGERS HOLD UP A MAIL COACH

away with gold and bank notes worth nearly £14 000. It gave much unholy pleasure among native-born democrats that the mounted police unable to catch the robbers were commanded by a new chum with the name of Sir Frederick Pottinger. A writer in the *Empire* said that it was difficult to know where the governor's rule ended and 'General' Gardiner's began, and offered the jocular forecast that 'ultimately those who object to being robbed, shot, or having their throats cut, may expect to find themselves cooped up in a small space around the shores of Botany Bay and Port Jackson.' In one of many ballads about the gang not even those shores were safe:

> 'And next to Sydney city we mean to make a call,
> For we're going to take the country,' says Dunn, Gilbert and Ben Hall.

Gardiner disappeared, and in 1864 was arrested in Queensland. He was tried in a crowded court in Sydney, found not guilty by a jury on one charge, arraigned on another charge, convicted, and sentenced to prison for thirty-two years. Gardiner's comrades stayed within New South Wales, teasing the police and discomforting the government. Ben Hall, born in 1837 of emancipist parents, led the gang after Gardiner left it and became the Jack Donohoe of his time. Hall, Gilbert, John O'Meally and two other young men occupied the town of Canowindra, south-west of Bathurst, for three days in October 1863, rounding up the population in a hotel and telling tales of their own exploits. 'The bushrangers treated all hands to grog,' the *Bathurst Free Press* reported, 'but we have not heard of their treating any one of them with violence or taking anything from them. Gilbert went out and

GILBERT, HALL AND DUNN
The gang is holding up a mail coach near Jugiong, and Gilbert is killing Sergeant Parry.

THE DEATH OF BEN HALL

purchased a box of cigars, which were placed upon the table for the use of all present; and when one person enquired as to the propriety of using stolen goods, Gilbert said they need not be under any apprehension on that score, as the cigars were bought and paid for. They then induced a young lady present to play the piano for them, two of them dancing to the music inside, while the others were scouting or watching outside.' The gang were less playful later when they killed a man at the house of a gold commissioner thirty miles from Bathurst, and a police sergeant from Gundagai who was escorting a mail coach on the southern road near Jugiong and a constable at Collector. Time and again Hall's and other gangs on their carefully stolen horses outrode the police who were chasing them. The *Sydney Mail* had a section each week headed 'Bushranging'. The robbery of mail coaches had become so common by 1864 that the postal authorities printed blank forms to be filled in by local officials announcing that the mails from . . . . to . . . . had been stolen.

The bushrangers were now a grave embarrassment to the ministry of Charles Cowper, which appeared impotent before them. Larger and larger rewards were offered for the apprehension of Hall, Gilbert and others. Troopers were taken out of their uniforms and put into bushmen's outfits; they were issued with new rifles and revolvers, better horses, and black trackers, and ordered to do nothing but hunt bushrangers. On 8 April 1865 the government had the New South Wales parliament pass a Felons Apprehension Act which drastically increased the penalties for helping men reasonably suspected of a felony, and authorized anybody to shoot a proclaimed outlaw, if it was reasonable to believe that he was armed, without calling on him first to surrender. Until now the bushrangers had been helped to keep ahead of the police by 'bush telegraphs'—a word-of-mouth warning system faster, more widespread and more flexible than the government's electric telegraph, for which there were only thirty-six stations in the colony by 1862. The increasing activity of the police made it riskier to be a bush telegraph, and the act of 1865 added greatly to the punishment for being caught at it. On 12 April Hall, Gilbert and Dunn were formally called upon to surrender to charges of murder by 29 April. On 5 May an informer and a black tracker led a party of mounted police to Hall's camp near Forbes, where they shot him dead. On 10 May Gilbert and Dunn were proclaimed outlaws, and

THE DEATH OF JOHN GILBERT

three days later Gilbert's grandfather took troopers to Gilbert and Dunn. Gilbert was shot dead; Dunn was wounded and escaped, to be captured early next year, convicted of murder, and hanged. The Cowper government could boast that its police had got the better of the bushrangers. One troublesome gang, led by Thomas and John Clarke, sons of a convict, remained at large somewhere near Braidwood when the ministry led by James Martin and Henry Parkes came into office in January 1866. Towards the end of the year Parkes enrolled as special constables four men who knew the Clarkes and their region, had them disguised as surveyors, and sent them off towards Braidwood as a secret police party. They were ambushed and shot dead. Troopers captured the gang in April 1867 with the help of a black tracker to whom white men had given the name Sir Watkin Wynne. When the chief justice, Sir Alfred Stephen, was sentencing them to death, he made a grim tally of the history of bushranging in the colony since 1863. Fifteen bushrangers dead, not counting the two men standing before him, and six others in prison for long terms; six citizens killed and ten wounded in the perpetration of robberies against them; seven policemen killed and sixteen wounded. The Clarkes were hanged at Darlinghurst Gaol on 25 June 1867 after receiving attentively the ministrations of the Catholic chaplain, Father Michael John Dwyer, whom Parkes was to dismiss in 1868 for releasing Henry James O'Farrell's alleged confession. The Clarkes and O'Farrell had been found guilty of the same offence—wounding with intent to murder—and it was under the Felons Apprehension Act of 1865 that in New South Wales, unlike England and other colonies, that crime was punishable by death.

No gang of bushrangers menaced anybody in New South Wales between 1867 and 1870. Only Frederick Ward, 'Captain Thunderbolt', was at large, holding up coaches, behaving kindly to the poor and respectfully to women. For a while he had the company of a lad—who was captured—but otherwise his only accomplice was a part-aboriginal woman, who to his grief died towards the end of 1867. On 25 May 1870 he was killed at Uralla, in the north of the colony, by a mounted trooper, Constable Alexander Walker.

Less than two weeks later the only other bushranger occupying policemen anywhere in Australia was captured. Harry Power, a man of Irish birth, had escaped from Pentridge Gaol, near Melbourne, where he was serving a sentence for wounding a policeman. He robbed travellers and settlers in the north-east of the colony, had £500 put on his head, and was captured by policemen on 5 June 1870. To the crowd gathered at Wangaratta to see him brought in, Power waved and said: 'They've caught Harry Power, but they had to catch him asleep!' There were rumours that he had been given away by a young bush telegraph named Ned Kelly.

This lad was the son of Irish Catholic parents, the father a convict and the mother a government emigrant. John, or Red, Kelly, from Munster, was a Vandemonian who crossed to Port Phillip after being emancipated. Ellen Quinn arrived from Ulster with her family in 1839 when she was three. The father looked for gold at Bendigo and then tried farming. Edward, or Ned, the first son and third child, was born at Wallan, near Melbourne, probably in 1854. Two more boys and three more girls were born to the couple before Red Kelly was sent to prison in 1865 for unlawful possession of a calf hide. It was no unusual experience for the Kellys and their relatives to be charged with stealing horses and cattle and attacking policemen. Ned went briefly to school, learning a little reading and writing but not much about those parts of the world which lay beyond the plains, mountains and towns of Victoria or the memory of battling Irish convicts and assisted emigrants. His father died in 1866 when Ned was probably twelve. His mother took her seven surviving children to a small selection she had bought at Eleven Mile Creek, near Greta, about a hundred and fifty miles north-east of Melbourne. Here Ned rode around with cousins and uncles, moving stock and working on farms. Evidence from relatives helped to get him aquitted when he first appeared in court, on 14 October 1869, charged with assaulting and robbing a Chinese named Ah Fook. He came to know Harry Power through two uncles who had met him in Pentridge. Ned was charged with highway robbery as an accomplice of Power in 1870, but was acquitted. 'He merely took charge of Power's horses at a distance', wrote a policeman, 'but he could not be recognised by any of the victims'. On 30 October 1870 Ned Kelly was convicted at Wangaratta of assault, for hitting a travelling butcher named McCormack, and of indecent behaviour, for sending Mrs McCormack, who had no children, a pair of calves' testicles and a note suggesting that they might be of use to her. He got three months on each charge and went into Beechworth Prison, where he remained until 29 March 1871.

Less than three weeks later, in Greta, a constable tried to arrest Ned Kelly on a charge of stealing a horse. 'I straddled him and rooted both spurs into his thighs', Kelly recalled in a statement dictated to a comrade, 'he roared like a big calf attacked by dogs . . . I got his hands at the back of his neck and tried to make him let the revolver go but he stuck to it like grim death to a dead volunteer'. Next day they took him to Wangaratta in a cart, handcuffed and roped. At Beechworth he was sentenced, as he put it later, to three years experience in Beechworth and Pentridge dungeons. When Ned Kelly came out in 1874 he was about twenty.

12 Rebels

IRISH CONVICTS

A riot or rebellion of prisoners had always to be considered a possibility in the penal settlements of Australia. It was likeliest among the convicts from Ireland, of whom about twelve hundred arrived by 1800. From the beginning some of their custodians found the Irish convicts villainous, superstitious and difficult to manage. After 1798 sedition was added to their iniquities. For in Ireland that year the United Irishmen rose in revolt, under a green flag inscribed 'Liberty or Death'. Their insurrection was put down quickly, but alarmed the rulers and hastened plans for the Union of Great Britain and Ireland. More than two hundred men were transported to New South Wales for proved or suspected complicity in the rebellion.

In September 1800 Governor Hunter heard rumours that a rising of Irish convicts was imminent, and called free men of property and good character to join 'loyal associations' of volunteers and stand ready at Sydney and Parramatta. When the supposed danger passed, Governor King disbanded the volunteers; but he enrolled them again for a week in November 1802 to make sure that a load of '400 Irish Convicts, (Mostly Rebels,)' was disembarked peacefully. Earlier in 1802 Irish convicts had been restless when two French ships appeared in Port Jackson; for to Irishmen here as at home, the French could appear as potential liberators. When ships of the East India Company off Norfolk Island were mistaken for a French fleet in 1804, the commandant had the Irish convicts locked up so that they could not give help to invaders.

A Catholic priest, James Dixon, was among men transported after the rising of 1798. He had been arrested near Wexford under suspicion of having commanded a company of rebels, convicted by court martial, sentenced to death and transported instead for life. Governor King, giving Dixon permission in May 1803 to work as a clergyman, imposed strict regulations on himself and his people, who were ordered to avoid seditious conversation at places of worship or anywhere else and to report any they heard among others. There must have been a good deal of it among Irish convicts in the days before Sunday 4 March 1804; for on that evening there began what King was to call 'the short-lived insurrection of those deluded Irish'. Their password was 'St Peter'. At the settlement of Castle Hill, north of Parramatta, a band of convicts suddenly overpowered officials, seized arms and ammunition, and gathered their fellows to hear an

Irishman named Philip Cunningham set out a plan to conquer the colony. An official who escaped from the rebels ran in to Parramatta towards nine o'clock in the evening with news of the rising. A messenger carried it to Government House in Sydney, where King ordered fifty-six men of the New South Wales Corps under Major George Johnston to march to Parramatta while another 160 waited at Sydney in case of insurrection there. Sixty soldiers already stationed at Parramatta were joined during the night by armed civilian volunteers.

The rebels marched to Parramatta, other men joining them on the way. They assembled outside the town, but instead of attacking it they withdrew before dawn and headed west towards Toongabbee. There they decided to move north-west towards the settlement on the Hawkesbury, where they hoped other convicts would join them. At Government House in Parramatta, King proclaimed a state of rebellion, established martial law, and produced a plan of campaign. Major Johnston and about forty men rode off after the rebels, taking with them the priest James Dixon. More than two hundred men were plodding towards the Hawkesbury in the hot morning sun when Dixon, under Johnston's orders, approached on horseback and urged them to surrender. The advice was declined. Then Major Johnston and a soldier rode up and called out for the rebels' leaders. Philip Cunningham and another man came forward, armed only with swords. When Johnston advised them to surrender, Cunningham's reply was an antipodean version of the United Irishmen's cry in 1798: 'Death or Liberty!' That meant death. Johnston and his companion drew pistols and seized the two leaders. Soldiers were ordered to charge. 'The detachment immediately commenced a well-directed fire,' as Johnston reported, 'which was but weakly returned, for the rebel line being soon broken they ran in all directions. We pursued them a considerable way, and have no doubt but that many of them fell. We have found 12 killed, 6 wounded, and have taken 26 prisoners.' The soldiers captured twenty-six muskets, one pistol, one fowling piece, four bayonets on poles, two swords, eight reaping hooks and a pitchfork.

Cunningham was hanged publicly without trial at the Hawkesbury. A court-martial held immediately at Parramatta convicted ten men of armed rebellion and gave them sentences of death which King approved in all but two cases. The exemplary hangings were distributed so that many people could see them: three at Parramatta on 8 March, three next day at Castle Hill, two as a Saturday spectacle in Sydney on 10 March. Nine men were tried by magistrates and sentenced to heavy floggings. Another thirty or so were held in chain gangs by magisterial order and sent off to revive a mining settlement in the north which had been called Coal River in 1796, Hunter River in 1797, and was now endowed with the name of the Duke of Newcastle.

'Their cry was death or liberty', wrote a settler, 'and a ship to take them Home.' The planners of the rising perhaps thought that they could steal a ship in Port Jackson and sail it to Ireland. Others possibly hoped to escape by land and walk to China or Ireland or the fabled colony where nobody worked. Whatever their visions, the rebels appeared to have had no clear military plan. They killed and wounded nobody. Untrained and poorly armed though they were, they could still have inflicted some casualties either at Parramatta during the night or on the road from Toongabbee to the Hawkesbury next morning. Possibly they knew that their rebellion was doomed but were determined to act it out, preferring a spasm of freedom to years of slavery in exile, and making before they went down an act of communion with their brothers of 1798 and all their ancestors who had fought and lost for Ireland. The place where the soldiers' muskets felled and scattered

THE REBELLION OF CONVICTS

*'Major Johnston and Quarter-Master Laycock One Serjeant and Twenty five
Privates of ye. New S. Wales Corps defeats Two Hundred and Sixty six Armed
Rebels 5th March 1804.' In the background Father Dixon cries: 'Lay down yr.
Arms my deluded Countrymen.' To Cunningham's 'Death or Liberty Major',
Johnston replies 'You Scoundrel I'll liberate you'. Some rebels fall and others scatter as
the soldiers shoot. At the left a later moment is depicted: the hanging of rebel leaders.*

the rebels came to be known as Vinegar Hill, after the hill near Wexford where the Irish
rebels had been defeated by the British on 21 June 1798.

King could report that all was perfectly quiet by 12 March; he was sure that
Irish minds would still be employed on insurrection, but also that they would not try it
again unless a foreign enemy actually landed in the colony. The executions and floggings
and expulsions to Newcastle were followed by other measures intended to deter them.
Catholic worship was prohibited. Irish communal memory preserved a scene in which
James Dixon was forced to witness the flogging of rebels and to put his hand on their
bleeding backs until he fainted. The priest was allowed to go back to Ireland in 1808.
The 'loyal associations' of citizens in arms, revived at Sydney and Parramatta, were not
disbanded. King asked the Colonial Office for more soldiers. A citadel, Fort Phillip, was
built on the western side of Sydney Cove as a refuge for the garrison against foreign and
internal enemies. Of its six sides, one faced the harbour, one the town, and one the road
to Parramatta.

Major Johnston was given two thousand acres out at Cabramatta for his part in the episode. Four years later he himself was the leader, or at least the figurehead, of a rebellion against the governor of New South Wales.

BRITISH OFFICERS

Ever since Phillip's day the officers of the New South Wales Corps, a regiment raised at home for service in the colony, had been very important men in its affairs. The first members of the corps sailed out in 1789, and by 1792 they replaced entirely the two hundred marines who had come in the first fleet. Both officers and men were below the average of the British army in character and competence; for new regiments such as this one always had difficulty in attracting good officers, and service in the colonies was regarded as the lowest form of military employment. The ranks of the corps included men who had joined in order to get out of military prison, and who therefore had cause to be touchy when Phillip, on the king's birthday in 1792, treated them as if they were on a level with convicts.

Commanding officers of the corps, Major Francis Grose and Major William Paterson, acted as governors of the colony between Phillip's departure in 1792 and Hunter's arrival in 1795. In that time a grant of a hundred acres of land was made to every officer, military and civil, who asked for it. Unlike the marine officers of the first fleet, those of the New South Wales Corps were permitted to bring their wives. Family men among them soon aspired to becoming landed gentry. Before long some were rich men, selling not only produce from their own land but also goods—including spirits—bought in bulk from trading vessels, and mixing the powers of office with commercial enterprise to hamper their competitors.

The naval men who governed from 1795 to 1806, Hunter and King, did what they could to control the officers' trafficking. Hunter had Johnston, who was his aide-de-camp, arrested and sent home on a charge of illegal dealing in spirits; but correspondence from other officers persuaded the authorities in London that Hunter was governing imprudently, and Johnston returned in 1802 without having faced a trial. King reduced the amount of spirits landed by sending some cargoes away, and had goods offered to settlers at prices lower than the officers' ring charged. Officers of the corps were at odds with King on other issues, including the social position of former convicts: the issue which was to give birth to the names 'exclusionist' and 'emancipist' was already causing friction as officers demanded a society in which they had the rights of gentlemen and freed convicts did not. The governor had one of the officer-magnates, Captain John Macarthur, sent to England in 1801 for court-martial after fighting a duel with his commander. He escaped trial by resigning his commission, and returned with not only a clear reputation but the grant of land on which he was to raise his merinoes.

Another sailor, Captain William Bligh, became governor in 1806. He was appalled by much about the colony, including the place spirits had attained in its affairs. In Bligh's view the future of New South Wales lay not with Macarthur and his sheep, nor with foreign trade, but with agriculture; and he feared that the trade in spirits could be the colony's undoing. He prohibited the use of liquor as payment for any other commodity or service and laid down heavy punishment for any breach of the order. Bligh was a despot. Men under him on H.M.S. *Bounty* had mutinied near Tahiti in 1789, and in 1805 a court-martial found charges of tyrannical behaviour in charge of another ship 'in part proved'. John Macarthur, for his part, had quarrelled with everybody set in authority over him; 'scarcely anything short of the full power of the Governor', Hunter had said, 'wou'd be consider'd by this person as sufficient for conducting the dutys of his office'. In this tiny and isolated society the two men were bound to collide.

It was Macarthur's trading activities that led him and Bligh to a showdown at the end of 1807. He wanted to land two stills, but the governor ruled that they must stay in bond. The working parts were duly lodged in the bond store, and the copper boilers in a warehouse owned by Macarthur. When Bligh had the boilers taken away to be shipped back to England, Macarthur argued successfully in court that the seizure was illegal. When a convict escaped from the colony in a schooner of which Macarthut was part-owner, Bligh had the ship placed under arrest and ordered him to forfeit a bond; but Macarthur said that as he had been dispossessed of the vessel he had no responsibility for it. He abused the chief constable who tried to serve a warrant on him. Macarthur was arrested on 16 December and charged with offences relating to the stills, the schooner, and the language he had used to the chief constable. In court on 25 January 1808 the accused asked that the judge advocate, Richard Atkins, step down from the bench on the ground that he was a swindler and owed Macarthur money. Macarthur told the six military officers who made up the court that the public were trembling for the safety of their property, their liberty and their lives. The court adjourned in confusion, and Macarthur went free. Next morning Bligh had him arrested. When the six officers of the court asked Bligh to release Macarthur on bail and appoint another judge advocate instead of Atkins, he charged them all with treasonable practices. That was his last act as governor; for it provoked Major George Johnston, acting commander of the New South Wales Corps, to declare himself lieutenant-governor, sign in that capacity an order for the release of Macarthur on bail, and send a message to Bligh calling on him to submit to arrest. Then he marched at the head of the corps, its colours flying and its band playing 'The British Grenadiers', to seize Bligh at Government House. It was 26 January 1808, the twentieth anniversary of the first landing at Sydney Cove.

Bligh declared later that if he had escaped to the Hawkesbury, the whole body of people there would have flocked to his standard; and perhaps farmers who were victims of the trading ring would have accepted him as champion. But the governor made no serious effort to escape anywhere, and raised no standard to which anybody could rally. None of his subordinates resisted the soldiers as they marched into Government House and rushed up the stairs. 'Without ceremony they broke into all parts of the house' Bligh wrote to the secretary of state, Lord Castlereagh. 'Nothing but calamity upon calamity was to be expected, even Massacre and secret Murder. I had only just time to retire upstairs to prevent giving myself up, and to see if anything could be done for the restoration of my Authority; but they soon found me in a back room, and a daring sct of Ruffians under arms, intoxicated by spirituous liquors, which was given them for the purpose, and threatening to plunge their bayonets into me if I resisted, seized me.' Castlereagh heard it differently from Johnston. 'After a rigid Search, the Governor . . . was at last discovered in a situation too disgraceful to be mentioned . . . As soon as Governor Bligh made his Appearance, I assured him of his personal Safety'. Martial law was proclaimed overnight, but only good-natured carousing went on in the streets as it customarily did on this day of the year. No shots were fired at anybody, and nobody suffered the slightest injury.

Johnston and Macarthur argued that the bloodless character of their coup, the absence of any resistance to their seizure and overthrow of Bligh, showed that they were acting with the support of the colony. Certainly the cantankerous governor had

THE ARREST OF BLIGH AS DEPICTED BY HIS ENEMIES
More than one version of this cartoon was displayed in Sydney soon after Bligh was deposed. It may have been the work of Lieutenant William Minchin, leader of the party of soldiers which entered Government House and found Bligh.

antagonized people other than the officers of the court and Macarthur, but there was no evidence that most free citizens of New South Wales preferred the new rulers. The affair of 26 January 1808 was very different from that of 4 March 1804. Castle Hill was a real insurrection, a straightforward defiance of the established order, to be met by shooting and hanging and flogging. The deposition of Bligh was a symbolic scuffle among gentlemen who avoided violence and then appealed to an umpire in London. Nothing was destroyed except paper, as both Bligh and his enemies tore up such documents as they feared could damage their case when it was heard at home. They all knew that the episode was far from unique on the frontiers of empire. Members of the Council of Madras had deposed and imprisoned their governor in 1776; and elsewhere, in colonies without representative institutions, allegedly unpopular governors had been replaced by their subordinates. Men of sense in the capital learned to take a mild view of mutiny by officers in these remote and factious outposts.

Before the removal of Bligh was given judicial investigation in London, the secretary of state had decided to put the colony under a military governor rather than another naval man, and to bring home the New South Wales Corps. Lieutenant-Colonel Lachlan Macquarie was to be both governor and commanding officer of the 73rd Regiment, 'a very respectable Battalion', as he described them, 'and complete in a very good and genteel Corps of Officers'. He had orders to restore Bligh for twenty-four hours and then replace him, to send home Johnston under close arrest, and to try Macarthur for high treason; but at Rio de Janeiro he learned that Johnston and Macarthur had just passed through on their way to England. On the last day of 1809 Macquarie landed officially at Port Jackson and proclaimed His Majesty's 'utmost regret and displeasure on account of the late tumultuous proceedings' and 'mutinous conduct'. On New Year's Day 1810 the bands of the New South Wales Corps and the 73rd Regiment played 'God Save the King' harmoniously together, soldiers of both corps fired volleys, and Macquarie had himself proclaimed governor. It was 'extremely difficult', he reported of the rebellion, 'to form a just judgment on this delicate and mysterious subject, Party rancour having run so high as to preclude the possibility of arriving at the truth without a very minute and legal investigation.' Bligh was 'uncommonly harsh and tyrannical in the extreme', but had done nothing Macquarie could discover to warrant mutiny. Macarthur, he thought, had been the 'real author of the Revolution and disturbances.'

Bligh and the New South Wales Corps and witnesses of the disturbances sailed off together on 12 May 1810 for Cape Horn and home. Johnston was court-martialled and convicted, but the court found extenuating circumstances which earned him no penalty worse than being dismissed from the army. He was allowed in 1813 to return to his acres in the colony, whose governor was directed to treat him as he would any other settler. Lawyers advised that Macarthur, as a civilian, could not be charged with treason in England for his part in the rebellion. He was permitted in 1817 to go out again to New South Wales on condition that he take no part in public affairs. Bligh died that year in retirement. The New South Wales Corps, now called the 102nd Regiment, was disbanded in 1818.

THREATS FROM FREE MEN

No convicts rose and no officers rebelled in the time of Macquarie. He gave convicts more to hope for than any previous governor, and if any contemplated insurrection, they knew from memories of Castle Hill how it would end. The former officers and other settlers who disliked his policies kept to constitutional forms of protest. No longer was there a division to exploit between the governor and the military, and in due course the discontented could put their grievances peaceably to the imperial emissary John Thomas Bigge.

The possibility of 'Internal Insurrection or Commotion' was nevertheless in Macquarie's mind, as well as 'a Recurrence of Hostilities on the part of the Native Blacks', when he tried to convince his superiors in 1817 that as the colony grew in population and extent, a military force of fewer than a thousand men was not enough to

keep it secure. Blacks, bushrangers, convicts and army officers had been the disturbers
so far. William Charles Wentworth foreshadowed in 1819 a new threat, from free men.
Unless the people of New South Wales were granted representative institutions, he warned
in his book on the colony, the imperial government might have to fight another colonial
war of independence. In case readers at Westminster thought that an extravagant
fantasy, Wentworth the politician invoked the authority of Wentworth the explorer.
'To those . . . who have traversed the formidable chain of mountains by which it is
bounded from north to south . . . the independence of this colony, should it be goaded into
rebellion, appears neither so problematical nor remote, as might be otherwise imagined.
Of what avail would whole armies prove in these terrible defiles, which only five or six
men could approach abreast? . . . If the colonists should prudently abandon the defence of
the sea-coast, and remove with their flocks and herds into the fertile country behind these
impregnable passes, what would the force of England, gigantic as it is, profit her?' This
minatory passage was retained in the second edition of Wentworth's book which
appeared in 1820.

Whether or not his vision of a revolutionary war impressed anybody at the
Colonial Office, the act of parliament which gave the colony its first legislature, in 1823,
did provide clearly for putting down domestic violence. In case of rebellion or insurrection
the governor could promulgate any law or ordinance necessary to suppress or prevent it,
even if every member of the Legislative Council dissented. The native-born patriot who
had imagined rebellion in 1819 might have been expected to protest at the governor's
having this power; but when Wentworth rewrote his book in 1824 he removed the
passage altogether. He was far from satisfied with the act of 1823; but even a short step
towards an elected legislature, and the granting of equal recognition to propertied
emigrant and propertied emancipist for service on juries, sufficed to make him erase the
picture of his countrymen withdrawing across the Blue Mountains beyond range of
British guns. His antagonist Governor Darling nevertheless remembered the passage: 'he
speaks as he wrote when compiling his book,' Darling said in 1826, 'of the independence of
the colony, and compares it to the situation formerly of America and the probability of its
being driven, as America was, to shake off the yoke.'

In 1825 the Colonial Office invited an opinion on the security of New South
Wales by a man uniquely placed to offer it, an experienced officer in the British army who
had grown up in the colony. Edward Macarthur, son of John, had been close to his
father's own rebellion in 1808 just before he sailed to join the British army and serve in
Spain. Captain Macarthur proposed for the colony of 1825 an auxiliary military force
modelled largely on the yeomanry which since its formation in 1794 had been helping the
rulers of England to suppress protest and disorder. The regular military force, Edward
Macarthur argued, was too small to protect the inhabitants of a scattered penal colony.
A militia raised from among the peasantry, and commanded by men whose property and
connexions gave them a strong local interest in preserving the peace, could be used both
to repress insubordination and riot and to resist the sudden attack of a foreign enemy. The
men should if possible be volunteers; but if too few offered they should be levied by ballot,
each district providing a quota. Former convicts would not be admitted to the force,
which would 'afford the means of training and disciplining the free inhabitants, and
gradually inculcate that respect for their superiors, that observance of the various
gradations of society, and that loyal attachment to the Crown, the acquisition of which is

unfortunately too little facilitated by their present habits and situation.' The men of Macarthur's exclusionist yeomanry would thus be training both to put down disorder and to become good deferential Britons.

They would have yet another value. Macarthur knew that many people in New South Wales, especially the emancipists and their sons, regarded the imperial soldiers in the barracks as likelier to use their arms against fellow-Britons than against any foe from distant Europe. 'The Australians', Alexander Harris wrote, 'uniformly take pains to exhibit a contemptuous dislike of the British military.' A militia such as he now proposed would be a means, Macarthur argued, of 'connecting the regular forces of the Crown with the great body of free inhabitants, by similarity of duties and feelings, and thus repressing the jealously and dislike, which are too apt to arise when the preservation of the public peace is entrusted to strangers.' Members of the force should be called away to muster and drill only sparingly, and with careful reference to the needs of agriculture; for the authorities must take into account the 'prejudices of a population who are widely dispersed, whose personal attention to their property is constantly required and who will, therefore, be unwilling to subject themselves to much military duty in time of peace.' Here lay one large obstacle to the whole plan, which Governor Darling saw at once when it was sent out to him for comment. 'What man in his senses', Darling asked, 'would leave his family and his property for any length of time at the mercy of convict servants?' Darling preferred the new force of mounted police, supported from time to time by the resident imperial soldiers and in extremity by citizens enrolled into loyal associations. Edward Macarthur's plan remained on the shelf, expressing a view of public order and defence in New South Wales by a professional soldier who was also a pure merino, and who was probably the first person to recommend that Australian men should be enrolled in a citizen military force, raised if necessary by compulsion.

Wentworth and his friends believed that the only serious obstacle to liberty in the colony was Governor Darling. Once he was removed, Wentworth assured the motherland that Australians were not only utterly loyal, but would rally to the old country if ever she were in danger. At the party held on his estate at Vaucluse to celebrate Darling's departure, guests listened to a song composed for the occasion applauding the end of 'tyranny's dire scourge' and assuring the old lion that

> Our native youth shall show,
> Their loyalty's bright glow,
> And first in battle stand.

From now on Wentworth was more and more inclined to see himself among the custodians of order, and to fear the threats to domestic peace offered by new men of the towns.

Sydney and Melbourne experienced seasons of disorder in the 1840s. Competent and honest policemen were uncommon in the towns; for the hours were long, the pay was low, and their job was popularly regarded as a last resort. The police force had to be composed, Bishop Polding said in 1838, out of 'wretched materials . . . the very refuse of

EDWARD MACARTHUR
Advocate of a citizen military force, 1825. He is shown here as lieutenant-general and commander-in-chief of the military forces in Australia, 1858.

other callings.' It had the reputation of being a haven for old lags. W. A. Miles, commissioner of police in Sydney from 1841 to 1848, had to tell a select committee of the Legislative Council on the Insecurity of Life and Property that former convicts under his command tended to collaborate with the criminals they were supposed to catch. Sydney was enough of a metropolis now to have mobs. The inadequte policing of its streets enabled a gang known as the 'cabbage tree mob'—they wore the broad-brimmed hats woven from cabbage-tree leaves which were popular out here—to roam at night abusing and assaulting people. Sydney and Melbourne were beginning to have democratic politics, which provoked riots in both towns during elections in 1843 and 1845. In Sydney one person was killed. The collision of Orange and Green in Port Phillip was beyond the power of policemen to control. Governor FitzRoy advised the secretary of state in 1847 that a force of a hundred soldiers had to be kept at Melbourne on account of 'the occasional religious Riots between the lower orders of the Catholic and Protestant portion of that Town'. In Sydney, he reported, 'Mobs of the most turbulent character have assembled which it has been found totally beyond the power of the local Police to overawe, and nothing but the interference of the Military has dispersed.'

None of these disorders carried seeds of insurrection. Crowds were gathering in Sydney, however, which contained within them, so it seemed to custodians of order, a darker menace than the cabbage-tree mob or the election rioters or the factious Irish. Bishop Broughton feared that a revolutionary movement was gathering. 'The people', he wrote in 1844, 'already talk of resistance and rebellion.' The eloquent young emigrant lawyer Robert Lowe seemed to Broughton to be stirring sans-culottist sentiments in the colony; and Lowe certainly used fiery language when he demanded that Englishmen be allowed to exercise out here the rights they enjoyed before emigrating. To the anniversary gathering on 26 January 1846, at which Wentworth was guest of honour, Lowe said: 'deeply avenged as were the outraged liberties of America, if the Colonial Office perseveres in its present policy, the bloody and expensive lesson will have to be read again in every quarter of the globe.' John Dunmore Lang exhorted colonists to declare their independence and call if necessary on France or America for help.

When Henry Parkes, Robert Lowe and others held their 'Great Protest Meeting' against the unloading of convicts from the *Hashemy* on 11 June 1849, the superintendent of the Sydney police sat on his horse watching the crowd, a double guard of soldiers with fixed bayonets protected Government House, and it was said that cannon were trained on the meeting place. The protest, delivered to FitzRoy by a deputation next day, was a careful mixture of loyalty and menace: 'being firmly and devoutly attached to the British Crown, we greatly fear that the perpetration of so stupendous an act of injustice by Her Majesty's Government will go far towards alienating the affections of the people of this colony from the mother country.' Parkes organized another meeting for 18 June, a day celebrated throughout the empire as the anniversary of the battle of Waterloo. The democrats' newspaper, the *People's Advocate*, exhorted all lovers of freedom to attend and '*win* THE BATTLE OF NEW SOUTH WALES.' The superintendent of police put the crowd at a thousand, the *Sydney Morning Herald* at five or six thousand. At the Circular Quay, in sight of the *Hashemy*, Parkes ridiculed people who said that the agitators were trying to rule by intimidation, but he spoke with admiration of American revolutionaries. Lowe declared that the injustice forced upon the Americans 'was not half so great as that forced upon this colony', and called on his hearers to free their necks from the yoke of 'the odious domination' to which they had been subjected. Parkes later looked back on 'that glorious

18th of June' as 'one of the brightest days in Australia's history.' Conservative men compared the protesters with Jacobins. FitzRoy wrote in August that he was afraid of the violence which 'such a mob as Sydney would produce did circumstances encourage its organisation.'

It was a fear shared by Wentworth, who told the Legislative Council in 1850, his sixtieth year, that a British military presence would remain necrssary until the colony had 'a body of gentlemen to supply their place—a yeomanry, or national guard—persons who had some property, and who would fight to defend it against the rapine and violence of lawless mobs.' In Wentworth's imagination these mobs were responding to the democratic and subversive ideas of men such as Lang. He told the council that he 'was afraid of those socialist and chartist principles, which the honorable and reverend member had advocated and continued to advocate in his speech and writings to that mob whom he had at his beck and call.' It was indeed true of Lowe and Parkes, if not of Lang, that they hoped to influence policy at home by arousing popular protest out here; but their talk of America and rebellion and blood was calculated hyperbole. 'If we were in open rebellion,' said Lowe in 1845, 'Her Majesty *might* hear of it; if we only talked high treason and stopped the supplies, we think it probable it might come to the ears of Lord Stanley; but being only in a civil, constitutional, gentlemanly state of disgust, we apprehend our complaints will penetrate no higher than Mr. Under-Secretary Stephen.' Back home in 1850 he spoke candidly about the manipulation of Australian crowds by reformers determined to get a hearing at home. 'We are obliged, in order to make an impression on the British Government, to stimulate the passions and inflame the minds of the masses in the colonies . . . to turn agitators, and stir up all the elements of the community, which, if we had a free government, every one would wish should lie dormant.'

It was no wonder that the opponents of Lowe and Parkes accused them of being hostile to the motherland. But Parkes denied indignantly 'the slanderous charges of native turbulence and anti-British feeling', declaring that he and his allies had 'a true British resolve to eradicate those seeds of dissension which would speedily lead to separation'. Their rhetoric did differ in one large respect from that of the revolutionary Americans whom they invoked with admiration. As the men who were to found the United States came closer to making their declaration of independence, they tended to speak less about the rights of Englishmen and more about the rights of man. The agitators against transportation did not make that shift. They felt themselves to be Britons abroad, and they knew in their hearts that the secretary of state would give in if only they shouted long and loudly enough.

John West thought that some of his friends who talked wildly of seizing independence were ignoring a stark fact about power. Towards the end of his *History of Tasmania*, West wrote: 'The American revolutionists had an army: they had thrust out the Indians and beaten the French . . . But Australia has not a soldier or a gun.' When America resisted, moreover, the military resources of England were feeble. 'Since then she has conquered Napoleon, subdued India, and established her military power in every region of the world . . . Independence may be desired; but it is well to remember that those who will attain it must fight for it, and that in this war they will not only contend with the most benign and just, but with the most powerful government on the earth.' But in what circumstances would a British government of the mid-nineteenth century send that army against British colonists? Certainly not to enforce the landing of convicts in Australia: when the secretary of state advised the governor of Van Diemen's Land in 1852 to expect no more convict transports, he said that England should not force the colonists 'into a furious opposition . . . extinguishing all loyalty and affection for the mother country'. Wentworth himself knew what it was like to use the language of insurrection while being in one's heart a thoroughly loyal Briton. Not only when demanding representative institutions in 1819, but even when calling for responsible government in 1850, Wentworth could sound as if he was prepared if necessary for a war of independence. He believed that the Canadians had been granted responsible government in 1846 because they threatened force, and he thought that Australians might gain it by talking similarly. No less than the democrats whose politics he deplored, Wentworth was willing to go in for rebellious bluster, confident that the imperial government would back away from it.

Some of West's fellow-colonists might have made another comment on his passage about military force. It did not follow from the overwhelming might of British arms that a body of British subjects would submit to any provocation, however iniquitous they found it, on the part of the imperial government or its proconsul. Given sufficient cause, men might rebel even if they were bound to lose.

13 Diggers

EUREKA

When the mail coach from Bathurst reached Sydney on 15 May 1851 with news of the first gold rush, some people pressed the government to proclaim martial law and prohibit digging; but Governor FitzRoy knew that a few hundred soldiers could no more stop diggers now than they could have stopped squatters a decade earlier. Major-General William Stewart believed that the colony urgently needed more soldiers. As commander of the military forces in 1825 Stewart had organized the first mounted police force, which rode out to offer protection against bushrangers around Bathurst. Having retired to live in that district, the old general had nearly all his horses stolen by men on their way to Ophir. On 21 May he wrote urging FitzRoy to send home for 'an Infantry Regiment of the Line from 500 to 600 strong, of superior Military discipline and good conduct; for the express purpose of preserving good order in the Mining District'. That might help by 1852; but what was the governor to do in May 1851? After some days of indecision FitzRoy proclaimed the crown's right at common law to all the gold in New South Wales and threatened to prosecute anybody who sought or dug it without permission. On 23 May the executive council authorized a system of licensing. If a man wanted to seek gold he must take out a licence, which would cost him thirty shillings a month at a time when a rural labourer was paid about two pounds a month and keep. The fee was expected to deter many men, and to be payable without hardship by those who were finding gold; but it was soon apparent both that few were kept away by having to pay the fee, and that thousands of diggers were finding it onerous. In Victoria a government confronted with gold rushes in the first weeks of separation from New South Wales introduced on 1 September 1851 the same system of licensing.

In both colonies the licence was proclaimed before there was anybody to administer it on the goldfields. At Ballarat, seventy miles west of Melbourne, informal meetings of diggers made their own arrangements for law and order before any official or policeman arrived, and resolved late in September to pay no more than five shillings a month for a licence. In October fewer than half of the six thousand men digging at Ballarat paid their fees. Governor La Trobe feared complete anarchy. Most of the policemen in his capital deserted to the diggings; Melbourne's force of forty constables had dwindled to two when the diggers came roistering into town for Christmas. There were only forty-four soldiers in the whole of Victoria, some of whom were riding beside the gold as it was carried from the fields while others guarded the gaol and the powder magazine in Melbourne. La Trobe asked the governors of New South Wales and Van Diemen's Land for reinforcements and begged the authorities at home to send at least one regiment of picked men who could be trusted not to throw down their arms and go off after gold. During 1852 FitzRoy sent down thirty soldiers from Sydney, and from Van Diemen's Land 130 military pensioners who had chosen to retire in the colony were signed on to work as policemen in Victoria for a year. A corps of mounted police—twelve officers and 250 troopers—was formed and equipped. A force of goldfields police was organized, working under officers of a new body called the Gold Commission. Many of the gold commissioners and officers of the mounted police were gentlemanly emigrants, and some were apt to antagonize diggers as they looked down from their saddles with an air of being officers in charge of unruly troops. William Howitt on the Ovens diggings in 1852 was appalled to see the commissioners in gold-laced uniforms and caps, with white gloves and silver-mounted whips, riding about with orderlies behind them. He wrote to La Trobe about it, and was pleased to see that after a while only the chief commissioner in each camp was allowed an orderly. Some officers in the goldfields police had spent their best years superintending convicts, and many of the rank and file had been convicts themselves. Among their duties until 1854 was to enforce a prohibition of alcohol on the goldfields.

HUNTING FOR LICENCES IN NEW SOUTH WALES, 1852
J. R. Hardy, chief gold commissioner for the colony, writes out a licence as some miners hide and others flee.

GOLD COMMISSIONERS ISSUING LICENCES
AND WEIGHING GOLD DUST IN BALLARAT

A former convict in uniform raiding the tent of a free man for illegal booze had not much chance of being respected as an agent of law and order, especially when the government, hoping to encourage zeal and save money, allowed the policeman responsible for a conviction to keep half the proceeds of a fine for sly grogging. A similar arrangement applied to fines for not paying licence fees; and in both cases the practice encouraged blackmail, perjury, and the neglect of less profitable tasks such as protecting diggers from robbery. When mounted police and goldfields police collaborated to sweep on a body of miners and demanded to see their licences, it was rather like a tiger-hunt or a military raid. 'It is hardly congenial to British feelings', a chief commissioner reflected, 'to have a tax or fee collected at the point of the bayonet.' Two-thirds of them were nevertheless paying it in Victoria by April 1852. La Trobe considered the administration of the gold fields to be running well by the later months of 1852, when the emigrant ships began to discharge thousands of intending diggers. One of these ships, arriving in October, carried men of the 40th Regiment, sent from England in reply to La Trobe's request.

The population of Victoria rose from 97 000 in 1851 to 168 000 in 1852, and increased by about 60 000 in each of the next three years. The colony, and especially its goldfields, became predominantly a society of very new emigrants. Some people feared that the torrent of gold-seekers would cause violence and chaos such as they heard was normal on the fields of California. The lawlessness of San Francisco was much exaggerated in Australian minds; but in any case, every goldfield in Victoria and New South Wales was closer than the Californian diggings to a centre of government from which officials, policemen and soldiers could be dispatched. Most of the newcomers, moreover, were law-abiding people who had paid their own way to a British colony in order to improve their fortunes. Order was kept largely by public sentiment among the miners themselves. A gold commissioner testified that when he went to hear two parties to a disputed claim, a thousand or more men gathered around to listen with him: 'it was not difficult to tell by a sort of popular feeling generally,' he wrote, 'if one *really* was in the wrong.' Mutual protection associations were formed to prevent lawlessness. Sundays were days of rest and religion. Most of these diggers would live and work in peace unless they were provoked to do otherwise. But the licence system was a provocation. As long as it remained, nobody could be sure whether or not violent protest would occur on the goldfields.

In the valley of the Turon River in New South Wales, men were outraged in February 1853 that not only miners but tradesmen and servants on the diggings were required to take out the licence, and that foreigners had to pay three pounds a month, not thirty shillings, for it. Hundreds of armed men led by an Englishman and a German resolved not to take out licences and threatened rebellion. Governor FitzRoy responded by intimidation and conciliation, sending soldiers to the Turon but also meeting the miners' complaints. On the Ovens River diggings in Victoria early in 1853 the government camp was attacked and police were disarmed by diggers after a trooper's musket had accidentally shot a miner. At Bendigo, the largest field in Australia, where nearly twenty thousand of Victoria's fifty thousand diggers were working, an Anti-Gold-Licence Association was formed in June 1853. In August an angry meeting of more than ten thousand men resolved to offer only ten shillings for next month's licence. The chief of police hurried the eighty miles to Melbourne and told the governor that Bendigo was in a state of revolution. La Trobe, fearing that thousands of men would march on his capital, increased the soldiers at Bendigo to three hundred and sent an officer to borrow three hundred more from Van Diemen's Land. But like FitzRoy earlier in the year, he tried also to remove the miners' grievance. In the Legislative Council, La Trobe announced a bill to replace the licence system by an export duty on gold, which would tax a man only in proportion to his actual earnings. 'The Government of Victoria', said *The Times* when news of La Trobe's response reached London, 'is humbled in the dust before a lawless mob.' That was not how it seemed to the commander of the 40th Regiment, who reported from Bendigo that the diggers were the 'most orderly and well disposed body' he had ever seen; when they heard that the governor meant to abolish the licence, they took off their hats and gave him three respectful cheers.

The licence system nevertheless stayed longer than La Trobe. Many members of the Legislative Council opposed his plan for an export duty both as an improper restriction on freedom of commerce and as a device impossible to administer because gold would be smuggled out through Sydney or Adelaide. The Goldfields Management Act of November 1853 reduced the licence fee to one pound a month or eight pounds a year, a sum higher than the men at Bendigo had demanded but low enough to keep the fields peaceful for the time being, especially as little effort was made for some months to pursue men who did not pay it. Franchise of a kind was offered to diggers in the draft constitution for Victoria which passed the council and went to England for approval in 1854. Miners could vote for the Legislative Assembly if they stayed in one place for six months and if they took out a licence for a whole year. They were thus recognized as having political rights, but only on terms that would exclude a great many of them.

La Trobe went home in May 1854. Vice-Admiral Sir Charles Hotham came out reluctantly to replace him, feeling that it would be fitter for a man of his naval experience to be fighting the queen's Russian enemies at the Crimea than presiding over the squabbles of her colonial subjects. An under-secretary at the Colonial Office said later of Hotham that 'he had never met with a man who had so little idea of what he was about to do in a colony.' Melbourne greeted him with flags, triumphal arches, 'Rule Britannia', 'God Save the Queen' and a banner declaring: 'Victoria welcomes Victoria's choice.' At Ballarat, too, he was received loyally. After touring the goldfields he observed that if the men there should become rebels they would be difficult, entrenched in their holes, for soldiers to fight. They must be governed, he thought, by tact and management. But if he ever needed armed force he would have plenty of it. Since 1788 the military headquarters of the Australian colonies had been in Sydney. But Victoria was now becoming the largest colony, Melbourne was the most nearly central point in the colonies, and the mail from England was landed there before Sydney. Early in 1854 the military headquarters moved from Sydney to Melbourne. The new governor had more than a thousand soldiers to call on.

Hotham was appalled to discover how much money was being lost by evasion of licence fees, and on 13 September he ordered that searches for licences be made at least twice a week. But fees were more onerous than ever now, as gold was proving harder to find. At Bendigo the licence hunts provoked men to found a Goldfields Reform League. At Ballarat, miners indignant at the searches were made even angrier by demands that they take off their hats to officials. Henry Kingsley, who worked in the mounted police on New South Wales goldfields, observed that 'an Australian never touches his hat if he is a free man, because the prisoners are forced to'. The diggers of Ballarat had by this time even more cause than men elsewhere to dislike the licence system. At Ballarat the gold was buried more than a hundred feet down, a great deal of it in three ancient stone riverbeds known as the Canadian, Gravel Pits, and Eureka leads. Digging so deep made the job more of a lottery than working in shallower holes. A team of eight or twelve men at Ballarat might dig a hole for six months or more, finding no gold but having to pay their licence fees each month. The deeper the hole, moreover, the more harassing it was to be called up from the bottom by a policeman on a licence hunt. Climbing out to show the document could delay work at Ballarat for more than half an hour. Even at best the licence system was inequitable and irritating. At Ballarat, where more than ten thousand men were enduring it late in 1854, the system was operating at its very worst. Any small act of official folly or delinquency might turn individual grievances into mass disaffection; and in October something happened which showed that men appointed to administer justice could not be trusted.

A man named James Scobie was kicked to death after drinking in the Eureka Hotel. The proprietor, James Bentley, and two other men were arrested and charged before three magistrates on 12 October. Despite much evidence, two of three magistrates found the accused not guilty. One of the two magistrates was known to be both corrupt and associated with Bentley. The other, Robert Rede, was the gold commissioner in charge of Ballarat. An orderly gathering of diggers on 17 October set up a committee to campaign for further proceedings against Bentley. After the meeting a crowd of men went to the Eureka Hotel and burned it down.

Governor Hotham ordered Bentley and the other two men to be arrested again. He began an inquiry into the administration of Ballarat, demanded the arrest of the men who destroyed the hotel, and reinforced the officers and men of the 40th Regiment who were camped already in the district. The three men were duly found guilty of manslaughter. The corrupt magistrate and a police sergeant were dismissed. Of the hundreds present at the burning of Bentley's hotel, three men were arrested and convicted of riot. Demands for their release mingled in Ballarat with the more general complaints of diggers. A Ballarat Reform League, formed by men with experience in the chartist movement at home, was launched in the last days of October. As at home, there was a variety of judgments at Ballarat about how reforms were best achieved. Five thousand men listened on 1 November to moderate advice from organizers of the league, republican agitation from a German named Vern, and incitement to physical force by a Scottish chartist, Kennedy, who recited a blunt couplet:

MEETING CALLED BY THE BALLARAT REFORM LEAGUE,
11 NOVEMBER 1854

Moral persuasion is all a humbug
Nothing convinces like a lick in 'the lug'.

A meeting of ten thousand men called by the Ballarat Reform League on 11 November adopted more drastic demands than had been made yet on any field. The licence must be abolished, and the Gold Commission with it; the three prisoners must be released; three points of the chartist programme—manhood suffrage, payment for members of parliament, and no property qualification for candidates—must be introduced into the colony. Like the arrival of the *Hashemy* at Port Jackson in 1849, the acquittal of Bentley and his associates had ignited large grievances and aspirations. In the Ballarat Reform League, as in the Australasian League for the Abolition of Transportation, men talked of the American revolution. A radical newspaper, the *Ballarat Times*, hailed the league as the 'germ of Australian independence'. The statement of principles accepted by the meeting of 11 November drew on memories of what the Americans had declared in 1776: 'That it is the inalienable right of every citizen to have a voice in making the laws he is called upon to obey. That taxation without representation is tyranny.' Whether this movement went further than anti-transportation would depend on how Hotham and his advisers responded to it.

Later in November a delegation of three men left for Melbourne to put the grievances of Ballarat before the governor. He told them that they must await the findings of a commission of inquiry which he had appointed on 16 November to report on the goldfields. To their most urgent demand, the release of the prisoners, Hotham replied that he would not pardon men whom a jury had convicted. One delegate, Kennedy the Scot, begged the governor to change his mind, 'if it were for no other reason than that of keeping back the spilling of blood'. But Hotham was ready to embrace that possibility. Every available policeman and soldier in the colony was now in Ballarat or on the way there. Major-General Sir Robert Nickle, commander-in-chief of the imperial military forces in Australia, was about to take personal charge of them. As some of the soldiers in chartered waggons passed a group of Irish miners at the Eureka lead on the evening of 28 November, they were hooted and pelted. One waggon was turned over, and the men in it were robbed of ammunition and bayonets. Shots were fired, and a drummer boy was hit and died. The leaders of the Ballarat Reform League, who knew nothing of this affray until it was over, condemned the miners who had begun it.

Next day, Wednesday 29 November, miners gathered on Bakery Hill to hear the delegates report on their visit to Melbourne. During the morning several men had built a platform for speakers and planted a pole eighty feet high. To the editor of the *Ballarat Times*, as to others who hoped that the Ballarat Reform League would do here what the chartists had been attempting at home, it was a historic moment when a flag bearing the stars of the southern cross was hoisted up the pole. 'There is no flag in Europe, or in the civilised world half so beautiful', the paper said, 'and Bakery Hill, as being the place where the Australian ensign was first hoisted, will be recorded in the deathless and indelible pages of history. The flag is silk, blue ground with a large silver cross; no device or arms, but all exceedingly chaste and natural.' Some of the ten thousand men who assembled under it must have remembered the flag that the anti-transportationists had flown in 1851. Both flags displayed the southern cross; but this one had no Union Jack. Vern, the German republican, moved that they should all burn their licences and protect anybody arrested

SOLDIERS FROM MELBOURNE
MARCH INTO THE GOVERNMENT CAMP, BALLARAT
Withers says that the scene is 'historical—not imaginary. The artist, Mr. Huyghue,
saw what he has depicted'.

for not having one. Two Catholic priests, Patrick Smyth and Frank Downing, moved that
the licences be not burned. Smyth had written anxiously to his superiors in Melbourne
about this rally, warning that 'everything tends to an insurrection'. His bishop, Dr Alipius
Goold, was so alarmed at the part that Catholics appeared likely to play at Ballarat that
he had ridden up from Melbourne all through the night before the meeting and told the
two priests what to do and say at it. They were not chaplains, and could not be given
orders by the secular authorities as James Dixon had been at Castle Hill in 1804; but
prudent Catholic clergy were no less likely now than half a century earlier to counsel
obedience. The priests' advice at Bakery Hill was rejected, as Dixon's had been on the road
to Toongabee. The Irish chairman of the meeting, Timothy Hayes, asked men to think
seriously about the consequences of Vern's motion before voting on it. Would a thousand,
two thousand, four thousand of them volunteer to liberate any man dragged to the lock-up
for not having a licence? Were they ready to die? The roars of 'Yes! Yes!', and the
cheers, moved Hayes to speak verse which connected this meeting with the insurrections
of his homeland:

> On to the field, our doom is sealed,
>   To conquer or be slaves;
> The sun shall see our country free,
>   Or set upon our graves.

Vern's resolution was passed almost unanimously. Revolvers and pistols were fired in the air, and licences blazed.

Despite Timothy Hayes's wild recitation, the men did not see their burning of licences as an act which would lead inevitably to an encounter of arms. Raffaello Carboni, a digger who knew what revolution was, and who suffered still from a leg wound sustained in fighting for the Roman republic in 1849, judged that Wednesday's crowd was disposed to use bluster rather than guns. 'The general impression', he wrote, 'was, that as soon as government knew in Melbourne the real state of the excited feelings of the diggers, the licence-hunt would be put a stop to.' Hotham, they assumed, would respond to agitation as the Legislative Council of New South Wales and then the secretary of state had responded to the petitions against transportation. But they were wrong. Commissioner Rede had instructions from Hotham 'to use force whenever legally called upon to do so, without regard to the consequences that might ensue'. On the morning after the licences were burned, Rede ordered a search for them. When diggers met him and the police with abuse and stones, he read the Riot Act and thus commanded them to disperse. Cavalrymen then charged among the miners and foot soldiers fired over their heads. Some men without licences were arrested. 'It was meant for a challenge', wrote an Irish digger, John Lynch, 'and as such was accepted.'

In the afternoon a crowd gathered on Bakery Hill under the Southern Cross. This meeting of Thursday 30 November was to be like none before it, and for the first time the mass of diggers threw up a single leader. Peter Lalor, a civil engineer from Queen's County in the province of Leinster, had left Ireland in 1852, and worked on the Geelong and Melbourne railway line and dug for gold at the Ovens before coming to Ballarat. At home in the 1830s his father had organized other farmers to refuse paying tithes to the established church and to resist eviction. His elder brother was planning armed revolt against English rule when he died in 1849. At Wednesday's meeting Peter Lalor had proposed a motion, which was carried, that the Ballarat Reform League meet on Sunday afternoon to elect a central committee. Carboni called him 'the earnest, well-meaning, no-two-ways, non-John-Bullised Irishman'. A poster offering a reward for information about him was soon to describe Lalor as: 'Height 5 ft. 11 in., age 35, hair dark brown, whiskers dark brown and shaved under the chin, no moustache, long face, rather good looking, and is a well made man.' It was an attractive portrait, from a source with no motive for flattery. Its only error, made by friends as well as enemies, was a tribute to Lalor's maturity of appearance: he was twenty-seven, not thirty-five. Lalor was surprised to become suddenly the leader of these outraged free emigrants. 'We waited for some time,' he recalled a few months later, 'expecting some of our public speakers to come forward and address us; but, through some accident or other, not one of them was present . . . I looked around me; I saw brave and honest men, who had come thousands of miles to labor for independence . . . The grievances under which we had long suffered, and the brutal attack of that day, flashed across my mind; and, with the burning feelings of an injured man, I mounted the stump and proclaimed "Liberty!"' With a rifle in his hand he called volunteers to fall in, and he asked Carboni to tell men who did not understand English that, if they were unable to get firearms, 'let each of them procure a piece of steel, five, or six inches long, attached to a pole, and that will pierce the tyrants' hearts.' A sort of military organization took shape during the afternoon: 'divisions' of men were formed under 'captains', a 'council of war' was appointed, and Lalor himself was elected 'commander-in-chief'. There followed an act of consecration. About five hundred armed men knelt with Lalor to take an oath. Head bare, right hand pointing up to the flag and the sky, he said: 'We swear by the Southern Cross to stand truly by each other, and fight to defend our rights and liberties.' 'Amen!' they responded. Two by two they marched behind their flag to the Eureka lead. If they were attacked, Lalor said, they should resist from the holes which, as Hotham had observed, offered much protection. Lalor was to be accused of inciting men 'to take up Arms, with a view to make war against Our Sovereign Lady the Queen.' He would always deny it, and so would his aide and war historian Carboni. 'It was perfectly understood, and openly declared,' Carboni wrote of the diggers' council of war, 'that we meant to organize for *defence*, and that we had taken up arms for no other purpose.'

On a hill at the Eureka lead, a place occupied by Irish miners, the men began on Thursday afternoon to raise a stockade made from the slabs of timber they used to line the sides of their shafts. It enclosed, in what Carboni called a higgledy-piggledy fashion, about an acre of easily accessible ground. Some of its builders thought that they were making not a fort but merely a screen to drill behind. 'I make no pretensions to military knowledge', Lalor had said earlier in the day. Nor did anybody else in the stockade. A veteran of Waterloo, watching them drill, described Lalor's men as an awkward squad. Carboni recalled 'marching, counter-marching, orders given by everybody, attended to by nobody.' It was a proof, he suggested, that the diggers had no revolutionary intent. Whatever it was they intended, the number of armed men in the stockade rose to about eight hundred by Thursday evening. A German blacksmith was making pikes, boasting of what he had done in the Mexican wars and swearing that his weapons would fix the red-toads of soldiers and the blue pissants of policemen.

Late on Thursday night the council of war decided on an action which showed that they still hoped for a peaceful outcome. Two men, accompanied by Father Smyth, were sent to the government camp to demand the release of the diggers who had been locked up that morning and a pledge to end licence-hunting. They reported grimly that Commissioner Rede had dismissed the agitation about licences as 'a mere cloak to cover a democratic revolution.'

On Friday 1 December nobody dug for gold. The stockade now enclosed about a thousand men, drilling and talking. Three hundred more marched in from Creswick, twelve miles away, accompanied by a band playing the 'Marseillaise' and led by the pugnacious Kennedy waving a sword and ready to deal out a lick in the lug. If the council of war was planning a rational military campaign, these men were valuable reinforcements; for as Father Smyth warned the occupants of the stockade, seven to eight hundred men were under arms in the government camp and more were coming from Melbourne. But the contingent from Creswick decided that they were not wanted and went away.

Hour by hour during Saturday, men slipped out of the stockade, some persuaded to withdraw from a hopeless venture, others thinking that they could return if an attack appeared imminent. Commissioner Rede was not pleased to observe them leaving. 'I am convinced', he wrote to Hotham on Saturday, 'that the future welfare of this Colony depends on the crushing of this movement in such a manner that it may act as a warning ... I should be sorry to see them return to their work.' With Lalor's permission, Smyth warned Catholic diggers against useless bloodshed and said that he hoped to see them at mass next morning. Despite the priest's exhortation, Irishmen tended to hang on longer than others. For them the tradition of glorious failure ran deep. It was as if they were preparing less for a fight than for an act of communion with the heroes of earlier defeats by English soldiers. They would carry the pikes as the men of 1798 carried them. Lalor even introduced on Saturday night a password—'Vinegar Hill'—which reminded them of those martyrs and which may in some memories have recalled Castle Hill. The rush for gold, the licence system, the police force, Scobie's murderers, the magistrates, Governor Hotham, the love of freedom and the wrongs of Ireland had brought a hundred and fifty men to lie down and sleep beside guns, pistols and pikes in the Eureka stockade on the night of 2–3 December 1854. Most of them were still asleep when nearly twice as many armed soldiers and policemen charged the stockade from north and south at dawn on the Sabbath. There were thirty cavalrymen and eighty-seven foot soldiers of the 40th Regiment, sixty-five foot soldiers of the 12th Regiment, seventy mounted police and twenty-four policemen on foot. On Lalor's count the defenders had about seventy guns, thirty pistols and twenty pikes,

SOLDIERS AND TROOPERS CHARGE THE EUREKA STOCKADE
*C. H. Currey writes that the artist 'was on the spot a few hours after the riot, The uniforms of the soldiers and the dress of the miners are correctly portrayed.'**

* See C. H. Currey, *The Irish at Eureka*, Sydney 1954, facing p. 56.

many of the men with arms having only one or two rounds of ammunition. When the attackers were about 150 yards off, the men in the stockade fired, hitting several soldiers. The soldiers and troopers fired two volleys back. Lalor, waving to his men to get down into holes, was shot in the left shoulder and fell. The men with pikes stood firm at the barricade, an easy target for muskets. Soldiers and policemen fixed bayonets and charged the stockade, and in ten minutes the battle was over—too quickly for some of the mounted police, who stuck their bayonets into dead and wounded bodies. Father Smyth moved around administering last rites to the dying. Of the living, those who could walk were marched in chains to the lock-up, guarded by cavalrymen with drawn swords. An Irish policeman tore down the Southern Cross to the cheers of his mates. Soldiers dragged the flag as a prize to the government camp, where it was thrown from hand to hand and trampled on.

Except at Castle Hill, there had been no other such encounter between white men in the history of Australia. For people who saw it and people who heard and read about it in the days ahead, the scene was almost incredible. On Sunday morning a correspondent of the *Geelong Advertiser* was among those who stood and stared at the wounded and the dead. 'They all lay in a small space with their faces upwards, looking like lead; several of them were still heaving, and at every rise of their breasts, the blood spouted out of their wounds, or just bubbled out and trickled away. One man, a stout-chested fine fellow, apparently about forty years old, lay with a pike beside him: he had three contusions in the head, three strokes across the brow, a bayonet wound in the throat under the ear, and other wounds in the body—I counted fifteen wounds in that single carcase. Some were bringing handkerchiefs, others bed furniture, and matting to cover up the faces of the dead. O God! sir, it was a sight for a sabbath morn that, I humbly implore Heaven, may never be seen again.' On Tuesday in Melbourne the *Age* said 'the mind refuses to believe that those scenes were really enacted within a few miles of Melbourne and that the actors in them were our fellow colonists'. Between thirty and forty of the actors were dead or dying. Captain H. C. Wise of the 40th Regiment and four private soldiers were killed. Twelve other soldiers and one policeman were wounded. Of the diggers, twenty were buried at Ballarat and perhaps another ten died later of wounds. Two of the dead soldiers, and ten of the dead miners, were Irish. Of other rebels killed, three were from England, two from Scotland, and one each from Canada, Nova Scotia, Hanover and Prussia. Only one was Australian-born. It was, as Lalor said, a movement of men who had come thousands of miles to labour for independence. Lalor himself escaped on Father Smyth's horse and arrived secretly on Sunday evening at the priest's house, where an Irish doctor took off his left arm. Confused as he admitted to being by events, Smyth was playing a complex part in them: on Friday the governor sent him thanks 'for the earnest efforts which, in your professional calling, you are making to allay the disturbances'; but here he was on Sunday harbouring the rebels' commander-in-chief. Bishop Goold made it strenuously clear that the Catholics in the stockade had no sanction from their church for rebellion. They had been deceived, he announced, by able intriguers against peace and order, whose evil counsel they preferred in a moment of weakness to the peace-inspiring instructions of ecclesiastical authority. The bishop said that he wept to consider 'the deeds of blood which now, for the first time, stain the annals of our adopted country'.

Sir Charles Hotham received news of the engagement in Melbourne as he came out of Sunday service at St James' Church. An official version was issued by Commissioner Rede in Ballarat the same day. 'Her Majesty's forces were this morning fired upon by a large body of evil-disposed persons of various nations, who had entrenched themselves in a stockade on the Eureka, and some [sic] officers and men killed. Several of the rioters have paid the penalty of their crime, and a large number are in custody . . . God Save the Queen.' The *Geelong Advertiser*'s man reported another interpretation: 'All whom I spoke to were of one opinion,' he wrote, 'that it was a cowardly massacre.' Carboni mocked himself as chronicler for thinking to describe such a one-sided affair as if it were a proper battle: 'What a nonsense of mine to endeavour to swell up the Eureka stockade to the level of a Sebastopol!! Good reader, I have to relate the story of a shocking murder, a disgrace to the Christian name.' To Charles Thatcher the emigrant entertainer, singing each night to audiences of diggers, comparing Eureka and Sebastopol seemed a happy conceit:

> Don't talk about Sebastopol,
>   The Russian War is flat now.
> Just listen to despatches
>   Just come from Ballarat now
> Our noble Governor, Sir Charles,
>   And where is there a better,
> Has permitted us to publish
>   Captain Bumble's private letter.

Captain Bumble's dispatch described the capture of two drayloads of potatoes, the inadvertent killing of a woman and a child in a tent, and a 'bold and desperate charge' against the sleeping rebels.

Hotham told the Colonial Office that the action at Eureka had restored and guaranteed order. One of the rebels, Vern, prophesied on the contrary that greater upheavals would follow. 'Victoria! thy future is bright', he wrote to the *Age* as he escaped from the colony. 'I confidently predict a Bunker's Hill, or an Alma as the issue of your next insurrection.' There was to be no insurrection, and perhaps Hotham was right to think that repression had deterred anybody else from resorting to arms. But he and his subordinates betrayed anxiety on that score for some time, and a swell of popular sympathy with the diggers forced his government into measures of conciliation. On Tuesday 5 December a meeting in Melbourne called by the mayor to endorse Hotham's policy was taken over by critics and ended with cheers for the diggers. Next day speakers at another public meeting condemned the government's resort to force. Hotham had three hundred police, a hundred gaol warders, a hundred volunteers and a body of soldiers standing by in case the meeting provoked disorder; but it did not. He urged the commission of inquiry on the condition of the goldfields to meet quickly. He asked Bishop Goold to go to Ballarat, and authorized him to say that the governor would do all he could both to restore order and to redress the miners' grievances. On Commissioner Rede he urged the utmost moderation. Martial law was proclaimed in Ballarat on Wednesday 6 December, when the town was visited by the commander-in-chief of the forces, Major-General Sir Robert Nickle, and Colonel Edward Macarthur, who was about to succeed him, and who was inspecting now the scene of the first insurrection to occur in Australia since he had been invited in 1825 to offer advice on how to deal with one. Nickle and Macarthur talked tactfully with diggers and advised the withdrawal of martial law after three days. At Bendigo and Castlemaine miners met to mourn, protest, and refuse to pay for licences. At Castlemaine they condemned military rule; at Bendigo they demanded the recall of

LET IT BURN, I'M ONLY A LODGER.

SIR CHARLES HOTHAM AND EUREKA

Hotham. On no field did commissioners think it prudent during December and January to conduct licence hunts. The commission of inquiry recommended a general amnesty for men involved at Eureka; but Hotham had thirteen of the prisoners, Carboni among them, arraigned for high treason.

Carboni was much pleased with the style of his judge, Redmond Barry, 'a man of the old-gentleman John Bull's stamp', who always addressed him with kindness. One by one, all the accused men were found not guilty by juries of Melbourne citizens, each dozen of them a fair sample of the colony's population. Carboni's was composed of two farmers, three gardeners, two carpenters, a joiner, a painter, a butcher, a grocer and a baker. When they found him not guilty, people in the court 'telegraphed the good news to the crowd outside, and "Hurrah!" rent the air in the old British style.'

The commission of inquiry reported on 27 March. Its six members represented, as Hotham had intended in appointing them, a broad range of respected colonial opinion. They included the Irish Catholic leader John O'Shanassy and the anti-Catholic, anti-squatting pioneer of settlement John Pascoe Fawkner. Their chairman was William Westgarth, a calm and liberal-minded merchant interested in the improvement of his fellow man. The commissioners deplored both the diggers' resort to arms and the measures that had provoked it. 'The tendencies to serious outbreak amongst masses of population', they wrote, 'are usually a signal that the government is at fault as well as the people.' Victoria's government was at fault in exposing British colonists 'to laws unsuited to their national character, and certainly most unsuitable to the circumstances in which they were placed upon the Gold Fields.' They recommended that an export duty on gold replace the licence fee, and that a 'miner's right', costing a pound a year, should entitle a man both to dig and to vote for parliament. Hotham acted promptly on the commissioners' advice. A service of wardens replaced the Gold Commission. Once the licence had gone, most of the officials and half the police on the goldfields were no longer needed. The export duty was not evaded after all by widespread smuggling. The governor was not recalled, but he worried himself to death. In a society requiring skilful civil government he saw himself as a simple beleaguered swordsman. 'I stand with my back to the wall and fight single handed', he told his wife. 'I may fall but if I go down it shall be with my colours flying.' In the event, Vice-Admiral Hotham did lower his colours. In November 1855 he wrote a letter of resignation which he meant to take effect a year later, but died in Melbourne on 31 December. As it was customary for the commander-in-chief of the military forces to administer a colony between governors, it fell to the son of John Macarthur to preside genially over the transition to responsible government in Victoria.

If the export duty had been introduced earlier there would have been no Eureka stockade. If there had been no Eureka stockade the government of Victoria in 1855 would not have given a vote to every purchaser of a miner's right and thus granted virtual manhood suffrage on the goldfields. The new constitution for the colony was well on its way to Westminster before the end of 1854. Eureka made it more nearly democratic.

Peter Lalor stayed in hiding until he was no longer wanted for treason, and became a farmer on the proceeds of concerts held for him in Ballarat and Bendigo. Later in 1855 he and another leader of the reformers stood for the electorate of Ballarat in the Legislative Council and were returned unopposed. He was elected to the new Legislative Assembly in 1856 and shocked radical friends by accepting official patronage as inspector of railways, supporting the motion for a plural property franchise, and being absent when the principle of manhood suffrage was voted on. To charges that he was a turncoat he replied, at the end of 1856: 'I would ask these gentlemen what they mean by the term "democracy"? Do they mean Chartism, or Communism or Republicanism? If so, I never was, I am not now, nor do I ever intend to be a democrat. But if democracy means opposition to a tyrannical press, a tyrannical people, or a tyrannical government, then I have ever been, I am still, and I ever will remain a democrat.' He was, it appeared, a man of conservative temperament, roused by particular obstacles to liberty, and content with the polity of his new homeland once they were removed. Lalor was returned by electors for more than thirty years. For the last nine years he was speaker of the Legislative Assembly, presiding over the democratic deliberations with his left sleeve empty as a reminder that there were other means than discussion to achieve political ends.

Melbourne appeared to Charles Gavan Duffy a peaceful place when he arrived to live there in 1856. 'It resembled a settlement in the American Far West in its external aspect,' he wrote, 'but with the external aspect the resemblance ceased. There was no violence or disorder, no roughs or rowdies. No man carried arms; every man knew all those whom he met, as he might know his neighbours in an English country town.' Duffy's picture was a little too cosy. Roughs and rowdies did sometimes disturb Melbourne's tranquillity. There were moments when hunger for land threatened to break the bounds of law and order. When the Victorian parliament failed in 1858 to meet the demands of a Land Convention, one of its leaders, Graham Berry, urged the people of Victoria 'to follow Garibaldi's example'. On the night of 28 August 1860 the debate about land very nearly turned into a battle in the streets of Melbourne. Radical politicians had gathered a crowd outside Parliament House to demonstrate in favour of a bill which was supposed to open the land to small farmers, and which had been blocked by the Legislative Council. 'Let them come peaceably, orderly,' said one of the organizers, 'with a determination to preserve the peace, but with a firm countenance.' The government ordered field guns to be trained on Prince's Bridge in case the crowd tried to cross it and rush the Victoria Barracks. People jammed the entrances to Parliament House and filled its yard. Some carried stones, and a few may have thrown them at windows. The premier, William Nicholson, ordered troopers and foot police to break up the crowd. They charged the yard three times, swinging truncheons and drawing blood. A dozen or more policemen were injured by stones, while inside the house popular members nervously insisted that they had tried to disperse their supporters. More than a thousand special constables were sworn in during the next few days, ready to be summoned in daylight by the Union Jack flying at the Town Hall, and at night by red lamps and rockets. A Disorderly Meetings Act forbade political assemblies within a prescribed part of the city. The danger passed; and so, in drastically weakened form, did Nicholson's land act, opening up the land to very few diggers. The struggles over land and other issues of colonial politics were pursued after 1860 in parliaments elected by manhood suffrage. With rare exceptions, such as when Orange met Green in Melbourne on the night of Prince Alfred's ball, differences between groups of the queen's white subjects were not expressed in public violence between 1860 and 1870.

CHINAMEN

When people spoke of Eureka as the last violent encounter on the goldfields, they were forgetting the Chinese. During 1854 thousands of Chinese men appeared on Victorian diggings, having been carried from Hong Kong in ships which had gone to China for cargoes after bringing emigrants from England. There were about 3500 of them in the colony by June. At Bendigo, where they made up some 2000 of 15 000 miners, public sentiment among white diggers was divided about whether or not to drive the Chinese off. A rally was organized to expel them on 4 July, postponed to 8 July when Americans protested against that mode of celebrating their national day, and abandoned after the police force on the field was strengthened and a meeting of miners voted against violence. The authorities promised to investigate grievances against the Chinese, which included complaints that they wasted water and ignored regulations and conventions of mining. The main source of trouble, according to the police magistrate at Bendigo, was that the Chinese were arriving just as the gold was running out.

They kept on arriving: 10 000 in Victoria by the end of 1854, 18 000 by June 1855. Governor Hotham reported in June that 'disputes and broils' were 'of daily occurrence.' His commission of inquiry into the goldfields reported that the number of Chinese, though 'almost incredible', was 'likely to increase still more upon the publication of the abolition of the licence fee.' Their presence in such large numbers 'must certainly tend to demoralise colonial society, by the low scale of domestic comfort, by an incurable habit of gaming and other vicious tendencies, and by the examples of degrading and absurd superstition.' The commissioners had no wish to exclude absolutely either the Chinese 'or any other branch of the great human family', but they did recommend that their entry be restricted immediately. Hotham tried to do so in an act of 1855 limiting the number of Chinese passengers a ship could land and imposing a tax of ten pounds, and another pound a year, on each Chinese head. Entrepreneurs responded by shipping Chinese passengers to Robe in South Australia and putting them ashore to walk two or three hundred miles to a Victorian goldfield. Sixteen shiploads of Chinese arrived at Robe in two months of 1857, and altogether 14 600 landed there. 'They were winding across the plain like a long black mark,' wrote a white observer of their trek towards the gold, 'and as I passed them, every one behind seemed to be yabbering to his mate in front in a sing-song tone.' In May 1857 the yabbering of one party became animated, for on their way to known fields they had found a new one, at Ararat. The Canton lead, as their discovery was called, was one of the richest shallow alluvial deposits in the colony. In the rush that followed, white miners attacked the Chinese and burned their tents.

The most systematic campaign to expel Chinese miners from a Victorian field was launched on the Buckland River, a tributary of the Ovens, in July 1857. As at Bendigo three years earlier, 4 July was chosen as a good date for a robust initiative, and this time it was carried through. The one police constable on the field that day, Constable Duffy, advised the Europeans not to attack and the Chinese to stand firm; but between fifty and a hundred men carrying pick-handles moved forward and the Chinese fled down the gorge. Their tents and joss-house were burned, and their bedding was thrown into the river. Three of the aggressors were wounded by shots from the Chinese. An unknown number of Chinese were drowned or died later from wounds or exposure. Policemen from Beechworth under the command of their superintendent, Robert O'Hara Burke, persuaded Chinese diggers to return from hiding in the bush and arrested a number of white men, most of whom were acquitted by juries in Beechworth and cheered as heroes when they left the court house. Three men convicted of unlawful assemblage and one of riot were sentenced to gaol for nine months.

The Chinese were actually a majority of the miners at the Buckland. If they kept coming at this rate, what was to stop the golden colony turning yellow? In the Legislative

REVIVAL OF THE FINE OLD AUSTRALIAN SPORT OF LICENSE-HUNTING.

HUNTING CHINESE DIGGERS
*An artist imagines a hunt at Beechworth under the proposed Victorian law to control
Chinese immigration.*

Council John Pascoe Fawkner moved for a committee to frame 'a Bill to control the flood
of Chinese immigration setting in to this Colony, and effectually prevent the Gold Fields of
Australia Felix from becoming the property of the Emperor of China and of the Mongolian
and Tartar hordes of Asia.' The emperor, labouring to resist the intrusion of European
powers, would have been amazed to know of his alleged designs on Victoria; but Fawkner's
committee found that more than 40000 of his subjects, all except four of them males, had
come to Victoria and were causing discord in the colony. Chinese petitioners to parliament
tried to make British colonists understand their strange ways. Why did they not buy land
and work farms? Because too much capital was required. 'We Chinamen who are here get
no gold only by washing, headings and tailings, and from old holes abandoned by
Europeans, and from which we can but barely make a living.' Why had they not brought
wives and children? Because 'we wish to leave some of the family to look after our aged
parents'. They asked only a brief indulgence, for as soon as they got a little money they
would try to return to those parents. The task of saving gold to take home appeared to be
made harder in 1857 when the cost of a licence to reside in the colony was increased from a
pound a year to a pound every two months; but as no penalty was provided for not paying
the fee, few Chinese took out licences.

There were about 42000 Chinese miners in Victoria at the end of 1858, nearly all of them men, and representing about 15 per cent of the male population. South Australia had imposed in 1857 restrictions similar to Victoria's of 1855 and thus stopped untaxed Chinese passengers from being unloaded at Robe; but as New South Wales imposed no limits, ships travelled from Hong Kong to Twofold Bay, north of the Victorian border. About 9000 Chinese newcomers entered Victoria from that direction in 1858. The government of John O'Shanassy resolved early in 1859 to police the entry tax and the residence licence. Parliament passed a bill imposing heavy fines or imprisonment for men who did not pay. Like white miners a few years earlier, Chinese miners protested at what seemed to them an unjust system of licensing. They formed a United Confederacy of Chinese which had aims not unlike those of the Ballarat Reform League. They threatened not to pay. At Bendigo in May 1859 a crowd of 700 Chinese gathered when goldfields police arrested some of their comrades who had refused to pay. Policemen were jostled and knocked down, and their prisoners escaped. There was a scuffle with the police at Beechworth. At Castlemaine nearly 3000 Chinese miners resolved to suspend all business with Europeans. 'Why this tax on Chinamen?' they asked. 'Chinamen pay for what they eat, Chinamen work very hard, but little money earn, and can't afford to pay tax . . . We obey law, we make no noise, we have feelings like other men, we want to be brothers with Englishmen—why not let be so?' The only answer from the democratic politicians in charge of the colony was to lay thousands of charges: by early 1860, 4000 Chinese had been fined and 2000 imprisoned for not paying their licence fees. As they had no votes and little support among white colonists, they could only resist by violence, or submit, or try to evade, or go away. Thousands went back to China, thousands moved on to New South Wales, and by 1861 Victoria's Chinese population was down to about 25000, nearly 24000 of them in mining areas. As their numbers went on declining in the 1860s, the restrictions on them were removed.

Many Chinese miners from Victoria walked into trouble across the border. In September 1856, when there were only some 1300 Chinese in New South Wales, a group who had travelled from Hong Kong to Sydney and made for the Rocky River field, near Armidale, were attacked by a party of white men under a leader who called himself Captain X. Several Chinese miners died of injuries; but there were only two troopers on the field, and no charges were laid. At Adelong, in the south, Chinese refugees from the Buckland River were driven off in 1857. Diggers at a western field, Tambaroora, tried in March 1858 to expel Chinese miners but were stopped by troopers under a commissioner who 'came forward like a lion', the *Sydney Morning Herald* reported, 'crying he would stand to be shot before he would allow a Chinaman to be touched.' The number of Chinese in the colony was now increasing rapidly, and so was hostility to them on the goldfields. By March 1861 there were 13000, or about 7 per cent of the male population. That was a lower proportion than in Victoria; but more were landing every month, and among the gold miners of New South Wales they were actually more numerous than white diggers.

Europeans and Chinese rushed in April 1860 to a new field at Lambing Flat, 265 miles across the ranges from Sydney and 60 miles north-west of Yass. White diggers organized a vigilance committee and drove out five hundred Chinese in November, just before the area was proclaimed a goldfield and became the base for a resident commissioner and policemen. Some of the Chinese returned; and in a drive against criminals, Chinese and other men deemed undesirable, some Chinese diggers were injured on 12 December. It was alleged, and denied, that one or two Chinese were killed in this episode. Official reports on it lacked precision, for the nearest agents of law and order, a commissioner and two troopers, were stationed at this time twelve miles away from the diggings. The police were closer and more numerous by Sunday 27 January, when a meeting decided to force all the Chinese—more than 1500 now—off the field. White diggers formed a Miners' Protective League, which had among its objects getting rid of the Chinese. Three weeks later, on 18 February, the police could not prevent assaults on Chinese miners. Messages reached Sydney suggesting that the field was dangerously close to anarchy. A detachment of 130 soldiers of the 12th Regiment and a squad of artillery set off for Lambing Flat on 25 February. The premier himself, Charles Cowper, arrived on 2 March.

A premier in 1861 had more cause than a governor in 1854 to avoid a confrontation with miners. As the leader of a democratically elected ministry, Cowper was reluctant to send police and soldiers into action against thousands of voters who had on the Chinese question the sympathy of many thousands more. He told a meeting of diggers that they must obey the law, that the Chinese must be allowed to work their claims, and that the government would look into the grievances of the Miners' Protective League. Then Cowper returned to Sydney pleased with the temper of his exchange with the miners and confident that the trouble would subside. The soldiers, arriving soon after he left, camped at Lambing Flat until they were recalled on 24 May. There were only about twenty policemen on the field on 30 June, when more than two thousand men mustered to solve the Chinese problem once and for all.

Like earlier days of violence in the area it was a Sunday, when by custom men did not look for gold and were free to sleep, to worship, to talk, and if the mood took them, to fight. The public mood on 30 June 1861 was belligerent, festive and patriotic. Sleeping men were roused by cries to rally with bludgeons and pick handles around a flag which like the flag of Eureka bore the stars of the southern cross, and which carried also the message ROLL UP ROLL UP NO CHINESE. They marched to the music of a band playing 'Rule Britannia' and the 'Marseillaise' and swarmed into the Chinese camp, smashing and burning tents. Then men on horseback hunted the fleeing Chinese and rounded them up, so it seemed to a correspondent of the *Sydney Morning Herald*, 'the same as they would a mob of cattle.' Pigtails were cut off. The correspondent 'saw one tail, with a part of the scalp the size of a man's hand attached, that had been literally cut from some unfortunate creature; another had his back broken.' Who among the British people, asked the paper in a leading article, 'could ever believe that men of their own country—Britons, would take the Chinese pigtails *with the scalp attached.*'

Foot police and troopers were summoned from surrounding districts. There were nearly sixty of them at Lambing Flat on the second Sunday after the rampage, when three men alleged to have led the attack were arrested and locked up. Like the diggers at Ballarat after the burning of the Eureka Hotel, the comrades of these three men demanded that they be released. Unlike members of the Ballarat Reform League, the men at Lambing Flat decided that they themselves would release the prisoners. The Riot Act was read in heavy rain as a crowd of men advanced on foot police and troopers who were guarding the lock-up. Policemen sent a volley over their heads; and when shots were fired at the troopers' horses, the foot police were ordered to shoot at the miners and the troopers to charge with drawn swords. One miner, William Lupton, was shot in the head and died. His comrades retired carrying Lupton's body back to the Empire Hotel. Fearing another attack next morning, the police withdrew to Yass, taking the three prisoners with them. On Tuesday Lupton's body was buried with informal military honours at a ceremony attended by more than three thousand people. The *Sydney Morning Herald*, whose correspondent was sending dispatches by messenger to Yass and thence by telegraph to Sydney, reported on Wednesday that Lambing Flat was 'in the hands of the insurgents.'

Cowper's government decided that it must establish a presence of overwhelming force. From Sydney it sent not only seven infantry officers and 123 men of the 12th Regiment and a force of artillery, but also seventy-four men and a naval gun from a British warship. The progress of this expeditionary force was well advertised. By the time it arrived, nobody at Lambing Flat was disposed to resist its weapons. Thirteen miners submitted quietly to arrest on charges of riot, but a court at Goulburn decided that only in one case had police found the right man. The Chinese returned to work. Lambing Flat became Young, in honour of a new governor.

Bills to restrict the entry of people from China into New South Wales had been before the new parliament on and off since 1857. The Legislative Assembly passed in 1858 a bill copied from the Victorian act of 1855, but adding a provision, for which some diggers had petitioned, making it impossible for Chinese residents ever to become British subjects. The measure was rejected by the Legislative Council on the ground that the Chinese were harmless and that discrimination proposed against them was inexpedient and inhuman. The affrays at Lambing Flat finally secured majorities in both houses for Cowper's Chinese Immigrants Regulation and Restriction Act of 1861, which like the earlier bill denied Chinese the right to be naturalized. That clause had been supported all along by Henry Parkes and Daniel Deniehy. The Chinese, Parkes thought, 'fondly cherished the belief that eventually this country would be theirs'; their unregulated entry would lead to 'future discord, anarchy and civil war.' The Colonial Office judged the denial of naturalization 'unnecessary and impolitic', but conceded that it was better to 'prevent the arrival of the immigrants than to discourage or harass them after they are arrived.' The act of 1861 hastened the homeward journey of many Chinese and deterred others from coming. The Chinese population of New South Wales fell by nearly half in ten years, to 7000 by 1871. As in Victoria, the politicians repealed the restrictive legislation once the tide had turned. Parkes was reluctant to see it go, arguing that it protected the British character of the colony; but he agreed by 1867 that it could always be restored if the Chinese threatened again to become too numerous.

Of the Chinese who stayed in Australia, many moved from prospecting into other occupations such as storekeeping and gardening. A remarkable number were victims of bushrangers in the 1860s, perhaps because it was a fair bet that a Chinaman on the road would be carrying gold. One Chinese, known in official records as Sam Poo, himself became a bushranger. He left the diggings at Mudgee, held up travellers, killed a trooper from Coonabarabran and was executed at Bathurst.

The Chinese who stayed in Australia were protected by policemen, evangelized by missionaries, tolerated by some people and persecuted by others. They were known with varying mixtures of affection and contempt as Chinkies, Chows, Celestials and John Chinaman. In 1870 there were still hard times ahead for them, especially on goldfields. 'All diggers have a horror of Chinamen', wrote a colonist of Queensland in 1872, 'though I doubt if half of them could tell you for what reason'.

How many Chinese miners were killed by white competitors was a matter for dispute: if the policemen who could have done the authoritative counting had been on the spot, the violence which broke out in their absence might never have happened. People who lived elsewhere than on goldfields tended to forget or not to learn that relations with the Chinese had ever been a serious issue in colonial society.

14 The Sound of Distant War

OUTPOSTS OF EMPIRE

England was at war with no other nation when the first fleet left home, peace having been concluded with the Americans, the French, the Spanish and the Dutch in 1783; but a war against one or other of these antagonists appeared by no means impossible. When Captain Arthur Phillip first entered Port Jackson, he imagined a thousand warships riding there 'in the most perfect security'. Soon after landing he appointed Lieutenant William Dawes as engineer and artillery officer and had him make a redoubt at the eastern end of the cove to provide a shelter for guns and men. The commander of the marines, Major Robert Ross, thinking of foreign men-of-war, pressed the governor in July to provide a 'kind of place for defence to retire to in case of an alarm or surprise.' Phillip thought that unnecessary; but when the *Sirius* went off in search of food she left eight guns behind on the western edge of the cove, which was named Dawes Point. Phillip ordered some fortification of this battery at the end of 1790, when a Dutch ship delivered a rumour from Batavia that England was at war with Spain; and by November 1791 the guns pointed across a low stone wall to the harbour.

 News that Frenchmen had begun a revolution in July 1789 travelled eleven months before it reached Sydney, and news of England's declaration of war against the revolutionary government on 1 February 1793 took almost as long to cross the world. Hearing of such things out in New South Wales was rather like watching in the night sky an explosion which had really happened a very long time ago. The lapse of time left imagination free to run wild until the next ship subdued it. What if English Jacobins had done to George III what their French friends had done to Louis XVI? What if dispatches from New South Wales were being read at home by French officials? 'By the capture of a ship off the coast of Brazil', wrote John Macarthur's wife on 1 September 1795, 'we were left without any direct intelligence from Europe for twelve months. We firmly believed that a Revolution or some national calamity had befallen Great Britain, and we should be left altogether to ourselves, until things at home had resumed some degree of order and the tempest a little subsided. These fears, however, have by a late arrival proved without foundation.'

 Elizabeth Macarthur did not anticipate the tumult of war in her new home. 'It seems to be the only part of the Globe', she wrote, 'where quiet is to be expected.' But what if French men-of-war should actually sail into Port Jackson? Governor Hunter had guns from a warship set up at the eastern end of the cove and nearby at Garden Island. He asked London for more guns, and received some in 1799. His successor, King, not impressed by the defences of the port, asked in August 1801 for eight twelve-pounders 'to prevent it from insult by the smallest vessels belonging to an enemy.' When the guns arrived, some of them were installed at George's Head, near the entrance to the harbour, where if they were fired accurately they could stop ships approaching Sydney Cove. King also began the construction of Fort Phillip, the citadel intended to protect the settlement against both insurgency and invasion.

Two French ships, *Le Géographe* and *Le Naturaliste*, entered Port Jackson on 20 June 1802. The names proclaimed their peaceful intentions, and news had reached Sydney before them that France and England had signed the Peace of Amiens; but one of the French party, guessing that the peace was merely a pause, sent robust advice to Captain-General Charles De Caen, military governor at Mauritius, that the British settlement at Port Jackson should be destroyed as soon as possible. 'Today we could destroy it easily; we shall not be able to do so in twenty-five years' time.' King did not guess that such a plan was in any French mind, but he did suspect the visitors of an aggressive design. Soon after the French ships left Port Jackson on 18 November 1802, King heard a rumour that some of their officers had spoken of making a settlement in Van Diemen's Land. The discovery of Bass Strait by Flinders and Bass had given ships travelling from Europe and India to Sydney a way safer and shorter than the route around the bottom of the island. King, determined that England should control this strait, sent in pursuit of the French the schooner *Cumberland*, the first ship ever built in the colony. It followed them to King Island, where men from the *Cumberland* raised the Union Jack on a tree as the French made scientific observations. The French watched with amusement, both because they had no plan for a settlement—the rumours reaching King had been untrue—and because the English flag was hoisted upside-down.

The first minister to hold office as secretary of state for war and the colonies, Lord Hobart, warned Governor King in February 1803 that the establishment of a foreign power at Port Phillip 'might, in the event of hostilities, greatly interrupt the communication with Port Jackson, and materially endanger the tranquility and security of our possessions there.' Two months later a party of convicts, soldiers and free settlers under Captain David Collins was dispatched from home for Port Phillip. Finding the site too dry and sandy and the entrance too perilous, Collins moved his people to the estuary of the Derwent River in Van Diemen's Land, where the landing of convicts had begun in September 1803 from Sydney. A settlement in the north of Van Diemen's Land, established in 1804 under Lieutenant-Colonel William Paterson, was made on orders which left England the month after war with France resumed in May 1803. Nobody in Sydney knew that the war was on again when Matthew Flinders sailed for home on 21 September 1803 in command of the *Cumberland*. The little ship had not been built to cross oceans. It leaked so badly that Flinders had to put in at Mauritius, where Captain-General De Caen, suspecting the English navigator of some hostile purpose, made him a French prisoner of war for six years.

The *Sydney Gazette*, first published on 5 March 1803, advised readers on 18 December that for the past seven months their nation had been at war again with France. The editor hoped for fresh reports from every ship. When Nelson's achievement and death at Trafalgar on 21 October 1805 became known in Sydney on 13 April 1806, the paper announced that the next Sunday would be a day of general thanksgiving. As in all its ceremonies so far, the colony was following the motherland, where a similar day of rejoicing for victory had been held late in 1805. A Scottish settler, John Bowman, gave the celebration a local character by flying at his property on the Hawkesbury a flag made from his wife's wedding dress. It bore not only a rose, shamrock and thistle surmounted by the word 'Unity', and not only the hero of Trafalgar's message 'England expects every man will do his duty', but also an emu and a kangaroo. It was perhaps the first time anybody had used the native animals as symbols of nationality.

Later in 1806 a plan made in London would have had soldiers and convict labourers from New South Wales take part in the war by joining a military expedition to Panama and Peru, where local populations had risen against Spanish rule after Spain was conquered by France. Once that enterprise was called off, the only way a man from the colony could get to war was by joining the army at home. Edward Macarthur did so in

FORT MACQUARIE
At Bennelong Point, Sydney Cove

1808, when he was nineteen. He was the first person raised in the colony to become a professional soldier, and the only one to serve against Napoleon. The first man actually born in the colony to gain a commission in the army was William Charles Wentworth's younger brother Darcy; but he was too late for the wars.

In Macquarie's time there was some danger that war might come to New South Wales. Napoleon did order De Caen to capture Port Jackson in 1810; but he had not the resources to do so, and at the end of the year a British force occupied Mauritius. In 1812 England went to war again with the Americans. A convict ship bound for Sydney, the *Emu*, was captured at sea by an American privateer. Wentworth was surprised that Sydney itself was not held to ransom or plundered by American ships. 'A vessel of ten guns', he wrote in 1819, 'might have effected this enterprise with the greatest ease and safety; and that the inhabitants were not subjected to such an insulting humiliation, could only have arisen from the enemy's ignorance of the insufficiency of their means of defence.' A report reached Sydney in April that a French squadron was preparing with American help to seize New South Wales and make it a base for trading with South America and the East Indies. Macquarie asked at once for a detachment of artillery, and for small arms to put into the hands of trustworthy settlers 'as a temporary Militia on any sudden Emergency or Invasion by a Foreign Enemy.'

Just before Macquarie dispatched this request, Napoleon's enemies had overthrown him and occupied Paris. The news reached Sydney five months later by a Russian ship which had picked it up in Rio de Janeiro, and was proclaimed in an extraordinary edition of the *Sydney Gazette*. Colonists were spared anxiety about his return from Elba, for the ship that reported it carried also news of the allied victory over him at Waterloo on 18 June 1815. That event was celebrated at Government House on the night of 17 January 1816 by eating, drinking, and dancing until dawn, and on the next Sunday by services of thanksgiving. Five months earlier people in Sydney had heard that the war with America was over. There was no threat for the time being from any foreign enemy; but among Macquarie's public works was the strengthening of the battery at Dawes Point, the reconstruction of Fort Phillip, and the beginning of a new fort on Bennelong Point, at the eastern side of the cove, to be named after himself. Commissioner Bigge was not impressed: 'the defence of New South Wales against Foreign Invasion, or even against internal Commotion,' he wrote to Macquarie on 2 October 1820, 'will ultimately depend upon other sources than those that may be afforded in the Town of Sydney.' Bigge meant that a battery out near the ocean would be more useful than the forts that embellished the cove. In the decade after Macquarie retired, the governors gave less attention to planning the defence of settled areas than to anticipating foreign landings and claims of possession at other places around the continent. Settlements at Western Port, King George Sound, the Swan River and elsewhere originated in efforts to forestall imagined initiatives by the French and the Americans.

The society of New South Wales had a military stamp. In Macquarie's day one in ten of the population was a soldier. Brisbane, Darling, Bourke and FitzRoy had all served in the wars against Napoleon: in the years of peace all the colonies were convenient places for old soldiers to be sent. The barracks housing the imperial regiments stood at George Street in the centre of Sydney. Soldiers contributed largely to ceremonies, games and brawls. Many became settlers, and others formed durable attachments: the builders of St Mary's church thought it worth sending an agent to India to solicit money from Catholics who had been stationed in Sydney. But colonists sometimes wondered what

THE BARRACKS, GEORGE STREET, SYDNEY

resistance the defenders of New South Wales could offer to an outside enemy. When two Russian ships visited Sydney on a cruise of exploration in 1829, the *Australian* said 'that gingerbread work, Macquarie Fort, and all the pop-guns at Dawes's Battery, could not for one hour oppose an armed force of any power, Russian or American'. Governor Bourke asked for more guns and was promised some, but Gipps complained in 1839 that they had still not arrived. Gipps received anxious petitions about them from time to time, and the Legislative Council debated whether or not the defences of the colony were adequate.

On the evening of 29 November 1839, a few days after one of these debates, two ships of the United States navy sailed into Port Jackson and dropped anchor in Sydney Cove. 'When the good people of Sydney looked abroad in the morning', wrote Commander Charles Wilkes, 'they were much astonished to see two men-of-war lying among their shipping, which had entered their harbour in spite of the difficulties of the channel, without being reported, and unknown to the pilots.' The Americans felt thoroughly at home among the friendly, English-speaking and acquisitive people of New South Wales; but Wilkes's professional eye could not help noticing what opportunities lay here for a less peaceful expedition. He saw that the guns of Fort Macquarie, which Gipps lent him to use as an observatory, were in no condition for service. Nor did any of the other defences impress him. 'Had war existed, we might, after firing the shipping, and reducing a great part of the town to ashes, have effected a retreat before daybreak, in perfect safety.'

The Americans' undetected entry made it easier to imagine such a devastation. When guns arrived in 1840, Gipps planned to have them set up in new batteries, one at Bradley's Head on the north shore of the harbour and the other on Pinchgut Island near the entrance to Sydney Cove. Preparations for housing the guns appeared to the *Sydney Herald* 'both warlike and business-like'; but despite requests from Gipps there was nobody from the Royal Artillery to man them. At the end of 1841, when a French warship was visiting Sydney and travellers brought tales that England and the United States were at war, the *Sydney Gazette* demanded a company or two of artillery. The paper, which was no longer under official patronage, offered an argument which was to be put vehemently later in the century by colonists aware that as Australians they had interests distinguishable from those of England: 'whilst rumours of war are constantly wafted to this distant land, from both Europe and America,' it declared, 'we really think that we have a right to that protection, the necessity for which only arises from our connexion with the Mother Country.' The faint threat of separation aroused no concern at home in 1841. Far from agreeing to strengthen the defences of New South Wales, the Colonial Office under Lord John Russell in 1841 and Lord Stanley in 1842 rebuked Gipps for spending three hundred pounds at Bradley's Head and Pinchgut without authority, and told him to stop. At the Colonial Office it appeared more important to keep down expenditure in New South Wales than to assure its inhabitants of protection against imaginary attack. But for many years after Wilkes's visit, some colonists were troubled by a spectral man-of-war which evaded or silenced the batteries and bombarded Sydney. John Dunmore Lang derided the 'tertian ague or regular intermittent fever about the "defences of Port Jackson"', the fear of 'some "predatory attack," of which it seems we are perpetually in danger from those pirates and robbers of the dark ages, the modern French and Russians and Americans!' He suspected that the colonial government pretended anxiety about a foreign

DAWES BATTERY
Fort Macquarie is across Sydney Cove, and Government House is on the far right.

attack 'merely to get a body of troops stationed in or near Sydney, to maintain and perpetuate the present monstrous system of government against the interests of the people.' But there was more behind the fever than that. Australian colonists were so far from their motherland that if ever they had to cry for help, her response would take the best part of a year. News from the rest of the world was so delayed by distance that nobody knew for certain whether the empire was at war or at peace. For a while in 1848 there was fever in Sydney about the French. The flight of King Louis Philippe from revolutionaries in February was reported in Sydney four months later. The *Sydney Morning Herald* expressed fear on 19 June that a general war might be on the way, and announced in a special edition on 14 July that Europe was ablaze. England and France had declared war on Russia, Austria and Prussia after an Austrian invasion of the papal states. The paper had the news from a ship's captain who in turn had been given it, he said, off Madeira on 28 April. For more than three weeks the paper and its readers believed that England was at war, until on 8 August the paper reported that she was not and hoped that the inaccurate captain would be dealt with.

As colonial self-government approached, it became likelier that whenever people in Australia asked for guns or soldiers they would be told to think about providing their own. In 1847 the number of soldiers in New South Wales was reduced by nine hundred, who were sent across to New Zealand to help subdue the Maoris. That would leave New South Wales with fewer than nine hundred soldiers—quite enough, Earl Grey told FitzRoy, when no foreign enemy endangered the colony, no native tribes were engaged in serious hostilities, and no rising of convicts need now be guarded against. 'Under these circumstances,' the secretary of state concluded, 'there is no part of Her Majesty's Dominions in which there is less occasion for a large body of Troops.' The *Sydney Morning Herald* protested that New South Wales was being sacrificed. When the Legislative Council deplored the decision, the secretary of state replied that the imperial soldiers had been there primarily to guard convicts, and that the garrisons must be reduced as the penal establishments were dismantled. The fortification of Sydney and Melbourne must now be largely a local responsibility. People in Sydney were less indignant at the loss of their defenders when they learned that the soldiers and their weapons really had been needed in the campaign against the natives of New Zealand.

Local resources contributed to military defence for the first time when a new barracks was provided for soldiers in Sydney. As the old barracks in George Street was now in the centre of a bustling city, it seemed to the advantage of both urban commerce and military discipline to use the site for civil purposes and move the soldiers farther out. The Legislative Council resolved that up to sixty thousand pounds could be used out of land revenue towards constructing the new quarters, and in 1848 the soldiers moved to Victoria Barracks, built on a common to the south of the city.

Late in 1849 Grey warned that the imperial garrison would be reduced to a guard in Sydney and one in Melbourne, whose pay would be sent from home. If a colony wanted more troops, it must pay for them. All barracks, forts and other military buildings were to be handed over to colonial governments, which must maintain them properly or lose the soldiers. Some members of the Legislative Council resisted the new policy; but when it was objected that the imperial government should pay for fortifications whose purpose was to deter foreign bombardment, Grey observed that a colony rich enough to tempt raiders could afford to protect itself against them. In 1851 the council resolved not to contribute to the fortification of Port Jackson until it was given full control of colonial revenues. That issue remained unresolved until the bill for a constitution, guaranteeing such control, was sailing for home in 1854; then the Council approved the building of forts at each side of the entrance to Port Jackson.

The presence of gold, carried from the fields to colonial treasuries and put on ships for Europe, became a new source for anxiety in minds inclined to worry about aggressors. A contributor to the *Sydney Morning Herald* saw the Australians as the people of a modern El Dorado, lacking the power to ward off a Cortes or a Pizarro. Governor La Trobe warned the Colonial Office that there was nothing to stop a ship anchoring in Port Phillip and holding Melbourne and its gold to ransom. The Legislative Council of Victoria appointed a committee in January 1854 to report 'as to the probable manner in which the Colony might be attacked by an enemy, and to devise the best means of meeting such a calamity.' The committee reported in March that Victoria was almost defenceless; that the French, established lately in New Caledonia, might be tempted to attack; and that the means to respond might include a war steamer, some guns from Woolwich arsenal, some troops from India, and the raising of local volunteers. A major war had begun in Europe when this committee met, though news of it was still a long way from Australia.

THE CRIMEA

Colonists learned in May 1854 that Russia and Turkey had gone to war and that England might become involved. In Sydney on 22 May more than two thousand people attended a public meeting to consider the news. They adopted an address assuring the queen of their devotion, their support for her government's stern posture towards the Russian invasion of Turkey, and their resolve to uphold the British flag and defend New South Wales. It was an emigrants' carnival. The address was proposed by J. B. Darvall, educated at Eton and Cambridge before coming out in 1839 to be a barrister. Other resolutions were moved by Sir Thomas Mitchell, veteran of the wars against Napoleon, and Henry Parkes, bounty emigrant. Parkes, serenely loyal now that transportation was dead, the new constitution safe, and England on the edge of war, moved that the citizens of Sydney were prepared to support the government 'in all needful measures for the protection of the colony against foreign invasion.' John Dunmore Lang offered radical but unpopular ridicule of the address to the queen, arguing in vain that the war was no business of people in Sydney. The meeting closed with cheers for the queen and her ministers and the sultan of Turkey. With every incoming ship it seemed likelier that England's long peace was about to end. A poet from Parramatta wrote verses entitled 'Our Defences' for the *Sydney Morning Herald* of 31 May:

> Sons of Australia, hear ye not
> The sound of distant War—
> Arise! prepare the sword and shield
> While yet 'tis heard afar.

The author saw the best of Britain assembling to defend their country, and wanted people out here to do likewise:

> Australians! guard thy native land
> E'er yet 'tis grasped by Tyrant hand.
> Let love of *Gold* be laid aside,
> And love of *Country* rise!

On 26 June the *Sydney Morning Herald* and its rival morning paper, Henry Parkes's *Empire*, announced that for the past three months England and France had been at war with Russia.

Colonists responded to the war as patriotic and imitative Britons. At home the queen proclaimed 26 April as a day of fast, humiliation and prayer for victory; so governors proclaimed days four months later for the same purposes. Sydney's day, Friday 18 August, was quieter than a Sunday. It must have pleased every real British Christian in the city, the *Sydney Morning Herald* said next morning. At home a Patriotic Fund was established for widows and orphans of British soldiers; so people in Australia, prompted by their leaders, subscribed to similar funds. Sir William Denison presided as governor at a public meeting in Sydney on 20 February 1855 to launch the fund in New South Wales. Six thousand pounds were subscribed on the spot as people in the gallery and the pit alike gave cheers for the queen, the governor and Lady Denison, Lord Raglan and Napoleon III, and three groans for the tsar. The merchant Daniel Cooper gave a thousand pounds of the fortune he had lately inherited from his emancipist uncle. The meeting had been his idea, and the initiative would earn him a baronetcy. Another emigrant merchant, T. S. Mort, gave £250. Charles Harpur, who agreed with Lang about the war, believing it 'craft and folly, blame and blunder', saw the contributors to the Patriotic Fund as engaged in ostentatious competition. In the weekly *People's Advocate* he wrote:

> Squire Sham . . .
>   Thumped down fifty pound!
> Several more, with Mort the Thrifty,
> Gave *five times* fifty!
> One Bank down thundered
> *Twice that*—five hundred!
>   But to its store
> Dan Cooper flung a *thousand*!

By September sixty thousand pounds had been raised in New South Wales. Parkes rebuked Harpur in the *Empire* for writing against British involvement. Harpur and Lang were more isolated in their dissent out here than they would have been in England.

Vendors of pleasure made money out of recreating the war. Thousands of people in Melbourne paid to see in the Cremorne Gardens an exhibition depicting the siege of Sebastopol, and an entrepreneur engaged the designers of this display to make 'a grand pictorial entertainment, illustrating the principal events of the campaign in the Crimea.' The war was commemorated by officials who had to think of names for the suburbs and country towns which burgeoned in these years of high immigration and gold. Fifteen streets in Sydney and twenty-one in Melbourne were named after the allied victory at the Alma River. Charles Dilke in 1867 could reconstruct the spread of settlement across Victoria by knowing the history of the war. 'The dates run in a wave across the country', he found. 'St. Arnaud is a town between Ballarat and Castlemaine, and Alma lies near to it, while Balaklava Hill is near Ballarat, where also are Raglan and Sebastopol. Inkerman lies close to Castlemaine, and Mount Cathcart bears the name of the general killed at the Two-gun Battery, while the Malakhoff diggings, discovered doubtless towards the end of the war, lie to the northward, in the Wimmera.' News of the war was awaited with a hunger that profited the makers of newspapers. The London press was flourishing as gentlemen read at breakfast what the correspondents had sent by telegraph from Inkerman or Balaklava the day before. There was no telegraph wire in Australia when the war began, and only one line by the time it ended; but even though the news of war came slowly by sea it was snapped up in Australian cities. The *Sydney Morning Herald* and the *Empire* kept boats ready night and day to take reporters out to board any ship approaching from Europe. They would race each other back to the city, where the printers rushed to be out with an 'Extraordinary' war issue. After several months of war news the proprietor of the *Sydney Morning Herald*, John Fairfax, boasted that the paper's circulation—6620—exceeded that of all but two daily papers in London.

It was not merely a disinterested loyalty to the empire that led more people to buy papers during the war. Rumours reached the colonies that a Russian warship had been sighted off Cape Horn, that four were expected at Valparaiso, that fourteen were at Vladivostok, that a squadron had arrived at Manila and was moving south. When Sir William Denison moved from Hobart to Sydney as governor in January 1855, he found his new capital in a state of panic. Denison was a military engineer who had served in the Admiralty, supervising the building and repair of naval works at home and in Bermuda, and he had caused batteries to be constructed for the protection of Hobart. He did not expect the Russians to attack Sydney—'our friends the French, and our relations the Americans' seemed to him likelier sources of danger—but he was pleased that fear of tsarist raiders was making colonists more interested in defending Port Jackson. 'The access to this harbour is so easy', he wrote to a friend on 21 May 1855, 'that unless we have some heavy batteries ready to open fire upon vessels lying off the town, a few frigates might run in under cover of the night, and the first notice I should have of their arrival would be a 32 lb shot, crashing through the walls of my house.' The batteries under construction out near the ocean seemed to him a mistake, and he had them dismantled. The fortification of Pinchgut, suspended in 1841, was resumed with imperial permission on the understanding that the money for it was raised in the colony. Eight thousand tons of sandstone were carried to the island and made into a battery, tower and barracks. The name Pinchgut, reeking of convictism, seemed to the engineer in charge of construction unworthy of the island's new dignity; and as Fort Denison, manned by members of the Royal Artillery sent out at colonial expense, the island joined the batteries at Dawes Point, Fort Macquarie and Bradley's Head to protect the city, the ships at its wharves, and the walls of Government House. The colony embarked also on the building of its first gunboat, a wooden ketch named the *Spitfire*.

In Victoria work began on batteries at Williamstown and Sandridge to protect the port of Melbourne, and the imperial authorities were asked for the protectors which a committee of the Legislative Council had recommended early in 1854. Even if the French were allies and not enemies, the colonial government still wanted from England an enlarged garrison, heavy guns, and a vessel more formidable than the *Spitfire*. Victoria's warship, for which her government was to pay thirty-eight thousand pounds, was the first ever built to the order of a British colony. When she was launched at Limehouse on 30 June 1855 *The Times* saw the event as marking 'the foundation of a great navy in Southern seas.' Her Majesty's Colonial Ship *Victoria*, of 580 tons and eight guns, could oppose any Russian men-of-war that might threaten Melbourne, if only she reached Port Phillip before they did.

On land, as in England, volunteers were enrolled and drilled as infantry, cavalry and artillery. Henry Parkes was enthusiastic about the movement as a means of encouraging colonial self-defence. The *Sydney Morning Herald* described with pleasure 'the

GRAND MILITARY REVIEW, SYDNEY
Imperial soldiers and colonial volunteers at the time of the Crimean War.
Volunteers are at left and right, red-coats in the centre.

gallant fellows in bottle-green' drilling in the Domain. The volunteers of Melbourne were called out on the night of 7 September 1854 when gunfire was heard in Port Phillip Bay and many people were convinced that war had come at last to this continent. 'Presently', the *Melbourne Morning Herald* reported next day, 'the ascent of several rockets stimulated the prevailing excitement to a higher pitch, and the exclamation, "The Russians!" was passed from mouth to mouth.' Men of the Volunteer Rifle Regiment, some armed with sticks and pick-handles, tumbled towards the bay. At the barracks in St Kilda Road, bugles were sounding and drums beating as the imperial soldiers were got under arms. The *Melbourne Morning Herald* was reminded of Brussels on the eve of Waterloo; and as at Brussels the officers were at a ball. A pale messenger entered the ballroom. The music stopped. Then another messenger arrived to say that the guns and rockets had been fired from the steamer *Great Britain* to celebrate her release after three weeks in quarantine for smallpox. Hurrahs were shouted across the floor. The band played inspiriting airs; but nobody wanted to resume the dance. Tomorrow's papers could report the spasm of terror with comic hyperbole, but tonight, as one guest at the ball wrote, 'every ear was strained to catch the first sound of the carriage-wheels, and to be on the road home seemed the only relief for the panic-stricken company.'

Rumour gave false cheer as well as false alarm. Early in December 1854 the *City of Sydney* steamed into Port Jackson with the words 'Fall of Sebastopol' across her bows and information on board, which the newspaper boats rushed ashore for 'Extraordinaries', that the Russian city was captured at last, eight thousand defenders having been killed or wounded and twenty-two thousand taken prisoner. When the same news reached Melbourne a few days earlier Governor Hotham had it proclaimed on posters and put around town in the hope that it would divert public attention from the rebellion at Eureka. Later in the month a steamer from New York brought news that Sebastopol had not fallen; and on the first day of 1855 the *Sydney Morning Herald* apologized to its readers. Accurate reports of the capture of Sebastopol in September 1855 were published the following December. From Melbourne the news travelled forty-five miles to Geelong by the first telegraph wire in the continent, and was picked up at Geelong by a mail steamer leaving for Sydney. Early on 11 December, Lady Denison at Government House in Sydney heard guns firing, looked out the window and saw the steamer coming in, dressed with flags and cheered from ships in the harbour. Sir William Denison ordered a salute of 101 guns and a general holiday. The Legislative Council, meeting for the last time before the coming of responsible government, resolved to congratulate the queen on the success of her arms. Lady Denison noted with pleasure that the colonists took such pride in England's glories.

The volunteers, here and at home, were enrolled only for service against invaders of their own soil. The popular chartist poet Gerald Massey, delighted by reports from Australia of colonial enthusiasm for the war, had the Gold Land say to the Old Land:

> We shall come, too, if you call,
> We shall Fight on if you fall . . .

In the event, no call went out from the old Britannia to the new for anything more than money to help the soldiers' widows and orphans. A military man might nevertheless set out for the Crimea on his own initiative. The superintendent of police at Beechworth in

VOLUNTEERS AT THE TIME OF THE CRIMEAN WAR
New South Wales Volunteer Artillery and Yeomanry Cavalry

Victoria, Robert O'Hara Burke, whose father and elder brother were army officers and who had himself been a captain in the army of Austria, sailed for England seeking a commission that would take him to the war. His brother became a posthumous hero as the first British officer to be killed at the Crimea. But the distance which had so far protected Australia against wars also made it difficult for anybody from the colonies to get to one in time. The struggle against Napoleon had lasted long enough for Edward Macarthur to be in it; but the Crimean War was too short for Robert O'Hara Burke. Told in England that fresh officers were no longer needed, he returned to Australia and waited for providence to open another path to glory. Back at Beechworth he would sometimes sit and stare at a portrait of his dead brother.

News of the war actually slowed down in its last phase, as the P. & O. mail steamers were diverted to carry troops to the Crimea and the mails for Australia came again in sailing ships. There was 'impatience and mortification' everywhere at the slow mails, the *Sydney Morning Herald* said on 29 March 1856. 'A hundred and eleven days! . . . we are all tired of conjecturing about the Crimea.' As far as the people of Melbourne knew, the war was still on when H.M.C. [for Colonial] S. *Victoria* steamed into Port Phillip on 31 May to protect them. In fact the Peace of Paris had been concluded on 30 March, as colonists learned three months later. The news reached Sydney on a Sunday, causing the Nonconformist proprietors of the *Sydney Morning Herald* to publish on the Sabbath for the first time. Copies of a single sheet headed GLORIOUS NEWS FROM EUROPE were sent to all the clergy, who passed the message to their congregations on Sunday evening. A copy was delivered to Government House, where Lieutenant-Colonel Sir William Denison reflected that men in Australia even more than Englishmen should thank God for peace. 'War is an unmitigated evil, throwing society back for years and years; in these colonies we have not even the shadow of glory to comfort us.'

SELF-DEFENCE

Before the war in the Crimea was over, newspapers from England spoke of a possible encounter with the United States. That supposed threat remained for most of 1856, freshening memories of the night in 1839 when American ships had sailed into Sydney Cove. Then it passed, to be replaced by rumours of trouble with the recent ally and old enemy, France. Reports reached the colonies that the French intended to place a large naval force at New Caledonia, twelve hundred miles from Sydney. The mails brought news in 1859 that France was at war with Austria and speculation that she might soon be at war with England. Governor Denison welcomed the prospect of a war in which soldiers and sailors based in Australia might gain a little glory. To Lieutenant-General Edward Macarthur, commander-in-chief of the imperial forces, Denison proposed that as soon as war was known to be declared, a force should be sent to seize New Caledonia. Did the French have matching intentions for Australian colonies? At some time during Lord John Russell's term as foreign secretary, between 1859 and 1865, he received a document purporting to show that Napoleon III was thinking about an expedition to conquer Australia. Although that report was unknown in the colonies, some people were sure that the French must be planning such an enterprise. In the event of a rupture in Europe, Henry Parkes told parliament in December 1859, 'one of the first movements would be a well-organised attack on the Australian colonies.' France, he observed, now had 'a port of refuge within a very few days' sail of our own harbour'. In order to resist invasion from

SELF-DEFENCE, 1859   **OBEYING THE CALL OF DUTY**

such a quarter, Parkes believed that the government of New South Wales ought to 'habituate the subjects of the Queen in this colony to the use of arms, and to foster among all classes a loyal and patriotic spirit of reliance on their own valour and military organisation.'

When Parkes called for a nation in arms he was following the latest fashion to arrive from home. The possibility of a war with Bonaparte's nephew had provoked the volunteer movement to sweep England in 1859 like a religious revival. The poet laureate, Tennyson, wrote for *The Times* of 9 May a poem telling the men of England that they must defend their country before improving its politics:

> Let your reforms for a moment go!
> Look to your butts and take good aims!
> Better a rotten borough or so
> Than a rotten fleet or a city in flames!

Within three months, a hundred thousand men had bought their own uniforms and were marching around drill grounds and practising to shoot French invaders. In Australia the volunteer forces raised in 1854 had fallen away when peace returned; but they flourished again now. Henry Kendall stood in for Tennyson, calling to colonists in his 'Australian Volunteer Song':

> Fathers of an infant nation
> Founders of a glorious State,
> Men, from every rank and station,
> Form and form, and watch and wait!

In 'Australian War Song', published in the *Empire*, Kendall put it to colonists that by joining the volunteers they would be both deterring an aggressor and answering a slanderous opinion that they were not ready for war:

> Men have said that ye were sleeping—
>   Hurl—Australians—back the lie;
> Whet the swords you have in keeping,
>   Forward stand to do or die.
> Hear ye not—across the ocean,
>   Echoes of the distant fray,
> Sounds of loud and fierce commotion,
>   Swiftly sweeping on the way?
>
> Patriot fires will scorch Oppression
>   Should it dare to draw too near;
> And the tide of bold Aggression
>   *Must* be stay'd from coming here.

To such appeals many men responded in 1859 and 1860, and volunteer rifle corps appeared in suburbs and country towns. Victoria had nearly four thousand volunteers at the end of 1860. Denison inspected fourteen hundred in Sydney on 19 January 1861. There were nearly ten thousand volunteers in the Australian colonies by 1863, drilling before and after work and on Saturday afternoons and public holidays, camping over Easter, and parading on the queen's birthday. They bought their own uniforms and arms, and if mounted they supplied their own horses. In England Charles Kingsley described the volunteer corps in 1862 as 'centres of cordiality between class and class'; and in the colonies, too, officers who were used to commanding gave orders to men in the ranks who did not mind being subordinate at leisure as well as at work. James Fairfax, son of John and partner in the firm that owned the *Sydney Morning Herald*, was a missionary for the movement and a captain in it; and one company of volunteers was composed almost entirely of the paper's employees. On the drill ground a man might make useful connexions as well as learn to defend his country: James Balfour, a merchant from Scotland, became a captain in a Victorian artillery company in 1864 under the command of James McCulloch, had his interest in politics aroused there, and by 1866 was sitting behind McCulloch in the Legislative Assembly. The volunteer movement had also an aspect of sport. The first rifle association in Australia was formed by volunteers in Sydney on 5 October 1860, and shoots between teams from New South Wales and Victoria were held annually from 1862. Adam Lindsay Gordon, who had studied for a while at the Royal Military College, Woolwich, before emigrating, joined a corps in Ballarat and another at Brighton, Victoria. He greatly enjoyed the drilling and the shooting. It was with his volunteer's rifle that Gordon committed suicide in 1870.

Apart from France and the United States, the most feasible enemy for the volunteers to resist was Russia. Reports of activity on Russia's Pacific coast, as well as concern about the French presence in New Caledonia, led the government of Victoria in 1858 to put twenty-five thousand pounds on the estimates for defence and to resume the construction of batteries at Williamstown and Sandridge which had been started during the Crimean war and stopped in 1856. A detachment of Royal Engineers under Captain Peter Scratchley arrived in Melbourne in 1860 to put the making of batteries in professional hands. Before Scratchley went home in 1863 the two batteries close to Melbourne were completed and another had been built near the ocean at Queenscliff. But when a frigate of the Russian navy steamed unexpectedly into Port Phillip on 4 January 1862 no salute greeted her, for the guns had no powder. Admiral Popov and the men of the *Svetlana*, on their way from Shanghai to Russia by way of Cape Horn, were met hospitably and stayed for two weeks. 'The only artillery practice witnessed', said the *Argus*, 'was the popping of champagne corks'. Early in 1863 the Russian admiral was around again in the corvette *Bogatyr*, this time visiting both Port Phillip and Port Jackson. Again the defences of Melbourne could offer no salute, though Sydney raised one. A young officer on the *Bogatyr* doubted whether his hosts would ever devote much of their resources to guns and powder. The French, he noted, began their settlements with batteries and garrisons; the Australian colonists, in his judgment, were too intent on material improvement to spend enough money on defence.

The Russian visitors aroused anxiety. The *Argus* reflected that the *Bogatyr* 'had the shipping at the anchorage at her mercy', and suspicion about why she had really come was revived in 1864 when war seemed possible between England and Russia over insurrection in Poland. A Polish agent who had deserted from the *Bogatyr* in Melbourne told the Victorian government that the Russians were planning to damage British trade by bombarding colonial harbours. The governor of Victoria, Sir Charles Darling, nephew and once aide-de-camp of the Darling who had governed New South Wales, passed the report in July 1864 to other governors and to the Colonial Office, where it was taken seriously. Darling advised that his colony was 'absolutely without the means of preventing a hostile Naval Force from occupying Pt. Phillip and from shelling Melbourne.' The alleged Russian designs became public knowledge in the colonies when *The Times* of 17 September arrived in November. In a leading article which was reprinted by Australian papers, *The Times* related the Russian danger to recent petitions from colonists against the continued dispatch of convicts to Western Australia. It argued that if the colonies, as threatened in some of these petitions, broke away from Britain, an enemy such as the Russians would know that it could attack them without bringing on itself the power of British arms. The *Argus* was outraged by the argument. 'It is really too bad that we should be expected to take charge of British criminals for no better reason than this, that we might otherwise receive worse injury from some other sort of people . . . It is a virtue of our character as British colonists that we seek protection from both the epauletted warriors of Europe and the trained felonry of England.' If the mother country could protect colonists against Russia, the *Argus* asked, why need they be concerned? If she could not, why should they obediently take convicts in gratitude?

In the event, there was no war with the Russians, the transportation of convicts to Western Australia stopped four years later, and the only foreign warship that actually gave trouble to colonists in the 1860s was American.

The civil war that began in the United States in 1861 was of very keen interest to Australians, living as they did in British communities that had remained colonies and had embarked a little later than the Americans on the road to democracy. At the beginning of 1862, moreover, war appeared imminent between the northern states and England. The crisis was precipitated when Charles Wilkes, Sydney's intruder of 1839, stopped a British mail steamer, the *Trent*, near the Bahamas on 8 November 1861 and took from it two diplomats who were on their way to represent the Confederacy in London and Paris. The British government demanded that the two men be released and that Abraham Lincoln's government apologize for violating British neutrality. All this news reached Australia in January 1862. 'However much absorbed the public mind may have been in watching the progress of the civil war in America,' said a New South Wales paper, 'the prospect of ourselves being involved in hostilities with one of the contending parties is far more exciting.' The same mail carried dispatches advising governors that war was indeed likely and reminding them of Wilkes's visit to Port Jackson. Batteries were inspected. British warships in port were made ready. Volunteers drilled, the South Australian government asking Victoria for the loan of tents in which men of Adelaide could camp for training in the parklands. The British demands had actually been met, and the prospect of war had vanished, before anybody in Australia had heard of the *Trent*. That news reached the colonies early in March. The secretary of state suggested to governors that the alarm would not have been useless if it impressed on colonial ministries the need for preparing to defend themselves in a crisis.

A war with the Union would have been painfully divisive in the colonies, as at home. Sympathy for the south was common among men who had made fortunes before the coming of responsible government. Edward Wilson was such a man; and his paper the *Argus*, which admirers liked to call *The Times* of the colonies, followed its English model in favouring the Confederates, whom it saw as gallant men fighting against long odds. The tariff, not slavery, seemed to the *Argus* the main cause of the war. The newer men in colonial politics tended to prefer Abraham Lincoln. In Melbourne the *Age*, and in Sydney both the *Sydney Morning Herald* and the *Empire*, supported the north, the *Age* approving both its hostility to slavery and its faith in tariffs.

It was not easy for the reader in Australia to follow the intricate course of the American war, especially as the news that reached him expressed different prejudices according to the direction from which it came: reports that passed through England tended to acquire an anti-northern bias, while messages travelling across America by telegraph and from California by sea were inclined to be hostile to the south. 'The South is up, and the North is down', observed the *Yass Courier* late in 1862. 'No: the North is up, and the South is down. Aby Lincoln has carried the day on Jeff. Davis. No; Jeff Davis has completely squashed old Aby Lincoln. And so wages this American war.'

By the beginning of 1865 the north was up and staying up; but that was by no means clear to anybody in Melbourne when on 25 January a warship flying the Confederate ensign and bearing the name *Shenandoah* steamed into Port Phillip. Close observers, who rowed out to look when she anchored at Sandridge, could see the remains of another name, *Sea King*, which the ship had borne when she left England, flying a British flag, ostensibly to carry coals to Bombay but really to sink and ransom ships belonging to the Union. The chronometers of nine victims were displayed on board as trophies. The commander, Captain James Waddell, sent his compliments to Government House and asked permission to make repairs, take on coal, and land prisoners. Governor Darling summoned his executive council, which agreed to let Captain Waddell do as he asked but resolved to remind him that Victoria was strictly neutral towards the American war. The premier, James McCulloch, and his ministers, and indeed the whole Victorian parliament, showed a striking reluctance to take any initiative towards the *Shenandoah*. She represented foreign relations of a bewildering complexity, and Governor Darling was welcome to deal as freely with her as if he were Governor Phillip.

Lincoln's government had a consul in Melbourne, William Blanchard, who demanded that the *Shenandoah* be seized as a pirate. Darling replied that his government

THE CONFEDERATE RAIDER IN MELBOURNE
Colonists inspect the raider Shenandoah, *anchored at Sandridge and flying the Confederate flag.*

was bound to treat her as a ship of war belonging to a belligerent power. The consul alleged that Waddell was violating international law by recruiting men in Melbourne for his crew. It was true: the ship was short of men, and the commander was enlisting as many as he could while she was being repaired. Waddell nevertheless denied that he was doing so. For a while the guns of the battery and of the colony's one warship, the *Victoria*, were ordered to be trained on the intruder; but high ground intervened between the battery and the water in which the *Shenandoah* was berthed. According to a newspaper, much amusement was caused by the appearance of the little *Victoria*, moored close to the raider and pointing one gun at her.

She was an object of great interest. Special trains took about seven thousand people from the city to Sandridge on her first Sunday in port. According to the *Argus*, 'the visitors showed their Southern sympathies by cheering the vessel heartily'. They may have been showing an indiscriminate liking for Americans, or a determination to enjoy themselves on a Melbourne Sunday; but sixty members of the colony's elite made their partisanship quite plain when they entertained Waddell and his officers at a dinner in the Melbourne Club and gave them three lusty cheers. The *Age*, which described Waddell and his men as a gang of respectable pirates, said that 'the soft-headed flunkeys who are recognised as the leaders of the Melbourne Club are entitled to any misdemeanour against common sense and good taste', but that officials of the colony who attended the dinner had committed a breach of the neutrality enjoined by Her Majesty.

Whatever their sympathies, colonists could be relieved to see the raider go on 18 February after twenty-four days among them. It was not that she had offered any immediate danger to Melbourne: there was no prospect of Jefferson Davis's government going to war against England, and therefore no fear that the *Shenandoah* would turn her guns on the city or on British shipping in port. But she might have brought the civil war to Port Phillip. Union flags were flying on several ships at anchor when she arrived, though they were lowered quickly to avoid provocation. Some American residents of northern allegiance were said to be plotting the ship's destruction; according to one story, an explosive device was actually fitted to the side but failed to go off. Even if she was no direct threat, she was a troublesome presence. The *Argus*, though approving Waddell's cause, was pleased to see the last of his ship: 'she, in the fulfilment of a warlike errand, was most unwelcome in our most peaceful port, and we are unfeignedly glad of her departure.'

Victorians would hear of the *Shenandoah* again. She headed for northern Pacific waters and set about destroying enemy whaling vessels. When masters of neutral ships told Waddell that the government whose flag he flew had capitulated, he was not convinced, and went on bombarding and burning. At Geneva in 1872 a tribunal held that because the authorities in Melbourne had permitted the *Shenandoah* to enlarge her crew, the government of Great Britain was responsible for all the damage she did after leaving Port Phillip. The tribunal was also considering damage done by two other Confederate raiders. For all three, it required Great Britain to pay the United States compensation of which about a quarter, or some eight hundred thousand pounds, represented the bill for the *Shenandoah*.

When the Confederate raider had gone, the *Argus* said that its visit had taught one practical lesson: 'If we want protection to our shipping and the city, we must find it ourselves.' Victorian politicians had been seeking greater naval protection for years. Until 1859 the Royal Navy patrolled the waters around Australia with four sailing ships and two small paddle-wheeled steamers, based on Sydney and attached to the East Indian station. It was because the Victorian government believed the security offered by these ships to be inadequate that it had paid for its own warship the *Victoria*. In London members of the General Association for the Australian Colonies formed a deputation to the Admiralty to ask for greater protection; and in 1859 the squadron at Sydney was enlarged and an Australian station of the Royal Navy was created. The purpose of the squadron, the Admiralty said, was to protect sea lanes as well as colonial ports. In a war it would 'give periodical convoys to treasure ships proceeding home either by the Cape of Good Hope or by Cape Horn.' Imperial officials in 1859 foresaw only treasure, not men, sailing home in time of war. What the squadron did in peace as well as war was entirely up to the British government.

Victorian politicians of the 1860s believed that the largest and richest colony in the empire needed, and could afford, a warship more powerful than the *Victoria* and likelier than the ships of the imperial squadron to be within range when a hostile vessel steamed up to raid or to ransom. They asked about the newly invented iron-clad turret steamships,

HER MAJESTY'S COLONIAL SHIP *CERBERUS* ARRIVES
TO PROTECT MELBOURNE

designed to defend harbours. After much correspondence about naval technology, imperial
law, and money, the Colonial Naval Defence Act of 1865 made it possible for Victoria to
get her iron-clad. The legal status of the *Victoria* had bothered officials at home: outside the
territorial waters of her own colony, it seemed to them doubtful whether she could claim to
be recognized as a British man-of-war. The act of 1865 allowed a colony to have warships
and crews of its own, which in time of war could become part of the Royal Navy. The
Victorian treasurer, George Verdon, went to London in 1866 to ask for a ship which the
colony would man, maintain, and in part pay for. Derby's cabinet liked the Victorians'
scheme. It was conceived, one minister said, 'in a spirit of independence and loyalty
which the Government ought to appreciate and encourage.' The navy would arrange
construction of a ship costing up to £125 000, of which the colony would pay £25 000.
Victoria would also bear the cost of arming it. The ship was to protect imperial as well as
colonial interests, and would therefore be placed in wartime under the command of the
senior officer on the Australian station, who might withdraw her from the waters of the
colony if he judged that to be absolutely necessary. Victoria was also to be given an old
wooden steamship, the *Nelson*, to use for training a local naval force.

The turret ships, big and ugly, were named after monsters of classical antiquity.
Victoria's was *Cerberus*; her younger sisters were *Cyclops*, *Gorgon*, *Hecate* and *Hydra*. *Cerberus*

sailed from Plymouth on 7 November 1870. She was perhaps the first ship bound for Australia to pass through the new Suez Canal and certainly the fattest to negotiate it so far, touching the side three times. After stopping at eight ports for coal and rolling dangerously in heavy gales, she lumbered into Port Phillip on 9 April 1871 and was escorted up the bay by the old *Victoria*—brought out of retirement for the occasion—and the training ship *Nelson*, to be greeted by a crowd of the people whom she was to guard. A Victorian flag flew from her stern. The act of 1865 had allowed colonial warships to be identified by a blue ensign with an emblem of the colony in the fly. Victoria chose to add five white stars of the southern cross, and thus devised for the *Cerberus* a flag rather like that of the League for the Abolition of Transportation. She weighed more than two thousand tons, and her four muzzle-loading ten-inch guns could fire a four-hundred-pound shot more than two miles. As she was a floating fort rather than a cruiser of oceans, she could not manoeuvre easily with the Australian squadron of the Royal Navy. Except for training journeys around the bay she floated at moorings close to the port, waiting.

The last imperial soldiers were on the sea for home when the *Cerberus* set off for Victoria. Since the 1850s the cost of keeping them in Australia had been a subject of negotiation and dispute between colonial governments and London. Colonial ministries, though accepting that they should pay something, argued that as colonies gave Britain wealth and strength and were at the mercy of imperial decisions about war and peace, they had a right to some protection at Britain's expense. But governors and men at the Colonial Office thought that colonists were inclined to exaggerate what the empire owed them. The argument that their trade was valuable to the mother country was—so Sir Henry Barkly, governor of Victoria, told the secretary of state in 1857—'usually amplified by the Colonial Press into the startling assertion that without the supply of gold from Victoria Great Britain could not have carried on the late war with Russia, or continue prosperous now Peace is restored but for the outlet for her Manufactures here afforded.' The House of Commons settled the matter. In 1862 it adopted without division a resolution whose effect, before long, was to bring the redcoats home from self-governing colonies: 'That this House (while fully recognising the claims of all portions of the British Empire to Imperial aid in their protection against perils arising from the consequences of Imperial policy) is of opinion that Colonies exercising the rights of self-government ought to undertake the main responsibility of providing for their own internal order and security, and ought to assist in their own external defence.'

What that meant for New South Wales, Tasmania, South Australia, Victoria and Queensland (Western Australia being not yet self-governing) was that they could borrow, between them, fifteen companies of imperial infantry—thirteen hundred men—at an annual cost of forty pounds a man. If they wanted more than that, or preferred artillery to infantry, they must pay seventy pounds a man. The arrangement struck nobody as satisfactory or stable. Colonial politicians disliked having to pay such money for imperial soldiers without gaining any control over their movements. In 1858 imperial troops had been withdrawn from Australia to help put down a mutiny of native soldiers in India, and in 1860 every available soldier in the Australian colonies was sent to New Zealand to repress the persistent Maoris. There was no guarantee that the soldiers for whom colonial governments were paying forty or even seventy pounds a head would not be sent to the Waikato or Calcutta or Hong Kong. The Victorian government told the Colonial Office in 1869 that the Legislative Assembly was opposed to paying any longer, 'except under the explicit understanding that the troops so supported would remain in the Colony as well in times of war as in those of peace.' That condition, as everyone knew, was not acceptable at home.

When Gladstone's ministry decided to withdraw all imperial soldiers from self-governing colonies, it caused little regret in either England or Australia. Men of both parties at Westminster agreed now that the less colonies cost, the better. Some misgivings were expressed in Tasmania, where proportionately more British soldiers had been maintained to the end in case of an outbreak by the ageing convicts of Port Arthur. On the mainland the news was greeted with resignation or pleasure. The music of their bands would be missed on festive occasions. Some people were sorry, no doubt, that redcoats would no longer march up and down outside Government House; and some ladies must have sighed to think that British officers would no longer sign their cards at queen's birthday balls. But in parliament and press the departure of the regiments was accepted as having become inevitable. Among the majority of colonists who did not read newspapers, one may guess that those who heard of the decision were not made unhappy by it. These soldiers had never fired a shot on their behalf at a foreign enemy; the only military engagement on Australian soil in living memory was against the diggers at Eureka. When E. W. O'Sullivan was a small boy in Hobart he watched imperial soldiers go off as reinforcements for the Victorian goldfields. 'It was this skirmish,' he recalled of Eureka, 'that accentuated the hostile feeling between the colonists and the military.'

The withdrawal of the British soldiers could even be welcomed as a blessing. To Charles Dilke in 1867 the old system appeared to prevent 'the development of that self-reliance which is requisite to form a nation's greatness.' Arthur Mills, the member of the House of Commons who moved the resolution of 1862, supported it by rebuking the imperial government for 'keeping the colonies in a state of everlasting minority and childish dependence.' Henry Parkes agreed with such critics, and had indeed anticipated them in 1859 when he told the Legislative Assembly that 'it would be . . . denationalising the country, stripping it of its highest attributes, emasculating it of the British spirit which was its safety—if they depended upon the troops of the Imperial Government.' Parkes was not at all clear what he wanted in their place; he simply felt that it would be more national and more manly and more British for Australian colonists to send the redcoats home and produce soldiers of their own. By 1870 it was generally agreed among people who thought about it that imperial garrisons gave colonies inadequate protection and deterred local initiative. When the last British soldiers sailed from Port Jackson on 6 September 1870, the *Sydney Morning Herald* hailed their going as Australia's 'first step towards nationality'.

The paper looked forward to full participation by colonies in imperial affairs, and went on to consider how they might prepare themselves for wars in which the empire was likely to be involved. But colonists with a less deferential approach towards the imperial relationship could put a different interpretation on the departure of the regiments. 'The British Colonies from which Imperial troops have been wholly withdrawn', said a Victorian royal commission in 1870, 'present the unprecedented phenomenon of responsibility without either corresponding authority or adequate protection. They are as liable to all the hazards of war as the United Kingdom; but they can influence the commencement or continuance of war no more than they can control the movements of the solar system; and they have no certain assurance of that aid against an enemy upon which integral portions of the United Kingdom can confidently reckon. This is a relation so wanting in mutuality that it cannot safely be regarded as a lasting one'. The dominant voice on this royal commission was Charles Gavan Duffy's. He and his colleagues were asking for the Australian colonies to be given either a better guarantee of imperial protection than was afforded by a naval squadron which might sail away at any moment, or the right to make their own foreign policy, including the right to stay out of an imperial war.

In Duffy's mind the return of the imperial soldiers had yet another implication for Australian nationality: it strengthened the case for federation. A federated Australia, he told the Legislative Assembly in 1870, could resist foreign aggression more powerfully than separate colonies. The threats he imagined, however, were not very persuasive. He foresaw a French or Yankee privateer overhauling an Australian clipper laden with gold, or attacking 'the ill-defended capital of a gold country'. But an assault on the high seas was a job for the Royal Navy, not for any colonial or even inter-colonial force; and if a raider bombarded Sydney or Melbourne, its commander would have not much to fear from soldiers who had to travel five hundred miles by sea to help resist him. George Higinbotham, replying to Duffy's speech, said that 'the necessity for a common defence is absent in the case of the Australian colonies, at the present stage of their existence.' Not until Australia had intercolonial railways and more apparent threats in her neighbourhood would many politicians see defence as a serious incentive to federation.

The rights and responsibilities of Australian colonists in the event of an imperial war were to be much debated in the years ahead. But what would happen if the American or French privateer, or a Russian man-of-war, or the Fenians rumoured during 1870 to be on their filibustering way from California, were to attack a colonial capital? After 6 September 1870 only volunteers and policemen would stand between them and the colonial treasury, or Government House, or whatever it was they were after. In New South Wales blocks of land were offered from 1867 to men who would join the volunteer force and stay in it for five years, and a similar reward was held out in Queensland. Hundreds of men responded in each colony, some of whom sold their Volunteer Land Orders to speculators. But the volunteer movement had been conceived as an auxiliary to the full-time armed forces, not a substitute. Volunteers could come and go pretty well as they pleased. They were distributed not according to any professional judgment of military need but to the vagaries of local enthusiasm. Just before Christmas 1870 the Ballarat Volunteers had the gas cut off from their orderly room because the corps was insolvent.

If distance was a powerful enough protector of the Australian colonies, then perhaps the imperial soldiers need not be replaced at all. 'We are situated at a remote corner of the world', said the Victorian politician Higinbotham in 1869. 'I believe that our police force would be able to annihilate any land force that might land and attempt to take possession of this country.' On other occasions, however, Higinbotham (who was himself a volunteer) assumed dangers which would require more than foot police and troopers to meet; and so did most people who engaged in public discussion of defence. Forts were still in fashion among British strategists, especially military engineers, on grounds which could appear relevant in Australia. Men inside forts, it was argued, could withstand much larger forces of invaders. A commission on defence appointed by Sir James Martin's ministry advised in November 1870 an elaborate system of fixed defences for Port Jackson. But would the forts be manned by volunteers? Or by citizen soldiers raised in some other way? Or by men of a New South Wales permanent military force? In one imagined version of a professional force it was a 'standing army', associated in British minds both with ancient tyranny at home and with the modern 'militarism' (a word which came into English in the 1860s) of illiberal regimes abroad. 'The influence most inimical to peace', said the *Sydney Morning Herald*, 'is that of a standing army.' The

British army was seen as an imperial police force rather than a standing army, far smaller than that of continental powers and much of it on guard at posts around the empire. That alone made it a model not readily applicable for colonists wondering how to organize their own defence. The British army was composed, moreover, of noble commanders, officers who were gentlemen, and other ranks who were virtually of another race. That was not a hierarchy easily reproduced in a society which had no aristocracy and in which the army would be under the control of ministers elected by manhood suffrage.

A retired officer of the Indian army argued as the last British soldiers left that New South Wales needed a militia act, by which specified numbers of men could be raised from the community, made subject to military law, given an annual retainer, and committed to stay in the force for two, three or four years. There was precedent for such a force in British history, but not lately; for the militia had disappeared at home after 1815. The *Sydney Morning Herald* preferred better incentives for men to join the volunteers, but looked above all to the education system established by the Public Schools Act of 1866. In England the rush to arms in 1859 had produced 'cadet corps' in public schools as a junior version and supplier of the volunteers. In New South Wales, four of the colleges which in England would have been called public schools established cadet corps between 1866 and 1870. The paper foresaw this system of training in arms extended to all the boys in all the elementary public schools of the colony. It would make them manly, self-reliant and obedient. It would produce the ideal army—wholly defensive, formed of citizens, and competent. After 1870 the military training of schoolboys would appeal to many people as a means of producing good citizens and good soldiers, solving in due course the problems of both delinquency and defence.

At the end of August 1870 colonists learned that France and Prussia were at war and that people at home were wondering whether England would be drawn in. The war cast a shadow over the opening of Sydney's Metropolitan Intercolonial Exhibition. Members of the volunteer artillery manned guns at Fort Macquarie and other points around Port Jackson. When a flag went up in Sturt Street, Ballarat, to announce that the European mail was in, crowds gathered outside the office of the *Star*, and a mass of men burst into the building, smashing office fixtures as they rushed the counter for copies of the first edition. A story circulated in New South Wales that England had gone to war with Russia and America, and that an army of citizens was assembling at Newcastle to defend Australia. As in all the world's wars since the French revolution, it was frustrating for people in Australia to be forced to wait so long for information. 'It is no use to write about this dreadful war, as your news is so much later than ours', Rachel Taylor, née Henning, wrote home on 30 November 1870. 'The last account that reached us was that Paris was surrounded and the bombardament to begin in two days. You know the results long ere this, and we have to wait another three weeks for further news.' In 1870, as when Charles Lamb wrote to Barron Field, news took so long to get from England to Australia that it turned into history on the way. That would not be true for much longer. If nations fought each other or revolutionaries overthrew a government after October 1872, the electric telegraph would let Australians know almost as soon as people in Europe. The messages would be too short to render complexities, and sometimes the line would break; but essential information, about such matters as war and peace and the price of wool, would come nearly every day, by three thousand miles of overland wire and nine thousand miles of cable, taking hours instead of months to travel from London via Land's End, Gibraltar, Malta, Alexandria, Suez, Aden, Bombay, Madras, Penang, Java and Port Darwin to

Adelaide. Later generations, including historians, would take the cable for granted; but to people using the electric messenger for the first time it gave a wonderful sense of liberation. Henry Parkes, who had just become premier of New South Wales when transmission began, called it 'a magical business, uniting us hand-in-hand, as it were, to the parent land.' Among other great changes, the cable would make it far more practicable for Australian colonists, if they wished, to go and serve the empire at war.

From the heart of empire in 1870 the mail steamers carried extremely cautious assurances to colonies which for the first time in their history were naked of imperial soldiers. The secretary of state told governors that if England should become involved in the war between France and Prussia, or appeared likely to be involved, the different parts of the empire would if possible be given warning and protection. That was the sort of message that provoked Duffy to demand for colonies the right to stay out of Britain's wars. It was far less reassuring than the promise of an English statesman who had said that Great Britain would defend her colonies with her last ship, her last shilling, and her last man. A prescient citizen of Ballarat suggested in September 1870 that the help would flow the other way. 'I am of opinion', he wrote of the motherland, 'that should she be entangled in hostilities, the colonies will have to help her with all their ships, their shillings, and their men.' In the half-century ahead, no enemy would attack any part of Australia, but three times Australians would volunteer to fight in an imperial war. In 1885, when the government of New South Wales offered troops for a campaign in the Sudan, a Sydney newspaper ridiculed the gesture in a cartoon which had John Bull receiving a Valentine card inscribed:

> I'd give my last shilling, I'd give my last man
> To aid thee, J. Bull
> In the war at Sudan.
> > Ever fondly NSW.

In the event, the contingent amounted to only seven hundred men. But to the war that broke out in South Africa at the end of the century the Australian colonies would send nearly sixteen thousand fighting men; and when a great European war appeared imminent at the end of July 1914, in the middle of a federal election campaign, the Scottish emigrant who was parliamentary leader of the Labor Party would promise that whoever won, 'Australians will stand beside our own to help and defend her to our last man and our last shilling.'

Australian colonists in 1870 were inclined to exaggerate the tranquillity of their history so far. They found it easy to forget both the aborigines and the Chinese. Eureka was a single episode not much noticed outside Victoria and regarded there as ancient history almost as soon as it was over, an incident of the dark ages before responsible government and democracy. Bushranging caused scores of deaths; but it belonged partly to the history of crime, partly to romance, and in some minds it was a postscript to a history best forgotten, of Botany Bay and Van Diemen's Land, rather than a chapter in the true history of Australia. The bloodless coup at Sydney in 1808 and the bloody suppression at Castle Hill in 1804 were part of that older history, meaning nothing outside New South Wales and little even there. Drought and fire and water were enemies which took lives, but it was a figure of speech to say so. What people meant above all when they spoke of Australian history as peaceful was that these colonies had not experienced true warfare.

The Stuff of History

If the history of Australia were to be counted from the time when James Cook named New South Wales and took possession of it for King George III, then in 1870 that history was a century deep. The centenary did not pass unrecognized, but the urge to celebrate it was mild. Cook had, after all, come and gone; the history of British settlement began in 1788, and then only in New South Wales. As people in other colonies made clear when they declined to notice the anniversary of Arthur Phillip's landing at Sydney Cove, they had no wish to lengthen their own history by connecting it to the story of Botany Bay. In New South Wales itself, writers and orators seeking to interpret the decades of colonial experience, to make an Australian history, found it no easy task to accommodate the age of convictism. Schoolteachers in 1870 did not have to try; for all history since the time of the Apostles was excluded from the classroom in case it made trouble between Catholics and Protestants.

Let us now praise famous men, and our fathers that begat us. *Every community wants to know and celebrate its makers. Europeans of the nineteenth century were encouraged by their literature to admire, even worship, heroes. In the United States, the quest for heroes—actual, mythical or both—was part of the task of making, preserving and reconstructing the nation. Had Australians by 1870 any candidates for a national pantheon? Which men among them, dead or alive, did colonists praise by raising statues or other monuments, by performing ceremonies of honour, by reciting odes or singing ballads? Whom did they choose to recollect as makers of their world? A few governors were remembered when most were forgotten. One currency lad was recognized throughout his life as the largest of native sons to walk the Australian earth, and was given in death an almost whole-hearted homage. Men who explored the mysteries of the interior were admired for enterprise, endurance and courage. If he not only risked but lost his life, the explorer was mourned; and to the dead Burke and Wills colonists gave the most heartfelt of tributes. Outside the circle of official and respectable recognition, bushrangers attracted a measure of regard as heroes. The events at Eureka lived on in many memories, and the defenders were honoured. So, by friends and beneficiaries, were the makers of the eight-hour day. But to no man did the colonists of Australia offer what Thomas Carlyle would have thought true hero-worship.*

British settlement over most of the continent was so recent that men not yet white-haired could remember it all, and compared with the occupiers of other lands the colonists had lived in tranquillity. As matter for history, their experience so far lacked mellowness and density. When some among them were moved to speak of history, they found it more inspiring to look forward than back.

15   Australian Heroes

MEN OF EMPIRE

The colonists of Australia shared with other citizens of the British empire a regard for great men who were its makers and preservers. In the first generation of settlement the wars against Napoleon had given the mother country two new heroes, Nelson and Wellington. At home the dead sailor and the living soldier were offered grander tributes in monument and ceremony than any citizen before them; and in the colonies their victories at Trafalgar and Waterloo were celebrated on each anniversary as reminders that even the most far-flung subjects of the kingdom were heirs to power and glory.

In 1822 a body of officials and settlers in Sydney met to commemorate two Englishmen, honoured at home, who were the first of their country's worthies to have a place in the history of this continent. Members of the Philosophical Society of Australasia, formed lately to pursue scientific learning, resolved in 1821 to put up a tablet at Botany Bay commemorating the visit of James Cook and Joseph Banks in 1770, and thus to proclaim that this land had now experienced half a century of British history. For several meetings members considered whether the inscription should be in Latin or English, what it should say, and exactly where it should be put. English, they decided, would be the more appropriate language here. Frederick Goulburn, the colonial secretary, submitted a draft which was adopted except for the words 'This spot saw them land'; nobody could be quite sure in 1821 where Cook and Banks did step ashore. Sir Thomas Brisbane reached Sydney in time to have his name on the tablet as president of the society. His coming connected the gesture more closely with the world of science; for the new governor was a fellow of the Royal Society, a serious astronomer attracted to Sydney by the prospect of southern stars. As the brass tablet was fixed to a sheltered rock the company drank to the immortal fame of Cook and Banks. The inscription said:

UNDER THE AUSPICES OF BRITISH SCIENCE
THESE SHORES WERE DISCOVERED
BY
JAMES COOK & JOSEPH BANKS
THE COLUMBUS AND MAECENAS OF THEIR TIME
THIS SPOT ONCE SAW THEM IN THE PURSUIT OF KNOWLEDGE
NOW
TO THEIR MEMORY THIS TABLET IS INSCRIBED
IN THE FIRST YEAR
OF
THE PHILOSOPHICAL SOCIETY OF AUSTRALASIA

A newcomer reading the tablet would not have guessed that he was in a penal colony; but the more recent associations of Botany Bay were faced in a sonnet about the ceremony by Judge Barron Field. Like the convict laureate Michael Massey Robinson before him and William Charles Wentworth after him, Field applied to Sydney Virgil's reflection on Rome: that it had risen high from low beginnings. The poet imagined Cook and Banks looking at this memorial:

> Erected by their own compatriots born,
>   Colonists here of a discordant state,
> Yet big with virtues (though the flow'ry name
>   Which Science left it, has become a scorn
>   And hissing to the Nations), if our Great
> Be wise and good.—So fairest Rome became.

In a second sonnet for the day, Field described the place where Cook and Banks landed as 'classic ground'.

It was also sandy ground, remote from settlement. The Philosophical Society disappeared. The tablet remained on its rock, rarely seen and not widely remembered. Cook's name was not among those toasted by the emancipists and natives at their Anniversary Day dinners, for they did not think of him as a maker of *their* Australia. John Dunmore Lang proposed in 1847 the name Cooksland for a province in the north-east; but that area became part of Queensland. Sydney's new university thought of him in 1859, setting as subject for a prize poem in English heroic metre 'Cook, meditating on Australia's future'. The winning entry was by an undergraduate, William Yarrington, who read it at a ceremony opening the Great Hall. It pleased Cook, he declared, to foresee a time when Australia's sons would defy

> All dangers that their onward course withstood,
> Until they'd won whate'er was great and good ...

Gazing down the years at the University of Sydney, Yarrington's Cook prayed that

> Sages and poets should, within these walls,
> Be nurtured; and from out those college halls
> Men, who in wisdom learned should watchful stand,
> And guard with sacred care their native land ...

What dangers faced the sons of Australia, or against what the graduates would guard her, remained obscure in these verses. It was not easy to write heroic poetry in a society which had provided so little scope for heroism. About Cook himself the poet could not think of much to say. Nor could Henry Kendall. Determined though he was to address the muse in a local accent, Kendall's four sonnets about Cook at Botany Bay were cloudy exercises, vague about both the man and his place in Australian history. A visitor of the 1860s found that the continent had only one monument to Cook, a drinking fountain in Geelong. It had been installed in 1859 by W. S. Jenkins, a recent English emigrant, and dedicated to Cook in order, he said, to 'shame the Australian people into erecting a more enduring monument', and also to discourage the youths of Geelong from destroying the fountain: 'the deeds of that hero are so imperishably written upon the hearts of all British lads', Jenkins declared hopefully, 'that I fancy everything bearing his name will be held sacred by young Australians and not be battered down and demolished as heretofore'. The drinking fountain survived, but did not evidently provoke people in Geelong or elsewhere to any larger commemoration.

As the hundredth anniversary of Cook's journey approached, he was given some recognition in New South Wales. In 1863 a committee arranged to have a 'grand commemoration festival' on 28 April, the anniversary of his landing. There was to be a picnic, a review of volunteers, and an excursion by water to Botany Bay to express, as a Sydney journal put it, 'the debt of gratitude that New South Wales owed to the memory of Captain Cook'. The scheme, said the journal, went up like a rocket and down like a stick; the festival was abandoned for want of public interest, 'and the debt is still unpaid.' All that happened was a luncheon at Botany Bay for members of the organizing committee on 16 May. They drank to the discoverer's memory. They inspected the old tablet and heard Dr Henry Grattan Douglass, who had been there as secretary of the Philosophical Society the day in 1822 it was put up, insist that he and his colleagues had fixed it at the exact spot where Cook landed. The 73-year-old doctor's listeners were sceptical. It seemed likelier, most of them thought, that the discoverer had landed on a smaller beach farther up the bay; and in the centenary year, 1870, Thomas Holt had a sandstone obelisk erected about half a mile from the tablet and inscribed: CAPTAIN COOK LANDED HERE 28 APRIL A.D. 1770. Holt, like Cook, came from Yorkshire. He had made a fortune as a wool merchant and financier since emigrating in 1842. He served briefly as colonial treasurer in the first Legislative Assembly and by 1870 he was a member of the Legislative Council. The monument to Cook's memory was one of many gifts Holt made to the people of his adopted home before he left it in 1881 to go back to England. When the obelisk was ready, Holt took the governor, the Earl of Belmore, and a distinguished company of colonists by steamer around from Port Jackson to Botany Bay. Their ship stopped as close as possible to the spot where Holt guessed the *Endeavour* had anchored, and when the guests went ashore they 'expressed their gratification in respect to the monument both as to its appearance and site.'

Holt's column was the tribute of one citizen, raised in a place still sparsely settled. In 1868 a public appeal was launched in Sydney to pay for a centennial statue of Cook in Hyde Park. Its sponsor was the Australian Patriotic Association, a body formed during the outburst of imperial and anti-Irish sentiment that followed the shooting of Prince Alfred. A great man of empire was an apt hero for Protestant loyalists; and when the prince himself laid the foundation stone during his second and quieter visit to the colony in 1869, he described the discoverer as 'among the chief of those who have helped to cement in one powerful brotherhood the subjects of the British Empire in every part of the world.' He hoped that many sons of Australia would emulate Cook 'and gild with noble deeds the name of this great country and the fame of England.' But by 28 April 1870 the Captain Cook's Statue Committee was a long way from having enough money for its monument. The *Sydney Morning Herald* noticed no public celebration on or near the day in the city or anywhere else in the colony except at Albury, on the Murray River. Later in 1870 the Metropolitan Intercolonial Exhibition in Sydney was deemed to be honouring Cook's memory. It was an afterthought, encouraging orators and editors to marvel at a century of progress. The hundredth year passed without revealing any strong popular will to celebrate the man who had found and named New South Wales. At the end of 1872 the Statue Committee, having less than £200 in hand, petitioned Henry Parkes as premier to find public money for the enterprise. Parkes put £1800 on the estimates and personally

THE DISCOVERER
Prince Alfred lays the foundation stone for the statue of Captain Cook.

commissioned the making of a statue by Thomas Woolner, the returned emigrant who was now as highly respected for his public effigies as any sculptor in England. When the statue of Cook arrived eventually it was nine years late for the centenary.

For respectable colonists in search of a history, Cook had the advantage of being unconnected with convictism; but he had no part either in reputable chapters of the Australian past. He belonged to pre-history. The Columbus of his time, and of the south, yes; but finding America in the fifteenth century was an achievement more marvellous than finding New South Wales in the eighteenth; and as a national hero for some citizens of the new world Columbus had one thing over Cook. In the United States Columbus was to become one day a sort of Italian St Patrick, the patron of an underprivileged mass of immigrants who could magnify themselves by reminding the Angle-Saxon Protestants on Columbus Day that the European discoverer of their land came from Genoa. Cook served no comparable purpose for any body of Australians in search of heroes. For the designers of school syllabuses after 1870, on the other hand, James Cook was a very suitable great man.

He was British, unsectarian, rose by merit from modest beginnings, sailed the world, enlarged scientific knowledge, prevented scurvy *and* discovered Australia. He was only too well fitted to be a secular and compulsory hero of the classroom.

The celebrants on 26 January did offer tributes to some men of empire who had come out as governors. At the dinners in the 1820s they drank to Phillip as the father of the country. In 1862 a prophetic vision of its future was attributed to him by Roderick Flanagan in *The History of New South Wales*. Flanagan was a bounty emigrant who arrived from Ireland as a child in January 1840, a few months after Henry Parkes, and who later edited Parkes's paper the *Empire*. Though declaring in the title of his book, which was published in London just after he died in 1862, that it was 'compiled from official and other authentic and original sources', Flanagan in fact exercised the licence enjoyed by ancient historians and invented a speech four pages long for the first governor to make at the ceremony of proclamation on 7 February 1788. Flanagan's Phillip expressed the colonial imperialism which was becoming popular in the historian's own lifetime, proclaiming that 'Australia'—a word never used by Phillip in real life—would 'ere many generations have passed away, become the centre of the southern hemisphere—the brightest gem of the southern ocean.' Because the speech was believed by readers to be Phillip's own, it encouraged anniversary orators to remember the first governor as a prescient founder of their nation. The *Sydney Morning Herald*'s leading article for 26 January 1870 drew on it, observing that Phillip's vision 'doubtless awakened in some enthusiastic hope, and in others an incredulous smile.' Flanagan's version remained in currency after 1870.

No statue or other material monument was raised to Phillip by 1870. For Macquarie, who like Phillip was often called the father of the nation on 26 January, a piece of ground was set aside to be the site of a memorial, but none was built. Macquarie himself had hoped that Australia would have a memory for its makers: '*my name*', the governor said, explaining why he had let it be put on so many natural and man-made features of the

THE DISCOVERER
The base awaiting the statue of Captain Cook, 1870

THE DISCOVERER
Thomas Woolner's statue of Captain Cook in place at last, 1879

land, from Macquarie Harbour to Macquarie Place, 'will not readily be forgotten after I have left it'. Wentworth, toasting him as father on 26 January 1832, declared it disgraceful to the colony that it had put up no monument to Macquarie. The site chosen for one remained vacant because the community of which he had been a maker was deeply divided about the wisdom of his policies, and especially his clemency towards the convicts.

The first statue to be erected in the continent, and as Mrs Charles Meredith observed 'the first specimen of high art which the colony has obtained,' was a heroic effigy of Sir Richard Bourke. A public fund for the monument was opened just before Bourke left

THE GOOD GOVERNOR
Statue of Sir Richard Bourke, Sydney

Sydney at the end of 1837, as a demonstration of sympathy on the part of those colonists who saw him as the friend of liberty. Wentworth was prominent among men who subscribed more than £1300 within a week and £2500 altogether. A correspondent in the *Sydney Herald*, which was hostile to Irish Catholics and emancipists, reported that names in these categories were generously represented among eight hundred or so contributors. The paper advised friends of the departing governor 'not to have the statue constructed of any precious material; or they may rest assured that the thieves will come in the night time and steal what they subscribed for in the day.'

It was constructed of bronze, in London, by E. H. Baily, R. A., and unveiled by Bourke's successor Gipps on 11 April 1842. 'At an early hour in the day,' reported the *Sydney Gazette*, 'groups gaily dressed in their holiday attire might be seen strolling about the town, whilst other groups of sturdy sires and portly matrons in carts and on foot came pouring in from the suburbs to hail the festive day. In fact all Sydney was alive'. The *Sydney Morning Herald* estimated the crowd at between seven and ten thousand people—the largest ever seen in Sydney. Roger Therry welcomed Gipps on behalf of the initiators. Gipps, determined to dodge controversy, remarked that the view from the site equalled in loveliness any scene in the known world. The statue stood beside Macquarie Street, above the Domain and the botanical gardens over whose trees sparkled the white turrets of the new Government House which Bourke had persuaded the Colonial Office to approve. On the base of the statue was carved a stone pamphlet: three hundred words praising Bourke for his competence, fairness and liberality; and between the lines, as any but the newest chum could see, abusing his predecessor Darling and his Tory enemies.

The only other governor for whom a memorial was built by popular subscription before 1870 was Sir John Eardley-Wilmot of Van Diemen's Land, who was dismissed in 1846 for alleged maladministration of the convict system and sexual misconduct. When he died in Hobart early in 1847 of no diagnosed disease, the *Colonial Times* said that he had been murdered and many people gave money for a Gothic mausoleum which was built in St David's Park in 1850. Except by falling foul of officials at home or powerful men in the colony, a governor could not easily become a popular hero. Even if he did, little of his fame would survive the generation who felt grateful to him. Nor could an itinerant imperial official be recommended easily to the youth of Australia as a man they might try to emulate.

THE GREAT NATIVE

William Charles Wentworth, born two years after 1788, was still alive in 1870. From the day he returned to Sydney in 1824 he was a hero among the native-born and the emancipists, honoured above all other men at the festivals of 26 January and feared by colonial Tories as a demagogue and destroyer. By the time he left the colony in 1854 to see the constitution bill through the imperial parliament, his friends and his enemies had changed, and it was now the pastoral magnates who were keenest to offer him public regard. James Macarthur and other political friends met at the Royal Hotel and launched a Wentworth Testimonial Fund. They resolved to commission a statue of the departing colonist which would 'animate the future patriots and statesmen of Australia', James Macarthur said, 'steadfastly to pursue the path of duty . . . assured that public opinion seldom fails, sooner or later, justly to award honour and distinction to those who deserve well of their country.' Seven hundred pounds were subscribed at once, committees were

THE GREAT NATIVE
Medallion of William Charles Wentworth by Thomas Woolner, 1854

set up to receive donations in country districts, and the sum needed was quickly in hand.
Thomas Woolner, lately back in London, hoped that he might get the job; but when the
committee asked Wentworth himself to nominate the sculptor he chose instead an eminent
Italian, Pietro Tenerani. The white figure in Carrara marble, slightly larger than life, was
unloaded at Sydney in November 1861 and unveiled in the Great Hall of Wentworth's
university on 23 June 1862. The subject was himself present, having returned to the colony
in his seventy-first year after seven years away. Even now it seemed not impossible to some
of the men in charge of the university that Wentworth might be involved in rancorous
controversy; the senate permitted the ceremony on the understanding that 'there would
be nothing of a party-political nature in the Proceedings.' They had no need to worry.
James Martin spoke with admiration and gratitude of the old man, and the occasion was
wholly amiable.

In the chamber where the young Legislative Assembly met, Wentworth could
inspect a new portrait of himself by Richard Buckner, accepted by the Assembly itself
in 1859 on the motion of Henry Parkes in consideration of his eminent services in obtaining
free institutions for the colony. The subject's pleasure at this recognition by the
democratically elected politicians must have been tempered by the knowledge that
exactly half of them had opposed the motion, and that the portrait was hung in the
chamber only on the casting vote of the Speaker.

There had also been conflict over his return. A motion that parliament should
adjourn on the day he came ashore divided the politicians, as the motion to order his
portrait had done. The opponents, said the *Sydney Morning Herald*, were 'inspired by a

WILLIAM CHARLES WENTWORTH

childish jealousy' and a 'brutal and turbulent spirit.' The motion was carried after debate, and Sydney enjoyed a general holiday when Wentworth landed from the P. & O. mail steamer *Benares* on 18 April 1861. A band played 'See the Conquering Hero Comes!' and 'Willie, We have Missed You!' The *Sydney Morning Herald*, which had often quarrelled with Wentworth, greeted him now as the great native. A leading article, presumably written by John West, observed that other Australians 'saw in the strength of his intellect and the extent of his services the first declaration of a national life. They point to him as an example that the mental powers of that nation, which is distinguished for vigour of its intellect, will bear transplanting to the antipodes . . . They saw that the eloquence of an Australian tongue could rival those of eminent orators who in ancient and modern times have held nations in suspense.' The oldest of currency lads had become a symbol of Australian nationality. In the Darwinian idiom which was soon to be fashionable, he was living proof that the race had not degenerated out here. It was in June 1861 that he accepted the presidency of the Legislative Council after becoming one of those members nominated for life whom he had believed to be an essential part of the constitution. But it was understood all round that he would sit in the chair only for a short season, and in October 1862 he resigned and sailed back to England. The *Sydney Morning Herald* wished him mild and genial suns—if he could find them in old England—and declared that he had drawn around him 'the warmest admiration and the strongest passions of the Anglo-Australian race.' It hoped that the young people of the colony would emulate him, but with discrimination. 'It is easy to storm like Wentworth, to copy his daring, to imitate his freedom of speech, but it was intellectual vigour, strong sense, and earnest toil that secured him a place in history'. Young colonists, hearing their elders dispute about the great man, might well wonder whether it was his younger or his older self that they ought to take as exemplar.

After his return to England, so it was said in the colony, Wentworth was offered a baronetcy and declined it. He intended to cross the world once more and die in his native land; but he became too ill, and died in England on 20 March 1872 after requesting that his body be buried by the harbour at Vaucluse. The news reached Sydney on 6 May. The *Empire*'s account was short and cool, saying no ill of the dead, acknowledging him 'the first great Australian', but clearly written from the vantage-point of those who regretted the latter part of his political career. Wentworth's wish to be buried at Vaucluse, the paper remarked, 'will be regarded as a proof that his attachment to the land with which his early and his best days were associated continued to the last.' The *Sydney Morning Herald* published a fuller and warmer obituary, which acknowledged that 'his political ideas were latterly thought to be somewhat modified by his sense of the great local importance of pastoral pursuits.' Henry Kendall dwelt on Wentworth's earlier years when he composed words for a song which was first sung at a concert in Sydney on 30 August:

> Honor the Hero! the laurelled Australian
> He who stood out in the dark elder days,
> Fighting our battles, when Freedom, an alien,
> Paled in false splendour, in Tyranny's blaze.
> Honor the Hero! the fine, fearless spirit,
> Liberty's grandest Hierophant here,
> He through whose sacrifice, lo, we inherit
> All that the sons of old England hold dear.

THE GREAT NATIVE
Statue of William Charles Wentworth in the Great Hall of the University of Sydney

The body travelled home on a sailing ship, the *British King*, to be given the first state funeral in the history of New South Wales. Sir James Martin, who had first heard Wentworth speak more than forty years earlier, proposed the funeral to parliament. 'We can remember how he stood', Martin said in the Legislative Assembly, 'in his old grey suit of tweed (for he always encouraged local industries) in sometimes an ungraceful attitude, but at all times showing the powers he was possessed of, and I think it is proper for us in this room that we should now ... crown the edifice, as it were, by receiving in a national kind of way his body, and accompanying it to its last resting-place, so that it may not be said that we are unmindful of our duty to the greatest of Australia's sons.' Not be said by whom? The double negative hinted at some unnamed judge—God, perhaps, or posterity—who would hold it against the politicians if they gave too little honour to the hero. It implied that the colony was discharging an unavoidable obligation to him rather than offering the tribute of a whole heart. Even when dead, Wentworth could make his fellows uneasy. But they were determined not to disagree about him today. Henry Parkes, who had opposed the adjournment of parliament for his return in 1861, seconded Martin's motion for the state funeral, making clear that he and Wentworth were not friends—saying, indeed, that they had never exchanged a word—but acknowledging that 'the early services of Mr. Wentworth were of a priceless character in repelling arbitrary power', and praising him as a model for young Australians. The motion was carried unanimously.

Parkes was now premier, and in charge of arrangements for the ceremony. A public holiday was proclaimed for Tuesday 6 May 1873. The route from St Andrew's Cathedral in George Street out to Vaucluse was lined by tens of thousands of people who fell silent as the procession passed. It was led by mounted police and volunteers, for there were no redcoats available now for public ceremonies. Then came members of friendly societies, fire brigades, and more than three hundred men, eight abreast, who walked in a section reserved for 'native Australians'. The phrase was apparently misunderstood by half a dozen aborigines. 'They were barefooted and barelegged, 'the *Sydney Morning Herald* reported, 'and their dresses were quaint and motley enough. The spectators were highly amused at the appearance of an item of which no mention had been made in the programme; but it is questionable whether this amusement was shared by the white natives of the Colony, whose claims to figure in the procession as 'the natives' were thus publicly disputed.'

The coffin, escorted by more mounted police, was followed by carriages bearing relatives, the governor—Sir Hercules Robinson—the clergy, members of parliament and leading citizens. Out at Vaucluse Sir James Martin, enrobed as a member of the university senate, gave a long and generous address. He saw around him, he said, representatives of three generations of Wentworth's fellow-colonists: the few who had grown up with him; their children, the present rulers and legislators, who learned from him how to discharge their duty to their country; and the more numerous young, who could estimate his character and services by the teachings of their fathers. As a member of the middle generation who felt himself to be a native, Martin spoke eloquently about the dead hero. 'We have no Westminster Abbey in which to place the bones of our illustrious dead; but here, under the bright Australian sky, and by the shores of the broad and blue Pacific, and in a corner of one of Nature's loveliest landscapes, we are about to lay his remains, where it was his own wish that they should repose.' Some of the old and the middle-aged might have remembered Wentworth's oration on the hustings in 1848. 'You may put it out of my power to serve you again', he had said, 'you cannot erase from memory the services of the

THE GREAT NATIVE
Funeral of William Charles Wentworth. The procession has left St Andrew's
Cathedral and is approaching the Town Hall.

past. I can truly say the love of my country has been the master-passion of my life.' The
Bishop of Sydney, Frederic Barker, read the words from the Church of England's burial
service, and the coffin was lowered into a vault hollowed from rock on which Wentworth
had liked to stand and look across his estate and out to the harbour.

When Kendall and others spoke of Wentworth as a hero, they cast him as a crusader
for liberty against named or unnamed tyrants. In his speech on the constitution bill in
1853, Wentworth had said: 'there is one heroic achievement open to us, and that is to
confer upon this country that large measure of freedom, under the protecting shade and
influence of which an ennobling and exalted patriotism may at last arise'. His own standing
as a hero was limited by disagreements about how far he had enlarged his country's

THE GREAT NATIVE
Portrait of William Charles Wentworth by Richard Buckner

freedom. It was limited also by his preference for England as the place to spend so much of his life. The public funeral was a vast and heartfelt tribute, and a national occasion of which colonists were proud. 'A similar pageant', the *Sydney Morning Herald* could blow, 'has not hitherto been witnessed in the Southern hemisphere'. But no truly public monument was erected to Wentworth. His portrait by Richard Buckner hung in Parliament House, whose members knew that half the legislators of 1859 had voted not to have it. The statue paid for by his friends of that day was confined within a university which had hardly begun to make a mark on its society. His body was buried at a place not easily seen except by deliberate pilgrimage.

Even if his politics had been more pleasing to liberal-minded men of the second and third generations, and even if he had returned to his compatriots before rather than after dying, how ardently would they have embraced him as a hero? Wentworth himself felt that heroic feats were tepid or incomplete when performed in an arena which was not, except in metaphor, a battlefield. 'Sir', he said in speaking on the constitution, 'it has not only been my misfortune, but it has been the misfortune of all my countrymen, that we have not lived in troublous times, when it became necessary, by force, to repress domestic faction or treason, to repel invasion from without, or, perhaps, to pour out our chivalry to seek glory and distinction in foreign climes. This is a privilege which has been denied to us. It is a privilege which can only belong to our posterity. We cannot, if we would, sacrifice our lives upon the altar of public good.' Like many of his compatriots then and later, the great native believed that Australia could not have adequate heroes until men shed blood for their country.

THE EXPLORERS

Although conquering the desert and the bush was a less fulfilling task for the soldier turned explorer than fighting the French, many men who led expeditions into country so far unknown by Europeans carried with them the hope of honour and even glory. Sturt, Mitchell and Leichhardt all aspired to being knighted for their discoveries. Sturt wanted to be made governor of Victoria or Queensland. The first marble bust executed in Australia, by the emigrant sculptor Charles Abrahams, was of Mitchell, commissioned by the subject himself in 1842. Leichhardt hoped for statues of himself. 'The greatest honour a man can obtain', he wrote in 1846, 'is to have his image placed in a public institution to become the silent preacher of great and noble actions to the present and future generations.' Leichhardt, far from having been a soldier, had evaded conscription into the Prussian army; but it was his practice on expeditions to celebrate the anniversary of the battle of Waterloo, 'and to revive our own ambitious feelings', as he wrote in June 1845, 'at the memory of the deeds of our illustrious heroes'. Edmund Kennedy had gone to Australia in 1840 as a young man described by his father as having 'an almost mad ambition to distinguish himself.' The explorer was often his own historian, writing a journal each day with an eye to dispatching the manuscript to a publisher who would make him a reputation among the reading public of the empire.

In the cities which they left and to which, if skilful and fit and lucky, they returned, explorers were celebrities. When John McDouall Stuart rode into Adelaide in January 1863, six months after washing his hands in the Indian Ocean, the government declared a public holiday and, as the leader and his men were carried to a banquet in their honour, a band played 'See the Conquering Hero Comes!' Leichhardt had the dreamlike experience of returning, after twenty months of travelling, to a city in mourning for him. There was jubilation in Sydney that he had not been taken after all by the land or the blacks. Prince of Explorers, he was called; no king, he wrote, could have been received with more joy and affection. Even down in Melbourne a public meeting celebrated Leichhardt's return, and Judge William à Beckett wrote verses which suggested that he may have been stirred by Thomas Carlyle's *On Heroes, Hero-worship and the Heroic in History* (1841), with its gospel of great men as 'the modellers, the patterns, and in a wide sense creators, of whatsoever the general mass of men contrived to do or attain'. Carlyle's heroes, from Odin and Mahomet to Rousseau and Napoleon, were a long way from a world where greatness was displayed by discovering grass and water; but in praise of Leichhardt, à Beckett declared that the explorer was an even nobler hero than the warrior:

> A 'monster meeting' let us have, where all may crowd around,
> And 'hero-worship' find its vent in one commingled sound;
>
> His mission was not to destroy, nor comes he back to tell
> Of fields, in which, though nobly won, our best and bravest fell;
> Far higher conquests his than these . . .

Leichhardt was soon to turn from a hero into a man of mystery: in 1848 he disappeared, and the search for him and his companions occupied other exploring parties for decades.

Fifteen thousand people saw Robert O'Hara Burke and William John Wills leave the Royal Park, near Melbourne, with their men and horses and camels on 20 August 1860 to cross the continent from south to north. The mayor stood on a dray to lead cheers for the party as it moved off. It was 'the largest and best appointed expedition yet organised in the Australian colonies', the *Age* boasted. 'Victoria, alone,' Dr David Wilkie had said at a meeting in 1858, 'had hitherto seemed to forget the claims of science and the future interests of Australia, but ought, from her large and rapidly increasing population, to take the lead in geographical discovery.' From that meeting came the Victorian Exploring Expedition, sponsored by the Royal Society of Victoria and paid for by public subscription. All sections of society were behind it. A government led by John O'Shanassy sent to India for the camels in 1858, and the ministry of William Nicholson, an immigrant from England, voted six thousand pounds early in 1860. A. C. Gregory, who had done much exploring in Western Australia, turned down an offer to lead this expedition, saying that the command should go to a man 'more closely identified with the Victorian community.' When the leadership was advertised, an experienced South Australian explorer, P. E. Warburton, declined to apply on the ground that he should not compete for 'honours, which many might think belonged exclusively to Victorians'. Burke was less well qualified for it than Warburton except by living in Victoria. The enterprise was prepared in great haste because a South Australian team led by Stuart was known to be getting ready to strike north for the sea. *Melbourne Punch* had a cartoon in which Burke on a camel and Stuart on a pony were engaged in 'The great Australian exploration race'. The last message ever sent to Burke from Melbourne told him that Stuart's party had reached the centre of the continent and added: 'The Honour of Victoria is in your hands.' Burke the police superintendent and Wills the surveyor were immigrants of the gold rushes, Burke a Protestant from Ireland in 1853 and Wills from England in 1852. Burke was thirty-nine years old, Wills twenty-six. They were champions of the colony no less than Wills's namesake Tom who was leading the Victorian cricketers against New South Wales.

Their disastrous expedition was to make Burke and Wills the most famous of all Australian explorers. They reached the Gulf of Carpenteria on 11 February 1861, having left the rest of their men in camps along the way. The journey took months longer than they had planned. Coming back, they and two companions ran out of supplies, and one of the two, tied to the back of a camel, died in the Stony Desert. On the evening of 21 April 1861 Burke, Wills and John King staggered into their depot at Cooper's Creek, so named by Sturt in 1845, nearly a thousand miles from the Gulf. 'Coo-ee!', Burke called as they approached; but nobody was there. Seeing the word 'Dig' cut into a tree, they dug, and found a message that members of their party had withdrawn that very morning for the camp at Menindie, five hundred miles away on the Darling River. If they had arrived a few hours earlier or the others had left a few hours later, Burke and Wills and King would have been safe. 'We proceed on to-morrow slowly down the creek to Adelaide, but we are very weak', Burke wrote. He put that message with Wills's diary in a bottle and buried it near the tree. On 8 May other members of the expedition, searching for the long overdue advance party, returned to Cooper's Creek. If they had found Burke's note, they would have known where to look for him and his companions. But Burke had not thought to leave any sign above ground that his note was there; and as the tree near the bottle bore only the old message 'Dig', and as the searchers saw no sign that anybody had been at the camp since they themselves left, they withdrew again towards the Darling. When the advance party was known to have disappeared, searchers left Melbourne, Adelaide and Brisbane, and the warship *Victoria* sailed for the Gulf of Carpentaria. A party under Alfred Howitt, sent out by the Royal Society of Victoria, found King living with aborigines and Burke and Wills dead. Some of Wills's remains were missing—probably disturbed by native dogs, Howitt thought. Burke's skeleton was entire except for the hands and feet, his loaded pistol rusty beside it. Howitt wrapped the bones in a Union Jack, put them in a grave, and read over them the words 'I am the resurrection and the life'. The story sounded from start to finish like an epic contrived by an author with a profoundly bleak vision of the universe.

It reached Melbourne in an extraordinary issue of the *Argus* on Sunday 3 November and was soon causing anguish throughout the colony. Motions of sorrow were passed in parliament and city council. Howitt, the discoverer of the tragedy, and King, the survivor, were stared at and interrogated in the streets. By 7 December, Howitt wrote, 'no less than 5 artists have commenced grand historical pictures of me burying Burke (from a sketch of the place I made)'. The mourning spread beyond Victoria. On 9 December in Sydney the *Empire* published 'The Fate of the Explorers', a narrative poem by Henry Kendall based on reports that had come from Melbourne by telegraph. The poet imagines the travellers, their 'glorious work' finished, looking towards 'a nation's well-earned cheers' when weariness and death overtake them. He calls for poets to write of the martyrs:

> Ye must rise, and sing their praises, O ye bards with souls of fire!
> For the People's voice shall echo through the wailings of your lyre;
> And we'll welcome back their comrade, though our eyes with tears be blind
> At the thoughts of Promise perished, and the shadow left behind
> Now the leaves are bleaching round them—now the gales above them glide,
> But the end was all accomplished, and their fame is far and wide:
> Though this fadeless glory cannot hide a grateful nation's grief,
> And their laurels have been blended with a gloomy cypress wreath.

Bewilderment and anger contended with grief. Who, if anybody, was to blame? Alfred Howitt thought the main cause of the disaster was that neither Burke nor Wills was really a bushman. A royal commission cut up the blame and spread it around: some to the Exploring Committee of the Royal Society, some to Burke, some to his subordinates. Since serious misjudgments and terrible misfortunes had both contributed to the tragedy, a man might as plausibly attribute it to fate.

Howitt was sent again to Cooper's Creek to bring back the bones he had buried. Camels carried them to Adelaide, where they were packed in a box covered with black cloth for shipment to Melbourne. Thousands of people watched the box pass through Adelaide. 'For a time all business was suspended and the streets were silent,' Howitt wrote, 'making most audible the slow tread of the crowd who followed the hearse and the solemn sounds of the military band playing Dead March in Saul.' A ship flying her flag at half mast carried the bones to Melbourne, where they were landed on 20 December 1861. In the hall of the Royal Society a doctor sorted them into coffins as best he could. Men, women and children passed through the hall day after day to look at the bones through

THE DEAD EXPLORERS
Funeral of Robert O'Hara Burke and William John Wills

a glass slide let into the lid of each coffin. 'No doubt it is a much higher feeling than mere curiosity', wrote the *Illustrated Melbourne Post* on 17 January 1863, 'which attracts the immense crowds of visitors every day to see poor Burke and Wills "lying-in-state" . . . Few will regret seeing the relics of the illustrious dead at last laid at rest, out of the bungling hands of the "Royal" Committee.' An ode in the same issue, 'The Burial of Burke and Wills', spoke of the bones as a funeral orator of Athens or Sparta might have spoken over the bodies of warriors who had died for their city:

> Raise high the bier! that in the sight of all
> This proud example to the world be shown.
> Bury their dust within the sculptured tomb;
> And when thy children yet unborn shall ask,
> What sacred relics rest beneath the stone?
> Tell them,—and, telling, let thy words strike deep,
> Deep as the sufferings they once endured,—
> How glorious BURKE and no less noble WILLS
> Gave their last breath, Victoria, for thee!

On Wednesday 21 January Burke and Wills were given Victoria's first state funeral, ten years before William Charles Wentworth was awarded that honour in New South Wales. The government closed the public offices from noon and invited all civil servants to attend the solemnities. The bronzed wheels of the funeral car, which was a copy of the one that bore the Duke of Wellington's body through London in 1852, began to roll from the hall of the Royal Society soon after one o'clock, and carriages of mourners moved off behind it for the next hour and a half. About 40000 people—in a city of some 130000—watched the procession go by, standing silent behind redcoats with reversed arms. The shops along the route were shut, and buildings were draped in purple and black. Among the polished and ornate memorials in the Melbourne General Cemetery was placed a rugged monolith weighing thirty-four tons. On each side of its base a message was inscribed:

IN MEMORY OF ROBERT O'HARA BURKE AND WILLIAM JOHN WILLS
LEADER AND SECOND IN COMMAND OF THE VICTORIAN EXPLORING EXPEDITION
DIED AT COOPER'S CREEK JUNE 1861
COMRADES IN A GREAT ACHIEVEMENT COMPANIONS IN DEATH AND ASSOCIATES IN RENOWN
THE FIRST TO CROSS THE CONTINENT OF AUSTRALIA
BURKE
WILLS
GRAY
KING *survivor*

The stone over their grave was neither the first nor the grandest monument to Burke and Wills. Before the funeral, memorials were erected by public subscription in three country towns: at Castlemaine an inscribed monolith, in Ballarat a clock-tower, at Bendigo a column surmounted by an urn, on a pedestal bearing, as many tributes did, the word 'ill-fated'. The people of Wills's birthplace in Devon put up a memorial to him in 1864. The most elaborate monument of all was a statue of the two men unveiled in Melbourne on 21 April 1865. Like their expedition, it was paid for by a public fund and a contribution—of four thousand pounds—from the colonial government. The sculptor was

THE DEAD EXPLORERS
Monument to Burke and Wills at Ballarat, 1863

Charles Summers, a student of the Royal Academy who had come out to dig for gold and stayed to make busts, medallions, and carvings for public buildings. This was the first bronze statue ever executed in the colony, made of copper from South Australia and tin from Beechworth, where Burke had served.

Friday 21 April was chosen as the day to unveil Summers's work because it was the fourth anniversary of the explorers' return to Cooper's Creek. As it happened also to be the ninth anniversary of the day when stonemasons struck for their eight hours, many people in the crowd of some eight to ten thousand who assembled on the corner of Collins and Russell Streets in the afternoon had already marched through town behind banners in the morning. A force of five hundred volunteers from suburbs and country towns was mustered by four o'clock on the site of the new monument. The governor, Sir Charles Darling, unveiled it to reveal the heroes twice as large as life, Wills seated holding his diary and Burke, bearded and bare-headed, standing with a hand on his companion's shoulder, both gazing into the distance that doomed them. It was a monument to blow about, and the governor was the first to do so: 'if I did not fear that I might afford ground for charging this colony with an exhibition of that 'swelling' greatness, which is sometimes imputed to us,' Darling told the crowd, 'I would add that I believe a work, including a figure in bronze of such magnitude as that before us, cast in a single piece, has never before been sent forth from any studio in the world.' Richard Horne, back in England in 1873, said that London had no public statue to equal this one.

Gazing at the Burke and Wills statue was a rich experience for John Forrest, one of the few natives to win fame as an explorer. When he and his companions reached Adelaide on 3 November 1874 after travelling overland from Western Australia, they were cheered through streets decorated with flags and flowers and greeted as 'the heroes from the west'. A newspaper published verses placing Forrest in the great tradition:

> And he, their leader, youthful still,
>   Our Western sister's gallant son,
>   The noblest title well has won
> That young Australia's hopes can fill.
>
> Explorer! Name oft earned by men
>   To whom too soon Death's message came,
>   Whose deeds upon the scroll of fame
> Stand writ as with a golden pen.
>
> Lost Leichhardt, Stuart, Burke and Wills,
>   McKinlay—heroes of the past!
>   Then grey-haired Warburton, and last
> A space thy name, brave Forrest, fills.

Forrest took a month's leave, sailed from Adelaide to Melbourne, and made a pilgrimage to the statue of Burke and Wills; 'that memorial', as he called it, 'of two brave men who sacrificed their lives in the cause of exploration . . . Several times afterwards during my stay in Melbourne I went to look at this monument, and it always sent a thrill through my very soul.'

It provoked Adam Lindsay Gordon to meditate on death. 'All the poetry of a new land will not escape in action', the first English reviewer of Kendall had written in 1862. 'If a Burke lives his poem, some Tennyson may arise to write it.' The statue of Burke and

THE DEAD EXPLORERS
The Burke and Wills monument, Melbourne

Wills moved Gordon to write verses which he entitled 'Gone', saying that few who fell in battle had fallen as stout and steady of soul as Burke:

> The storm was weathered, the battle was won,
>   When he went, my friends, where we all must go.

The poet asked God to grant that we might all meet fate as steadily and straight

> As he whose bones in yon desert bleach'd.

The lines sang doubly of death to readers who knew how Gordon himself had gone; but a colonist without any tendency to suicide might well look at the figures of Burke and Wills and draw the hard lesson that this land was more than a match for the white newcomers. The lesson could be drawn readily from other chapters in the annals of exploration, such as Eyre's coming on the dry bed of what he was to call Lake Torrens in 1839 and sensing that the land was forbidding him to approach, or Sturt's confessing his disappointment— 'if such a word can express the feeling'—as he turned his back on the centre of Australia in 1844 after having so nearly gained it. Eyre and Sturt survived. The explorers remembered most vividly were men who perished on their journeys. In Henry Kingsley's fable *The Boy in Grey*, the hero lands on a coast resembling the Great Australian Bight and sleeps by 'the Creek of the Lost Footsteps', where 'lay a human figure on its side, withered long since by rain and sun, with the cheek pressed in the sand. So lies Leichhardt, so lay Wills.'

Did a democratic taste in heroism lead Australian colonists to savour the man who dared and was overwhelmed? Walt Whitman, the poet of American democracy, offered a robust salute to the unsuccessful:

> Vivas to those who have failed!
> And to those whose war-vessels sank in the sea!
> And to those themselves who sank in the sea!
> And to all generals who lost engagements, and all overcome heroes!
> And to the numberless unknown equal to the greatest heroes known.

When the writer in colonial Australia celebrated failure he was apt to sound less hearty. Melancholy, indeed, was said to be his trade mark, especially when he wrote about the bush. 'The music to which he has set his impressions of Nature', a critic remarked of Kendall in 1866, 'is invariably of a gloomy and despondent tone. One would think he had been "lost in the bush" at an early period of his life, and thus had learned to associate thoughts of horror with the fairest scenes. No poet in the language, from Chaucer to Tennyson, draws such dismal meanings from the external world.' Ten years later a reviewer of Kendall's verse wrote of the bush: 'Its vastness, its thick undergrowth, its monstrous trees, its desolation, its silence, all produce a depressing effect, which every one who has travelled through it must have observed . . . The vein of sadness is not peculiar to Mr Kendall, but is apparent in Harpur, Gordon, and indeed all our poets who have passed much of their time in the bush.' If Gordon in 'Gone', Kendall in 'The Fate of the Explorers', and the author of the ode on 'The Burial of Burke and Wills' were speaking for the thousands who watched the bones go by or queued to see them in the coffin, then there was among colonists of the 1860s a disposition to venerate dead civic heroes as victims of fate, annihilated rather than awaiting resurrection, and living on in the memories of their compatriots. It was an elegiac mode of commemoration, more in harmony with the stoicism of classical antiquity than with the doctrines of the Christian churches to which most colonists gave adherence.

Burke and Wills entered rapidly into folk history: the *Age* could observe in 1865 that in Australia 'no nursery rhyme or story of ancient chivalry or modern romance is kept in memory one-tenth as well as the simple tale of how these two brave gentlemen, whom nearly all of us remember in vigorous life a few years ago, went out upon their desolate mission; accomplished it, and perished of starvation in the moment of success.' Few writers or orators put the explorer in a higher place of honour than the soldier, as William à Beckett had done in his tribute to Leichhardt; but it could be said of Burke and Wills, as of few other worthies in these colonies, that they had (in Wentworth's phrase) sacrificed their lives upon the altar of public good. That fitted the two men to be made into exemplary heroes for the nation's children—that is to say, for the male half of them, who would grow up to be the workers, the voters, and if need be the warriors; girls were commonly assumed to need no other model than their mothers. In the year the statue was unveiled, J. E. Tenison Woods published his two-volume *History of the Discovery and Exploration of Australia* which closed with an expression of hope that the inland sea for which so many explorers had searched might after all be there, and might prove to be the seed of a vast empire. 'If it does,' the author wrote, 'it will be owing to the energy and activity of its sons, who may perchance be spurred to emulation by the deeds of daring their fathers have performed in obtaining the knowledge detailed in these volumes.' Before long the bleak truth would be established that there was no inland sea. After the journeys of Ernest Giles and Forrest, not much of the continent remained to be discovered, and the great explorers receded into the past. They could be commended to the young, however, for their displays of character. 'Australian parents', said Sir Charles Darling beside the Burke and Wills statue in 1865, 'pointing to that commanding figure, shall bid their young and aspiring sons to hold in admiration the ardent and energetic spirit, the bold self-reliance, the many chivalrous qualities which combined to constitute the manly nature of O'Hara Burke.' Gazing at Wills, they might teach their sons 'to emulate the thirst for science, the deep love of the Almighty's works in nature, the warm filial and family affections, the devotion to duty, self-control, and submission of his own judgment to authority, which he regarded as rightfully conferred and exercised'. Speaking nearly a decade before education was compulsory, the governor thought of parents rather than schoolmasters as the teachers of youth. For the next and later generations of children the stories of exploration were to be told in reading books and illustrated on school walls.

The tales might or might not inspire an Australian boy. If he was of Irish Catholic stock he would be likely to find the explorers alien figures; for the heroes were seldom of his faith, and men who embarked on long, lonely and punishing journeys far from their fellows were more readily accommodated to the ethic of Protestant individualism than to the communal tradition of the Irish. Catholic or Protestant, emigrant or native, there was a danger that the stories might provoke not imitation but dread. Most Australian boys lived in suburbs; and the story of Burke and Wills might incline a lad never to go near the dry inland, associated as it was with deprivation and with death at the hands of an ingeniously cruel fortune. The greater danger was indifference. Hunger and weariness were enemies more difficult to animate for young minds than Sepoys or Frenchmen or Russians. How could a teacher make the return to Cooper's Creek as exciting as the charge of the Light Brigade, especially when he had Tennyson's rattling lines to help him with the one, and only Gordon's 'Gone' with the other? Despite the English critic's prophecy, no colonial Tennyson arose to catch the action of exploration. Unless some writer or artist should discover how to do so, the explorers would fade so steadily in Australian minds that it would not be easy for later generations to comprehend the sentiment that led those thousands of people to see Burke and Wills off at the Royal Park, or the passion with which their bones were seen to the grave.

THE WILD COLONIAL BOY

The bushranger, like the explorer, could imagine himself as hero of a new history. 'It is the boast of most of them, that their names will live in the remembrance of the colony', Peter Cunningham wrote in 1827, noting that songs were often made about their exploits by 'sympathizing brethren'. The names of bushrangers did live in Australian memories, thanks not only to their comrades but to respectable people who made them celebrities. When Michael Howe was clubbed to death in 1818 after leading his gang for five years, his head was put on show in Hobart Town and the lieutenant-governor's secretary published a book entitled, hopefully, *Michael Howe, the Last and Worst of the Bush Rangers*. It was the first work of general literature to be published in the island. When Lieutenant-Colonel G. C. Mundy visited the colony thirty years later, he found Howe 'without dispute, and without disparagement to other public characters who, on more reputable grounds may deserve a memoir . . . the historical great man of this island.' Jack Donohoe's death in 1830 was greeted by the *Sydney Gazette* with rejoicing on behalf of all respectable citizens. But pipes moulded to resemble his dead head, with bullet-holes in the forehead, were bought and smoked in Sydney; and so solid a colonist as the surveyor-general, Thomas Mitchell, drew a tender sketch of the corpse's head and shoulders. When Frank Gardiner was awaiting trial in Sydney in 1864 a number of gentlemen visited him; Darlinghurst Gaol, it was said, became a curiosity shop as people found excuses to get in. Gardiner's horse fetched a high price as a relic. The courtroom at his first trial was crowded. James Martin, prosecuting, was so sure of the crown's case that he said to the jury: 'no one will be better pleased than myself if you acquit the prisoner.' The twelve citizens of Sydney did just that, and were clapped and cheered by other spectators with an enthusiasm beyond the power of tipstaves and constables to quell. Though the chief justice, Sir Alfred Stephen, sentenced Gardiner to thirty-two years after his conviction at the second trial, public agitation persuaded the government to let him out after ten.

Of all bushrangers Gardiner was the easiest for law-abiding people to admire: handsome, elegant, and apparently a reformed character by the time the police caught him in Queensland. For native sons of convict stock, Ben Hall was the bushranger on whom legend could most easily build. Both his parents were convicts; and he had been a peaceable squatter, it was said, until his wife went off with a policeman. His gang's festive capture of Canowindra and their frequent humiliation of the police made fine stories for anybody who enjoyed seeing authority defied. But the fame of such men went far beyond a regard for their personal qualities, real or imagined.

The bushrangers of balladry were larger, gentler and more sinned against than in life. No song about Donohoe reported that he killed a man with whom he had lived, and burned his body. Daniel Morgan, who was described by the bushranger John Gilbert as a bloodthirsty wretch, became in song 'the traveller's friend'. Songs about Ben Hall and his gang did not record their acts of homicide. Hall was known to have stolen from the poor—a shearer, an old shepherd, a toll-keeper—but folk memory affirmed that he 'never robbed a needy man'. When the police caught Hall he was wide awake and on his feet, but legend preferred him otherwise:

> Come all Australian sons with me
> For a hero has been slain,
> And cowardly butchered in his sleep
> Upon the Lachlan Plain.

Their reputations were enhanced by the press. Most newspapers were editorially hostile to bushranging; but from the *Sydney Gazette* on they found the gangs irresistible as news. That paper's first competitor, Wentworth's and Wardell's *Australian*, was launched in 1824, the year before Jack Donohoe was transported; the *Monitor* began in 1826. One of the ballads about Donohoe gave these journals an important place in his story:

> For every week in the newspapers there was published something new
> Concerning this dauntless hero, the bold Jack Donohoe!

His deeds were reported fully and even magnified: 'we fancy', said the *Australian*, 'he has more credit given to him for outrages than he is deserving of'. Decade after decade newspapers denounced the bushrangers and rebuked governments for not exterminating them, but showed them as dashing fellows. 'Daring Robbery by Bushrangers', an account would be headed; and if the robbers had shown a measure of chivalry, compassion or wit, the reporter might dwell on it with relish. 'Outrage on St Kilda Road', the *Argus* proclaimed on 19 October 1852. On a high road close to Melbourne, in broad daylight, a gang had coolly robbed and bailed up everyone who came along on foot, on horseback or in a cart for more than two hours, then galloped off at sunset. The episode was preserved for history by William Strutt. In 'Bushrangers on the St Kilda Road', one of the colonial

THE WILD COLONIAL BOY:
BUSHRANGERS ON THE ST KILDA ROAD

works painted after Strutt returned to England, the respectable victims sit helpless in a row, several of them looking up at their swaggering guard.

The bushrangers were the earliest subjects of an Australian drama. A romantic version of the career of Matthew Brady, hanged in Van Diemen's Land in 1826, was given by David Burn in his play *The Bushrangers*, written in the colony and performed at Edinburgh in 1829. Henry Melville's play of the same name, staged at Hobart in 1834, was the first drama with a local theme to be published and performed in the colonies. In 1833 Charles Harpur, aged twenty, wrote *The Tragedy of Donohoe*, and published another version in 1853 as *The Bushrangers*. These authors were aspiring antipodean Byrons or Shakespeares who discerned in the bushranger the one colonial type fit for a heroic literature. They worked less skilfully in their chosen medium than the anonymous makers of ballads, for whom Donohoe was the most attractive of the bolters:

> 'Resign to you—you cowardly dogs: A thing I ne'er will do,
> For I'll fight this night with all my might,' cried bold Jack Donahoe.
> 'I'd rather roam these hills and dales, like wolf or kangaroo
> Than work one hour for Government!' cried bold Jack Donahoe.
>
> Then come, my hearties, we'll roam the mountains high!
> Together we will plunder, together we will die!
> We'll wander over mountains and we'll gallop over plains—
> For we scorn to live in slavery, bound down with iron chains.

These verses were paid the official tribute of having their public singing prohibited by law. The bushrangers' fame itself became in folklore a matter for pride. One ballad had Ben Hall much discussed in high places of the old world:

> The records of this hero bold
> Through Europe have been heard,
> And formed the conversation
> Between many an Earl and Lord.

Of how many other colonists could that be sung? To tunes transported from Ireland, balladists celebrated the deeds of heroes from Bold Jack Donohoe to Brave Ben Hall in verses which were sung all over the country and outlived their makers. They created a misty figure called the Wild Colonial Boy, in early versions a convict and later native-born, who embodied all the bushrangers' defiance of authority and lust for freedom.

'To hear some persons speak during the bushranging era', wrote Charles White in his *History of Australian Bushranging*, 'one might imagine that the members of the police force . . . were engaged in a conspiracy against the happiness of mankind—and that whatever happened to them "served them right" '. A preference for bushrangers over policemen was widespread but by no means universal. It was stronger among Irish Catholics than among the population at large; for many of the bushrangers were their kinsmen, and it was easy for the Irish to feel sympathy for any wild man on the run. The common crowd of the city, according to the *Sydney Morning Herald*, received with pleasure news of highway robberies and the shooting of police. In the countryside squatters and diggers had good cause not to like men who bailed up stations and coaches; among rural workers bushranging was regarded as different from ordinary crimes and the outlaw was commonly a hero. The attitudes of small farmers varied from hatred to complicity. Some country people hostile to bushrangers were reluctant to say so because they lived in fear of them.

The government of New South Wales, troubled by the popularity of criminal gangs, had medals struck in 1870—in gold for private colonists and silver for policemen—to encourage the view that the true heroes in the battles of the bush were not the outlaws but their opponents: not John Gilbert, but William MacLeay, who fought off his gang near Goulburn; not 'Captain Thunderbolt', but Constable Alexander Walker, who clubbed him to death in a waterhole with his empty revolver. In all seven gold and three silver medals were awarded, each inscribed with the name of the recipient and an account of his feat.

Australians of later generations, drawing their knowledge from a folklore that softened the bushrangers, could easily exaggerate the public esteem for them and under-estimate the sympathy for their pursuers and still more their victims. William Charles Wentworth and Charles Harpur (both, as it happened, sons of men charged with highway robbery at home) shared a strong antipathy to bushrangers. To Wentworth, writing in 1819, they were 'wretches' who 'endangered the person and property of every one that has evinced himself hostile to their enormities.' They stirred Harpur's imagination but appalled his moral sense. In April 1829, when he was sixteen, a settler on the Hunter River was shot dead by two bushrangers. Harpur shared a common opinion that one of the killers was Donohoe. As he showed by writing verses mourning both the blacks massacred at Myall Creek and the whites slaughtered at the Creek of the Four Graves, Harpur was readily moved to grieve for any human being put to death by another. He searched for the grave of the murdered settler, found it, and wept. A short poem, 'The Grave of Clements', was made from the experience, and a longer one, 'The Glen of the White Man's Grave', years later. In *The Tragedy of Donohoe*, 'Written by an Australian' and published in the *Monitor* during 1835, the bushranger was an utter villain. The play imitated Shakespeare in structure and style. While writing it Harpur may have seen the first performance in Sydney of *Richard III*, and the character of Donohoe certainly has resemblances to that of Richard. He is a wicked man, displaying no nobler emotion than remorse. 'Clements—ye're avenged!' he cries as he is dying. When the play was revised and published in 1853 as *The Bushrangers*, Donohoe had become Stalwart in name but remained vicious by nature. Once he says that he became an outlaw after a tyrant had hurled 'the opprobrious term of *convict*' in his teeth; but that is in a speech whose purpose is to deceive a maiden. When he is honest he says that 'a wild, ungovernable heart' has driven him to crime. He speaks of unnamed 'burning wrongs' which have stung him to commit deeds terrible to name; but he sees himself as destined for hell and deserving it. Harpur hoped to find in the bushranger the stuff of an Australian literature; but the man who shed tears at Clements's grave could not make Donohoe a hero. Harpur's bushranger bore no resemblance to the Wild Colonial Boy. In real life, as a gold commissioner, Harpur joined a party of volunteers who hunted the Clarke gang after they had killed a policeman at Nerrigundah, near Braidwood, in 1866.

Even if Harpur's play had been written in nimbler language than he could manage when attempting blank verse, it might still have failed to find a public; for his perception of the bushranger could not be palatable to people who saw him as a figure of romance, while other readers deemed bushranging unfit matter for proper literature. In 1866 G. B. Barton, a native lately appointed reader in English literature at the University of Sydney, published his *Literature in New South Wales*. Of Harpur's *The Bushrangers* he wrote: 'A more unfortunate selection of a plot could hardly have been made. There is no scope for poetry, and it would be difficult for any mind, not accustomed to feed on sensation, to interest itself in the fortunes of a bushranger.'

When Barton offered that prim judgment, many adults were worrying about the seductive power of the bushranger over colonial lads. Some boys, like Ned Kelly, were taken on as apprentices by experienced outlaws. Others fancied themselves as wild colonial boys. Henry Lawson, born in 1867, wrote later that his brother Charlie 'was undecided as to whether he'd join the bushrangers or the mounted troopers—a state of indecision not uncommon amongst boys before our time, for both troopers and bushrangers came from the same class.' It was during the epidemic of bushranging that Henry Parkes canvassed support for the public schools bill of 1866 on the ground that native lads not civilized by education were in danger of turning to crime and being hanged. Properly schooled, they might choose their heroes with more discrimination, looking up not to bandits but to liberal statesmen or manly explorers. In the crowd which destroyed the decorum of the court by applauding the jury's acquittal of Gardiner in 1864, Judge Wise was especially appalled to notice a boy of about fifteen clapping with great vigour. Edward Wise's own schooling had been at Rugby, and his son Bernhard would go to Rugby and Oxford, learning to be an English gentleman before spending his adult life in colonial law and politics. Unfortunately for history, the judge did not ask this young admirer of Gardiner where he had been or not been to school before committing him to Darlinghurst Gaol for contempt of court.

Three years later the chief justice, Sir Alfred Stephen, spoke with concern about the boys of the colony at the end of the Clarke brothers' trial. He rebuked the jury which had found Gardiner not guilty and said that the expressions of rejoicing in court on that day 'would disgrace any community on earth.' When he pronounced the death sentence Stephen was addressing not merely Thomas and John Clarke but everybody who perceived the bushrangers as heroes and especially youths who might be attracted to emulate them. How was it, he asked, that 'these bushrangers, the scum of the earth, the lowest of the low, the most wicked of the wicked, are occasionally held up for our admiration?' The judge's answer lay back in the darkness of Botany Bay (to which, though he may not have known it, the Clarke brothers' father had been transported in 1825). 'It is the old leaven of convictism not yet worked out'. But brighter days were coming. 'Others who may think of commencing a course of crime such as yours', the chief justice told the condemned men, 'may rely on it that . . . there will be no longer that expression of sympathy with crime which sometime disgraced the country, and sunk it so low in the estimation of the world.'

The bushrangers would soon disappear from Australian society, beaten by universal schooling and efficient policing. They would ascend into mythology. The most famous bushrangers, like the most famous explorers, were men who had been led to death by their occupation, and folklore dwelt on the bravery or dignity of their dying. Relics from them were cherished. Boys played games about them. Only after they had gone did the custodians of order stop worrying about their popularity among the young. When Sir Redmond Barry was sentencing the last of the bushrangers in 1880 he spoke with deliberation about the danger of allowing boys to take such a man as a model. 'In new communities', said the judge, 'where the bonds of society are not so well linked together as in older countries, there is unfortunately a class which disregards the evil consequences of crime. Foolish, inconsiderate, ill-conducted, unprincipled youths unfortunately abound, and unless they are made to consider the consequences of crime they are led to imitate notorious felons, whom they regard as self-made heroes'. Ned Kelly had therefore to be hanged.

HEROES FOR DEMOCRACY

　　When Wentworth cited as an impediment to heroism in Australia the absence of any 'domestic faction or treason' which had to be repressed by force, he was demonstrating how far, by 1853, he had drifted from the colonial democrats. Had the contest over the renewal of transportation led to bloodshed it would have been the opponents, not the defenders of public order, who supplied any popular heroes; and when an insurrection did occur in Victoria the year after Wentworth spoke, the only participants to be honoured were rebels.

　　A sense of destiny settled on men of the Ballarat Reform League as their encounter of arms approached: it was expressed in the *Ballarat Times*'s prophecy that Bakery Hill would be recorded in the deathless pages of history. Raffaello Carboni had the first pages of his own sizzling celebration of the rebels printed in time for the anniversary of the battle on 3 December 1855, and sold them that day on the site of the stockade. A monument paid for by a citizen of Geelong was erected in 1856 at the Ballarat cemetery. It bore the names and birthplaces of the dead diggers and an inscription affirming that their cause was righteous: 'Sacred to the memory of those who fell on the memorable 3rd

MARTYRS FOR DEMOCRACY
Eureka monument at Ballarat

MONUMENT IN THE BALLARAT CEMETERY TO THOSE WHO FELL AT THE
EUREKA STOCKADE

of December 1854 in resisting the unconstitutional proceedings of the Victorian Government.' This memorial became an object of pilgrimage on the second anniversary, when two hundred people assembled on the ground where the martyrs had fallen to hear a speech in praise of them by John Lynch, one of Lalor's 'captains'. Then they walked in mourning procession to the cemetery, where they crowned the diggers' monument with garlands of flowers. Not far from it stood a broken column in memory of James Scobie, the man who had in a sense begun it all by being kicked to death near the Eureka Hotel.

The Melbourne General Cemetery housed an ornate monument over the grave of Sir Charles Hotham, who had ordered the soldiers and police to Eureka. It was made in England by the most eminent sculptor of the Gothic revival, George Gilbert Scott. 'VOTED BY THE LEGISLATIVE COUNCIL, JANUARY 10 1856', an inscription recorded. It was an anti-popular rather than a popular memorial, a gesture of sympathy for the governor made ten days after his death and two months before the old council dissolved for the last time. Peter Lalor had been elected for Ballarat in time to vote with six other digger members against the tribute to Hotham; as Lalor put it, there was 'sufficient monument already existing in the graves of the thirty individuals slain at Ballarat.'

Other occupants of the stockade beside Carboni set down their recollections of Eureka, and men who had been in it were honoured for the rest of their lives. If the soldiers killed in the charge were remembered in legend, it was as opponents and victims. 'It is next to impossible to get any two versions of what transpired to tally', a writer in the *Ballarat Star* observed in 1870; 'there are at least a score of people, all of whom not only shot at but struck down Captain Wyse [sic].'

It was a modest and local regard that the heroes of Eureka enjoyed. The issues that had ignited at Ballarat were so quickly put out, and the most prominent of the rebels, Lalor, became so evidently moderate a politician, that Eureka did not occupy any large place in the rhetoric of Victorian politics after responsible government began in 1856. Outside Victoria it seemed a remote affray. It was not a subject that commended itself straightforwardly to instructors of the young. Colonists who took up arms against servants of Queen Victoria, whatever the provocation, were less easily rendered into figures fit for the classroom than Captain Cook or Burke and Wills.

Pioneers of the eight-hour day were given respect by their comrades as heroes of labour. The flag of 1856 was kept at Melbourne's Trades Hall as a precious relic, to be brought out on anniversaries. James Stephens and other leaders had places of honour in the procession. Supporters of the eight-hours movement resolved at a meeting in Williamstown on 30 June 1869 to place a memorial over the grave of James Galloway, who had been buried in the Melbourne General Cemetery in 1860. It was lofty and classical and bore a tribute to 'the valuable services he rendered in establishing the eight hours system in this colony'. None of the eight-hours men was well known outside his own range of occupations or his own city.

Every colony had worthies of its own. Victoria had John Batman and John Pascoe Fawkner, each of whom was regarded by one faction of the people as the true founder of their community. Batman, as Charles Gavan Duffy wrote, was 'the type of the Squatters', and Fawkner 'a type of the Squatters' opponents, the dwellers in towns, the men of enterprise and movement.' There was talk of a statue to Fawkner in Melbourne, but the plan was ridiculed in *Melbourne Punch* (which showed him as Napoleon, Hercules and Pallas Athene) and abandoned. Few people outside Victoria ever heard of either him or his rival; and within Victoria the Irish quarter of the population preferred Long John

O'Shanassy to either of them. O'Shanassy's stature was recognized in death as in life, for the Celtic cross on his grave would soar over all others in the Roman Catholic section of the Melbourne General Cemetery. His own hero was Daniel O'Connell, the Liberator, of whom a statue was to be erected in the grounds of St Patrick's Cathedral.

In activities of leisure as well as in politics, the scattered and separated character of Australian settlement made it difficult for anybody to gain a more than parochial fame. The beginning of intercolonial contests and of reporting by telegraph helped to make outstanding men of sport more widely known; but no truly national reputation was to be had from games until colonists competed overseas and the cable brought rapid news of their achievements. In that sense F. R. Spofforth, champion bowler against English cricket teams in the 1870s and 1880s, was perhaps the first thoroughly Australian hero of leisure.

Were there no heroines? Apart from Queen Victoria, who was put on the throne by an inflexible rule of primogeniture, England had only one woman of heroic reputation between 1788 and 1870, and that was Florence Nightingale. The democratic colonies of Australia were no more hospitable than their homeland to women in public life. As far as Charles Dilke could see, the outnumbered females of the continent cheerfully accepted their subordination. 'In all our Southern colonies together', he wrote in 1868, 'there are a million of men to only three-quarters of a million of women; yet with all this disproportion . . . not only have the women failed to acquire any great share of power, political or social, but they are content to occupy a position not relatively superior to that held by them at home'. Members of a later generation, searching the record, might well discover a few women on whom to confer retrospectively the name of heroine: Mrs Macquarie's chair, on the headland between Farm Cove and Woolloomooloo Bay, might be made a shrine at which she and other notable wives of governors, among them Lady Franklin and Lady Denison, could be given honour; Mary Reibey, convict turned capitalist, could well be celebrated for her enterprise; Lucy Osburn, disciple of Miss Nightingale, who arrived in Sydney in 1868, could be shown to have transformed the craft of nursing; Mary McKillop, Mother Mary of the Cross, founder of the Sisters of St Joseph at Penola, South Australia, in 1867, might eventually be recognized as Australia's first saint. But none of these women would have been mentioned in any catalogue of important colonists compiled in 1870. Caroline Chisholm alone had surmounted the disadvantages of being a woman sufficiently to make a large mark on the man's world of Australia. The one female who gained national and even international fame in the 1860s was Jane Duff, aged seven, and that was for saving the lives of her two brothers when they were lost in the bush.

Among the public men of Australia none aspired more eagerly to be the hero of democracy than Henry Parkes. He was himself given to worshipping heroes, among them the master of the subject Thomas Carlyle, who detested democracy and saw the leadership of exceptional men as its only salvation. Parkes was committed to democratic politics as his means of access to eminence. In 1854, having won the seat in the Legislative Council just vacated by Wentworth, he let his delight show. 'I have been elected', he said floridly, 'the successor of the greatest man who ever trod this country' and 'you have made me by your votes the most distinguished commoner in the land.' Some of his democratic allies found that tone ominous. 'Professed liberals, when they get on in the world,' a group of his employees wrote in a letter to the *Sydney Morning Herald*, 'sometimes forget their antecedents and ape the tyrannical aristocrats they have been so long in denouncing. Is it so with Mr. Parkes?' His old comrade Charles Harpur was appalled. The praise of Wentworth struck him as 'false in feeling and philosophy'; Parkes' election had not made him 'a whit greater than he either was, or had it in him to be, before that event.' In the *People's Advocate* Harpur wrote:

> I like you, friend Parkes, but don't like the morality
>   Of your notion of greatness, so bloated and crude.
>
> Such a crochet, I fear, has made many a Nero;
>   Of all that's despotic, I know, 'tis the seed;
> And would make the *great* Czar, not a spoiler, but Hero—
>   And the devil a *very great fellow indeed.*

Parkes still had to learn that a democratic politician must conceal his sense of destiny if he wanted his peers to go on electing him. It was not easy for him to dissemble, since his purpose in life, as he confessed when standing for the first Legislative Assembly in 1856, was 'so to impress my name and my character and my influence on this country, that I may be remembered when I am dead and in my grave.' In 1870 he was among the small band of politicians whose reputation extended beyond one colony. He aspired to be leader of a larger nation than New South Wales. At fifty-five he looked every inch of his beard a patriarch, and he had two decades still to spend at the task which he described in the title of his autobiography, *Fifty Years in the Making of Australian History.* In 1888, the seventy-third year of his life and his forty-ninth as a colonist, he would propose a pantheon in Sydney as a means of celebrating a century of British settlement. It would be laughed out of Parliament House by opponents who suspected that he wanted only to create a monstrous mausoleum for himself, and who believed that this colony, this continent, had no men great enough for such grand commemoration.

The democratic Americans made heroes of their leaders. They came close to deifying their first president, George Washington; they named their capital after him and pierced its sky with the Washington Monument. On the fourth of July they celebrated the other founders of the republic as if the signing of the declaration of independence were rather like the last supper. They saw democracy as incarnate in Andrew Jackson, called him 'the Hero', and built equestrian statues of him all over the country. Walt Whitman wrote as reverently of Abraham Lincoln as other poets wrote of Jesus. The colonists of Australia were not disposed to look at any politician, or any other man, in that spirit. Charles Dilke, visiting both societies in 1866–7, found the democracy of the Australian colonies different in character from the democracy of the United States. For Americans, he observed, democracy was a general idea. In the Australian colonies it was merely an accident. 'The first settlers were active, bustling men of fairly even rank or wealth, none of whom could brook the leadership of any other. The only way out of the difficulty was the adoption of the rule "All of us to be equal, and the majority to govern;" but there is no conception of the nature of democracy'. One day, Dilke expected, democracy would strike roots in Australia. If he was right, then the people might one day give more honour to the men they chose to lead them.

The great American heroes were associated with war. Washington commanded the army of the revolution. Jackson was 'old Hickory' the soldier, and had a gold medal from Congress for winning the battle of New Orleans, before he went into politics. Lincoln led one half of the nation to war against the other half and became in legend Father Abraham, the saviour, martyred at the moment when he was sealing its reunion. Australian society provided by 1870 no comparable opportunity or need. For Wentworth it

was a matter of lament that the colonial patriot had been offered no civil war, no invasion
and no field for chivalry abroad. But might not the tranquillity of this continent be counted
a blessing rather than a deprivation? Henry Parkes devoted a poem, 'The Flag', to saying
so:

> Fling out the flag—our virgin flag,
>   Which foeman's shot has never rent,
> And plant it high on mount and crag,
>   O'er busy town and lonely tent.
>
> Where commerce rears her stately halls,
>   And where the miner rends the rock,
> Where the sweet rain on cornfield falls,
>   Where pastures feed the herd and flock.
>
> Still let it float o'er homes of peace,
>   Our starry cross—our glorious sign!
> While Nature's bounteous gifts increase,
>   And Freedom's glories brighter shine.
>
> Brave hearts may beat in Labour's strife,
>   They need no spur of martial pride;
> High deeds may crown a gentle life,
>   And spread their radiance far and wide.
>
> Fling out the flag, and guard it well!
>   Our pleasant fields the foe ne'er trod;
> Long may our guardian heroes dwell
>   In league with truth—in camp with God!
>
> In other lands the patriot boasts
>   His standard borne through Slaughter's flood,
> Which, waving o'er infuriate hosts,
>   Was consecrate in fire and blood.
>
> A truer charm our flag endears;
>   Where'er it waves, on land or sea,
> It bears no stain of blood and tears—
>   Its glory is its purity.
>
> God girdled our majestic isle
>   With seas far-reaching east and west,
> That man might live beneath His smile,
>   In peace and freedom ever blest.

What was the flag that floated untorn over these people living in comfort, freedom
and peace? Parkes's 'starry cross' was the blue and white standard which was employed
officially on occasions to represent the colony of New South Wales but which would not
have been recognized by most of her citizens. The flag familiar to Australians was the
Union Jack, which was by no means free of bloodstains. Was it the destiny of these colonies
to be mere extensions of the mother country, smiled upon by providence but having no

national identity of their own? How would 'guardian heroes' appear, as long as the far-reaching seas made the task of protecting these shores so easy?

For the time being, Australians who wanted heroes had to choose between Cook the remote discoverer, Wentworth the flawed patriot, the grim explorers of the interior, the disreputable outlaws of the bush, the makers of the Eureka stockade and the eight-hour day, and other men of such reputation as could be nurtured within the bounds of colonial settlement and experience.

16   She Is Not Yet

At Launceston, in Van Diemen's Land, a policeman with a taste for writing verse imagined a bachelor emigrant settler of the 1840s wondering why he had left home. In sickness he missed friends; at Christmas he missed the festive days of winter; all the year round his sense of exile was nourished by the inversions of nature. The land in which he had settled was empty of valour:

> The woods have never rang with War's loud crash,
>   No chivalry has swept the silent plains;
> Mailed bands of combatants, with courage rash,
>   Were never led to fight by gallant Thanes.

Australia had no 'tales of battle field, or martial fame' to fire the ardour of youth; nor had she any other kind of distinction to honour.

> Here are no storied tombs, nor sculptured shrines,
>   On which we read a Saint, or Hero's praise;
> The ancient Harper never poured his rhymes,
>   Nor Troubadour e'er sang melodious lays!

The American contemplating Europe could feel that the history of his own land was shallow, as when Nathaniel Hawthorne confessed in 1860 'the difficulty of writing a romance about a country where there is no shadow, no antiquity, no mystery, no picturesque and gloomy wrong, nor anything but a commonplace prosperity, in broad and simple daylight'. But Europeans had been settled in Hawthorne's Massachusetts for two centuries. America had a past rich and deep compared with a society in which first fleeters were still alive in the 1840s and their sons and daughters were among the citizens of 1870. 'As a section of the British Empire,' the committee of the Sydney Mechanics' School of Arts reported at its sixth annual meeting in 1838, 'our history is bounded by the recollections of the present generation. Everything around us is new'. The neo-Gothic style of such buildings as Sydney's Government House in the 1840s and the churches and universities of the 1850s had one purpose beyond those it served in both England and America: for Australian colonists, the imitation of mediaeval architecture was the only

visible reminder of a civilization earlier than 1788. The history that both emigrants and
natives carried in their heads was made up in large part of events in the old country.
'Most of us . . .' as an early settler of Port Phillip wrote in 1849 'have either brought with us
or inherited recollections of the past, which extend beyond our own lives, and crowd into
a present picture the storied memories of a nation.'

To the settler in the Tasmanian poem the figure of Time brings a message of
comfort. On the absence of warfare he speaks as Henry Parkes was to speak in 'The Flag',
saying:

> Thou should'st rejoice that no ensanguined mound
> Is seen to rise with slaughter's dreadful pile.

As for the other missing ingredients of colonial civilization, Time counsels patience and sees
a future in which Science will dawn, the arts will flourish, and the settler himself, no longer
a bachelor, will be ready to risk death for a woman's approving smile.

Like the policeman of Launceston, any poet or orator searching for grandeur in so
young and untried a society was bound to turn to the future. Erasmus Darwin began the
tradition when he made Hope see those 'tall spires, and dome-capt towers' at Sydney Cove
in 1789. Authors passed from pen to pen the conceit that this city would transcend its
origins as Rome had done. Wentworth at Cambridge saw the native's task as to 'Foretell
the glories' of his country. The men of letters who saw themselves as makers of an
Australian civilization in the 1840s and 1850s carried on the custom of patriotic prophecy.
W. A. Duncan published in the *Australian* an anthem for his adopted land, affirming that
posterity would honour his generation for beginning to build 'Australia the Wide and
the Free'. Charles Harpur had the young nation beckon the emigrant by gazing ahead to
a time of plenty and republican democracy:

> Till the future a numberless people shall see,
> Eager, and noble, and equal, and free,
> And the God they adore their sole monarch shall be—
> Then come, build thy home in Australia!

Harpur's admirer Deniehy avowed in 1853: 'I am a native of the soil and I am proud of
my birthplace. It is true its past has not been hallowed in history by the achievements of
men whose names reflected a light upon the times in which they lived. We have no long
line of poets or statesmen or warriors in this country. Art has done nothing but Nature
everything. IT IS OURS, THEN, TO INAUGURATE THE FUTURE.' The University of Melbourne,
which opened in 1855, took as motto Horace's words *Postera crescam laude*, or 'I shall grow
in the esteem of future generations.' Henry Kendall, inheritor of hopes indulged by
Harpur and his friends, entitled a poem of 1859 'The Far Future':

> Australia, advancing with rapid wing'd stride,
> Shall plant among nations her banner with pride,
> The yoke of dependence aside she will cast,
> And build on the ruins and wrecks of the Past.
> Her flag on the tempest will wave to proclaim
> 'Mong kingdoms and empires her national name.
> The Future shall see it asleep or unfurl'd,
> The shelter of Freedom and boast of the world.

The notion that Australia would build on the ruins of the past was not unlike the American revolutionaries' equation of Europe with senility and corruption. The Victorian politician George Verdon, who ordered the *Cerberus*, invoked this theme in 1858, declaring that while old countries 'have to knock down and root up the misshapen structure of centuries, before they can build as their experience teaches them, we, having nothing to undo can, if we will, make the last page of their history the first of our own, and complete to its finished perfection the temple of which they have but laid the foundations.' But Thomas Jefferson and his contemporaries had also an achievement to celebrate; and their sons and grandsons enjoyed triumphs and suffered disasters which gave the history of the United States by 1870 a density lacking on this side of the Pacific, where preachers, politicians and poets went on scanning the future for their innocent fellow colonists. The title of John Dunmore Lang's last work, published in 1870, with an almost millenarian ring announced what was in store: *The Coming Event! or Freedom and Independence for the seven united provinces of Australia.* At the official luncheon for Anniversary Day on 26 January 1870 the premier of New South Wales, Charles Cowper, looked forward not merely with confident hope, but with pride. 'This holiday was considered the holiday of the year,' he said, 'and he had never yet seen the day come round when we had not occasion to congratulate ourselves on the glorious future that lay before us.' When a politician talked as if the coming history of his country had happened already, and knew that there was glory in it, he was taking the colonial habit of blowing as far as it could go.

For many years after 1870 colonial patriots would find too little to celebrate in the present and the past, and would invite other Australians to believe that the real history of their nation lay ahead. This was the burden of 'The Dominion of Australia: a Forecast', a poem written in 1877 by James Brunton Stephens. The author had emigrated from Scotland to Queensland in 1866 and wrote the verses while he was teaching at a school near Brisbane.

> She is not yet; but he whose ear
> Thrills to that finer atmosphere
>   Where footfalls of appointed things,
>   Reverberent of days to be,
>   Are heard in forecast echoings
>   Like wave-beats from a viewless sea
> Hears in the voiceful tremors of the sky
> Auroral heralds whispering, 'She is nigh.'

The poet compares an underground river waiting to be divined with 'A viewless stream of Common Will' which

> At Wisdom's voice shall leap to light,
>   And hide our barren feuds in bloom,
> Till, all our sundering lines with love o'ergrown,
> Our bounds shall be the girding seas alone.

Stephens's dominion of Australia would be a fertile and united continent. When she would appear, and what she would then do, remained obscure in his verses, which were read and learned by children in all the colonies, and became perhaps the most widely known of poetic statements about Australian nationality between 1870 and 1900.

To British ears, unable to hear footfalls of a future barely audible to colonists on the spot, the name of Australia could still stand in 1870 for the farthest imaginable part of the world; and even so late in the century it might be associated with convictism. Henry Bournes Higgins, a young Protestant Irish emigrant of 1870, recalled that as a child in Killarney he and his brothers were sent on wet days to play in a garret at the top of the house. 'Being so remote from the street level', he wrote, 'it was called "Australia." ' And the only place the Higgins boys had heard of in that distant land was Botany Bay.

In the lifetime of Higgins and his fellow colonists events would happen, some of their own choosing and some not, which would make it easier for Australians to affirm that they had a history. Men of the labour movement would make governments. The people of six colonies would vote themselves into a new Commonwealth. They would be offered participation in a great war, and from that experience would emerge a solemn festival of nationality. Early in 1916 the director of education in New South Wales, Peter Board, would say of the landing at Gallipoli: 'On 25th April history and Australian history were fused . . . Never again can the history of this continent of ours stand detached from World history.' In Anzac Day, Australians would create a holiday not transplanted from elsewhere, not confined to one region, not an occasion for pleasure; commemorating the shedding of blood for nation and empire, and honouring heroes as nobody in Australia had ever been honoured before.

ABBREVIATIONS

ADB	*Australian Dictionary of Biography*
AE	*Australian Encyclopaedia,* 1958
AJPH	*Australian Journal of Politics and History*
HRA	*Historical Records of Australia*
HRNSW	*Historical Records of New South Wales*
HS	*Historical Studies*
JRAHS	*Royal Australian Historical Society, Journal and Proceedings*
SG	*Sydney Gazette*
SMH	*Sydney Morning Herald*

Bibliography

The following sources have been consulted for more than one chapter. Other sources are cited below in notes to each chapter. Biographical information not otherwise attributed is from the *Australian Dictionary of Biography*.

Contemporary works

Barlow, N. (ed.). *Charles Darwin's Diary of the Voyage of H.M.S. Beagle*. Cambridge 1933.

Barton, G. B. *Literature in New South Wales*. Sydney 1866.

Beaglehole, J. C. (ed.). *The Journals of Captain James Cook on his Voyage of Discovery. 1 The Voyage of the "Endeavour", 1768–1771*. Cambridge 1955.

Braim, T. H. *A History of New South Wales, from its settlement to the close of the year 1844.* 2 vols. London 1846.

Collins, D. *An Account of the English Colony in New South Wales.* 2 vols. London 1798, 1802.

Cunningham, P. *Two Years in New South Wales: a series of letters, comprising sketches of the actual state of society in that colony*. London 1827.

Denison, Sir W. *Varieties of Vice-Regal Life.* 2 vols. London 1870.

Dilke, C. W. *Greater Britain: a record of travel in English-speaking countries during 1866 and 1867.* 2 vols. London 1868.

Duffy, C. G. 'An Australian example', *Contemporary Review*, vol. 53, 1888.

—— *My Life in Two Hemispheres.* 2 vols. London 1898.

Emigrant Mechanic, An [A. Harris]. *Settlers and Convicts, or Recollections of Sixteen Years Labour in the Australian Backwoods*. Melbourne 1883.

Finn, E., *see* Garryowen.

Garryowen [E. Finn]. *The Chronicles of Early Melbourne 1835 to 1852. Historical, anecdotal and personal.* 2 vols. Melbourne 1888.

Hare, F. A. *The Last of the Bushrangers*. 3rd ed. London 1894.

Harpur, C. *The Bushrangers: a play in five acts, and other poems*. Sydney 1853.

—— *Poems*. Melbourne 1883.

Harris, A., *see* Emigrant Mechanic, An.

Heaton, J. H. *Australian Dictionary of Dates and Men of the Time: containing the history of Australasia from 1542 to May, 1879*. Sydney 1879.

Henning, R. *The Letters of Rachel Henning*. Sydney 1952.

Howitt, W. *Land, Labour, and Gold: or, Two Years in Victoria: with visits to Sydney and Van Diemen's Land*. 2 vols. London 1855.

[James, J. S.]. *The Vagabond Papers*. Melbourne 1878.

Kelly, W. *Life in Victoria, or Victoria in 1853, and Victoria in 1858*. 2 vols. London 1859.

[Kerr, J. H.]. *Glimpses of Life in Victoria by a Resident*. Edinburgh 1872.

Kingsley, H. *The Recollections of Geoffrey Hamlyn*. 3 vols. Cambridge 1859.

Lang, J. D. *Aurora Australis, or Specimens of Sacred Poetry for the Colonists of Australia*. Sydney 1826.

——— *The Coming Event! or Freedom and Independence for the Seven United Provinces of Australia*. Sydney 1870.

——— *Freedom and Independence for the Golden Lands of Australia : the right of the colonies and the interest of Britain and the world*. London 1852.

——— *An Historical and Statistical Account of New South Wales, both as a Penal Settlement and as a British Colony*. 2 vols. London 1834.

——— *An Historical and Statistical Account of New South Wales : including a visit to the gold regions, and a description of the mines etc.* 2 vols. 3rd ed. London 1852.

[Laye, E. P. R., Mrs]. *Social Life and Manners in Australia, being the notes of eight years' experience by a resident*. London 1861.

Mackaness, G. (ed.). *Odes of Michael Massey Robinson First Poet Laureate of Australia (1754–1826)*. Sydney 1946.

Marjoribanks, A. *Travels in New South Wales*. London 1847.

Massary, Isabel, Miss, *see* Laye, E.P.R., Mrs.

Mellersh, H. E. L. (ed.). *The Voyage of the Beagle*. Heron Books 1968.

Meredith, Mrs C. *Notes and Sketches of New South Wales During a Residence in that Colony from 1839 to 1844*. London 1844.

Michie, Sir A. *Readings in Melbourne ; with an essay on the resources and prospects of Victoria, for the emigrant and uneasy classes*. London 1879.

Milner, J. and Brierly, O. W. *The Cruise of H.M.S. Galatea, Captain H.R.H. the Duke of Edinburgh, K.G. in 1867–1868*. London 1869.

Parkes, H. *Fifty Years in the Making of Australian History*. 2 vols. London 1892.

——— *Speeches on Various Occasions Connected with the Public Affairs of New South Wales 1848–1874*. Melbourne 1876.

Phillip, Arthur. *The Voyage of Governor Phillip to Botany Bay ; with an account of the establishment of the colonies of Port Jackson & Norfolk Island ; compiled from authentic papers*. London 1789.

Reed, T. T. (ed.). *The Poetical Works of Henry Kendall*. Adelaide 1966.

Robb, F. M. (ed.). *Poems of Adam Lindsay Gordon*. Melbourne 1946.

Silvester, E. K. (ed.). *New South Wales Constitution Bill. The speeches, in the Legislative Council, on the second reading of the bill*. Sydney 1853.

Thatcher, C. *Thatcher's Colonial Minstrel : new collection of songs, by the inimitable Thatcher*. Melbourne 1864.

Therry, R. *Reminiscences of Thirty Year's Residence in New South Wales and Victoria*. London 1863.

Trollope, A. *Australia and New Zealand*. 2 vols. London 1873.

Wentworth, W. C. *A Statistical, Historical and Political Description of the Colony of New South Wales, and its Dependent Settlements in Van Diemen's Land*. London 1819. (2nd ed. 1820).

——— *A Statistical Account of the British Settlements in Australasia ; including the colonies of New South Wales and Van Diemen's Land*. 2 vols. 3rd ed. London 1824.

West, J. *The History of Tasmania*. 2 vols. Launceston 1853.

Wilkes, C. *Narrative of the United States Exploring Expedition during the years 1838, 1839, 1840, 1841, 1842*. 5 vols. Philadelphia 1844.

Withers, W. B. *The History of Ballarat*. 2nd ed. Ballarat 1887.

Later Works

Barrett, J. *That Better Country : the religious aspect of life in eastern Australia, 1835–1850*. Melbourne 1966.

Bassett, M. *The Hentys: an Australian colonial tapestry.* London 1954.

Bean, C. E. W. *Here, My Son: an account of the independent and other corporate boys' schools of Australia.* Sydney 1950.

Birch, A. and Macmillan, D. S. (eds). *The Sydney Scene 1788–1960.* Melbourne 1962.

Birt, H. N. *Benedictine Pioneers in Australia.* 2 vols. London 1911.

Blainey, A. *The Farthing Poet: a biography of Richard Hengist Horne 1802–84.* London 1968

Blainey, G. *The Rush that Never Ended: a history of Australian mining.* Melbourne 1963.

—— *The Tyranny of Distance: how distance shaped Australia's history.* Melbourne 1966.

A Century of Journalism: the Sydney Morning Herald and its record of Australian life 1831–1931. Sydney 1931.

Chisholm, A. H. *Strange New World: the adventures of John Gilbert and Ludwig Leichhardt.* Revised ed. Sydney 1955.

Clark, C. M. H. *A History of Australia. 1 From the earliest times to the age of Macquarie,* Melbourne 1962.

2 New South Wales and Van Diemen's Land, 1822–1838, Melbourne 1968.

—— (ed.). *Select Documents in Australian History 1788–1850.* Sydney 1950.

—— (ed.). *Select Documents in Australian History 1851–1900.* Sydney 1955.

—— *Sources of Australian History.* London 1957.

Cobley, J. *Sydney Cove 1788.* London 1962.

Crowley, F. K. *Forrest 1847–1918. 1 1847–91, apprenticeship to premiership,* Brisbane 1971.

Dunstan, K. *Wowsers: being an account of the prudery exhibited by certain outstanding men and women in such matters as drinking, smoking, prostitution, censorship and gambling.* Melbourne 1968.

Dutton, G. (ed.). *The Literature of Australia.* Penguin 1964.

Ellis, M. H. *John Macarthur.* Sydney 1955.

—— *Lachlan Macquarie: his life, adventures and times.* Sydney 1947.

Erdos, R. *The Sydney Gazette: Australia's first newspaper.* Melbourne 1961.

Feeken, E. H. J., Feeken, G. E. E. and Spate, O. H. K. *The Discovery and Exploration of Australia.* Melbourne 1970.

Grainger, E. *Martin of Martin Place . . . a biography of Sir James Martin (1820–1886).* Sydney 1970.

Grant, J. and Serle, G. (eds). *The Melbourne Scene 1803–1956.* Melbourne 1957.

Haydon, A. L. *The Trooper Police of Australia: a record of mounted police work in the Commonwealth from the earliest days of settlement to the present time.* London 1911.

Kiddle, M. *Caroline Chisholm.* Melbourne 1950.

—— *Men of Yesterday: a social history of the Western District of Victoria 1834–1890.* Melbourne 1961.

King, H. *Richard Bourke.* Melbourne 1971.

Knight, R. *Illiberal Liberal: Robert Lowe in New South Wales, 1842–1850.* Melbourne 1966.

Kunz, E. and E. *A Continent Takes Shape.* Sydney 1971.

La Nauze, J. A. *Alfred Deakin: a biography.* 2 vols. Melbourne 1965.

Lansbury, C. *Arcady in Australia: the evocation of Australia in nineteenth century English literature.* Melbourne 1970.

Life of a Pioneer: adventures of H. S. Wills first white settler in Ararat district. Rockhampton n.d.

Martin, A. W. 'Henry Parkes: man and politician' and 'Faction politics and the education question in New South Wales' in E. L. French (ed.), *Melbourne Studies in Education 1960–1961,* Melbourne 1962.

Melbourne, A. C. V. *Early Constitutional Development in Australia.* 2nd ed. Brisbane 1963.

—— *William Charles Wentworth.* Brisbane 1934.

Millar, T. B. *The History of the Defence Forces of the Port Phillip District and Colony of Victoria 1836–1900* (M.A. thesis, University of Melbourne, 1957).

Miller, E. M. *Australian Literature from its Beginnings to 1935.* Melbourne 1940.

Molony, J. N. *An Architect of Freedom: John Hubert Plunkett in New South Wales 1832–1869.* Canberra 1973.

—— *The Roman Mould of the Australian Catholic Church.* Melbourne 1969.

Moorehead, A. *Cooper's Creek.* London 1963.

Moran, Cardinal P. F. *History of the Catholic Church in Australasia : from authentic sources.* Sydney n.d. [1895].

Morris, E. E. *Austral English : a dictionary of Australasian words, phrases and usages.* London 1898.

—— *A Memoir of George Higinbotham, an Australian politician and Chief Justice of Victoria.* London 1895.

Mulvaney, D. J. *Cricket Walkabout : the Australian Aboriginal cricketers on tour 1867–8.* Melbourne 1967.

Murtagh, J. G. *Australia : the Catholic chapter.* New York 1946.

Nadel, G. *Australia's Colonial Culture : ideas, men and institutions in mid-nineteenth century eastern Australia.* Melbourne 1957.

Normington-Rawling, J. *Charles Harpur, an Australian.* Sydney 1962.

O'Farrell, P. (ed.). *Documents in Australian Catholic History.* 2 vols. London 1969.

Perry, T. M. *Australia's First Frontier : the spread of settlement in New South Wales 1788–1829.* Melbourne 1963.

Pike, D. *Paradise of Dissent : South Australia 1829–1857.* 2nd ed. Melbourne 1967.

Ramson, W. S. *Australian English : an historical study of the vocabulary 1788–1898.* Canberra 1966.

Reese, T. R. *The History of the Royal Commonwealth Society 1868–1968.* London 1968.

Reid, G. H. *My Reminiscences.* London 1917.

Ritchie, J. *Punishment and Profit : the reports of commissioner John Bigge on the colonies of New South Wales and Van Diemen's Land, 1822–1823 ; their origins, nature and significance.* Melbourne 1970.

Roberts, S. H. *The Squatting Age in Australia 1835–1847.* Melbourne 1935.

Robson, L. L. *The Convict Settlers of Australia : an enquiry into the origin and character of the convicts transported to New South Wales and Van Diemen's Land 1787–1852.* Melbourne 1965.

Roe, M. *Quest for Authority in Eastern Australia 1835–1851.* Melbourne 1965.

Sadleir, J. *Recollections of a Victorian Police Officer.* Melbourne 1913.

Scott, E. *The Life of Captain Matthew Flinders, R.N.* Sydney 1914.

Serle, G. *The Golden Age : a history of the colony of Victoria, 1851–1861.* Melbourne 1963.

Shaw, A. G. L. *Convicts and the Colonies : a study of penal transportation from Great Britain and Ireland to Australia and other parts of the British Empire.* London 1966.

—— *The Economic Development of Australia.* London 1944.

Smith, B. *Australian Painting, 1788–1960.* London 1962.

Turner, H. G. *A History of the Colony of Victoria from its Discovery to its Absorption into the Commonwealth of Australia.* 2 vols. London 1904.

Turner, I. (ed.). *The Australian Dream : a collection of anticipations about Australia from Captain Cook to the present day.* Melbourne 1968.

Walker, M. H. *Come Wind, Come Weather : a biography of Alfred Howitt.* Melbourne 1971.

Ward, R. *The Australian Legend.* Melbourne 1958.

—— (ed.). *The Penguin Book of Australian Ballads.* Melbourne 1964.

White, C. *History of Australian Bushranging. 1 The early days to 1862,* Sydney 1900. *2 1863–1880 Ben Hall and the Kelly Gang,* Sydney 1906.

Notes

Introduction

The first essay I published on the theme of this work was 'Anzac: the substitute religion', *Nation*, 23 April 1960. A revised version of the lecture given in Canberra appeared in *Meanjin Quarterly*, no. 1, 1965, pp. 25–44, and also in C. B. Christesen (ed.), *On Native Grounds* (Sydney 1968), pp. 205–21. On the subject of the pilgrimage to Gallipoli, I wrote 'Diggers in antiquity', *Nation*, 29 May 1965, and 'Return to Gallipoli', *Australian National University Historical Journal*, no. 3, 1966, pp. 1–10. Other pieces of work in progress are 'Anzac and Christian—two traditions or one?', *St. Mark's Review*, no. 42, November 1965, pp. 3-12; 'Australia Day', *HS*, vol. 13, 1967-9, pp. 20-41; 'Conscription in peace and war, 1911-1945' in R. Forward and B. Reece (eds), *Conscription in Australia* (St Lucia 1968), pp. 22-65; *C. E. W. Bean, Australian Historian*, John Murtagh Macrossan Lecture 1969 (St Lucia 1970); 'The Australians at Gallipoli', *HS*, vol. 14, 1970-1, pp. 219-30, 361-75.

The passage on tunnels is in J. H. Hexter, *Reappraisals in History* (London 1961), p. 194.

The People

1 Convicts

BOTANY BAY

Information on early discovery and mapping is drawn from Scott, *The Life of Captain Matthew Flinders, R.N.*, pp. 420-9; Feeken, Feeken and Spate, *The Discovery and Exploration of Australia*, pp. 33-47; Kunz, *A Continent Takes Shape*, pp. 8-30; Beaglehole (ed.), *The Journals of Captain James Cook on his Voyages of Discovery*, vol. 1, pp. 298-313, 387-8; entries 'Australia', 'Exploration by Sea' and 'Maps and Mapping' in *AE*.

The newspaper that placed the colony on the west side of New Holland is reported in Clark, *A History of Australia*, vol. 1, p. 71. Phillip's judgment of Port Jackson is quoted in Clark (ed.), *Select Documents 1788-1850*, p. 45. On the seasons at Botany Bay, see G. Blainey, 'Climate and Australia's history', *Melbourne Historical Journal*, no. 10, 1971, p. 5.

The colonial author quoted on the English public's perception of Botany Bay is James Macarthur, *New South Wales: its present state and future prospects* (London 1837), p. 23; the passage is quoted in Lansbury,

Arcady in Australia, p. 55. The quotation from D. Collins, *Account of the English Colony in New South Wales*, is at p. 502. West's comparison of the names 'Van Diemen's Land' and 'Tasmania' is in *The History of Tasmania*, vol. 1, pp. 3-4. The stamps are described in A. F. Basset Hull, 'History of Australian postage stamps', *JRAHS*, vol. 27, 1941, p. 314. Flinders's liking for 'Australia' is in *HRA*, ser. 1, vol. 9, pp. 867-9; Scott, *op. cit.*, pp. 424-8. Macquarie's preference for it is in *HRA*, ser. 1, vol. 9, p. 747; for his receipt of Flinders's book see p. 356. The inscription on his tomb is given in Ellis, *Lachlan Macquarie*, p. 491. Proposed names for South Australia are cited in Pike, *Paradise of Dissent*, p. 57.

THE TRANSPORTED

My account draws on Shaw, *Convicts and the Colonies*. Additional information about the convicts is taken from E. O'Brien, *The Foundation of Australia (1786-1800): a study in English criminal practice and penal colonisation in the eighteenth century* (London 1937), especially at p. 241; Robson, *The Convict Settlers of Australia*, especially at pp. 143, 147, 168-71, 192-3. Description of the ceremonies on 26 January and 7 February 1788 is based on Cobley, *Sydney Cove 1788*, pp. 60, 63; Clark, *A History of Australia*, vol. 1, pp. 88, 114; Phillip, *The Voyage of Governor Phillip to Botany Bay*, p. 66.

Phillip's instruction not to facilitate the return of convicts is quoted in Shaw, *op. cit.*, p. 66. West's judgment of Port Arthur is in *The History of Tasmania*, vol. 2, p. 244. The permission given governors to remit sentences is quoted in Shaw, *op. cit.*, p. 82. On Bigge's inquiry into Macquarie's administration, see Ritchie, *Punishment and Profit*, especially pp. 61-5, 218-22, 240-1, 247-50. The official who observed that a convict is estimated as a colonist, not a felon, is quoted in 'Papers relative to transportation and assignment of convicts', *Parliamentary Papers*, vol. 38, 1839, no. 582, p. 2. The judgment of the 1837 committee is in 'Report from the select committee on transportation', *Parliamentary Papers*, vol. 22, 1837-8, no. 669, p. xx. Lord John Russell's statement of 1839 is quoted in Shaw, *op. cit.*, pp. 288-9.

The remark about transporting a burglar to a gold mine is by Henry Parkes, quoted in Grainger, *Martin of Martin Place*, p. 55. The passage on convictism for English readers is quoted from *Realm*, 24 February 1864, in Morris, *Austral English*, p. 95. Trollope's visit to Port Arthur is described in his *Australia and New Zealand*, vol. 2, pp. 28-9, 36. S. Murray-Smith has an illuminating introduction to M. Clarke, *His Natural Life* (Penguin Books 1970).

EMANCIPISTS

Phillip's instructions are in Clark (ed.), *Select Documents 1788-1850*, p. 219. The surgeon observing former convicts in 1804 is James Thomson in *HRNSW*, vol. 5, p. 391. The visitor of 1805 writing about the national character is John Turnbull, quoted in Ward, *The Australian Legend*, p. 35. Macquarie's declaration of 1821 is quoted in Ellis, *Lachlan Macquarie*, p. 557. Joseph Harpur's tribute to Macquarie is quoted from *Australian*, 20 August 1830, in Normington-Rawling, *Charles Harpur, an Australian*, p. 7. Peter Cunningham's observations on 'convict' and associated words are in his *Two Years in New South Wales*, vol. 2, pp. 116-18. For 'Irish convict' as offensive, see Knight, *Illiberal Liberal*, p. 246; for 'prisoner', see Ward, *op. cit.*, p. 33. One version of the joke about the best judges in England is in Kelly, *Life in Victoria*, vol. 1, p. 112. 'Expiree' is noted in Morris, *Austral English*, p. 140. The wider connotations of 'emancipist' are observed in Knight, *op. cit.*, pp. 246-7. Mudie's views are expressed in his *The Felonry of New South Wales* (London 1837), pp. vi-viii. Cunningham explains 'exclusionist' in *op. cit.*, p. 118; *SG*, 27 October 1825, uses the word as if coining it. For 'exclusive', see *Colonist*, 28 January 1836, where it is used as a synonym for 'pure merino', which is elucidated in Therry, *Reminiscences of Thirty Years' Residence*, p. 58. For 'cross-breds', see Cunningham, *op. cit.*, p. 116.

The numbers of convicts and former convicts are drawn from Shaw, *Convicts and the Colonies*, p. 349; Ward, *op. cit.*, p. 14. The European visitor in Melbourne is a Russian naval officer quoted in Fitzhardinge, 'Russian naval visitors to Australia, 1862-1888', *JRAHS*, vol. 52, 1966, p. 137.

2 Emigrants

NEW CHUMS

The hostility of emancipists to emigrants is reported in Harris, *Settlers and Convicts*, p. 34; J. D. Lang, *Reminiscences of my Life and Times*, edited by D. W. A. Baker (Melbourne 1972), p. 114. The 1828 census figures are taken from R. B. Madgwick, *Immigration into Eastern Australia 1788-1851* (Sydney 1969, first published London 1937), p. 65. Numbers for later years are calculated from Clark (ed.), *Select Documents 1788-1850*, p. 214. On the balance of sexes, see entry 'Immigration' in *AE*; Ward, *The Australian*

Legend, p. 88. The passage on the relative advantages of New South Wales and North America follows closely Blainey, *The Tyranny of Distance*, pp. 151-2. On the meaning of 'settler', see Roberts, *The Squatting Age in Australia*, p. 80. The secretary of state's statement of policy in 1838 is Glenelg to Gipps, 9 August 1838, *HRA* ser. 1, vol. 19, pp. 537-8. On family emigration, see Kiddle, *Caroline Chisholm*; the Scottish clergyman, Lang, is quoted at p. 124. For Mrs Chisholm's vow, see Murtagh, *Australia : the Catholic chapter*, p. 69. The Vandemonian is quoted from *Cassell's Magazine*, 1867, in Morris, *Austral English*, pp. 220-1, 488. On 'new chum', see Morris *op. cit.*, p. 319. The character in Harris's novel is quoted in Ward *op. cit.*, p. 17. The traveller of 1847 is Marjoribanks, *Travels in New South Wales*, pp. 240-1, quoted in Nadel, *Australia's Colonial Culture*, p. 33.

AN EXCELLENT SYSTEM FOR POOR GENTLEMEN

The emigration of the Deakins is described in La Nauze, *Alfred Deakin*, vol. 1, pp. 5-6. James Henty is quoted in Bassett, *The Hentys*, pp. 34-6, and the Hentys' neighbour on p. 530. On Scottish settlers in Victoria, see Kiddle, *Men of Yesterday*, p. 14. On the Hentys and similar people, see G. C. Bolton, 'The idea of a colonial gentry', *HS*, vol. 13, 1967-9, pp. 307-26. On Barry, see P. Ryan, *Redmond Barry* (Melbourne 1965), pp. 3-8; on the Reids, see Sir G. H. Reid, *My Reminiscences* (London 1917), p. 5; on Lowe, see Knight, *Illiberal Liberal*, p. 21. Burke's question to his dancing partner is in Sadleir, *Recollections of a Victorian Police Officer*, pp. 75-6. Gordon's poem is in Robb (ed.), *Poems of Adam Lindsay Gordon*, p. 194. On possible royal parentage for Miles, see *ADB*; for de Mestre, see review of C. H. Currey, *Sir Francis Forbes*, in *Times Literary Supplement*, 14 August 1969; for Gibbes, see F. West (ed.), *Selected Letters of Hubert Murray* (Melbourne 1970), p. 165.

What Charles Darwin wanted most to know about the colony is set down in N. Barlow (ed.), *Charles Darwin's Diary of the Voyage of H.M.S. Beagle* (Cambridge 1933), p. 386. For his pride in being English, see N. Barlow (ed.), *Charles Darwin and the Voyage of the Beagle* (London 1945), pp. 135-6. His praise of the Macarthur house is in *Charles Darwin's Diary*, p. 386. His enthusiasm after riding to Bathurst is expressed in *Charles Darwin and the Voyage of the Beagle*, p. 132. His recognition of the success of transportation is in H. E. L. Mellersh (ed.), *The Voyage of the Beagle* (Heron Books 1968), p. 446. For his disgust at the confusion of relationships, see *Charles Darwin's Diary*, p. 386. His reflection on emigration is in *Charles Darwin and the Voyage of the Beagle*, p. 135. His farewell to Australia is in Mellersh, *op. cit.*, p. 451. His daydream of Van Diemen's Land is in F. Darwin (ed.), *The Life and Letters of Charles Darwin* (London 1887), vol. 1, p. 334. There is an account of the visit in A. J. Marshall, *Darwin and Huxley in Australia* (Sydney 1970).

Charles Dickens's thought of flying to Australia is reported in E. Johnson, *Charles Dickens : his tragedy and triumph* (London 1953), and quoted in Lansbury, *Arcady in Australia*, p. 124. On the emigration of his sons, see *ADB*. For Carlyle's vision of an emigrant queen, court and government, see Parkes, *Fifty Years in the Making of Australian History*, vol. 1, pp. 160-1; for the queen's own threat, see D. Duff, *Victoria Travels. Journeys of Queen Victoria between 1830 and 1900, with extracts from her journal* (London 1970), p. 12.

HENRY AND CLARINDA PARKES

My main source is A. W. Martin, 'Henry Parkes: man and politician'; his letter to the *London Charter* is quoted at p. 11. Campbell's 'Lines' are in his *Poetical Works* (London 1854), and in I. Turner (ed.), *The Australian Dream*, pp. 22-5; the last couplet is used on the title-page of Braim, *History of New South Wales*. The New South Wales Archives has the 'Indent of Bounty Emigrants per *Strathfieldsaye* 1839', from which B. Nairn supplied me with information. Lang's vision of drugged passengers is in his *An Historical and Statistical Account of New South Wales* (1834), vol. 2, pp. 241-2. Parkes's letter at sea is in his *An Emigrant's Home Letters* (Sydney 1896), p. 83; Martin warns that in editing for publication, Parkes's daughter inserted punctuation, corrected grammar and spelling, and omitted references to money. The poem about Pinchgut is in Parkes, *Stolen Moments : a short series of poems* (Sydney 1842), p. 127. His letters as an exile and colonial patriot are in *An Emigrant's Home Letters*, pp. 134, 136.

GOLD SEEKERS

I have made much use of Blainey, *The Rush That Never Ended*. On Horne, see A. Blainey, *The Farthing Poet*, pp. 190-6. For 'diggerdom', see Howitt, *Land, Labour, and Gold*, vol. 1, p. 43. The visitor to the Victorian diggings in 1853 is C. Clacy, quoted in Clark (ed.), *Select Documents 1851-1900*, p. 36. The midshipman is quoted in P. Thompson (ed.), *Close to the Wind. The early memoirs (1866-1879) of Admiral Sir William Creswell* (London 1965), p. 103.

SOJOURNERS AND STAYERS

The traveller quoted on emigrants is Marjoribanks, *Travels in New South Wales*, p. 234. Hotham's judgment is quoted in I. Getzler, Neither Toleration nor Favour: The Struggle of the Jewish Communities in the Australian Colonies for Equal Religious Rights in the 1840's and 1850's (M.A. thesis, University of Melbourne, 1960). p. 161 n. 23. Kingsley's character speaks in vol. 2, p. 193. Duffy recounts the talks in London in his *My Life in Two Hemispheres*, vol. 2, pp. 107-9. Wilson's English way of life is described in Serle, *The Golden Age*, pp. 18-19. Nicholson is quoted in D. S. Macmillan, 'The Australians in London, 1857-1880', *JRAHS*, vol. 44, 1958, p. 160. Higinbotham on absentee colonists is in Morris, *A Memoir of George Higinbotham*, p. 163. Michie on Childers is in his *Readings in Melbourne*, pp. 113-14. On the General Association for the Australian Colonies, see C. S. Blackton, 'The Cannon street episode: an aspect of Anglo-Australian relations', *HS*, vol. 13, 1967-9, pp. 520-32. On the Royal Colonial Institute, see Reese, *The History of the Royal Commonwealth Society*, especially pp. 19-22. In suggesting why emigrants stay I draw on Serle, *op. cit.*, p. 373. The girl from London is in Kiddle, *Caroline Chisholm*, p. 243. West is quoted from his *The History of Tasmania*, vol. 1, p. 214; his work as editor is recorded in *A Century of Journalism*, pp. 170-1. Michie's observation of 1844 is quoted in Nadel, *Australia's Colonial Culture*, p. 33. Kendall, 'The Australian emigrants', is in *Australian Home Companion*, 16 June 1860, and Reed (ed.), *The Poetical Works of Henry Kendall*, p. 253. Parkes writes of his visit to England in *Fifty Years in the Making of Australian History*, vol. 1, pp. 156-75; see also Martin, 'Henry Parkes: man and politician', pp. 20-1. On his colleagues' policies, see A. A. Hayden, Governmental Assistance to Immigration to New South Wales, 1856-1900 (Ph.D. thesis, University of Wisconsin, 1959), especially pp. 49-80; and A. A. Hayden, 'New South Wales immigration policy, 1856-1900', *American Philosophical Society Transactions*, new series 61, no. 5, 1971, especially pp. 13-18.

HOME

'The Bush' is defined in G. H. Wathen, *The Golden Colony: or Victoria in 1854* (London 1855), p. 117, quoted in Morris, *Austral English*, p. 51. Its fabulous inhabitant is the subject of C. Barrett, *The Bunyip* (Melbourne 1946). On imitation of English conventions, see C. G. Duffy, 'An Australian example', *Contemporary Review*, January 1888, p. 28; on reading of English poetry, see Dilke, *Greater Britain*, vol. 2, p. 37; on colonial seasons, see Henning, *Letters*, p. 34. The officer greeting the fleet in 1790 is Watkin Tench, quoted in Clark (ed.), *Sources of Australian History*, p. 88. The decline of *Punch* is noted in Henning, *op. cit.*, p. 61. The Swan River settler is quoted in Bassett, *The Hentys*, p. 156. The emigrant to Melbourne is quoted in Garryowen, *The Chronicles of Early Melbourne*, vol. 2, p. 642. Smith's recollection is in his 'Melbourne in the fifties', *Centennial Magazine*, December 1889, pp. 348-9. Numbers of letters abroad are given in K. Sinclair, 'Australasian inter-government negotiations 1865-80: ocean mails and tariffs, *AJPH*, vol. 16, 1970, p. 175n. Post offices are noticed in Trollope, *Australia and New Zealand*, vol. 2, p. 176. On news as history, see C. Lamb, 'Distant correspondents', *The Essays of Elia* (London 1906), pp. 121-3. The notion of emigrants as prematurely dead is in Garryowen, *op. cit.*, vol. 2, p. 642. The account of shipping services draws on Blainey, *The Tyranny of Distance*, especially pp. 216, 221-2. On the branch steamers see *SMH*, 11 January 1867.

3 Colonists

CURRENCY LADS

On usage of 'currency' and 'sterling', see Cunningham, *Two Years in New South Wales*, vol. 2, pp. 53-4. Bigge is quoted in Clark (ed.), *Select Documents 1788-1850*, p. 434. Population figures are in *ibid.*, p. 405; Ward, *The Australian Legend*, p. 14; K. Macnab and R. Ward, 'The nature and nurture of the first generation of native-born Australians', *HS*, vol. 10, 1961-3, p. 296. Lamb's question is in *The Essays of Elia* (London 1906), p. 126. Criminality of currency lads is estimated in Macnab and Ward, *op. cit.*, especially pp. 289, 301, On Bigge's native-born crew, see M. Phillips, *A Colonial Autocracy* (London 1909), p. 261n.

On currency speech, see Ward, *op. cit.*, index, 'Speech'. For 'bloody', see Grainger, *Martin of Martin Place*, p. 13; Marjoribanks, *Travels in New South Wales*, pp. 57-8. Fowler is quoted in Ward, *op. cit.*, p. 61. Cursing by aborigines is noted by a Russian navigator cited in V. Fitzhardinge, 'Russian ships in Australian waters 1807-1835', *JRAHS*, vol. 51, 1965, p. 131; the use of 'jirrand' is reported in Cunningham, *op. cit.*, vol. 2, p. 59.

For examples of usage of 'natives', see *Colonist*, 2 February 1837 ('two hundred natives of this colony'); *Australian*, 18 January 1842, quoted in *ADB* on W. C. Wentworth ('the natives of this colony');

SG, 29 January 1843 (writing about Anniversary Day). The explanation for English readers is in Meredith, *Notes and Sketches of New South Wales*, p. 50. The gawky girls are inspected in Henning, *Letters*. p. 61. The comparisons of Sydney and London are in Cunningham, *op. cit.*, vol. 2, p. 57; Meredith, *op. cit.*, p. 51; G. H. Reid, *My Reminiscences* (London 1917), p. 153. The shouts of "Coo-ee" are recorded in Morris, *Austral English*, pp. 96-7. For a later case of the untamed Australian native in London, see B. Humphries and N. Garland, *The Wonderful World of Barry Mackenzie* (London 1968). The English view that all Australians are aborigines is cited by John Woolley in Turner (ed.), *The Australian Dream*, p. 85. The police magistrate on 'home' is quoted in Ward, *op. cit.*, p. 58. H. Kingsley, *The Boy in Grey*, is quoted by F. H. Mares in G. Dutton (ed.), *The Literature of Australia*, p. 248. The passage on contests between currency and sterling is in Lang, *An Historical and Statistical Account of New South Wales* (1834), vol. 1, pp. 175-6. The effect of climate on beauty is considered in Braim, *History of New South Wales*, vol. 2, pp. 229-30.

RISE, AUSTRALIA!
Monitor on 'Australians' is quoted in Normington-Rawling, *Charles Harpur, an Australian*, p. 14. The Macarthur girls are reported in N. Barlow (ed.), *Charles Darwin's Diary of the Voyage of H.M.S. Beagle* (Cambridge 1933), p. 386. Wentworth on 'my country' is in *ADB*. My main source of information about his life is Melbourne, *William Charles Wentworth*. The passages on the 'aristocratic body' in Wentworth, *A Statistical, Historical and Political Description*, are at pp. 343, 346 and 356. His comment on the judges' verdict is in W. C. Wentworth, *Australasia: a poem* (London 1823), p. iv. Banks's question of 1797 is in *HRNSW*, vol. 3, p. 202. The officer at Port Phillip is quoted in Turner, *A History of the Colony of Victoria*, vol. 1, p. 29. On usage of 'Australasia', see Morris, *Austral English*, pp. 8-9; J. A. Ferguson, *Bibliography of Australia, 1, 1784-1830* (Sydney 1941), p. 77. The *Sydney Gazette*'s use of 'Advance Australia' is noted in P. Mander Jones, 'Australia's first newspaper', *Meanjin*, no. 1, 1953, p. 46. Wentworth on an independent paper is in his *A Statistical Account of the British Settlements in Australasia*, p. 20. Darling's views are in *HRA*, ser. 1, vol. 12, pp. 761, 765; ser. 1, vol. 13, p. 81. The rejoicing at his departure is quoted from *Australian*, 31 October 1831, in Birch and Macmillan, *The Sydney Scene*, pp. 60-2.

The title *Currency Lad* is explained in the issue of 12 January 1833. Harpur's 'The Emigrant's Vision' is in his *Poems*, pp. 197-9. The tribute to Harpur in *Colonial Literary Journal* is quoted in Roe, *Quest for Authority in Eastern Australia*, p. 151. Duncan and Stenhouse are mentioned in Normington-Rawling, *op. cit.*, pp. 73-4. Parkes's preface to *Stolen Moments* is quoted in Barton, *Literature in New South Wales*, p. 94; his tribute to Harpur and Duncan is in Parkes, *Fifty Years in the Making of Australian History*, vol. 1, p. 9. 'Sutherland's Grave' is in Reed (ed.), *The Poetical Works of Henry Kendall*, pp. 117-18. There is another poem on the grave in *ibid.*, p. 478. The muse commands Harpur in 'The Dream by the Fountain', *Poems*, pp. 136-40. See also J. Wright, *Preoccupations in Australian Poetry* (Melbourne 1966), pp. xv-xvi. On 'colonists', see *SG*, 27 October 1825; 'the true spirit of colonists' is W. C. Windeyer, 1883, quoted in Nadel, *Australia's Colonial Culture*, p. 36. Michie's lecture was published separately and also in his *Readings in Melbourne*, where the passage quoted is at p. 9.

DEMOCRACY
Parkes's declaration about the Great Protest Meeting is quoted in Knight, *Illiberal Liberal*, p. 219; the resolution from it is quoted in his *Fifty Years in the Making of Australian History*, vol. 1, pp. 15-16; his address to the crowd is in his *Speeches*, p. 4. Earl Grey's distaste is reported in Shaw, *Convicts and the Colonies*, p. 326. The anthem is in Harpur, *The Bushrangers*, pp. 114-15.

The *Australian*'s hostile verdict on its founder is in the issue of 18 January 1842, quoted in Melbourne, *William Charles Wentworth*, p. 61. Parkes's judgment of him is in *Fifty Years in the Making of Australian History*, vol. 1, pp. 27-8. Wentworth's sneer at the newcomers is quoted in Knight, *op. cit.*, p. 241; Lowe on nativity is in *ibid.* Parkes's use of 'Australian' is quoted in Nadel, *Australia's Colonial Culture*, p. 19. His denunciation of Wentworth is quoted in Grainger, *Martin of Martin Place*, p. 55; Harpur's attack is quoted in J. Normington-Rawling, 'Before Eureka', *Labour History*, no. 4, 1963, p. 15. FitzRoy's account of Wentworth's style of campaigning, and Wentworth's comment on the result, are quoted in Melbourne, *op. cit.*, p. 78.

Parkes writes of 'the reign of Nomineeism and Squatterdom' in *Fifty Years in the Making of Australian History*, vol. 1, pp. 24-5. The definition of 'squatter' heard by Darwin is in N. Barlow (ed.), *Charles Darwin's Diary of the Voyage of H.M.S. Beagle* (London 1933), p. 383; the change in meaning is described in Roberts, *The Squatting Age in Australia*, pp. 67-81; Therry's remark on settlers and squatters is quoted in *ibid.*, p. 80; Gipps on the squatting interest is in *HRA*, ser. 1, vol. 23, p. 510; Morris, *Austral English*, p. 434 shows 'squattocracy' by 1844. Harpur's sonnet is quoted in Roe, *Quest for Authority in Eastern Australia*, p. 75. Lowe's cry is quoted in Roberts, *op. cit.*, p. 331.

Wentworth's exposition of his views on the constitution is in Silvester (ed.), *New South Wales Constitution Bill*; the passages quoted are at pp. 26-8, 37-8, 223-4. For Deniehy's speech I have used the version in *SMH*, 16 August 1853, which is also in Clark (ed.), *Select Documents 1851-1900*; a slightly different version is in E. A. Martin, *The Life and Speeches of Daniel Henry Deniehy* (Melbourne and Sydney 1884), pp. 51-6. See also B. T. Dowd, 'Daniel Henry Deniehy', *JRAHS*, vol. 33, 1947, pp. 57-95; the family's return as bounty emigrant is described at p. 62. Harpur's lines on Deniehy are quoted in Normington-Rawling, *Charles Harpur, an Australian*, p. 188; his verdict on the bunyip is in *ibid.*, p. 191; for his judgment of Wentworth's poem see *ibid.*, p. 189, and Harpur's parody, *ibid.*, p. 190. Deniehy's belief in 'God's aristocracy' is expressed in the speech reported in *SMH*, 16 August 1853. Parkes on his supporters is in his *Speeches*, p. 42.

Michie's reflection that all men came out to work is in his *Readings in Melbourne*, p. 3; on the men near the top, see Trollope, *Australia and New Zealand*, vol. 1, p. 479; on the Australian conservative, see Dilke, *Greater Britain*, vol. 2, p. 39. Denison's observations on responsible government are in his *Varieties of Vice-Regal Life*, vol. 1, p. 497. On the comparative quality of politicians in England and Victoria, see Duffy, 'An Australian example', p. 25. On Parkes, see Dilke, *op. cit.*, vol. 2, p. 50.

What Trollope wrote for publication is in his *Australia and New Zealand*, vol. 1, p. 118; what he wrote privately is quoted in A. Trollope, *Australia*, edited by P. D. Edwards and R. B. Joyce (St Lucia 1967), introduction p. 33. The passages on 'blowing' are in Trollope, *Australia and New Zealand*, vol. 1, pp. 117, 387. The quality of Victoria's statistical records is observed in Dilke, *op. cit.*, vol. 2, p. 25.

SCHOOLING THE CHILDREN

The chaplain, Johnson, is quoted in J. F. Cleverley, *The First Generation: school and society in early Australia* (Sydney 1971), p. 10; Castlereagh is quoted on p. 11 and Mrs Macarthur on p. 118. My account of early schooling draws on this book. The senior Catholic priest, Polding, is quoted in Moran, *History of the Catholic Church in Australiasia*, p. 208. Wills on education is in *Currency Lad*, 26 January 1833; his diary is quoted in *Life of a Pioneer: adventures of H. S. Wills*, p. 4. The headmaster of Sydney College is quoted in G. C. Bolton, 'The idea of a colonial gentry', *HS*, vol. 13, 1967-9, p. 326. The prospectus for Sydney College is in Braim, *History of New South Wales*, vol. 2, pp. 212-21. On Victorian grants to church schools, see G. Blainey, J. Morrissey and S. E. K. Hulme, *Wesley College: the first hundred years* (Melbourne 1967), p. 19. Perry is quoted in Clark (ed.), *Select Documents 1851-1900*, p. 701.

Wentworth's speech proposing a select committee on a university is quoted in J. M. Ward, 'Foundation of the University of Sydney', *JRAHS*, vol. 37, 1952, p. 299. The committee's lament about the effects of education abroad is in *Report from the Select Committee on the Sydney University* (Sydney 1849), p. 4; I owe this reference to G. Fischer, Archivist, University of Sydney. Wentworth's speech to the council on his motion for the university bill is quoted in Clark, *op. cit.*, p. 697. The verse is quoted from W. Woolls, *Lines Written to Commemorate the Passing of 'A Bill to Incorporate and Endow a University, to be called the "University of Sydney"'* (Parramatta 1850), p. 5. Parkes's *Empire* is quoted in D. S. Macmillan, 'The University of Sydney—the pattern and the public reaction, 1850-1870', *Australian University*, July 1963, pp. 29-30. The *SMH* correspondent is quoted in A. Barcan, *A Short History of Education in New South Wales* (Sydney 1965), p. 156. The judgment of Australian youths is in Braim, *op. cit.*, vol. 2, p. 189. The praise of the Great Hall is in Trollope, *Australia and New Zealand*, vol. 1, p. 229. For numbers at Melbourne see G. Blainey, *A Centenary History of the University of Melbourne* (Melbourne 1957), p. 50; Barry is paraphrased in *ibid.*, p. 10.

The section on schools for the majority draws on A. G. Austin, *Australian Education, 1788-1900* (Melbourne 1961). The terms of reference for Lowe's committee of 1844 are quoted in J. Barrett, *That Better Country*, p. 105. Gipps on dispersion and education is quoted in Braim, *op. cit.*, vol. 2, p. 190. The schoolmasters' judgment of the dual system is quoted in Austin, *op. cit.*, pp. 57, 111. Parkes's *Empire* for 3 June 1854, on the state and education, is quoted in *ibid.*, p. 112. Parkes's speech moving the second reading of the Public Schools Bill, 12 September 1866, is in his *Speeches*, pp. 217-51; the speech is analyzed in Austin, *op. cit.*, pp. 118-19, and its delivery imagined in Grainger, *Martin of Martin Place*, p. 106. On Cleveland Street Public School as model, see Barcan, *op. cit.*, p. 129n. Wilkins's account of schools in the old days is quoted in Austin, *op. cit.*, p. 59. Parkes on 'a great and holy work' is in his *Speeches*, p. 277.

'September in Australia' is in Reed (ed.), *The Poetical Works of Henry Kendall*, pp. 66-8. The critic of Parkes's argument about ignorance and crime is William Forster, quoted in Grainger, *op. cit.*, p. 107. For larrikins and larrikinism, see Morris, *Austral English*, pp. 259-61; the South Australian politician is quoted in D. Pike, 'Education in an agricultural state', in E. L. French (ed.), *Melbourne Studies in Education 1957-8* (Melbourne 1958), p. 74. The Catholic bishops are quoted in Clark, *op. cit.*, p. 722.

Holidays Old and New

My approach to this subject is indebted to M. E. Curti, *The Roots of American Loyalty* (New York 1946), a historical study of Independence Day. The passage quoted at the beginning of the section is from 'Holidays', *North American Review*, April 1857, p. 336.

4 The Monarch's Birthday

A FESTIVAL OF EMPIRE

The aboriginal who inferred that 'king' was a drink is Bennelong, reported in J. Hunter, *Historical Journal of the Transactions at Port Jackson and Norfolk Island* (London 1793), p. 460. The first king's birthday in New South Wales is chronicled in Phillip, *The Voyage of Governor Phillip to Botany Bay*, pp. 116-17; the passage quoted about its celebration is at p. 117. Phillip's note on the observation is in Cobley, *Sydney Cove 1788*, p. 158; the officer quoted on the feast is G. B. Worgan, in *ibid.*, pp. 158-9; Phillip's pleasure is recorded in *ibid.*, p. 160. The diary of Richard Atkins, 1792-1810, is in the National Library, Canberra; it records the friction of 1792 as well as the parsimony of 1793. The festivity of 1801 is described in Clark, *A History of Australia*, vol. 1, p. 170. The ode for 1810 is in G. Mackaness (ed.), *Odes of Michael Massey Robinson*, pp. 21-3, and the ode for 1820 on pp. 92-5. Macquarie's indulgence is reported in *SG*, 5 June 1819. On the mourning and thanksgiving in 1820, see Clark, *op. cit.*, vol. 1, p. 352.

The *Sydney Herald* describes Queen Victoria's nineteenth birthday on 28 May 1838; Gipps's speech is reported in *SG*, 25 May 1838. On mourning for Prince Albert, see *Empire*, 28 February and 21 March 1862; *South Australian Advertiser*, 1 March 1862. The queen's liking for the statue of which Sydney's was a copy is reported in *SMH.*, 23 April 1866; the unveiling is described in *ibid.*, 24 April 1866. The chalked message to Prince Alfred is recorded in Milner and Brierly, *The Cruise of H.M.S. Galatea*, p. 173. Lang's plea for a republic is in his *The Coming Event!*, pp. 428-9. On Lord Granville's opening the mail, see Reese, *The History of the Royal Commonwealth Society*, p. 1. Higinbotham's judgment of colonial loyalties is in Morris, *A Memoir of George Higinbotham*, p. 188. The passage on the warmth of regard by loyal exiles is in Laye, *Social Life and Manners in Australia*, p. 161. The Presbyterian minister is A. J. Campbell, *Fifty Years of Presbyterianism in Victoria* (Melbourne [1889]), p. 25. The ceremony at the Swan is described in Bassett, *The Hentys*, p. 93, and the arrival of the emigrant ship on p. 366. On Leichhardt's observance, see Chisholm, *Strange New World*, p. 183; Burke's diary is quoted in Moorehead, *Cooper's Creek*, p. 121; Forrest's celebration is recorded in Crowley, *Forrest 1847-1918*, vol. 1, p. 43.

THE BEST PEOPLE

SG on the ball in 1826 is quoted in Erdos, *The Sydney Gazette*, p. 38; Mrs Forbes's judgment is quoted in Birch and Macmillan, *The Sydney Scene*, p. 59; Cunningham's is in his *Two Years in New South Wales*, vol. 2, p. 121. Mrs Forbes on the society of the 1820s is quoted in Birch and Macmillan, *op. cit.*, p. 59. On 'The Clerk's Lament', see Erdos, *op. cit.*, pp. 58-9. Government House is described in Braim, *History of New South Wales*, vol. 2, p. 293. On Lowe's attempt to have the levee boycotted, see Knight, *Illiberal Liberal*, pp. 121-2. The *SMH*'s concern about the length of the guest list is quoted in *A Century of Journalism*, p. 215. The offence given to the Catholic bishop is described in Moran, *History of the Catholic Church in Australasia*, p. 269; the offence given to Nonconformists in Adelaide is described in Pike, *Paradise of Dissent*, p. 486.

5 The Sabbath

SUNDAY MUSTER

The sergeant who said that the place was 'crisned' on 26 January 1788, is quoted in G. Mackaness, 'Australia Day', *JRAHS*, vol. 45, 1959-60, p. 267. The rhetorical question about that day is in W. W. Burton, *The State of Religion and Education in New South Wales* (London 1840), pp. 4-5. Johnson's first sermon is reported in Cobley, *Sydney Cove 1788*, p. 54; for the officer's resolve to keep the table, see *ibid.*, p. 78. On Johnson's work, see Clark, *A History of Australia*, vol. 1, pp. 114, 129. The Spanish priest is quoted in Moran, *History of the Catholic Church in Australasia*, p. 16. For Hunter's order, see *ibid.*; and for his interpretation of the fire, see Ward, *The Australian Legend*, p. 85. Macquarie's account of his policy is quoted in Clark (ed.), *Sources of Australian History*, pp. 125-6. On penalties for staying away from worship, and for misbehaving and sleeping during it, see Shaw. *Convicts and the Colonies*, p. 230; Robson, *The Convict Settlers of Australia*, p. 105.

Lang's judgment of Church of England domination is in his *An Historical and Statistical Account of New South Wales* (1834), vol. 2, p. 251. The clergyman who invited nobody to meet the governor is in Henning, *Letters*, p. 101.

GOD AND MAMMON

Lang's interpretation of the drought is cited in R. B. Walker, 'Presbyterian church and people in the colony of New South Wales in the late nineteenth century', *Journal of Religious History*, vol. 2, 1962-3, p. 60. The Sabbatarian postmaster at Perth is in Bassett, *The Hentys*, p. 472; Mitchell is quoted in Kunz, *A Continent Takes Shape*, p. 74. Lang's judgment of Sunday pleasures is in his *Lectures on the Sabbath* (Sydney 1841), p. 20; the downfall of the young clerk is recounted in his *An Historical and Statistical Account of New South Wales* (1834), vol. 2, p. 243. Broughton's report on Sabbath observance in outer districts is quoted in W. W. Burton, *The State of Religion and Education in New South Wales* (London 1840), pp. 278-9. On remoteness from churches see H. W. Haygarth, *Recollections of Bush Life in Australia* (London 1848), p. 94. The observer of squatters' negligence is C. J. Baker, *Sydney and Melbourne* (London 1845), p. 61-2. The view that Sunday is not generally sacred in the bush is in J. Hood, *Australia and the East* (London 1843), p. 164. Harris is quoted from A. H. Chisholm (ed.), *The Secrets of Alexander Harris* (Sydney 1961), p. 131. The Wesleyan minister beyond the range is J. E. Carruthers, *Memories of an Australian Ministry 1868 to 1921* (London 1922), p. 54. Scott's account of society in 1825 is in F. T. Whitington, *William Grant Broughton* (Sydney 1936), p. 17.

For à Beckett on Mammon in Victoria see Serle, *The Golden Age*, p. 31; Polding on gold is quoted in Moran, *History of the Catholic Church in Australasia*, p. 314. Lang's cheerier view is in the third edition of his *An Historical and Statistical Account of New South Wales*, vol. 2, p. 510. For Sunday on the goldfields, see G. Blainey, *The Rush That Never Ended*, p. 41; on emigrants of the 1850s as worshippers, see G. Serle, 'The gold generation', *Victorian Historical Magazine*, vol. 41, 1970, p. 271. On Methodist policy, see R. B. Walker, 'Methodism in the "Paradise of Dissent"', 1837-1900', *Journal of Religious History*, vol. 5, 1968-9, pp. 331-47, especially p. 332. The passage on Protestants and working men is in F. Barker, *A Charge Delivered at his Primary Metropolitan Visitation* (Sydney 1860), p. 63. On the habit of going to the country, see Kelly, *Life in Victoria*, vol. 1, p. 109; and on the beach, see C. Aspinall, *Three Years in Melbourne* (London 1862), p. 19. The prohibition of shooting on Sunday is mentioned in Braim, *History of New South Wales*, vol. 1, p. 292; and Marjoribanks, *Travels in New South Wales*, p. 45. On the Sabbatarian movement in England, see O. Chadwick, *The Victorian Church* (London 1966), vol. 1, pp. 455-68. The grief of colonial Sabbatarians is expressed in *Address to the Colonists from the Society for Promoting the Observance of the Lord's Day* (Sydney 1857), p. 7. On the Sabbatarian campaign, see Dunstan, *Wowsers*, pp. 16-22. Continental-inspired desecration is described in Braim, *op. cit.*, vol. 2, p. 159; Goold's concern over Catholics is quoted in O'Farrell (ed.), *Documents in Australian Catholic History*, vol. 1, p. 129.

RELIGION AND NATIONALITY

The wistful comparison with America is in Van Diemen's Land Colonial Missionary and Christian Instruction Society, *Eighth Report* (1843); it is used as epigraph to Barrett, *That Better Country*. For the American prayer, see A. de Tocqueville, *Democracy in America* (New York, Knopf, 1953), vol 1, p. 303. Perry's list of qualities for a clergyman is quoted in *Papers Read at the Church Congress* (Sydney 1889), p. 208. The clergyman who swam his horse through the river is described in Kerr, *Glimpses of Life in Victoria*, p. 100. Deakin's recollection of church is in La Nauze, *Alfred Deakin*, vol. 1, p. 16.

6 St Patrick's Day

ST PATRICK AND ST BENEDICT

For St Patrick's day as the Irish sabbath, see Garryowen, *The Chronicles of Early Melbourne*, vol. 2, p. 653. Therry's toast is in *SG*, 20 March 1832. On the St Patrick's Society ball, see *Sydney Herald*, 19 March 1839; Wilkes, *Narrative of the United States Exploring Expedition*, vol. 2, pp. 386-7. The version quoted of 'The Wearing of the Green', said to be from 1798, is in J. Cooke (ed.), *The Dublin Book of Irish Verse 1728-1909* (Dublin 1909), pp. 742-3, and the added verse is on pp. 351-2. The libations of 1795 are observed in Collins, *An Account of the English Colony in New South Wales*, vol. 1, p. 411; those of 1832 in *SG*, 20 March. News of a peaceful 17 March is in *Sydney Herald*, 21 March 1836; *Colonist*, 23 March 1837; *Hobart Town Courier*, 4 April 1849, quoted in J. N. Molony, 'The Australian hierarchy and the holy see, 1840-1880', *HS*, vol. 13, 1967-9, p. 179n. Darling's preference for English priests is in *HRA*, ser. 1, vol. 12, p. 543; McEncroe's advice to the Pope is quoted in Moran, *History of the Catholic Church in Australasia*, p. 779; the Benedictine diarist is quoted in T. L. Suttor, *Hierarchy and Democracy in Australia, 1788-1870* (Melbourne 1965), p. 83. Polding's pastoral letter of 1856 is quoted in Birt, *Benedictine Pioneers in Australia*, vol. 2, p. 352. The number of Irish bishops is given in Molony, *op. cit.*, p. 178n. Lanigan's view of national history is quoted in Birt, *op. cit.*, p. 352, The *Advocate* on 'Irish-Victorians' is 8 February 1868.

ORANGE AND GREEN

Sentinel is quoted in Roe, *Quest for Authority in Eastern Australia*, p. 137; Lang in J. N. Molony, 'The Australian hierarchy and the holy see, 1840-1880', *HS*, vol. 13, 1967-9, p. 182n. Polding's vision of a Catholic country is in Birt, *Benedictine Pioneers in Australia*, vol. 1, p. 292. The siege of Melbourne in 1846 is described in Garryowen, *The Chronicles of Early Melbourne.*, vol. 2, p. 684. The outsider's view of St Patrick's Cathedral is in [H. Willoughby], *The Critic in Church* (Melbourne 1872), p. 78. Bishop Murphy on friendly feeling is quoted in Pike, *Paradise of Dissent*, p. 276; Therry, in his *Reminiscences*, p. 147. The anti-popish emigrant is quoted in G. M. Tobin, The Sea-Divided Gael: a Study of the Irish Home Rule Movement in Victoria and New South Wales, 1880-1916 (M.A. thesis, Australian National University, 1970), p. 17 n.2. Michie's lament is in his *Readings in Melbourne*, p. 20. On Victorian governments' policy towards St Patrick in 1863 and 1864, see Serle, *The Golden Age*; *Victorian Parliamentary Debates*, vol. 10, 1864, p. 215. The regatta is interpreted and the day characterized in *SMH*, 18 March 1865.

HENRY JAMES O'FARRELL

For accounts of the episode see Milner and Brierly, *The Cruise of H.M.S. Galatea*; P. M. Cowburn, "The attempted assassination of the Duke of Edinburgh, 1868", *JRAHS*, vol. 55, 1969, pp. 19-42. The score of rabbits shot is in Kiddle, *Men of Yesterday*, p. 305. *The Times* of 14 January 1868 is quoted in Cowburn, *op. cit.*, pp. 28-9. The dress of Martin and Parkes is described in Grainger, *Martin of Martin Place*, pp. 111-12; Parkes's letter to his sister is quoted in Martin, 'Henry Parkes: man and politician', p. 22. The definition of 'corroboree' is cited in Morris, *Austral English*, p. 101. The services of intercession are mentioned in A. Pyne, *Reminiscences of Colonial Life and Missionary Adventure in Both Hemispheres* (London 1875), p. 400. Kendall's poems are also in Reed (ed.), *The Poetical Works of Henry Kendall*, pp. 348-50. The minister who called O'Farrell a foreign importation is quoted from *SMH*, 19 March 1868, in Cowburn, *op. cit.*, p. 32. *Freeman's Journal* of 28 March 1868 is quoted in Grainger, *op. cit.*, p. 115. Polding's pastoral letter is in O'Farrell (ed.), *Documents in Australian Catholic History*, vol. 1, pp. 426-8. The passage of the Treason Felony Bill is described in Parkes, *Fifty Years in the Making of Australian History*, vol. 1, pp. 224-5, and his observation of the lurid glare on p. 224; his judgment of Catholics while in England is quoted in Martin, 'Faction politics and the education question in New South Wales', p. 34. Carlyle's understanding of sectaries is quoted in Parkes, *op. cit.*, vol. 1, p. 202. Polding on Parkes is quoted in Birt, *Benedictine Pioneers in Australia*, vol. 2, p. 332. The offer of reward is quoted in P. Ford, *Cardinal Moran and the Australian Labor Party* (Melbourne 1966), p. 26. Blainey, *The Rush That Never Ended*, p. 97, has a summary of O'Farrell's life. The diary is quoted, with relish, in Parkes, *op. cit.*, vol. 1, p. 229. The confession is quoted in Milner and Brierly, *op. cit.*, p. 450. Charges under the act are reported in *SMH*, 25 March, 31 March and 1 April 1868. Polding's outburst is quoted in Birt, *op. cit.*, vol. 2, p. 337. The allegation at Kiama is in Parkes, *op. cit.* vol. 1, p. 232, and Parkes's motion on p. 236. Polding on the object of the Protestant Political Association is quoted in Birt, *op. cit.*, vol. 2, p. 361. Dalley's testimony is quoted in O'Farrell, *op. cit.*, vol. 1, pp. 428-30;

Duffy's letter and Parkes's reply are quoted in Martin, 'Faction politics and the education question in New South Wales', p. 40. The editor at Shoalhaven is quoted in *SMH*, 23 March 1869. Celebration in Sydney is reported in *Empire*, 18 March 1870; Ireland's Patriotic Sons are accused by *SMH*, 16 April 1870.

7 Christmas

THE GOOD OLD ENGLISH CUSTOM
For the phrase of Phillip's officer, see Clark, *A History of Australia*, vol. 1, p. 85; for the English Christmas at that time, see J. A. R. Pimlott, *Recreations* (London 1968), especially p. 42. The message from the newcomer to Adelaide is in J. Hayter, *The Landsman's Logbook* (London 1842), p. 136. Upper-class attitudes are reported in G. C. Mundy, *Our Antipodes* (London 1852), vol. 3, p. 24. On colonial goose, see Morris, *Austral English*, p. 94. The melancholy reflection from Geelong is in A. Polehampton, *Kangaroo Land* (London 1862), pp. 218-19. For the mail as Christmas box, see M. M. Doyle (ed.), *Extracts from the Letters and Journals of George Fletcher Moore* (London 1834), p. 214. The aborigines offering Christmas bush are mentioned in Grainger, *Martin of Martin Place*, p. 9; carts carrying greenery are observed in Meredith, *Notes and Sketches of New South Wales*, p. 127; on Christmas trees, see Denison, *Varieties of Vice-Regal Life*, vol. 1, p. 202.

THE HEAT
The curiosity of a hot Christmas is remarked in Henning, *Letters*, p. 14; Wilkes, *Narrative of the United States Exploring Expedition*, vol. 2, p. 292. Mrs Meredith is on the sofa in *op. cit.*, pp. 127-8. On snap-dragon, see G. C. Mundy, *Our Antipodes* (London 1852), vol. 3, pp. 24-5; Denison, *Varieties of Vice-Regal Life*, vol. 1, pp. 372-3; T. F. Thiselton Dyer, *British Popular Customs, Present and Past* (London 1875), p. 463. On the Thomas family in Adelaide, see P. Hope (ed.), *The Voyage of the Africaine* (Melbourne 1968), pp. 119-20. Christmas day 1852 in Melbourne is described in Laye, *Social Life and Manners in Australia*, p. 160; at Ballarat, in Howitt, *Land, Labour, and Gold*, vol. 1, p. 175. The Mahonys' day is in *The Fortunes of Richard Mahony* (Melbourne 1946, first published 1917), p. 218. On the ice industry see D. J. Boorstin, *The Americans: the national experience* (New York 1965), pp. 10-16; Kelly, *Life in Victoria*, vol. 2, pp. 102-4; Serle, *The Golden Age*, p. 123; J. Jervis, 'Thomas Sutcliffe Mort', *JRAHS*, vol. 24, 1938, p. 376. On adaptation to the Australian environment, see Mrs E. Millett, *An Australian Parsonage* (London 1872), pp. 114-15; D. Kennedy, quoted in Grant and Serle, *The Melbourne Scene*, p. 168. The indigestible plum pudding is described in Hare, *The Last of the Bushrangers*, p. 11; the fresh dessert in Dilke, *Greater Britain*, vol. 2, p. 94. The glamour of plum pudding is perceived in Kerr, *Glimpses of Life in Victoria*, p. 396.

THE HOLIDAYS
Martin's account is in Grainger, *Martin of Martin Place*, p. 9. Stupefied shepherds are reported in Henning, *Letters*, p. 66; absent and incapable servants in Meredith, *Notes and Sketches of New South Wales*, p. 128; the drunken clerk in J. D. Mereweather, *Diary of a Working Clergyman* (London 1859), p. 128. On the Christmas of 1851 in Victoria, see Blainey, *The Rush That Never Ended*, p. 33; G. H. Wathen, *The Golden Colony* (London 1855), p. 35. Boxing Day is described in *Empire*, 27 December 1870; in Melbourne, *Age*, 27 December 1870. On New Year larks see J. P. McGuanne, 'The humours and pastimes of early Sydney', *JRAHS*, vol. 1, 1901-6, p. 37; and on disorders, H. King, 'Some aspects of police administration in New South Wales, 1825-1851', *JRAHS*, vol. 42, 1956-7, pp. 222-3. New Year celebration in Scotland is described in Lang, *Aurora Australis*, p. 161. The speculation about family groups is in R. and F. Hill, *What We Saw in Australia* (London 1875), p. 385. The politician on the Christmas holidays is quoted in H. W. Arndt, 'The financial year', *Australian Quarterly*, June 1963, pp. 53-4. The report of Melbourne's holiday season is in *SMH*, 3 January 1870. The holiday-keeping of colonists is observed in Kerr, *Glimpses of Life in Victoria*, p. 392. For 'the Easter holidays' see *Argus*, 19 March 1856. The folks of Sydney are called work-shirking by 'Peter Possum' in *SMH*, 4 October 1871.

8 New Festivals of Leisure

THE SACRED GIFT OF TIME
I have made much use of H. Hughes, 'The eight hour day and the development of the labour movement in Victoria in the eighteen-fifties', *HS*, vol. 9, 1959-61, pp. 396-412; Galloway's declaration is quoted at p. 399. On England, see S. J. Webb and H. Cox, *The Eight Hours Day* (London 1891). The carpenter

speaking of stonemasons is quoted in J. Niland, 'The birth of the movement for an eight hour working day in New South Wales', *AJPH*, vol. 14, 1968, p. 77; on stonemasons, see also Serle, *The Golden Age*, p. 215. For information about Stephens I am grateful to the Archives Section of the State Library of Victoria and to Bede Nairn; see also Serle, *op. cit.*, p. 212. The stonemasons' protest is described by W. E. Murphy in *The History of Capital and Labour* (Sydney and Melbourne 1888), p. 123; Galloway's letter is in *Argus*, 22 April 1856. Lassitude is described in Harris, *Settlers and Convicts*, p. 85; Clarke is quoted in University of Sydney Archives, *Record*, vol. 1, no. 2, 1973, p. 10. Stephens's memory of the day is quoted in *The History of Capital and Labour*, p. 123; in checking it I am indebted to A. K. Hannay, Regional Director, Commonwealth Bureau of Meteorology, Melbourne. The argument that men need leisure for knowledge is cited in Serle, *op. cit.*, p. 23; 'the sacred gift of time' is quoted in Hughes, *op. cit.*, p. 400. The speech at the Trades Hall in 1859 is quoted in R. Gollan, *Radical and Working Class Politics: a study of eastern Australia, 1850-1910* (Melbourne 1960), p. 72. The *Herald*'s warning to workers is quoted in R. N. Ebbels, *The Australian Labor Movement 1850-1907* (Sydney 1960), pp. 65-6. Don's statement about the right to good housing is quoted in Hughes, *op. cit.*, p. 412; his introduction to parliament in Serle, *op. cit.*, p. 204; his view of the movement as panacea in Turner (ed.), *The Australian Dream*, p. 48.

Early agitation in Sydney is recalled in C. Thornton, 'How the eight-hour day was won', *Australian Worker*, 30 September 1915. O'Sullivan is quoted in *The History of Capital and Labour*, p. 43. On the progress of the movement in New South Wales, see Niland, *op. cit.*, pp. 75-87; T. A. Coghlan, *Labour and Industry in Australia* (Melbourne 1969), vol. 2, pp. 711-12. On Parkes, see his *Speeches*, pp. 70-5; C. Thornton, *op. cit.* On Brisbane and Adelaide, see Coghlan, *op. cit.*, vol. 2, pp. 1055, 1064, 1066. Saturday half-holidays are reported in *SMH*, 29, 30 April 1870. The anniversary toast in Melbourne is quoted in Gollan, *op. cit.*, p. 72; the procession is described in *The History of Capital and Labour*, pp. 140-1; Clarke's 'Paean' is in M. Pizer (ed.), *Freedom on the Wallaby: poems of the Australian people* (Sydney, n.d.), pp. 48-50.

'Australia versus England' is in Thatcher, *Thatcher's Colonial Minstrel*, pp. 99-101. Trollope is quoted from his *Australia and New Zealand*, vol. 1, pp. 399, 480; vol. 2, pp. 140, 499-500. The eight-hour man in Sydney denying that recreation meant drinking is writing to *SMH*, 16 February 1856, quoted in Ebbels, *op. cit.*, p. 59; the prophet of social elevation is speaking in 1856 and quoted in Niland, *op. cit.*, p. 81. On literacy, see Serle, *op. cit.*, p. 371; on booksellers in Sydney, Nadel, *Australia's Colonial Culture*, p. 76; on Melbourne's public library, *ibid.*, p. 84; Trollope, *op. cit.*, vol. 1, p. 390. Circulation figures for *Age* are in C. E. Sayers, *David Syme, a life* (Melbourne 1965), pp. 106-11. *Argus*, 21 April 1856, on the pleasures of home, is quoted in Clark (ed.), *Select Documents 1851-1900*, pp. 736-7. Jevons is quoted in O. H. K. Spate, 'Bush and city: some reflections on the Australian cultural landscape', *Australian Journal of Science*, May 1956, p. 180. On Australians' preference for mirth over prolonged labour, see Dilke, *Greater Britain*, vol. 2, p. 143.

CUP DAY

On Australians' pursuit of sport and pleasure, see Michie, *Readings in Melbourne*, p. 201. Early diversions are described in *A Century of Journalism*, pp. 225-7. *Argus* on 'muscular Christianity' is quoted in Grant and Serle, *The Melbourne Scene*, p. 113. The pedestrian contest on Easter Monday is reported in *SMH*, 19 April 1870. The Melbourne *Herald*'s greeting to the Victorian cricketers is quoted in Grant and Serle, *op. cit.*, p. 111. *Argus* of 26 December 1861, on the arrival of the English team, is quoted in K. Dunstan, *The Paddock That Grew: the story of the Melbourne Cricket Club* (Melbourne 1962), p. 21. On the Melbourne ground, see *ibid.*, pp. 22-3; H. S. Altham, *A History of Cricket*, vol. 1 (London 1962), p. 132; Bagot's work on it is reported in *Age*, 6 January 1862; attendance figures are in *Age*, 2, 3 January 1862. The English captain's question is quoted in Dunstan, *op. cit.*, p. 22. The scores at Beechworth, on which historians differ, are in *SMH*, 14 January 1862. For the comparison with the Crimean War, see *A Century of Journalism*, p. 292. The commercial success of the tour is reported in Dunstan, *op. cit.*, p. 26; D. J. Mulvaney, *Cricket Walkabout*, p. 4. The English judgment on the colonial players is quoted in Dunstan, *op. cit.*, p. 26. The massacre at Cullinlaringo is described in *Life of a Pioneer: adventures of H. S. Wills*, pp. 11-16. The country newspaper's account of the aboriginal team is quoted in Mulvaney, *op. cit.*, p. 35; the London *Daily Telegraph* is quoted in *ibid.*, p. 48, and *The Times* at p. 70; the 'Coo-ee!' is recorded at pp. 62-3, and the view that the visitors must be 'niggers' at pp. 70-1.

On the origins of 'Victorian rules', I draw on A. G. Daws, 'An institution in the metropolis: for the centenary of Australian rules football', *Quadrant*, Winter 1958, pp. 9-16. The newspaper reporting an 'epidemic' is quoted in Daws, *op. cit.*, p. 10; the cancellation for an English mail at p. 11. The usage 'Victorian rules' is cited in Bean, *Here, My Son*, p. 164. On the Brisbane Cup as the governor's memorial, see Lang, *An Historical and Statistical Account of New South Wales* (1834), p. 173. On factions and racing clubs, see Heaton, *Australian Dictionary of Dates and Men of the Time*, part 2, pp. 227-8. The ubiquity of race-courses is noticed in Trollope, *Australia and New Zealand*, vol. 2, p. 286. Attendance at the first Cup meeting is reported in *Argus*, 8 November 1861. On the formation of the Victoria Racing Club, see Kiddle, *Men of Yesterday*, p. 354; D. L. Bernstein, *First Tuesday in November: the story of the Melbourne Cup* (Melbourne 1969), p. 20. The letter from 'Pleasure' in *Daily Telegraph*, 31 October 1872, was spotted for me by H. Mayer. 'Cup fever' is diagnosed in James, *The Vagabond Papers*, second series, pp. 135-51. Clarke on the 1867 Cup in *Argus* is in L. T. Hergenhan (ed.), *A Colonial City: High and Low Life, selected journalism of Marcus Clarke* (St Lucia 1972); the passages quoted are at pp. 174, 177; his imaginary report in *Herald* is in *ibid.*, p. 184. Whiteman's verse is quoted in Bernstein, *op. cit.*, p. 22. Gordon's poem is 'Hippodramania; or whiffs from the pipe'; it is in Robb (ed.), *Poems of Adam Lindsay Gordon*, pp. 83-8. Robb misplaces the race in 1865. On Gordon as rider, see *Argus*, 12 October and 9 November 1868; Wilde on Babbler and babbling is in *Pall Mall Gazette*, 25 March 1889, and in O. Wilde, *Reviews* (London 1908), p. 456. A version of the story about Craig's dream is in M. Cavanough and M. Davies, *Cup Day: the story of the Melbourne Cup 1861-1900* (Melbourne 1960), p. 28; but the sceptical reader is invited to turn up *Age*, 9 November 1870. The Maori prophecy is reported in R. P. Whitworth and W. A. Windas, *Shimmer of Silk: a volume of Melbourne Cup stories* (Melbourne 1893), pp. 7-12. The reflection on horsemanship and racing is in 'Petrel', *In Southern Seas. A trip to the Antipodes* (Edinburgh 1888), p. 53. The creation of Flemington by nature is fancied in M. Longway, *London to Melbourne* (London 1889), p. 209; the observer of the hill is R. E. N. Twopeny, *Town Life in Australia* (London 1883), p. 211. On Bagot's work at Flemington, see James, *op. cit.*, second series, p. 132; Bernstein, *op. cit.*, p. 22. The passage on the Cup as the great gambling event is in Twopeny, *op. cit.*, p. 213. On the attractions of a handicap race for gamblers, I follow Dunstan, *Wowsers*, p. 206. Dilke's estimate of Victoria is in his *Greater Britain*, vol. 2, p. 21. The public favour of horse racing is affirmed in E. Davenport Cleland, 'The Melbourne Cup race', in E. E. Morris (ed.), *Cassell's Picturesque Australasia*, vol. 4 (London 1889), p. 134. The preacher of 1879 is W. P. Pearce, quoted in James, *op. cit.*, second series, p. 123.

9 Anniversary Day

THE LAND, BOYS, WE LIVE IN

The celebrations of 1818 are reported in *SG* of 24, 31 January. *SG*'s blowing on 22 January 1837 is quoted in Perry, *Australia's First Frontier*, p. 7. The odes are in Mackaness (ed.), *The Odes of Michael Massey Robinson*, pp. 91, 99-100, 106-7; on Wentworth's toast, see Clark, *A History of Australia*, vol. 2, p. 66. The cold toast to Darling is reported in *Monitor*, 27 January 1827; for the conflict at the Crown and Anchor, see *SG*, 29 January 1831. The emancipists' meeting in 1833 is described in Melbourne, *William Charles Wentworth*, pp. 52-3. Controversy over Wentworth in 1837 is reported in *SG*, 26, 28 January; *Sydney Herald*, 30 January; and *Colonist*, 2 February. On the dinner of 1846, see Knight, *Illiberal Liberal*, p. 115. Driver's tribute to Wentworth is in *SMH*, 28 January 1867.

Devotion to pleasure is described in *SG*, 28 January 1837; Presbyterian tolerance is expressed in *Colonist*, 24 January 1838; the indulgent court is reported in *SG*, 28 January 1837. For rain on queen's birthday regattas, see *Australian*, 25 May 1839; *SG*, 26 May 1842. The wish to make the day the grand festival is perceived in *SG*, 29 January 1842.

On the fiftieth anniversary, see *SG*, 23, 27, 30 January 1838; the phrase 'the Australian Jubilee' is used by a lamp contractor in the issue of 23 January. On the day as mitigating rancour, *Australian*, 25 January 1842, is quoted in Grainger, *Martin of Martin Place*, p. 29. Gipps's mistake is noted in *ibid.*, pp. 28-9; his grant to first fleeters is commended in *SG*, 29 January 1842. On the dinner of 1842, see Grainger, *op. cit.*, p. 32; *SG*, 29 January 1842. For 'the national holiday' see *Empire*, 28 January 1856; Parkes's toast is in *SMH*, 28 January 1867.

A NATIONAL HOLIDAY?

Lang's declaration is mentioned in Serle, *The Golden Age*, pp. 392-3; the mayor of Melbourne is quoted in J. D. Lang, *Historical Account of the Separation of Victoria from New South Wales* (Sydney 1870), p. 20. The Legislative Council of Victoria on the primacy of Melbourne is quoted in Serle, *op. cit.*, p. 207. The South Australian writer pleased to have escaped contagion is quoted in Pike, *Paradise of Dissent*, p. 459. West on federal union is in his *The History of Tasmania*, vol. 2, p. 345. Duffy in 1857 is cited in Serle, *op. cit.*, p. 314. On rail gauges, see Blainey, *The Tyranny of Distance*, pp. 245-53. The contrast with America is in Dilke

Greater Britain, vol. 2, p. 108. On usages of 'Australasia', see *ibid.*, vol. 2, pp. 4-5; K. Sinclair, 'Australasia inter-government negotiations 1865-80: ocean meals and tariffs', *AJPH*, vol. 16, 1970, p. 174. For Lang's view of New Zealand, see E. J. Tapp, 'New Zealand and Australian federation', *HS*, vol. 5, 1951-3, p. 244.

Denison's message by wire is in *SMH*, 30 October 1858. The 'great mechanical artery' is in Kelly, *Life in Victoria*, vol. 2, p. 358. Faults in the cable are described in F. R. Bradley, 'History of the electric telegraph in Australia', *JRAHS*, vol. 20, 1934-5, pp. 239-63. The telegram from Echuca is quoted in Hare, *The Last of the Bushrangers*, p. 52. Parkes's prophecy of 1867 is in his *Speeches*, p. 256. *Argus* on the failure of the intercolonial conference is quoted in Clark (ed.), *Select Documents 1851-1900*, p. 284; the South Australian representative in 1870 is quoted in *ibid.*, p. 290.

On Victoria's first exhibition, see Turner, *A History of the Colony of Victoria*, vol. 2, p. 220; on her invitation to other colonies, see *ibid.*; Sydney's exhibition is celebrated in *SMH*, 1 September 1870; the festival of music is described in *ibid.*, 6 October 1870; the rightness of Sydney as site is affirmed in *ibid.*, 31 August 1870, quoted in Birch and Macmillan, The *Sydney Scene*, p. 189. The comparison of federation with the millennium is in *Freeman's Journal*, 12 May 1866, quoted in *Catholic Weekly*, 12 May 1966.

On the maritime frontier, see J. M. R. Young, 'Australia's Pacific frontier', *HS*, vol. 12, 1965-7, pp. 313-14; D. Shineberg, *They Came for Sandalwood* (Melbourne 1967), p. 11. The 'Australian Anthem' is in Lang, *Aurora Australis*, pp. 149-50; the author's view of the French as unfit colonizers is in Lang, *The Coming Event!*, p. 317. Duffy's vision is quoted in Serle, *op. cit.*, p. 251n. Wentworth's farewell is reported in *SMH*, 21 March 1854. The vision of Australia as centre of empire is quoted from *Argus*, 21 September 1853, in L. G. Churchward, Australia and America: a Sketch of the Origin and Early Growth of Social and Economic Relations Between Australia and the U.S.A., 1790-1876 (M.A. thesis, University of Melbourne, 1941), p. 116. The *SMH* version is in an article on 'American independence', 5 July 1858. Dilke's scepticism is in *Greater Britain*, vol. 2, pp. 400-1. Duffy in 1870 is quoted in Clark (ed.), *Select Documents 1851-1900*, p. 451. Cowper's speech is reported in *SMH*, 27 January 1870. The passages from Trollope, *Australia and New Zealand*, are (in the order quoted) at vol. 2, p. 497; vol. 1, p. 152; vol. 2, pp. 497-8. The American in London is quoted in M. E. Curti, *The Roots of American Loyalty* (New York 1946), p. 139. The observation by 'the Vagabond', J. S. James or Julian Thomas, is in *The Vagabond Papers*, fifth series, p. 54.

War and Peace

10 Natural Enemies

THE ELEMENTS
Braim's rapture is recalled in his *History of New South Wales*, vol. 2, pp. 271-2; Horne is quoted in A. Blainey, *The Farthing Poet*, pp. 194-5. On the *Neva* and *Cataraqui*, see C. Bateson, *Australian Shipwrecks, 1 1622-1850* (Sydney 1972), pp. 110, 186-8; the number of wrecks off King Island is in Blainey, *The Tyranny of Distance*, p. 193. The wreck of the *Dunbar* is described in *A Century of Journalism*, p. 195; the loss of the *London* in Nadel, *Australia's Colonial Culture*, p. 48. For the wreck of the *Admella*, as for many other wrecks, different sources give different numbers of victims; the figure here is from I. Mudie, *Wreck of the Admella* (Adelaide 1966), pp. 145-6; 'From the Wreck' is in Robb (ed.), *Poems of Adam Lindsay Gordon*, pp. 126-31. Bigge's censure of the farmers is quoted in Clark (ed.), *Select Documents 1788-1850*, p. 139. Harpur's account is in Normington-Rawling, *Charles Harpur, an Australian*, pp. 212-13. On other floods, see Heaton, *Australian Dictionary of Dates and Men of the Time*, part 2, p. 103; Roberts, *The Squatting Age in Australia*, p. 386; entry 'Floods' in *AE*.

The warning against drought is in C. E. W. Bean, 'Willoughby Bean. A settler of the 1820's', *JRAHS*, vol. 31, 1945, p. 372. On the drought of 1812-13, see Perry, *Australia's First Frontier*, pp. 29-30; Sturt is quoted in *ibid.*, p. 36. The passage of prayer is in Church of England, N.S.W., *A Form of Prayer, with Fasting* (Sydney 1838), p. 5; the sermon at Maitland is J. Grigor, *Duties Appropriate to a Day of Public Fast and Humiliation* (Sydney 1838), p. 11. The rain in 1866 is reported in W. M. Cowper, *Episcopate of the Right Reverend Frederic Barker* (London 1888), pp. 187-8. The plea for divine moderation is in *Empire*, 24 May 1870.

Lang's sonnet is in his *Aurora Australis*, p. 145; Harpur's 'The Bush Fire' is in his *The Bushrangers*, pp. 72-5. Kendall's poem 'A Death in the Bush' is in Reed (ed.), *The Poetical Works of Henry Kendall*, pp. 84-5; it won a prize from the *Illustrated Australian Annual* (Melbourne) in 1869. Black Thursday is described in Kerr, *Glimpses of Life in Victoria*, pp. 101-3; the passage is quoted in Grant and Serle, *The Melbourne Scene*, pp. 66-7; the clergyman recalling it is J. H. L. Zillman, *Past and Present Australian Life* (London 1889), p. 39. On Strutt's painting, see B. Smith, *Australian Painting*, pp. 52, 54-5. Parkes's recollection of 1839 is in his *Fifty Years in the Making of Australian History*, vol. 1, pp. 3-4.

On explorers who had been professional soldiers, see K. E. Fitzpatrick, *Australian Explorers* (Melbourne 1958), p. 10. Sturt's reflection is in his *Narrative of an Expedition into Central Australia during 1884, 5 and 6* (London 1849), vol. 1, p. ii. The governor of Victoria, Sir Charles Darling, is quoted in *Age*, 22 April 1865; for this view of Burke, see K. E. Fitzpatrick, 'The Burke and Wills expedition and the Royal Society of Victoria', *HS*, vol. 10, 1961-3, pp. 475-6. On the wreck of the *Maria* in 1840, see Bateson, *op. cit.*, p. 145; on the *Maria* of 1872, J. Moresby, *Discoveries and Surveys in New Guinea* (London 1876), pp. 38-48. For aborigines using fire as weapon, see Bassett, *The Hentys*, p. 406.

ABORIGINES

Cook's encounter is in Beaglehole (ed.), *The Journals of Captain James Cook*, vol. 1, p. 305; Kendall's interpretation of it is in Reed (ed.), *The Poetical Works of Henry Kendall*, p. 477. Phillip's naming Manly Cove is in *HRNSW*, vol. 1, part 2, p. 129. The skirmish at Airds is described by Macquarie in *HRA*, Ser. 1, vol. 9, pp. 139-40; his disappointment is quoted in Ellis, *Lachlan Macquarie*, p. 405. The passage calling the exploring party an army is in T. L. Mitchell, *Three Expeditions into the Interior of Eastern Australia* (London 1838), vol. 2, p. 3; his judgment of the aborigines is quoted in *ADB*. On Stuart at the centre, see D. Pike, *John McDouall Stuart* (Melbourne 1958), p. 20. Gipps on outrages is quoted in *ADB*. 'A Convict's Lament on the Death of Captain Logan', by 'Frank the Poet', is in Ward (ed.), *The Penguin Book of Australian Ballads*, pp. 36-8. For the killings of 1838, see J. N. Molony, *An Architect of Freedom: John Hubert Plunkett in New South Wales 1832-1869* (Canberra 1973), p. 139; for the killings of 1842, Mulvaney, *Cricket Walkabout*, p. 16. 'The Creek of the Four Graves' is in C. Harpur, *Poems*, pp. 47-59; for the view that 'the history of Australian poetry begins' with this poem, see K. Slessor, *Bread and Wine* (Sydney 1970), pp. 67-71. On Brisbane's policy, see Perry, *Australia's First Frontier*, p. 92. The events in Van Diemen's Land are described in West, *The History of Tasmania*, vol. 2, pp. 28-55. See also *ADB* on Arthur; C. D. Rowley, *The Destruction of Aboriginal Society* (Canberra 1970), pp. 45-53. Henty is quoted in Bassett, *The Hentys*, p. 185; see also Rowley, *op. cit.*, p. 67; F. H. Goldsmith, 'The battle of Pinjarra', *JRAHS*, vol. 37, 1951, pp. 344-50.

Heaps of aboriginal bones, and killing for sport, are described in Roberts, *The Squatting Age in Australia*, p. 409; the comparison of aboriginal and emu is by J. L. Stokes, quoted in Morris, *Austral English*, p. 137. The colonist of Port Phillip is quoted in D. J. Mulvaney, 'The Australian Aborigines 1606-1929. Opinion and fieldwork: part 1: 1606-1859', *HS*, vol. 8, 1957-9, p. 142. Gipps's response to the request from Port Phillip is quoted in Molony, *op. cit.*, p. 139. FitzRoy on the case for a military force is in *HRA*, ser. 1, vol. 25, p. 532. On 'myall', Mitchell is quoted in Morris, *op. cit.*, p. 311. Gipps's account of the massacre at Myall Creek is in *HRA*, ser. 1, vol. 19, pp. 700-4. *SMH* is quoted in B. Harrison, The Myall Creek Massacre: White Aboriginal Relations in Early New South Wales (Seminar paper, University of Papua New Guinea, 1969), p. 19; Gipps on the black as fellow creature is quoted in *ibid.*, p. 24. On the massacre, see also Molony, *op. cit.*, pp. 140-8. Harpur's response is described in Normington-Rawling, *Charles Harpur, an Australian*, pp. 72-3, 158. Stephen's verdict on protection is quoted in the *ADB* entry on Gipps; that of Harris is in his *Settlers and Convicts*, p. 222. The retribution for Brown's death is described by J. C. Hamilton, quoted in Mulvaney, *Cricket Walkabout*, p. 17. Jackey Jackey is one of the few aborigines in the *ADB*. The praise for native police is reported in Sadleir, *Recollections of a Victorian Police Officer*, p. 294; on their taking to drink, see Kiddle, *Men of Yesterday*, p. 127; on the white officers travelling behind, see entry 'Police, native' in *AE*; A. Laurie, 'The Black War in Queensland', Royal Historical Society of Queensland, *Journal*, vol. 6, no. 1, September 1959, pp. 162, 172-3. The guide to Australia is quoted in Morris, *op. cit.*, p. 34. The massacre at Hornet Bank and the reprisals after Cullinlaringo are described in Laurie, *op. cit.*, pp. 161-2, 166; Heaton, *Australian Dictionary of Dates and Men of the Time*, part 2, p. 6. On the Jardines' expedition see Laurie, *op. cit.*, p. 166; Rowley, *op. cit.*, p. 170. The number of white men killed in the 1860s is estimated in G. C. Bolton, *A Thousand Miles Away: a history of North Queensland to 1860* (Canberra 1963), p. 38. For estimates of the number of aborigines killed in Queensland and elsewhere, see H. Reynolds, 'Violence, the Aboriginals, and the Australian historian', *Meanjin Quarterly*, no. 4, 1972, p. 475. The advice to shoot straight is quoted in Bolton, *op. cit.*, p. 38. Dilke's reflection is in his *Greater Britain*, vol. 2, p. 96. The need to restrain 'station blacks' in 1864 is described in Henning, *Letters*, p. 68. Darwin's observation is in H. E. L. Mellersh (ed.), *The Voyage of the Beagle* (Heron Books 1968), p. 434. *Age* is quoted in Mulvaney, *Cricket Walkabout*, pp. 14, 16. For population figures, see D. E. Barwick, 'Changes in the Aboriginal population of Victoria, 1863-1966', in D. J. Mulvaney and J. Golson (eds), *Aboriginal Man and Environment in Australia* (Canberra 1971), p. 288. For the Russian visitor's experience, see P. Mukhanov, 'Sydney', translated by V. Fitzhardinge, *JRAHS*, vol. 51, 1965, p. 303. The American visitor is Wilkes, *Narrative of the United States Exploring Expedition*, vol. 2, p. 197. 'Britons of the south' is in *Encyclopaedia Britannica*, eleventh edition, 1910-11, vol. 17, p. 628; Higinbotham's assessment of Maoris is in Morris, *A Memoir of George Higinbotham*, p. 164. On the award of the Victoria Cross, see Heaton, *op. cit.*, part 2, p. 119. The passage from Bonwick's book is at p. 400.

11 Bushrangers

BOLTERS

On 'bushranger' and other names, see Morris, *Austral English*, pp. 71-2; J. Fielding and W. S. Ramson, 'Further evidence on the early use of "bushranger"', *Australian Literary Studies*, vol. 5, 1972, pp. 316-21. On brutalizing punishment and bolters, see Ward, *The Australian Legend*, pp. 137-8; H. King, 'Some aspects of police administration in New South Wales, 1825-1851', *JRAHS*, vol. 42, 1956-7, p. 213. Cunningham's view is in his *Two Years in New South Wales*, vol. 2, p. 198. On belief in escape by land, see *ibid.*, pp. 199-204; Lang, *An Historical and Statistical Account of New South Wales* (1852), vol. 1, p. 43; Perry, *Australia's First Frontier*, p. 27. Donohoe's declaration is quoted in White, *History of Australian Bushranging*, vol. 1, p. 104. Jenkins's recommendation is quoted in Ward, *op. cit.*, p. 139. Brady's offer of reward is quoted in White *op. cit.*, vol. 1, pp. 42-3; for his attack on Launceston see *ADB* entry on William Balfour. Mosquito's career is in Heaton, *Australian Dictionary of Dates and Men of the Time*, part 2, p. 51. The commandant's report from Bathurst is in *HRA*, ser. 1, vol. 11, p. 898; Stewart's response is described in *ibid.*, ser. 1, vol. 12, p. 85; *SG*, 15 September 1825; King, *op. cit.*, p. 224; tranquillity is reported in *SG*, 1 December 1825. On the mounted police, see King, *op. cit.*, pp. 225-6; C. Jeffries, *The Colonial Police* (London 1952). On the Bushranging Act, see White, *op. cit.*, vol. 1, pp. 143-5; Ward, *op. cit.*, p. 146. The currency lad in handcuffs testifies in Harris, *Settlers and Convicts*, p. 81. Bourke's statement on the act is quoted in Shaw, *Convicts and the Colonies*, p. 198. The select committee's comment on convictions for highway robbery is quoted in Clark (ed.), *Sources of Australian History*, p. 213. On outrages around Bathurst in 1840, see J. N. Molony, *An Architect of Freedom: John Hubert Plunkett in New South Wales 1832-1869* (Canberra 1973), pp. 176-7. Mrs Meredith's account of bailing up is in her *Notes and Sketches of New South Wales*, p. 132; Marjoribanks's is in his *Travels in New South Wales*, p. 72.

GOLD ROBBERS

For information on the new men I am indebted to R. B. Walker, 'Bushranging in fact and legend', *HS*, vol. 11, 1963-5, pp. 206-21; see also White, *op. cit.*, vol. 1, pp. 26-7, 203-4. On Melville, see H. Reynolds, '"That hated stain": the aftermath of transportation in Tasmania', *HS*, vol. 14, 1969-71, pp. 20, 24. *Empire*'s forecast of 1862 about 'General' Gardiner is quoted in Grainger, *Martin of Martin Place*, pp. 88-9. The ballad is quoted in Ward, *op. cit.*, p. 163. Gardiner's arrest, trial and sentence are described in White, *op. cit.*, vol. 1, pp. 310-9. The Bathurst paper is quoted in *ibid.*, vol. 2, pp. 35-6; *Sydney Mail* in Walker, *op. cit.*, p. 214. The troopers in disguise are described in Haydon, *The Trooper Police of Australia*, p. 162. The ambush by the Clarkes is reported in *ibid.*, pp. 174-5; White, *op. cit.*, vol. 2, pp. 209-14. On Power's capture, see *ibid.*, vol. 2, pp. 248-60; Hare, *The Last of the Bushrangers*, p. 241. On Kelly's relationship with Power, see Hare, *op. cit.*, p. 93. Kelly himself is quoted in M. Brown. *Native Son: the story of Ned Kelly* (Melbourne 1948), p. 273.

12 Rebels

IRISH CONVICTS

Their number is given in Shaw, *Convicts and the Colonies*, pp. 363-4. Precautions against their rising are reported in *HRA*, ser. 1, vol. 3, p. 654; Clark, *A History of Australia*, vol. 1, p. 170; H. McQueen, 'Convicts and rebels', *Labour History*, no. 15, November 1968, pp. 5-6. On the incident at Norfolk Island, see Blainey, *The Tyranny of Distance*, p. 63. King on the 'deluded Irish' is in *HRA*, ser. 1, vol. 4, p. 611. For accounts of the rising, see *ibid.*, pp. 563-77; McQueen, *op. cit.*, pp. 3-30; R. W. Connell, 'The convict rebellion of 1804', *Melbourne Historical Journal*, no. 5, 1965, pp. 27-37. Johnston's account of the engagement is in *HRA*, ser. 1, vol. 4, 570. The settler reporting the rebels' cry is G. Suttor, quoted in Connell, *op. cit.*, p. 35. The memory of Dixon's punishment is reported in Clark, *op. cit.*, vol. 1, p. 173.

BRITISH OFFICERS
On the quality of the corps, see T. G. Parsons, 'The social composition of the men of the New South Wales Corps'. *JRAHS*, vol. 50, 1964, pp. 297-305; A. G. L. Shaw, 'Rum corps and rum rebellion', *Melbourne Historical Journal*, no. 10, 1971, pp. 15-17. King's measures against the officers are described in Clark, *A History of Australia*, no. 1, p. 162. Hunter is quoted in the *ADB* entry on Macarthur, whose conflict with Bligh is narrated in Ellis, *John Macarthur*, pp. 296-7. For events just before the rebellion, see Clark, *op. cit.*, vol. 1, pp. 217-18. Johnston's version of the rebellion is in *HRA*, ser. 1, vol. 6, pp. 208ff.; Bligh's is in *ibid.*, pp. 420ff. On similar events elsewhere, see J. J. Auchmuty, 'The background to the early Australian governors', *HS*, vol. 6, 1953-5, p. 309. Macquarie's description of his regiment is in Ellis, *op. cit.*, p. 195; his speech on landing, *ibid.*, pp. 206-7; his report on the rebellion, *ibid.*, pp. 216-17.

THREATS FROM FREE MEN
Macquarie's request for more soldiers is quoted in D. MacCallum, 'The early "Volunteer" Associations in New South Wales', *JRAHS*, vol. 47, 1961, p. 358. Wentworth's threat is in his *A Statistical, Historical and Political Description*, pp. 245-6. Darling's memory of the passage is quoted in Melbourne, *Early Constitutional Development in Australia*, p. 134. On the yeomanry in England, see F. C. Mather, *Public Order in the Age of the Chartists* (Manchester 1959), pp. 141-50. Edward Macarthur's recommendations are quoted in MacCallum, *op. cit.*, pp. 361-2. Harris on Australian dislike of the British military is quoted in Ward, *The Australian Legend*, p. 58. The song sung at Vaucluse is quoted in *Monitor*, 22 October 1831; I owe this reference to G. Shaw. Polding's judgment of the police is quoted in Birt, *Benedictine Pioneers in Australia*, vol. 1, p. 318. For Miles's testimony, and on the 'cabbage-tree mob', see H. King, 'Some aspects of police administration in New South Wales', *JRAHS*, vol. 42, 1956-7, pp. 221-2. For the death in Sydney, see Knight, *Illiberal Liberal*, p. 45. FitzRoy's dispatch on the need for troops in Melbourne is in *HRA*, ser. 1, vol. 25, pp. 532-3. Broughton on talk of rebellion is quoted in Knight, *op. cit.*, p. 120; Lowe's threat on 26 January 1846 is in *ibid.*, p. 117; Lang's exhortation is in *ibid.*, p. 121; the report that cannon were trained on the protest meeting is in *ibid.*, pp. 221-2. The protest is in Parkes, *Speeches*, p. 4. The *People's Advocate* is quoted in Knight, *op. cit.*, p. 223. Parkes on the American revolutionaries is in his *Speeches*, pp. 6-7. Lowe's speech, and Parkes's looking back on the day as historic, are quoted in Knight, *op. cit.*, p. 224. FitzRoy on the mob is quoted in J. N. Molony, John Hubert Plunkett in New South Wales. 1832-1869 (Ph.D. thesis, Australian National University, 1971), p. 247n. .

Wentworth's speech in the Legislative Council is reported in *SMH*, 13 September 1850. Lowe's remarks on the need to inflame the masses are in Knight, *op. cit.*, p. 120. Parkes's denial of anti-British feeling is in his *Speeches*, p. 15. The contrast between America and Australia is drawn in West, *The History of Tasmania*, vol. 2, p. 344. The secretary of state in 1852 is quoted in Shaw, *Convicts and the Colonies*, p. 350. There is much relevant to this chapter in A. G. L. Shaw, 'Violent protest in Australian history', *HS*, vol. 15, 1971-3, pp. 545-61, which I had not read when I wrote it.

13 Diggers

EUREKA
On FitzRoy's knowledge that his soldiers could not stop diggers, see G. Blainey, 'Gold and governors', *HS*, vol. 10, 1961-3, p. 134. Stewart's letter to the governor is in Colonial Secretary's Papers, N.S.W. Archives, bundle 4/1146; I owe this reference to J. N. Molony. On FitzRoy's decision, see Blainey, *op. cit.*, pp. 135-6. My main source on the Victorian diggings is Serle, *The Golden Age*; for the licensing system, see p. 19. Howitt's observation of gold commissioners is reported in Walker, *Come Wind, Come Weather: a biography of Alfred Howitt*, p. 50; the chief commissioner's reflection on Britons and bayonets is quoted in Serle, *op. cit.*, p. 101; the commissioner testifying about justice and popular feeling is quoted in Ward, *The Australian Legend*, pp. 110-11. On troubles at the Turon, and the Ovens, see Blainey, *The Rush That Never Ended*, pp. 52-3. On troubles at Bendigo, see Serle, *op. cit.*, pp. 109ff; *The Times* and the commander of the regiment are quoted at p. 112.

The colonial official's judgment of Hotham is quoted in *ibid.*, p. 156. The observation that the free

Australian does not touch his hat is in Kingsley, *The Recollections of Geoffrey Hamlyn*, vol. 2, p. 312. The peculiarities of digging at Ballarat are described in Blainey, *op. cit.*, pp. 49-50. On Hotham's sending military reinforcements, see T. B. Millar, The History of the Defence Forces of the Port Phillip District and Colony of Victoria, 1836-1900 (M.A. thesis, University of Melbourne, 1957), p. 25. Kennedy's couplet is quoted in Serle, *op. cit.*, p. 164. *Ballarat Times* is quoted in E. D. and A. Potts, 'American republicanism and the disturbances of the Victorian goldfields', *HS*, vol. 13, 1967-9, p. 153; the statement of principles is quoted in Clark (ed.), *Select Documents 1851-1900*, p. 58. Kennedy's plea to Hotham to avoid bloodshed is quoted in Serle, *op. cit.*, p. 165. *Ballarat Times* on the beauty of the flag is quoted in L. Fox, *The Strange Story of the Eureka Flag* (Sydney 1963), p. 5. Father Smyth's anxiety is quoted in *H.S. Eureka Centenary Supplement*, p. 94. Hayes's verse is quoted in R. Carboni, *The Eureka Stockade: the consequences of some pirates wanting on quarter-deck a rebellion* (Melbourne 1855), p. 41; the author's view that the government would yield is at p. 43. Rede's instructions to the contrary are quoted in Serle, *op. cit.*, pp. 163-4; Lynch on the challenge is at p. 167. On Lalor the non-John-Bullised, see Carboni, *op. cit.*, p. 46. Lalor's account of becoming leader is quoted in Serle, *op. cit.*, p. 167. His translated message is quoted in Carboni, *op. cit.*, p. 44; the oath, p. 50; the insistence that men were organizing only for defence, p. 49; Lalor's making no pretensions to military knowledge, p. 48; the account of marching and counter-marching is at p. 64. Rede's apprehension of a democratic revolution is reported in Serle, *op. cit.*, p. 167; his hope that the men would not return to work, p. 168. For Smyth's advice to Catholics, see Carboni, *op. cit.*, p. 60.

On the behaviour of the mounted police at Eureka, see 'Report of the commission appointed to enquire into the condition of the gold fields of Victoria', *Votes and Proceedings of the Legislative Council*, 1854-5, vol. 2, A 76, p. xxiv. The fate of the flag is described in Carboni, *op. cit.*, p. 77; Withers, *The History of Ballarat*, p. 158. The description of the dead and dying is quoted in Carboni, *op. cit.*, p. 77. The incredulity of *Age* is quoted in Grant and Serle, *The Melbourne Scene*, p. 95. On the dead, see 'Report of the commission appointed to enquire into the condition of the gold fields of Victoria', *op. cit.*, p. xxv; Withers, *op. cit.*, pp. 156-7. Hotham's thanks to Smyth is quoted in Carboni, *op. cit.*, p. 61. Goold's denunciation is in his Lenten Pastoral 1855, quoted in O'Farrell (ed.), *Documents in Australian Catholic History*, vol. 1, p. 235. The official version of the engagement is in *Argus*, 5 December 1854; *Geelong Advertiser*'s is quoted in Carboni, *op. cit.*, p. 78; Carboni's own, p. 62. The ballad comparing Sebastopol and Ballarat is in Ward, *The Penguin Book of Australian Ballads*, pp. 64-6. Vern's prophecy of greater upheavals is quoted in Carboni, *op. cit.*, p. 72. On Goold's mission to Ballarat, see Moran, *History of the Catholic Church in Australasia*, p. 750. For Barry's kindly manner, see Carboni, *op. cit.*, p. 108; the British 'Hurrah!' is reported at p. 117. The judgment that the government was at fault is in 'Report of the commission appointed to enquire into the condition of the gold fields of Victoria', *op. cit.*, p. liv. Hotham as beleaguered swordsman is quoted in Serle, *op. cit.*, p. 203. Lalor's reflection on democracy is quoted in *ibid.*, p. 260.

The peace of Melbourne in 1856 is described in C. G. Duffy, 'An Australian example', *Contemporary Review*, January 1888, p. 17. Barry's advice that Victorians should follow Garibaldi is quoted in A. G. L. Shaw, 'Violent protest in Australian history', *HS*, vol. 15, 1971-3, p. 556. Events in Melbourne on the night of 28 August are described in Serle, *op. cit.*, pp. 298-300; Grant and Serle, *op. cit.*, pp. 118-21.

CHINAMEN

On the Chinese coming in emigrant ships, see Blainey, *The Tyranny of Distance*, pp. 202-3. The numbers of Chinese are taken from C. A. Price, *The Great White Walls are Built* (Canberra 1974); the author has let me use an early draft, and has kindly supplied me with page references to the book, which had not appeared when this volume went to the publisher. Hotham's report of 'dispute and broils' is in Serle, *The Golden Age*, p. 323. The commission's judgment of the Chinese is in its 'Report', *Votes and Proceedings of the Legislative Council*, 1854-5, vol. 2, A 76, pp. l-lii. The white observer of the Chinese walking from Robe is quoted in Clark (ed.), *Select Documents 1851-1900*, p. 67; Fawkner's motion is in *ibid.*, p. 68; the Chinese petition is in *ibid.*, pp. 70-1. The Chinese at Castlemaine wanting to be brothers with Englishmen are quoted in Serle, *op. cit.*, p. 330. The *SMH* report of the commissioner at Tambaroora who protected the Chinese is quoted in Price, *op. cit.*, p. 78. The fact that Chinese diggers outnumbered white diggers is noted in Blainey, *op. cit.*, p. 88

The account of disturbances at Lambing Flat draws on D. L. Carrington, 'Riots at Lambing Flat, 1860-1861', *JRAHS*, vol. 46, 1960, pp. 223-49; P. A. Selth, The Government, the Chinese, and the Europeans at the Burrangong Gold Fields, 1860-1 (B.A. Honours essay, Australian National University, 1971). The passages quoted from *SMH* on violence done to Chinese are in issues of 2, 4, 20 July 1861, the last of which is quoted in Clark (ed), *Select Documents 1851-1900*, p. 73. The report that Lambing Flat is in the hands of insurgents is in *SMH*, 18 July 1861. Parkes's view that unregulated entry of Chinese would lead to civil war is quoted in Price, *op. cit.*, pp. 83-4; the judgment of the Colonial Office is quoted in *ibid.*, p. 87. Names of Chinese victims of bushrangers are given in Heaton, *Australian Dictionary of Dates and Men of the Time*, part 2, pp. 44ff; the career of Sam Poo is described in Haydon, *The Trooper Police of Australia*, p. 173. Terms used for Chinese are cited in Morris, *Austral English*, p. 86. The colonist of 1872 is C. H. Eden, *My Wife and I in Queensland* (London 1892), p. 266.

14   The Sound of Distant War

OUTPOSTS OF EMPIRE

Phillip's vision of the naval harbour is quoted in Cobley, *Sydney Cove 1788*, p. 31. Ross's request for a place for defence is quoted in M. Austin, 'The early defences of Australia', *JRAHS*, vol. 49, 1963-4, p. 192. Mrs Macarthur is quoted in S. Macarthur-Onslow (ed.), *Some Early Records of the Macarthurs of Camden* (Sydney 1914), p. 46. King's request of 1801 is quoted in Austin, *op. cit.*, p. 196. On the guns at George's Head, see G. P. Walsh and D. M. Horner, 'The defence of Sydney in 1820', *Army Journal* (Canberra), May 1969, p. 13. The French observer urging the destruction of Port Jackson is quoted in Scott, *The Life of Captain Matthew Flinders, R.N.*, p. 464. On the mission of the *Cumberland*, see Blainey, *The Tyranny of Distance*, pp. 76-7; Clark, *A History of Australia*, vol. 1, p. 190. On the scene at King Island when the English flag was hoisted upside-down, see E. Scott, 'Taking possession of Australia—the doctrine of "Terra Nullius" (No Man's Land)', *JRAHS*, vol. 26, 1940, p. 11 and n. Hobart's warning to King is in *HRA*, ser. 1, vol. 4, p. 9. On the settlement in the north of Van Diemen's Land, see Blainey, *op. cit.*, pp. 80-1.

For Bowman's flag celebrating Trafalgar with local imagery, see F. Cayley, *Flag of Stars* (Adelaide 1966), pp. 56-7. French plans for attack from Mauritius are cited in E. Scott, *Terre Napoléon: a history of French explorations and projects in Australia* (London 1910), p. 21.

The passage from Wentworth on how easily an enemy could enter Port Jackson is in his *A Statistical, Historical and Political Description*, p. 36. The report of a French plan to seize the colony in 1814 is in *HRA*, ser. 1, vol. 8, pp. 72-6. Macquarie's request is quoted in D. MacCallum, 'The early "Volunteer" Associations in New South Wales', *JRAHS*, vol. 47, 1961, p. 358. The route by which news of Napoleon's defeat reached Sydney is described in V. Fitzhardinge, 'Russian ships in Australian waters 1807-1835', *JRAHS*, vol. 51, 1965, pp. 119-20. For celebration of Waterloo, see Clark, *op. cit.*, vol. 1, p. 296; for the end of war with the Americans, see *SG*, 19 August 1815.

Bigge's critical view of Macquarie's defences is quoted in Walsh and Horner, *op. cit.*, pp. 22-3. On strategic motives for settlements, see Blainey, *op. cit.*, pp. 83-98. The defences of Sydney are derided in *Australian*, 8 April 1829. Gipps's complaint of 1839 is in *HRA*, ser. 1, vol. 20, pp. 305-6. The Americans' entry is described in Wilkes, *Narrative of the United States Exploring Expedition*, vol. 2, p. 168; Wilkes's judgment of how easily he might have done devastation is in *ibid.*, p. 169. Preparations for housing guns are approved in *Sydney Herald*, 12 February 1841, quoted in Birch and Macmillan, *The Sydney Scene*, p. 83. The demand for protection is in *SG*, 30 December 1841. For the Colonial Office rebukes to Gipps, see *HRA*, ser. 1, vol. 21, pp. 51-3; vol. 22, pp. 327-9, 770-1. Fear of bombardment is expressed by 'A Briton' in *SMH*, 22 September 1843, and ridiculed in Lang, *An Historical and Statistical Account of New South Wales* (1852), vol. 2, pp. 154, 158. On misinformation about war in 1848, see Molony, *The Roman Mould of the Catholic Church*, pp. 50-1. Earl Grey's grounds for moving troops from New South Wales to New Zealand are in *HRA*, ser. 1, vol. 25, p. 264; for *SMH*'s protest, and for subsequent recognition that the soldiers had been needed in New Zealand, see *A Century of Journalism*, p. 134. The move to Victoria Barracks is described in R. Vardanega, 'The Victoria Barracks at Paddington', *JRAHS*, vol. 50, 1964, pp. 58-74. On Earl Grey's warning of 1849, see the entry 'Military Defence' in *AE*. Grey's observation about riches and protection is cited in Lang, *op. cit.*, vol. 2, p. 155. The vision of Australia as El Dorado is in *SMH*, 11 July 1853, quoted in V. Fitzhardinge, Russian-Australian Relations in the Nineteenth Century (M.A. thesis, Australian National University, 1964), p. 106. The task of the Victorian committee of 1854 is quoted, and its findings are reported, in T. B. Millar, The History of the Defence Forces of the Port Phillip District and Colony of Victoria, 1836-1900 (M.A. thesis, University of Melbourne, 1957), pp. 37-8.

THE CRIMEA

The meeting of 22 May is reported in *SMH*, 25 May 1854. On the meeting to launch the Patriotic Fund, see Denison, *Varieties of Vice-Regal Life*, vol. 1, p. 306. Harpur's poem is quoted in Normington-Rawling,

Charles Harpur, an Australian, p. 198. On the Cremorne Gardens enterprise, see Serle, *The Golden Age*, p. 364; *Argus*, 26 May 1856. Dilke's observation is in his *Greater Britain*, vol. 2, p. 91. Fairfax's boast about the circulation of *SMH* is in *A Century of Journalism*, p. 168. For the governor's pleasure at fear of raiders, see Denison, *op. cit.*, vol. 1, p. 309. The elevation of Pinchgut into Fort Denison is described in A. B. Shaw, 'Fort Denison, Sydney Harbour', *JRAHS*, vol. 23, 1937, pp. 382-7; D. MacCallum, 'Some aspects of defence in the 1850's in New South Wales', *JRAHS*, vol. 44, 1958, p. 82. On the *Victoria*, see W. P. Evans, *Deeds Not Words* (Melbourne 1971), pp. 10-11.

Parkes records his enthusiasm for volunteers in his *Fifty Years in the Making of Australian History*, vol. 2, p. 268. *SMH* reports them drilling in bottle-green on 23 November 1854. The interrupted ball in Melbourne is described in Laye, *Social Life and Manners in Australia*, p. 128. The reception in Sydney of the news that Sebastopol had fallen is described in Denison, *op. cit.*, vol. 1, pp. 322-3. The poem 'Down in Australia' is in G. Massey, *My Lyrical Life: poems old and new* (second series, London 1889), p. 340. On Burke, see Moorehead, *Cooper's Creek*, p. 30. The diversion of mail steamers is described in J. W. Cell, *British Colonial Administration in the Mid-Nineteenth Century* (New Haven 1970), p. 235. The Sunday special of *SMH* is reported in *A Century of Journalism*, p. 194. The governor's reflection is in Denison, *op. cit.*, vol. 1, p. 354.

SELF-DEFENCE

The proposal to seize New Caledonia is in Denison, *Varieties of Vice-Regal Life*, vol. 1, pp. 463-4. The document received by Russell is cited in E. Scott, *Terre Napoléon: a history of French explorations and projects in Australia* (London 1910), p. 279. Parkes's thoughts on the danger of French invasion are in his *Speeches*, pp. 97, 101, 103. 'Australian Volunteer Song' was written in July 1860 and is in Reed (ed.), *The Poetical Works of Henry Kendall*, pp. 125-6; 'Australian War Song', published in *Empire*, 20 August 1860, is in *ibid.*, pp. 261-2. On the appearance of volunteer corps, see F. B. Boyce, *Four Score Years and Seven* (Sydney 1934), p. 12. Numbers are in the entry 'Military Defence' in *AE*. Kingsley is quoted in F. B. Smith, *The Making of the Second Reform Bill* (Canberra 1966), p. 12; on the English movement, see *ibid.*, pp. 11-12. On the *SMH* and volunteering, see *A Century of Journalism*, pp. 194, 273; Balfour's experience is recorded in A. Harper, *The Honourable James Balfour M.L.C.: a memoir* (Melbourne 1918), pp. 86-93; on Gordon as volunteer, see Robb (ed.), *Poems of Adam Lindsay Gordon*, introduction, pp. lxviii, lxxv.

Victorian defence preparations are described in T. B. Millar, The History of the Defence Forces of the Port Phillip District and Colony of Victoria, 1836-1900 (M.A. thesis, University of Melbourne, 1957), pp. 76, 111-15; B. A. Knox, 'Colonial influence on imperial policy, 1858-66: Victoria and the Colonial Naval Defence Act', *HS*, vol. 11, 1963-5, p. 64. The report of the Russians' reception in *Argus*, 20 January 1862, is quoted in D. MacCallum, 'The alleged Russian plans for the invasion of Australia, 1864', *JRAHS*, vol. 44, 1958, p. 304. The officer on the *Bogatyr* is P. Mukhanov; see 'Sydney', translated by V. Fitzhardinge, *JRAHS*, vol. 51, 1965, p. 308. The reflection of *Argus*, 25 March 1864, that *Bogatyr* had the shipping at her mercy is quoted in V. Fitzhardinge, 'Russian naval visitors to Australia, 1862-1888', *JRAHS*, vol. 52, 1966, p. 132. On the Polish agent's report, see MacCallum, *op. cit.*, pp. 308-11; Knox, *op. cit.*, p. 70. Darling's advice that the colony was so vulnerable is quoted in MacCallum, *op. cit.*, p. 314. The outrage of *Argus*, 14 November 1861, is quoted in *ibid.*, p. 313.

For Australian responses to the *Trent* episode, see J. H. Moore, 'New South Wales and the American Civil War', *AJPH*, vol. 16, 1970, pp. 31-4; M. V. Sapiets, Australian Press Coverage of America, 1850-65, with Specific Reference to New South Wales (M.A. thesis, Australian National University, 1970), pp. 260-4. The newspaper excited at the prospect of war is *Newcastle Chronicle*, 15 January 1862, quoted in Moore, *op. cit.*, p. 31. The South Australian request for tents is reported in *South Australian Advertiser*, 6 March 1862. The secretary of state's suggestion to governors is quoted in Millar, *op. cit.*, appendix A. On newspapers' views of the war, see Sapiets, *op. cit.*, pp. 257, 326. *Yass Courier*, 26 November 1862, is quoted in Moore, *op. cit.*, p. 35. On the visit of the *Shenandoah*, see E. Scott, 'The Shenandoah incident, 1865', *Victorian Historical Magazine*, vol. 2, 1926-7, pp. 55-75; C. Pearl, *Rebel Down Under: when the 'Shenandoah' shook Melbourne, 1865* (Melbourne 1970). *Argus* report of cheers for the Southerners is quoted in Scott, 'The Shenandoah incident, 1865', *op. cit.*, p. 58; *Age* rebuking officials who attended the dinner is quoted in E. Scott, *Historical Memoir of the Melbourne Club* (Melbourne 1936), p. 60. For the story of the explosive device, see Morris, *A Memoir of George Higinbotham*, p. 89. *Argus* expression of pleasure at the departure of the ship is quoted in Scott, 'The Shenandoah incident, 1865', *op. cit.*, p. 70; the paper's view that the visit had taught a lesson is quoted in Pearl, *op. cit.*, p. 132.

The Admiralty's statement of purpose for the squadron at Sydney is quoted in G. L. Macandie, *The Genesis of the Royal Australian Navy* (Sydney 1949), p. 15.

English appreciation of the Victorians' plan for a warship is quoted in Knox, *op. cit.*, p. 77. My account of the transaction draws on *ibid.*, pp. 62, 77; Macandie, *op. cit.*, pp. 24-5; W. P. Evans, *Deeds Not Words* (Melbourne 1971), pp. 56-61. On the *Cerberus* touching the side of the Suez Canal, see Blainey *The Tyranny of Distance*, p. 218. Sir Henry Barkly's view that the Victorian press inflated the mother country's debt to the colony is quoted in Serle, *The Golden Age*, p. 313. The House of Commons' resolution on colonial self-defence is in *Hansard*, ser. 3, vol. 165, p. 1060 (4 March 1862). The consequent arrangements are described in W. C. B. Tunstall, 'Imperial defence, 1815-1870', *Cambridge History of the British Empire, 2 The growth of the new empire 1783-1870* (Cambridge 1940), p. 834. Victorian opposition to paying for troops unless they stay in the colony is expressed in *Votes and Proceedings of the Legislative Assembly*, 1869, vol. 1, A 20, p. 523. Misgivings in Tasmania are reported in H. Reynolds, '"That hated stain": the aftermath of transportation in Tasmania', *HS*, vol. 14, 1969-71, pp. 24-5. O'Sullivan's recollection of Eureka is quoted in B. E. Mansfield, *Australian Democrat: the career of William Edward O'Sullivan, 1846-1910* (Sydney 1965), p. 5. Dilke's view that the old system retarded self-reliance is in his *Greater Britain*, vol. 2, p. 152; Mills is quoted in *Hansard*, ser. 3, vol. 165, p. 1036; Parkes in his *Speeches*, p. 108. On the general view in 1870, see A. Preston, *Canada and 'Imperial Defense'* (Durham, North Carolina 1967), pp. 212-13. The Victorian Royal Commission on Federal Union is quoted in Clark (ed.), *Select Documents 1851-1900*, p. 372. Duffy's argument for a federated and self-defending Australia is in *ibid.*, p. 451. Higinbotham's reply, *ibid.*, p. 448. The cutting off of gas is reported in *Ballarat Star*, 22 December 1870; for access to photocopies of this paper I am grateful to W. Bate. Higinbotham's remark on remoteness as protector is quoted in Morris, *op. cit.*, p. 169. *SMH*'s hostility to a standing army, expressed on 9 September 1870, is quoted in *A Century of Journalism*, p. 275. The retired officer proposing a militia is W. Chatfield in *SMH*, 3 September 1870. On cadet corps in Australia, see Bean, *Here, My Son*, pp. 176-7; *SMH*'s call for military training for all boys in elementary schools is quoted in *A Century of Journalism*, p. 274-5. Frustration at the slow news of war is in Henning, *Letters*, p. 103. Parkes's description of the telegraph as magical, 14 May 1872, is quoted in F. P. Clune, *Overland Telegraph: the story of the great Australian achievement and the link between Adelaide and Darwin* (Sydney 1955), p. viii. The secretary of state's cautious assurance is quoted in *Victorian Parliamentary Debates*, vol. 2, 1870, p. 754. The letter from the citizen of Ballarat is in *Ballarat Star*, 39 September 1870. The cartoon showing the Valentine card is in *Bulletin*, 21 February 1885; Fisher's promise is quoted in E. Scott, *Australia During the War* (Sydney 1936), p. 22.

The Stuff of History

In studying perceptions of the past among Australian colonists I have found some interpreters of American history helpful, especially D. Wecter, *The Hero in America* (New York 1941); D. J. Boorstin, *The Americans: the national experience* (New York 1965).

15 Australian Heroes

MEN OF EMPIRE

The ceremony in honour of Cook and Banks in 1822 is described in C. H. Bertie, 'Captain Cook and Botany Bay', *JRAHS*, vol. 10, 1924, pp. 240-8; Field's sonnets are in *SG*, 22 March 1822. The proposal to name a province is embodied in the title of J. D. Lang, *Cooksland, in North Eastern Australia: the future cotton field of Great Britain* (London 1847). The lines quoted from the prize poem are in W. H. H. Yarrington, *Captain Cook Meditating on Australia's Future* (Sydney 1908), pp. 3-6; for information about the contest I am grateful to G. Fischer, Archivist, University of Sydney. Kendall's verses are in Reed (ed.), *The Poetical Works of Henry Kendall*, pp. 117-18, 476-8. The visitor of the 1860s is quoted in *Sydney Punch*, 28 April 1866. Jenkins is quoted in W. R. Brownhill, *The History of Geelong and Corio Bay* (Melbourne 1955), pp. 345-6. On the effort at celebration in 1863, see *SMH*, 29 April 1863; *Illustrated Sydney News*, 16 June 1864. The ceremony at Botany Bay in 1870 is described in H. E. Holt, *An Energetic Colonist* (Melbourne 1972), pp. 111-12. The public appeal for a statue is recalled, and Prince Alfred's tribute to Cook is quoted, in *Sydney Mail*, 1 March 1879. On Parkes's part in creating the statue, see *SMH*, 5 May 1873; his *Fifty Years in the Making of Australian History*, vol. 1, pp. 170-1. Phillip the colonial imperialist speaks in R. Flanagan,

The History of New South Wales; with an Account of Van Diemen's Land (Tasmania), New Zealand, Port Phillip (Victoria), Moreton Bay, and other Australasian Settlements. The whole compiled from official and other authentic and original sources (London 1862), vol. 1, p. 33. The *SMH* version is not word-for-word Flanagan's, but it is so close that I assume him to be its source; *SMH*'s Phillip says on 7 February 1788 that the colony will 'before many generations shall have passed, become the centre of the civilisation of the southern hemisphere, and the most brilliant gem of the Austral ocean.' A letter from 'Critic' in *SMH*, 6 October 1886, argued that as nobody present at the ceremony had ever attributed to Phillip the words quoted by Flanagan, and no other historian appeared to have known of 'this singular speech', Flanagan himself must have been its author. I am grateful to Barbara Hau'ofa for discovering this piece of history-making. Macquarie on his name is quoted in *ADB*; for Wentworth's deploring the absence of a monument, see *SG*, 28 January 1832. For subscribers to the statue of Bourke, see *ibid.*, 24 February 1842; H. King, *Richard Bourke* (Melbourne 1971), p. 291 n.64. The observation about Irish names is quoted from *Sydney Herald* in *SG*, 16 June 1838. The advice to the governor's friends is in *Sydney Herald*, 7 December 1837. Accounts of the unveiling day are in *SG* and *SMH*, 12 April 1842; Braim, *History of New South Wales*, vol. 2, p. 294. For a critical discussion of the stone pamphlet, see A. G. L. Shaw, *Heroes and Villains in History: Governors Darling and Bourke in New South Wales* (Sydney 1966). On Eardley-Wilmot's dismissal, see Roe, *Quest for Authority in Eastern Australia*, pp. 20, 195.

THE GREAT NATIVE

The resolution to commission a statue of Wentworth is reported in *SMH*, 21 March 1854; on subscriptions for it, see G. B. Barton, 'The life and times of William Charles Wentworth', *Australian Star* (Sydney), 11 March 1899. The text of the motion for the portrait and the division of the house on it are reported in *SMH*, 12 October 1859. The university senate's conditional permission for the unveiling of the statue is recorded in its minutes for 15 May 1862, transcribed for me by G. Fischer. The *SMH*'s judgment of politicians who opposed the adjournment to welcome Wentworth home is quoted in *A Century of Journalism*, p. 253; the holiday is described and the paper's tribute quoted in *ibid.*; its farewell is quoted in *ibid.*, pp. 265-6. For the recommendation of a baronetcy, see Melbourne, *William Charles Wentworth*, pp. 105-6; *SMH*, 6 May 1872, says that he declined it. Kendall's poem is in Reed (ed.), *The Poetical Works of Henry Kendall*, p. 390. Martin's proposal for the funeral is in *Public Funeral of the Late William Charles Wentworth* (Sydney 1873), p. 17; Parkes's support, *ibid.*, pp. 17-18; the presence of unwanted aborigines is reported in *ibid.*, p. 52; Martin's remarks at the grave are in *ibid.*, p. 64. Wentworth's words of 1848 are quoted in Melbourne, *op. cit.*, p. 75; those of 1853 are in Silvester (ed.), *New South Wales Constitution Bill*, p. 227, and are quoted in Nadel, *Australia's Colonial Culture*, p. 60.

EXPLORERS

Leichhardt's hope for a statue is recorded in Chisholm, *Strange New World*, p. 229; his words on Waterloo are quoted in *ibid.*, p. 196. Kennedy's father is quoted in *ADB*. On Stuart's arrival in Adelaide, see D. Pike, *John McDouall Stuart* (Melbourne 1958), p. 29. á Beckett's poem 'Leichhardt's Return' is in Garryowen, *The Chronicles of Early Melbourne*, vol. 2, p. 666-7. *Age* on the departure of Burke and Wills is quoted in Grant and Serle, *The Melbourne Scene*, p. 122. Wilkie's view that Victoria should take the lead is quoted in K. E. Fitzpatrick, 'The Burke and Wills expedition and the Royal Society of Victoria', *HS*, vol. 10, 1961-3, p. 476. On support by governments, see Serle, *The Golden Age*, pp. 367-8. Gregory's and Warburton's grounds for declining leadership are quoted in Fitzpatrick, *op. cit.*, p. 477. The cartoon from *Melbourne Punch* is reproduced in Moorehead, *Cooper's Creek*, opposite p. 39. Burke's last message is quoted in Fitzpatrick, *op. cit.*, p. 476. My account of events at Cooper's Creek follows Moorehead, *op. cit.*, p. 84. Howitt on the five artists is quoted in Walker, *Come Wind, Come Weather: a biography of Alfred Howitt*, p. 132. Kendall's 'The Fate of the Explorers' is in Reed (ed.), *The Poetical Works of Henry Kendall*, pp. 46-9. For Howitt's view of why the disaster happened, see I. F. McLaren, 'The Victorian exploring expedition and the relieving expeditions, 1860-61: the Burke and Wills tragedy', *Victorian Historical Magazine*, vol. 29, 1959, p. 233. Howitt's account of the silent streets of Adelaide is quoted in Walker, *op. cit.*, p. 142. On the funeral, see Moorehead, *op. cit.*, pp. 193-4. On monuments, see McLaren, *op. cit.*, pp. 240-1. The unveiling of the statue is described, and Darling quoted, in *Age* and *Argus*, 22 April 1865; Horne's blowing about it is in a review of Trollope, *Australia and New Zealand*, in the *Contemporary Review*, October 1873, p. 719. The verses in praise of Forrest are quoted in Crowley, *Forrest 1847-1918*, vol. 1, pp. 73-4; his own words on the statue are quoted in *ibid.*, p. 75. The English review of Kendall is in *Athenaeum*, 27 September 1862, quoted in T. T. Reed, *Henry Kendall, a Critical Appreciation* (Adelaide 1960), p. 2. Gordon's 'Gone' is in

Robb (ed.), *Poems of Adam Lindsay Gordon*, pp. 7-9. Sturt's disappointment is quoted in Kunz, *A Continent Takes Shape*, p. 96. Kingsley, *The Boy in Grey* is quoted by F. H. Mares in Dutton (ed.), *The Literature of Australia*, p. 248. The judgment of Kendall is in Barton, *Literature in New South Wales*, p. 105. The depressing effect of the bush on poets is remarked by S. S. Topp in *Melbourne Review*, April 1876, quoted in Reed, *Henry Kendall*, p. 4. The estimation of the place of Burke and Wills in popular memory is in *Age*, 22 April 1865. The passage on the explorers and the sons is in J. E. Tenison Woods. *A History of the Discovery and Exploration of Australia* (London 1865), vol. 2, p. 513; Darling's remarks are quoted in *Age*, 22 April 1865. On the tendency for explorers to be English or Scottish rather than Irish, see Moorehead, *op. cit.*, p. 28.

THE WILD COLONIAL BOY
Cunningham's view that bushrangers were after fame is in his *Two Years in New South Wales*, vol. 2, p. 198; Mundy on Howe is quoted in Ward, *The Australian Legend*, p. 135. Respectable rejoicing at Donohoe's death is reported in Clark, *A History of Australia*, vol. 2, p. 176. On Gardiner's visitors in gaol, see Grainger, *Martin of Martin Place*, p. 98; on his first trial, see White, *History of Australian Bushranging*, vol. 1, p. 310. On Donohoe's killing, see Clark, *op. cit.*, p. 176; on Morgan, see R. B. Walker, 'Bushranging in fact and legend', *HS*, vol. 11, 1963-5, p. 220; on Hall, see *ibid.*, pp. 220-1. The ballad about Hall is in Ward (ed.), *The Penguin Book of Australian Ballads*, p. 73. The ballad which speaks of Donohoe as news is in *ibid.*, p. 45; the *Australian*'s view that his deeds were magnified is quoted in White, *op. cit.*, vol. 1, p. 102; on admiring reports of bushrangers, see Erdos, *The Sydney Gazette*, pp. 47-50. The *Argus* report of the incident on St Kilda Road is quoted in Grant and Serle, *The Melbourne Scene*, p. 89; on Strutt's painting, which was completed in 1889, see B. Smith, *Australian Painting*, pp. 36, 53. On the making of the Wild Colonial Boy, see Ward, *The Australian Legend*, p. 156. The view that the police were the villains is noted in White, *op. cit.*, vol. 2, p. 233. *SMH* on popular pleasure at news of bushranging is cited in Walker, *op. cit.*, p. 218. On the gold and silver medals, see Heaton, *Australian Dictionary of Dates and Men of the Time*, part 2, p. 48; Haydon, *The Trooper Police of Australia*, p. 158. Wentworth's view of bushrangers is in his *A Statistical, Historical and Political Description*, p. 132; Harpur's sentiments are recorded in Normington-Rawling, *Charles Harpur, an Australian*, pp. 33, 43-5. The passages quoted from Harpur, *The Bushrangers*, are at pp. 7, 9-10, 20, 59. On Harpur's pursuit of the Clarke gang, see Normington-Rawling, *op. cit.*, pp. 288-9. The rebuke to Harpur for writing about a bushranger is in Barton, *Literature in New South Wales*, p. 98. The indecision of Lawson's brother is reported in 'A fragment of autobiography', in C. Mann (ed.), *The Stories of Henry Lawson* (first series, Sydney 1964), p. 11. On the young admirer of Gardiner, see White, *op. cit.*, vol 1, pp. 310-1; Stephen at the trial of the Clarkes is quoted in *ibid.*, vol 2, p. 231; Barry at the trial of Kelly is quoted in Grant and Serle, *op. cit.*, p. 158.

HEROES FOR DEMOCRACY
On commemoration at Ballarat, see Withers, *The History of Ballarat*, pp. 156-7; on Lalor's opposition to the monument for Hotham, see Serle, *The Golden Age*, p. 210. The difficulty of getting consistent accounts of Eureka is observed in *Ballarat Star*, 4 March 1870. On the memorial to Galloway, see *Argus*, 1 July 1869. The characterizing of Batman and Fawkner is in C. G. Duffy, 'An Australian example', *Contemporary Review*, January 1888, p. 7. The contented dependence of women is perceived in Dilke, *Greater Britain*, vol. 2, p. 85. The achievement and fame of Jane Duff are described in L. J. Blake, *Lost in the Bush: the story of Jane Duff* (Melbourne 1964). Parkes's boast on election, and the responses by his employees and Harpur, are quoted in Normington-Rawling, *Charles Harpur, an Australian*, pp. 195-6. His confession of ambition is quoted in C. E. Lyne, *Life of Sir Henry Parkes* (Sydney 1896), vol. 1, p. 47. The comparison of American and Australian democracy is in Dilke, *op. cit.*, vol. 2, p. 56. 'The Flag' is in H. Parkes, *The Beauteous Terrorist and Other Poems* (Melbourne 1885), pp. 42-4.

16 She Is Not Yet

'The Lay of the Bachelor Settler', in *Headlong Rhymes by a Policeman* (Launceston 1843) is quoted in Nadel, *Australia's Colonial Culture*, p. 59; in this chapter I draw substantially on pp. 56-64 of Nadel's book. The committee of the Sydney Mechanics' School of Arts is quoted in *ibid.*, p. 58; the settler in Port Phillip, p. 41; Duncan's anthem, p. 61. 'The Emigrant's Vision' is in Harpur, *Poems*, p. 199. Deniehy is quoted in Normington-Rawling, *Charles Harpur, an Australian*, p. 129. 'The Far Future' is in Reed (ed.), *The Poetical Works of Henry Kendall*, p. 241; it was perhaps written jointly by the poet and his twin brother Edward.

Verdon on the advantages of a fresh start is quoted in Nadel, *op. cit.*, p. 64. J. B. Stephens, 'The dominion of Australia: a forecast, 1877' is in Turner (ed.), *The Australian Dream*, pp. 210-11. The young emigrant's notion of Australia is in H. B. Higgins, manuscript autobiography (National Library of Australia), pp. 11-12. Board's words are in an address, 'History and Australian history', *JRAHS*, vol. 3, 1915-17, p. 293.

Index

by Dorothy F. Prescott

Place names have been qualified by the current state name in order to facilitate identification in current locational guides, e.g. Melbourne (Victoria) rather than Melbourne (Port Phillip). 'Newspapers and journals' are grouped together under this heading, and 'ships' will be found likewise in one sequence. Abbreviations are as follows: G.B., Great Britain; N.S.W., New South Wales; N.T., Northern Territory; N.Z., New Zealand; Q., Queensland; S.A., South Australia; Tas., Tasmania; V.D.L., Van Diemen's Land; Vic., Victoria; W.A., Western Australia.

DATE			